The Piazza Tales

Webster's Italian
Thesaurus Edition

**for ESL, EFL, ELP, TOFEL®, TOEIC®, and AP® Test
Preparation**

Herman Melville

ICON CLASSICS

Published by ICON Group International, Inc.
7404 Trade Street
San Diego, CA 92121 USA

www.icongrouponline.com

The Piazza Tales: Webster's Italian Thesaurus Edition for ESL, EFL, ELP, TOFEL®, TOEIC®, and AP®
Test Preparation

This edition published by ICON Classics in 2005
Printed in the United States of America.

ISBN 0-497-25719-X

Contents

PREFACE FROM THE EDITOR

Webster's paperbacks take advantage of the fact that classics are frequently assigned readings in English courses. By using a running English-to-Italian thesaurus at the bottom of each page, this edition of *The Piazza Tales* by Herman Melville was edited for three audiences. The first includes Italian-speaking students enrolled in an English Language Program (ELP), an English as a Foreign Language (EFL) program, an English as a Second Language Program (ESL), or in a TOEFL® or TOEIC® preparation program. The second audience includes English-speaking students enrolled in bilingual education programs or Italian speakers enrolled in English speaking schools. The third audience consists of students who are actively building their vocabularies in Italian in order to take foreign service, translation certification, Advanced Placement® (AP®)[1] or similar examinations. By using the Rosetta Edition® when assigned for an English course, the reader can enrich their vocabulary in anticipation of an examination in Italian or English.

Webster's edition of this classic is organized to expose the reader to a maximum number of difficult and potentially ambiguous English words. Rare or idiosyncratic words and expressions are given lower priority compared to "difficult, yet commonly used" words. Rather than supply a single translation, many words are translated for a variety of meanings in Italian, allowing readers to better grasp the ambiguity of English, and avoid them using the notes as a pure translation crutch. Having the reader decipher a word's meaning within context serves to improve vocabulary retention and understanding. Each page covers words not already highlighted on previous pages. If a difficult word is not translated on a page, chances are that it has been translated on a previous page. A more complete glossary of translations is supplied at the end of the book; translations are extracted from Webster's Online Dictionary.

Definitions of remaining terms as well as translations can be found at www.websters-online-dictionary.org. Please send suggestions to websters@icongroupbooks.com

The Editor
Webster's Online Dictionary
www.websters-online-dictionary.org

[1] TOEFL®, TOEIC®, AP® and Advanced Placement® are trademarks of the Educational Testing Service which has neither reviewed nor endorsed this book. All rights reserved.

THE PIAZZA

"With fairest flowers,
Whilst summer lasts, and I live here, Fidele—"

When I removed into the country, it was to **occupy** an old-fashioned farm-house, which had no piazza—a **deficiency** the more **regretted**, because not only did I like piazzas, as somehow **combining** the coziness of in-doors with the freedom of out-doors, and it is so **pleasant** to **inspect** your **thermometer** there, but the country round about was such a picture, that in **berry** time no boy climbs hill or crosses **vale** without coming upon easels planted in every **nook**, and sun-burnt **painters** painting there. A very **paradise** of painters. The **circle** of the **stars** cut by the circle of the **mountains**. At least, so looks it from the house; though, once upon the mountains, no circle of them can you see. Had the site been chosen five rods off, this **charmed** ring would not have been.

The house is old. **Seventy** years since, from the heart of the Hearth Stone Hills, they quarried the Kaaba, or Holy Stone, to which, each Thanksgiving, the social pilgrims used to come. So long ago, that, in **digging** for the foundation, the workmen used both **spade** and **axe**, **fighting** the Troglodytes of those **subterranean** parts—**sturdy roots** of a sturdy wood, **encamped** upon what is now a long land-slide of **sleeping meadow**, **sloping** away off from my poppy-

Italian

axe: ascia, scure.	ispezioniamo, ispezionate,	**roots**: radici.
berry: bacca.	ispezionano, ispeziona, ispeziono,	**seventy**: settanta.
charmed: affascinato.	controllare.	**sleeping**: dormendo, addormentato.
circle: circolo, cerchio, compagnia.	**meadow**: prato.	**sloping**: inclinato.
combining: abbinando, combinando,	**mountains**: montagne.	**spade**: vanga, vangare.
conglobando, unendo.	**nook**: angolino, cantuccio.	**stars**: spighe.
deficiency: deficienza, mancanza,	**occupy**: occupare, occupano, occupo,	**sturdy**: robusto.
carenza, difetto, disavanzo.	occupiamo, occupate, occupa, occupi.	**subterranean**: sotterraneo.
digging: scavando, scavare.	**painters**: pittori.	**thermometer**: termometro.
encamped: accampato.	**paradise**: paradiso.	**vale**: valle.
fighting: lotta, combattente.	**pleasant**: piacevole, gradevole, ameno.	
inspect: ispezionare, ispezioni,	**regretted**: rammaricato.	

bed. Of that knit wood, but one **survivor** stands—an **elm**, lonely through steadfastness.

Whoever built the house, he builded better than he knew; or else Orion in the **zenith** flashed down his Damocles' sword to him some **starry** night, and said, "Build there." For how, otherwise, could it have entered the builder's mind, that, upon the clearing being made, such a purple prospect would be his?—nothing less than Greylock, with all his hills about him, like Charlemagne among his peers.

Now, for a house, so situated in such a country, to have no piazza for the **convenience** of those who might desire to **feast** upon the view, and take their time and ease about it, seemed as much of an **omission** as if a picture-gallery should have no bench; for what but picture-galleries are the marble halls of these same **limestone** hills?—galleries hung, month after month **anew**, with pictures ever **fading** into pictures ever fresh. And beauty is like piety—you **cannot** run and read it; **tranquillity** and **constancy**, with, now-a-days, an easy chair, are needed. For though, of old, when **reverence** was in **vogue**, and **indolence** was not, the devotees of Nature, **doubtless**, used to stand and adore—just as, in the cathedrals of those ages, the worshipers of a higher Power did—yet, in these times of failing faith and **feeble** knees, we have the piazza and the pew.

During the first year of my residence, the more **leisurely** to witness the **coronation** of Charlemagne (weather permitting, they crown him every **sunrise** and sunset), I chose me, on the hill-side bank near by, a royal lounge of turf—a green **velvet** lounge, with long, moss-padded back; while at the head, strangely enough, there grew (but, I suppose, for **heraldry**) three tufts of blue **violets** in a field-argent of wild **strawberries**; and a **trellis**, with **honeysuckle**, I set for **canopy**. Very majestical lounge, indeed. So much so, that here, as with the reclining **majesty** of Denmark in his **orchard**, a **sly** ear-ache **invaded** me. But, if damps **abound** at times in Westminster Abbey, because it is so old, why not within this **monastery** of mountains, which is older?

A piazza must be had.

Italian

abound: abbondare, abbondano, abbondate, abbondi, abbondiamo, abbondo, abbonda.	**feast**: banchetto, festa.	**reverence**: riverenza.
anew: di nuovo, ancora.	**feeble**: debole.	**sly**: furbo, astuto, scaltro.
cannot: non potere.	**heraldry**: araldica.	**starry**: stellato.
canopy: baldacchino, tettuccio, calotta.	**honeysuckle**: caprifoglio.	**strawberries**: fragole, fragola.
constancy: costanza.	**indolence**: indolenza.	**sunrise**: alba, levar del sole.
convenience: convenienza.	**invaded**: invaso.	**survivor**: superstite, sopravvissuto.
coronation: incoronazione.	**leisurely**: comodo.	**tranquillity**: tranquillità.
doubtless: senza dubbio.	**limestone**: calcare.	**trellis**: graticcio.
elm: olmo.	**majesty**: maestà.	**velvet**: velluto.
fading: svanendo, scolorimento.	**monastery**: monastero.	**violets**: viola.
	omission: omissione.	**vogue**: moda.
	orchard: frutteto.	**zenith**: zenit.

The house was wide—my **fortune** narrow; so that, to build a **panoramic** piazza, one round and round, it could not be—although, indeed, considering the matter by rule and square, the carpenters, in the kindest way, were anxious to **gratify** my **furthest** wishes, at I've forgotten how much a foot.

Upon but one of the four sides would **prudence** grant me what I wanted. Now, which side?

To the east, that long camp of the Hearth Stone Hills, fading far away towards Quito; and every fall, a small white **flake** of something peering suddenly, of a coolish morning, from the topmost cliff—the season's new-dropped **lamb**, its earliest **fleece**; and then the Christmas **dawn**, **draping** those **dim** highlands with red-barred plaids and tartans—goodly sight from your piazza, that. **Goodly** sight; but, to the north is Charlemagne—can't have the Hearth Stone Hills with Charlemagne.

Well, the south side. Apple-trees are there. Pleasant, of a **balmy** morning, in the month of May, to sit and see that orchard, white-budded, as for a bridal; and, in October, one green **arsenal yard**; such **piles** of **ruddy** shot. Very fine, I grant; but, to the north is Charlemagne.

The west side, look. An **upland pasture**, alleying away into a **maple** wood at top. Sweet, in opening spring, to **trace** upon the hill-side, otherwise **gray** and bare—to trace, I say, the **oldest paths** by their streaks of earliest green. Sweet, indeed, I can't deny; but, to the north is Charlemagne.

So Charlemagne, he carried it. It was not long after 1848; and, somehow, about that time, all round the world, these kings, they had the **casting** vote, and **voted** for themselves.

No **sooner** was ground broken, than all the **neighborhood**, neighbor Dives, in particular, broke, too—into a laugh. Piazza to the north! Winter piazza! Wants, of winter midnights, to watch the Aurora Borealis, I suppose; hope he's laid in good store of Polar muffs and mittens.

That was in the **lion** month of March. Not forgotten are the blue noses of the carpenters, and how they scouted at the **greenness** of the cit, who would build

Italian

arsenal: arsenale.
balmy: fragrante.
casting: assegnazione delle parti, getto, colata.
dawn: alba, aurora, albeggiare.
dim: oscuro, tenebroso, scuro, pallido.
draping: drappeggiando.
flake: scaglia, fiocco.
fleece: vello.
fortune: fortuna, sorte, patrimonio.
furthest: il più lontano.
goodly: bonariamente.

gratify: gratificare, gratificano, gratifico, gratifichiamo, gratifichi, gratificate, gratifica.
gray: grigio.
greenness: verde.
lamb: agnello, l'agnello.
lion: leone.
maple: acero.
neighbor: vicino.
neighborhood: vicinato, vicinanza, quartiere.
oldest: maggiore, il più vecchio.

panoramic: panoramico.
pasture: pascolo, pastura.
paths: percorsi.
piles: emorroidi.
prudence: prudenza.
ruddy: rubicondo.
sooner: prima.
trace: traccia, tracciare, delimitare.
upland: regione montagnosa, altopiano.
voted: votato.
yard: cortile, iarda, cantiere, pennone.

his sole piazza to the north. But March don't last **forever**; **patience**, and August comes. And then, in the cool elysium of my northern **bower**, I, Lazarus in Abraham's **bosom**, cast down the hill a **pitying** glance on poor old Dives, tormented in the **purgatory** of his piazza to the south.

But, even in December, this northern piazza does not repel—nipping cold and **gusty** though it be, and the north wind, like any miller, **bolting** by the snow, in finest flour—for then, once more, with **frosted beard**, I pace the sleety **deck**, weathering Cape Horn.

In summer, too, Canute-like, sitting here, one is often reminded of the sea. For not only do long ground-swells roll the **slanting** grain, and little wavelets of the grass **ripple** over upon the low piazza, as their beach, and the **blown** down of **dandelions** is wafted like the **spray**, and the **purple** of the mountains is just the purple of the billows, and a still August **noon** broods upon the deep meadows, as a calm upon the Line; but the **vastness** and the lonesomeness are so **oceanic**, and the silence and the **sameness**, too, that the first **peep** of a strange house, rising beyond the trees, is for all the world like **spying**, on the Barbary coast, an unknown **sail**.

And this recalls my **inland voyage** to fairy-land. A true voyage; but, take it all in all, interesting as if **invented**.

From the piazza, some uncertain object I had caught, **mysteriously** snugged away, to all appearance, in a sort of purpled breast-pocket, high up in a hopper-like **hollow**, or sunken angle, among the northwestern mountains—yet, whether, really, it was on a mountain-side, or a mountain-top, could not be determined; because, though, **viewed** from **favorable** points, a blue summit, peering up away behind the rest, will, as it were, talk to you over their heads, and plainly tell you, that, though he (the blue summit) seems among them, he is not of them (God forbid!), and, indeed, would have you know that he **considers** himself—as, to say truth, he has good right—by several cubits their superior, nevertheless, certain ranges, here and there double-filed, as in platoons, so shoulder and follow up upon one another, with their **irregular** shapes and heights, that, from the piazza, a nigher and lower mountain will, in most states of the atmosphere,

Italian

beard: barba.
blown: dischiuso.
bolting: bullonatura.
bosom: petto, seno.
bower: ancora di prora, pergolato.
considers: considera.
dandelions: dente di leone.
deck: coperta, ponte, piattaforma.
favorable: favorevole.
forever: per sempre.
frosted: brinato.
gusty: burrascoso, tempestoso.

hollow: cavo, cavità, vuoto, incavare.
inland: interno.
invented: inventato.
irregular: irregolare, saltuario.
mysteriously: misteriosamente.
noon: mezzogiorno, mezzodì.
oceanic: oceanico.
patience: pazienza.
peep: occhieggiare, pigolio, pigolare, sbirciare.
pitying: compatire, pietà.
purgatory: purgatorio.

purple: viola, porpora, rosso porpora.
ripple: ondulazione, increspatura.
sail: vela, veleggiare, la vela, salpare, navigare.
sameness: uniformità.
slanting: obliquo.
spray: spruzzare, spray, spruzzo, nebulizzare.
spying: spionaggio.
vastness: vastità.
viewed: visto.
voyage: viaggio.

effacingly shade itself away into a higher and further one; that an object, **bleak** on the former's **crest**, will, for all that, appear **nested** in the latter's **flank**. These mountains, somehow, they play at hide-and-seek, and all before one's eyes.

But, be that as it may, the spot in question was, at all events, so **situated** as to be only visible, and then but **vaguely**, under certain witching conditions of light and shadow.

Indeed, for a year or more, I knew not there was such a spot, and might, perhaps, have never known, had it not been for a **wizard** afternoon in autumn — late in autumn — a mad poet's afternoon; when the turned maple woods in the broad **basin** below me, having lost their first **vermilion tint**, dully **smoked**, like smouldering towns, when flames **expire** upon their prey; and **rumor** had it, that this smokiness in the general air was not all Indian summer — which was not used to be so sick a thing, however mild — but, in great part, was blown from far-off forests, for weeks on fire, in Vermont; so that no wonder the sky was **ominous** as Hecate's cauldron — and two sportsmen, crossing a red **stubble** buck-wheat field, seemed guilty Macbeth and **foreboding** Banquo; and the hermit-sun, hutted in an Adullum **cave**, well towards the south, **according** to his **season**, did little else but, by indirect reflection of narrow rays shot down a Simplon pass among the clouds, just steadily paint one small, round, **strawberry mole** upon the wan cheek of northwestern hills. Signal as a **candle**. One spot of **radiance**, where all else was shade.

Fairies there, thought I; some **haunted** ring where fairies dance.

Time passed; and the following May, after a gentle shower upon the mountains — a little shower islanded in **misty** seas of **sunshine**; such a distant shower — and sometimes two, and three, and four of them, all visible together in different parts — as I love to watch from the piazza, instead of **thunder** storms, as I used to, which **wrap** old Greylock, like a Sinai, till one thinks swart Moses must be climbing among scathed hemlocks there; after, I say, that, gentle shower, I saw a **rainbow**, **resting** its further end just where, in autumn, I had marked the mole. Fairies there, thought I; remembering that rainbows bring out the blooms, and that, if one can but get to the rainbow's end, his fortune is made in a bag of gold.

Italian

according: secondo.
basin: bacino, catino, vasca, bacinella, conca.
bleak: alborella, triste, freddo, afflitto, spiacevole, sgradevole, buio, scuro, brullo.
candle: candela, la candela, cero.
cave: caverna, grotta.
crest: cresta.
expire: scadere, morire, scadi, scadono, muoio, scadiamo, scadete, muori, muoiono, moriamo, scado.

flank: fianco.
foreboding: presentimento.
haunted: frequentato, perseguitato.
misty: nebbioso.
mole: talpa, molo, neo.
nested: intercalato.
ominous: sinistro, di malaugurio, infausto.
radiance: radianza.
rainbow: arcobaleno, l'arcobaleno.
resting: riposare.
rumor: diceria, voce, vociferare.

seas: mari.
situated: situato.
smoked: fumato, affumicato.
strawberry: fragola.
stubble: stoppia.
sunshine: luce del sole.
thunder: tuono, tuonare.
tint: tinta.
vaguely: vagamente.
vermilion: cinabro, vermiglio.
wizard: mago, stregone.
wrap: avvolgere.

Yon rainbow's end, would I were there, thought I. And none the less I wished it, for now first **noticing** what seemed some sort of glen, or **grotto**, in the mountain side; at least, whatever it was, viewed through the rainbow's medium, it glowed like the Potosi mine. But a work-a-day neighbor said, no doubt it was but some old **barn**—an abandoned one, its **broadside beaten** in, the **acclivity** its background. But I, though I had never been there, I knew better.

A few days after, a **cheery** sunrise **kindled** a golden **sparkle** in the same spot as before. The sparkle was of that vividness, it seemed as if it could only come from glass. The building, then—if building, after all, it was—could, at least, not be a barn, much less an abandoned one; **stale hay** ten years musting in it. No; if aught built by **mortal**, it must be a **cottage**; perhaps long **vacant** and **dismantled**, but this very spring **magically** fitted up and **glazed**.

Again, one noon, in the same direction, I marked, over **dimmed** tops of terraced **foliage**, a broader **gleam**, as of a silver **buckler**, held sunwards over some croucher's head; which gleam, experience in like cases taught, must come from a roof newly shingled. This, to me, made pretty sure the recent **occupancy** of that far cot in **fairy** land.

Day after day, now, full of interest in my discovery, what time I could spare from reading the Midsummer's Night Dream, and all about Titania, **wishfully** I gazed off towards the hills; but in **vain**. Either troops of shadows, an imperial guard, with slow pace and **solemn**, defiled along the **steeps**; or, routed by **pursuing** light, **fled broadcast** from east to west—old wars of Lucifer and Michael; or the mountains, though unvexed by these **mirrored sham** fights in the sky, had an atmosphere otherwise **unfavorable** for fairy views. I was sorry; the more so, because I had to keep my chamber for some time after—which chamber did not face those hills.

At length, when pretty well again, and sitting out, in the September morning, upon the piazza, and thinking to myself, when, just after a little **flock** of sheep, the farmer's banded children passed, a-nutting, and said, "How sweet a day"—it was, after all, but what their fathers call a weather-breeder—and, indeed, was become go sensitive through my illness, as that I could not bear to look upon a

Italian

acclivity: pendio.
barn: granaio, baracca, fienile.
beaten: battuto, picchiato.
broadcast: trasmettere, trasmissione, diffusione, teletrasmettere.
broadside: fiancata.
buckler: protezione, scudo.
cheery: allegro.
cot: lettino, branda.
dimmed: oscurato.
dismantled: smontato.
fairy: fata.

fled: fuggito.
flock: branco, stormo, bioccolo, gregge.
foliage: fogliame.
glazed: satinato.
gleam: luccicare, barlume.
grotto: grotta.
hay: fieno.
kindled: acceso.
magically: magicamente.
mirrored: replicato.
mortal: mortale.

noticing: notare.
occupancy: occupazione.
pursuing: perseguendo.
sham: simulare.
solemn: solenne.
sparkle: scintilla, sfavillare, brillare.
stale: raffermo, stantio, trito e ritrito.
steeps: immerge, bagna.
unfavorable: sfavorevole.
vacant: vacante, libero.
vain: vanitoso, vano.
wishfully: desiderosamente.

Chinese **creeper** of my adoption, and which, to my delight, **climbing** a post of the piazza, had burst out in starry **bloom**, but now, if you removed the leaves a little, showed millions of strange, cankerous worms, which, feeding upon those blossoms, so shared their **blessed hue**, as to make it unblessed evermore—worms, whose germs had doubtless lurked in the very **bulb** which, so hopefully, I had planted: in this ingrate peevishness of my **weary convalescence**, was I sitting there; when, suddenly looking off, I saw the golden mountain-window, **dazzling** like a deep-sea **dolphin**. Fairies there, thought I, once more; the queen of fairies at her fairy-window; at any rate, some glad mountain-girl; it will do me good, it will **cure** this **weariness**, to look on her. No more; I'll launch my yawl—ho, cheerly, heart! and push away for fairy-land—for rainbow's end, in fairy-land.

How to get to fairy-land, by what road, I did not know; nor could any one **inform** me; not even one Edmund Spenser, who had been there—so he wrote me—further than that to reach fairy-land, it must be **voyaged** to, and with faith. I took the fairy-mountain's **bearings**, and the first fine day, when strength permitted, got into my yawl—high-pommeled, leather one—cast off the fast, and away I **sailed**, free **voyager** as an autumn **leaf**. Early dawn; and, sallying **westward**, I sowed the morning before me.

Some miles brought me **nigh** the hills; but out of present sight of them. I was not lost; for road-side golden-rods, as guide-posts, pointed, I doubted not, the way to the golden window. Following them, I came to a **lone** and **languid** region, where the grass-grown ways were **traveled** but by **drowsy** cattle, that, less **waked** than stirred by day, seemed to walk in sleep. **Browse**, they did not—the **enchanted** never eat. At least, so says Don Quixote, that **sagest** sage that ever lived.

On I went, and gained at last the fairy mountain's base, but saw yet no fairy ring. A pasture rose before me. Letting down five mouldering bars—so **moistly** green, they seemed **fished** up from some sunken wreck—a wigged old Aries, long-visaged, and with **crumpled horn**, came snuffing up; and then, retreating, decorously led on along a milky-way of white-weed, past dim-clustering

Italian

bearings: cuscinetti.	accecante.	**lone**: solitario, solo.
blessed: benedetto, beato.	**dolphin**: delfino.	**moistly**: umido.
bloom: fiore, fiorire, fioritura.	**drowsy**: sonnolento.	**nigh**: vicino.
browse: sfogliare, brucare.	**enchanted**: incantato.	**sage**: salvia, saggio.
bulb: lampadina, ampolla, lampada,	**fished**: pescato.	**sailed**: navigato.
bulbo.	**horn**: corno, tromba, clacson.	**traveled**: viaggiato.
climbing: alpinismo.	**hue**: tinta.	**voyaged**: viaggiato.
convalescence: convalescenza.	**inform**: informare, informano,	**voyager**: passeggero, viaggiatore.
creeper: pianta rampicante.	informate, informi, informiamo,	**waked**: svegliato.
crumpled: sgualcito, spiegazzato.	informo, informa, insegnare.	**weariness**: fiacca.
cure: guarire, cura.	**languid**: languido.	**weary**: stanco, stancare, fiacco.
dazzling: abbagliare, abbagliante,	**leaf**: foglia, foglio, sfogliare.	**westward**: verso ovest.

Pleiades and Hyades, of small forget-me-nots; and would have led me further still his **astral** path, but for golden flights of yellow-birds — pilots, surely, to the golden window, to one side flying before me, from bush to bush, towards deep woods — which woods themselves were luring — and, somehow, lured, too, by their fence, banning a dark road, which, however dark, led up. I pushed through; when Aries, **renouncing** me now for some lost soul, **wheeled**, and went his wiser way.. **Forbidding** and forbidden ground — to him.

A winter wood road, **matted** all along with winter-green. By the side of **pebbly** waters — waters the cheerier for their **solitude**; beneath **swaying** fir-boughs, petted by no season, but still green in all, on I journeyed — my horse and I; on, by an old saw-mill, bound down and hushed with vines, that his **grating** voice no more was heard; on, by a deep **flume clove** through **snowy** marble, vernal-tinted, where freshet eddies had, on each side, spun out empty chapels in the living rock; on, where Jacks-in-the-pulpit, like their Baptist **namesake**, **preached** but to the **wilderness**; on, where a huge, cross-grain block, fern-bedded, showed where, in forgotten times, man after man had tried to split it, but lost his wedges for his pains — which wedges yet **rusted** in their holes; on, where, ages past, in step-like ledges of a **cascade**, skull-hollow pots had been churned out by **ceaseless whirling** of a flintstone — ever wearing, but itself unworn; on, by wild **rapids** pouring into a secret pool, but **soothed** by circling there awhile, issued forth serenely; on, to less broken ground, and by a little ring, where, truly, fairies must have **danced**, or else some wheel-tire been heated — for all was bare; still on, and up, and out into a hanging orchard, where **maidenly** looked down upon me a **crescent** moon, from morning.

My horse hitched low his head. Red apples rolled before him; Eve's apples; seek-no-furthers. He tasted one, I another; it tasted of the ground. Fairy land not yet, thought I, flinging my **bridle** to a **humped** old tree, that **crooked** out an arm to catch it. For the way now lay where path was none, and none might go but by himself, and only go by **daring**. Through **blackberry brakes** that tried to **pluck** me back, though I but **strained** towards **fruitless** growths of mountain-laurel; up

Italian

astral: astrale.
blackberry: mora.
brakes: freni.
bridle: briglia, freno, imbrigliare.
cascade: cascata.
ceaseless: incessante.
clove: chiodo di garofano.
crescent: mezzaluna.
crooked: storto, disonesto.
danced: ballato, ballavo ballava.
daring: osando, audace.
flume: canale.

forbidding: vietando, proibendo, ostile, spaventevole.
fruitless: infruttuoso, inutile.
grating: grata, griglia, stridente, carabottino, inferriata.
humped: gobba.
maidenly: puro, verginale.
matted: coperto di stuoie.
namesake: omonimo.
pebbly: sassoso.
pluck: rompere, staccare, cogliere, spennare, strappare, fegato.

preached: predicato.
rapids: rapide.
renouncing: rinunciando.
rusted: arrugginito.
snowy: nevoso.
solitude: solitudine.
soothed: calmato.
strained: teso.
swaying: oscillare.
wheeled: ruota.
whirling: turbinoso, vorticoso.
wilderness: regione selvaggia.

slippery steeps to **barren** heights, where stood none to welcome. Fairy land not yet, thought I, though the morning is here before me.

Foot-sore enough and weary, I gained not then my journey's end, but came ere long to a craggy pass, **dipping** towards growing regions still beyond. A **zigzag** road, half overgrown with **blueberry** bushes, here turned among the cliffs. A rent was in their **ragged** sides; through it a little track branched off, which, **upwards** threading that short **defile**, came breezily out above, to where the mountain-top, part **sheltered northward**, by a taller brother, **sloped** gently off a space, ere darkly plunging; and here, among **fantastic** rocks, reposing in a **herd**, the foot-track **wound**, half beaten, up to a little, low-storied, grayish cottage, **capped**, nun-like, with a peaked roof.

On one slope, the roof was deeply weather-stained, and, nigh the turfy eaves-trough, all velvet-napped; no doubt the snail-monks **founded mossy** priories there. The other slope was newly shingled. On the north side, doorless and windowless, the clap-boards, innocent of paint, were yet green as the north side of lichened pines or copperless hulls of Japanese junks, **becalmed**. The whole base, like those of the **neighboring** rocks, was rimmed about with **shaded** streaks of richest **sod**; for, with hearth-stones in fairy land, the natural rock, though housed, **preserves** to the last, just as in open fields, its **fertilizing charm**; only, by **necessity**, working now at a remove, to the sward without. So, at least, says Oberon, **grave** authority in fairy lore. Though setting Oberon aside, certain it is, that, even in the common world, the soil, close up to farm-houses, as close up to pasture rocks, is, even though untended, ever richer than it is a few rods off — such gentle, nurturing heat is **radiated** there.

But with this cottage, the shaded streaks were richest in its front and about its entrance, where the ground-sill, and especially the doorsill had, through long eld, quietly settled down.

No **fence** was seen, no **inclosure**. Near by — ferns, ferns, ferns; further — woods, woods, woods; beyond — mountains, mountains, mountains; then — sky, sky, sky. Turned out in **aerial** commons, pasture for the mountain moon. Nature, and but nature, house and, all; even a low cross-pile of silver **birch**, piled **openly**,

Italian

aerial: antenna, aereo.
barren: sterile.
becalmed: acquietato.
birch: betulla.
blueberry: mirtillo, bacca di mirtillo.
capped: avente come limite superiore.
charm: fascino, incanto.
defile: gola.
dipping: immersione.
fantastic: fantastico.
fence: recinto, staccionata.
fertilizing: concimando.

founded: fondato.
grave: tomba, grave.
herd: mandria, gregge, branco, gruppo, armento.
inclosure: recinzione.
mossy: muschioso.
necessity: necessità, bisogno.
neighboring: vicino.
northward: verso nord.
openly: apertamente.
preserves: conserve.
radiated: irradiato.

ragged: cencioso, logoro.
shaded: ombreggiato, ombroso, sfumatura.
sheltered: riparato.
slippery: sdrucciolevole, scivoloso.
slope: pendio, pendenza, inclinazione, pendice.
sloped: inclinato.
sod: zolla erbosa.
upwards: verso l'alto.
wound: ferita, ferire.
zigzag: zigzagare, zigzag.

to season; up among whose **silvery** sticks, as through the **fencing** of some **sequestered** grave, sprang **vagrant raspberry** bushes — willful assertors of their right of way.

The foot-track, so **dainty** narrow, just like a sheep-track, led through long ferns that **lodged**. Fairy land at last, thought I; Una and her lamb **dwell** here. Truly, a small abode — mere palanquin, set down on the summit, in a pass between two worlds, **participant** of neither.

A **sultry** hour, and I wore a light hat, of yellow sinnet, with white duck trowsers — both relics of my **tropic** sea-going. Clogged in the muffling ferns, I softly **stumbled**, **staining** the knees a sea-green.

Pausing at the **threshold**, or rather where threshold once had been, I saw, through the open door-way, a lonely girl, **sewing** at a lonely window. A pale-cheeked girl, and fly-specked window, with wasps about the mended upper panes. I spoke. She **shyly** started, like some Tahiti girl, **secreted** for a **sacrifice**, first **catching** sight, through palms, of Captain Cook. **Recovering**, she bade me enter; with her **apron brushed** off a **stool**; then silently **resumed** her own. With thanks I took the stool; but now, for a space, I, too, was **mute**. This, then, is the fairy-mountain house, and here, the fairy queen sitting at her fairy window.

I went up to it. Downwards, directed by the tunneled pass, as through a **leveled telescope**, I caught sight of a, far-off, soft, **azure** world. I hardly knew it, though I came from it.

"You must find this view very pleasant," said I, at last.

"Oh, sir," **tears** starting in her eyes, "the first time I looked out of this window, I said 'never, never shall I weary of this.' "

"And what **wearies** you of it now?"

"I don't know," while a tear fell; "but it is not the view, it is Marianna."

Some months back, her brother, only seventeen, had come **hither**, a long way from the other side, to cut wood and burn coal, and she, elder sister, had accompanied, him. Long had they been orphans, and now, sole inhabitants of the sole house upon the mountain. No guest came, no **traveler** passed. The zigzag,

Italian

apron: grembiule, grembiale.
azure: azzurro.
brushed: spazzolato.
catching: contagioso, prendendo, infettivo, colpendo, prendere.
dainty: delicato.
dwell: abitare, dimorare, dimorate, dimoro, dimori, dimorano, dimora, abitiamo, abiti, abitate, abitano.
fencing: scherma.
hither: qui, quà.
leveled: livellato.
lodged: alloggiato.
mute: muto.
participant: partecipante.
raspberry: lampone, pernacchia.
recovering: ricuperando.
resumed: ripreso.
sacrifice: sacrificio, sacrificare, offrire.
secreted: secreto.
sequestered: confiscato, sequestrato.
sewing: cucendo, cucito.
shyly: timidamente.
silvery: argenteo.
staining: mordenzatura.
stool: sgabello, feci.
stumbled: inciampato.
sultry: soffocante, afoso.
tear: strappo, lagrima, strappare, lacerare, lacrima.
telescope: telescopio, cannocchiale.
threshold: soglia.
traveler: viaggiatore.
tropic: tropico.
vagrant: vagabondo, ambulante.
wearies: stanco.

perilous road was only used at seasons by the **coal wagons**. The brother was **absent** the **entire** day, sometimes the entire night. When at evening, fagged out, he did come home, he soon left his **bench**, poor **fellow**, for his bed; just as one, at last, **wearily quits** that, too, for still deeper rest. The bench, the bed, the grave.

Silent I stood by the fairy window, while these things were being told.

"Do you know," said she at last, as **stealing** from her story, "do you know who lives yonder? — I have never been down into that country — away off there, I mean; that house, that **marble** one," **pointing** far across the lower **landscape**; "have you not caught it? there, on the long hill-side: the field before, the **woods** behind; the white shines out against their blue; don't you mark it? the only house in sight."

I looked; and after a time, to my **surprise**, **recognized**, more by its position than its **aspect**, or Marianna's **description**, my own **abode**, glimmering much like this **mountain** one from the piazza. The **mirage haze** made it appear less a farm-house than King Charming's **palace**.

"I have often **wondered** who lives there; but it must be some happy one; again this morning was I thinking so."

"Some happy one," returned I, starting; "and why do you think that? You judge some rich one lives there?"

"Rich or not, I never thought; but it looks so happy, I can't tell how; and it is so far away. Sometimes I think I do but **dream** it is there. You should see it in a **sunset**."

"No doubt the sunset **gilds** it **finely**; but not more than the sunrise does this house, perhaps."

"This house? The sun is a good sun, but it never gilds this house. Why should it? This old house is **rotting**. That makes it so mossy. In the morning, the sun comes in at this old window, to be sure — boarded up, when first we came; a window I can't keep clean, do what I may — and half burns, and nearly **blinds** me at my sewing, **besides setting** the **flies** and wasps astir — such flies and wasps as only lone mountain houses know. See, here is the curtain — this apron — I try to

Italian

abode: residenza, appartamento, alloggio, dimora.	**finely**: bellamente.	**quits**: abbandona.
absent: assente.	**flies**: vola.	**recognized**: riconosciuto.
aspect: aspetto, apparenza, aria.	**gilds**: dora, indora.	**rotting**: marcendo.
bench: panchina, banco, panca.	**haze**: foschia, caligine.	**setting**: regolazione.
besides: inoltre, d'altronde.	**landscape**: paesaggio, panorama.	**stealing**: furto, rubare.
blinds: acceca.	**marble**: marmo, pallina.	**sunset**: tramonto.
coal: carbone.	**mirage**: miraggio.	**surprise**: sorprendere, sorpresa, meraviglia, stupore.
description: descrizione.	**mountain**: montagna, monte, la montagna.	**wagons**: carri.
dream: sogno, sognare.	**palace**: palazzo, il palazzo.	**wearily**: stancamente.
entire: intero, completo, totale, tutto.	**perilous**: pericoloso.	**wondered**: domandato.
fellow: uomo.	**pointing**: indicare.	**woods**: bosco.

shut it out with then. It **fades** it, you see. Sun **gild** this house? not that ever Marianna saw."

"Because when this **roof** is **gilded** most, then you stay here within."

"The hottest, weariest hour of day, you mean? Sir, the sun gilds not this roof. It leaked so, brother **newly** shingled all one side. Did you not see it? The north side, where the sun strikes most on what the **rain** has **wetted**. The sun is a good sun; but this roof, in first scorches, and then **rots**. An old house. They went West, and are long dead, they say, who built it. A mountain house. In winter no **fox** could **den** in it. That chimney-place has been **blocked** up with **snow**, just like a hollow stump."

"Yours are strange fancies, Marianna."

"They but **reflect** the things."

"Then I should have said, 'These are strange things,' rather than, 'Yours are strange fancies.' "

"As you will;" and took up her sewing.

Something in those quiet words, or in that quiet act, it made me mute again; while, noting, through the fairy window, a **broad shadow** stealing on, as **cast** by some **gigantic condor**, **floating** at **brooding poise** on **outstretched wings**, I **marked** how, by its deeper and **inclusive dusk**, it **wiped** away into itself all **lesser** shades of rock or **fern**.

"You watch the **cloud**," said Marianna.

"No, a shadow; a cloud's, no doubt—though that I cannot see. How did you know it? Your eyes are on your work."

"It dusked my work. There, now the cloud is gone, Tray comes back."

"How?"

"The dog, the **shaggy** dog. At noon, he **steals** off, of himself, to change his shape—returns, and lies down awhile, nigh the door. Don't you see him? His head is turned round at you; though, when you came, he looked before him."

"Your eyes rest but on your work; what do you speak of?"

Italian

blocked: bloccato.
broad: largo, ampio.
brooding: cova.
cast: calco, fuso, getto.
cloud: nube, nuvola, nuvolo.
condor: condor.
den: tana.
dusk: crepuscolo.
fades: svanisce.
fern: felce.
floating: galleggiante, galleggiamento, fluttuante.

fox: volpe, la volpe.
gigantic: gigantesco.
gild: indorare, dorare.
gilded: dorato.
inclusive: inclusivo, compreso.
lesser: minore.
marked: marcato, contrassegnato.
newly: nuovamente.
outstretched: disteso.
poise: equilibrio.
rain: pioggia, piovere, la pioggia.
reflect: riflettere, rifletti, riflettiamo,

rifletto, riflettono, riflettete.
roof: tetto, volta.
rots: marcisce.
shadow: ombra.
shaggy: ispido, peloso, irsuto.
shut: chiudere, chiuso.
snow: neve, nevicare, la neve.
steals: ruba.
wetted: bagnato.
wings: diritti d'acquisto di titoli negoziabili del Governo.
wiped: pulito, strofinato, asciugato.

"By the window, crossing."

"You mean this shaggy shadow—the nigh one? And, yes, now that I mark it, it is not **unlike** a large, black Newfoundland dog. The **invading** shadow gone, the invaded one returns. But I do not see what casts it."

"For that, you must go without."

"One of those **grassy** rocks, no doubt."

"You see his head, his face?"

"The shadow's? You speak as if *you* saw it, and all the time your eyes are on your work."

"Tray looks at you," still without glancing up; "this is his hour; I see him."

"Have you then, so long sat at this mountain-window, where but clouds and, vapors **pass**, that, to you, shadows are as things, though you speak of them as of phantoms; that, by **familiar** knowledge, working like a second **sight**, you can, without looking for them, tell just where they are, though, as having mice-like feet, they **creep** about, and come and go; that, to you, these **lifeless** shadows are as living friends, who, though out of sight, are not out of mind, even in their faces—is it so?"

"That way I never thought of it. But the friendliest one, that used to **soothe** my weariness so much, **coolly quivering** on the ferns, it was taken from me, never to return, as Tray did just now. The shadow of a birch. The **tree** was **struck** by **lightning**, and brother cut it up. You saw the cross-pile out-doors—the **buried root** lies under it; but not the shadow. That is **flown**, and never will come back, nor ever **anywhere stir** again."

Another cloud here **stole** along, once more blotting out the dog, and **blackening** all the mountain; while the **stillness** was so still, **deafness** might have **forgot** itself, or else **believed** that **noiseless** shadow **spoke**.

"Birds, Marianna, singing-birds, I hear none; I hear nothing. Boys and bob-o-links, do they never come a-berrying up here?"

Italian

anywhere: dovunque, in qualche luogo, da qualche parte.	**forgot**: dimenticato.	**soothe**: calmare, calmano, calmiamo, calmi, calmate, calmo, calma, placare, lenire.
believed: creduto.	**grassy**: erboso.	
blackening: annerendo.	**invading**: invadendo, invadere.	
buried: seppellito, sepolto.	**lifeless**: esanime.	**spoke**: raggio.
coolly: frescamente.	**lightning**: fulmine, baleno, lampo.	**stillness**: calma, immobilità, tranquillità, quiete.
creep: strisciare, strisci, strisciamo, strisciano, strisciate, strisciamento, striscia, striscio.	**noiseless**: silenzioso.	**stir**: mescolare, agitare, muovere.
	pass: passare, passaggio, lasciapassare, passata, trascorrere, passo.	**stole**: stola.
deafness: sordità.	**quivering**: tremare.	**struck**: colpito.
familiar: familiare.	**root**: radice.	**tree**: albero, l'albero.
flown: volato.	**sight**: vista, aspetto, avvistare, aria, apparenza.	**unlike**: diversamente da, a differenza di.

"Birds, I **seldom** hear; boys, never. The **berries mostly ripe** and fall — few, but me, the wiser."

"But yellow-birds showed me the way — part way, at least."

"And then flew back. I **guess** they play about the mountain-side, but don't make the top their home. And no doubt you think that, living so **lonesome** here, knowing nothing, **hearing** nothing — little, at least, but sound of thunder and the fall of trees — never reading, seldom speaking, yet ever **wakeful**, this is what gives me my strange thoughts — for so you call them — this weariness and wakefulness together Brother, who stands and works in open air, would I could rest like him; but mine is mostly but **dull** woman's work — sitting, sitting, **restless** sitting."

"But, do you not go walk at times? These woods are wide."

"And lonesome; lonesome, because so wide. Sometimes, 'tis true, of **afternoons**, I go a little way; but soon come back again. Better feel lone by **hearth**, than rock. The shadows **hereabouts** I know — those in the woods are strangers."

"But the night?"

"Just like the day. Thinking, thinking — a **wheel** I cannot stop; **pure** want of sleep it is that **turns** it."

"I have heard that, for this wakeful weariness, to say one's **prayers**, and then lay one's head upon a fresh **hop pillow** — "

"Look!"

Through the fairy window, she pointed down the **steep** to a small garden **patch** near by — mere **pot** of rifled **loam**, half **rounded** in by sheltering rocks — where, side by side, some feet **apart**, nipped and **puny**, two hop-vines climbed two poles, and, gaining their tip-ends, would have then joined over in an **upward clasp**, but the **baffled shoots**, **groping** awhile in empty air, trailed back **whence** they sprung.

"You have tried the pillow, then?"

"Yes."

Italian

afternoons: pomeriggi.
apart: separato, separatamente, a parte.
baffled: sconcertato.
berries: bacche.
clasp: fermaglio.
dull: opaco, smussato, spuntato.
groping: brancolando.
guess: supporre, indovinare, supposizione, congettura.
hearing: udendo, sentendo, udito, udienza, ascolto.

hearth: focolare.
hereabouts: qui vicino.
hop: luppolo.
loam: argilla.
lonesome: solitario.
mostly: maggiormente, soprattutto.
patch: toppa, pezza, patch.
pillow: guanciale, cuscino.
pot: vaso.
prayers: preghiere.
puny: gracile.
pure: puro.

restless: inquieto, irrequieto.
ripe: maturo.
rounded: rotondo, arrotondato.
seldom: raramente.
shoots: spara.
steep: ripido, erto, scosceso.
turns: gira, svolta, cambia.
upward: ascendente, verso l'alto, in alto.
wakeful: sveglio.
wheel: ruota.
whence: da dove, donde.

"And prayer?"

"Prayer and pillow."

"Is there no other cure, or charm?"

"Oh, if I could but once get to **yonder** house, and but look upon **whoever** the happy being is that **lives** there! A **foolish** thought: why do I think it? Is it that I live so lonesome, and know nothing?"

"I, too, know nothing; and, therefore, cannot answer; but, for your **sake**, Marianna, well could **wish** that I were that happy one of the happy house you dream you see; for then you would **behold** him now, and, as you say, this weariness might leave you."

— Enough. **Launching** my yawl no more for fairy-land, I **stick** to the piazza. It is my box-royal; and this **amphitheatre**, my theatre of San Carlo. Yes, the **scenery** is magical — the **illusion** so complete. And Madam Meadow Lark, my prima donna, **plays** her **grand engagement** here; and, **drinking** in her sunrise **note**, which, Memnon-like, seems struck from the **golden window**, how far from me the weary face behind it.

But, every night, when the **curtain falls**, **truth** comes in with **darkness**. No light **shows** from the mountain. To and fro I **walk** the piazza deck, haunted by Marianna's face, and many as real a story.

Italian

amphitheatre: anfiteatro.
behold: guardare.
curtain: cortina, tenda, tendina, sipario.
darkness: oscurità, tenebre.
drinking: bere.
engagement: fidanzamento, assunzione.
falls: cade.
foolish: sciocco, stupido, stolto, ignorante, fesso.
golden: dorato, aureo, d'oro.

grand: grande, grandioso.
illusion: illusione.
launching: lancio, lanciare, varo.
lives: vive, abita.
note: nota, biglietto, appunto, annotazione, notare, annotare.
plays: gioca, suona.
sake: causa.
scenery: paesaggio.
shows: mostra.
stick: bastone, appiccicare, bastoncino, attaccare, incollare, ficcare, bacchetta.

theatre: teatro.
truth: verità.
walk: camminare, cammino, cammina, camminano, camminate, cammini, camminiamo, camminata, passeggiare, passeggiata.
whoever: chiunque.
window: finestra, sportello, finestrino, la finestra.
wish: desiderio, volere, desiderare, volontà, voglia.
yonder: là, laggiù.

BARTLEBY

I am a rather **elderly** man. The nature of my avocations, for the last thirty years, has brought me into more than ordinary contact with what would seem an interesting and **somewhat singular** set of men, of whom, as yet, nothing, that I know of, has ever been written—I mean, the law-copyists, or scriveners. I have known very many of them, **professionally** and **privately**, and, if I **pleased**, could **relate** divers histories, at which **good**-natured gentlemen might smile, and **sentimental** souls might **weep**. But I **waive** the biographies of all other scriveners, for a few passages in the life of Bartleby, who was a scrivener, the strangest I ever saw, or heard of. While, of other law-copyists, I might write the complete life, of Bartleby nothing of that sort can be done. I believe that no materials exist, for a full and **satisfactory biography** of this man. It is an **irreparable** loss to **literature**. Bartleby was one of those beings of whom nothing is **ascertainable**, except from the original sources, and, in his case, those are very small. What my own **astonished** eyes saw of Bartleby, *that* is all I know of him, except, indeed, one **vague** report, which will appear in the **sequel**.

Ere **introducing** the scrivener, as he first appeared to me, it is fit I make some **mention** of myself, my *employés*, my business, my chambers, and general **surroundings**; because some such description is **indispensable** to an **adequate** understanding of the chief character about to be **presented**. Imprimis: I am a man who, from his **youth** upwards, has been **filled** with a **profound conviction** that

Italian

adequate: adeguato, sufficiente.
ascertainable: accertabile.
astonished: stupito, si stupito.
biography: biografia.
conviction: convinzione, condanna.
elderly: anziano.
filled: pieno.
good-natured: gradevole, cortese.
indispensable: indispensabile.
introducing: presentando, introducendo.
irreparable: irreparabile.

literature: letteratura.
mention: menzionare, menzione, cenno.
pleased: contento, soddisfatto.
presented: presentato.
privately: privatamente.
professionally: professionalmente.
profound: profondo, fondo.
relate: raccontare, raccontiamo, racconta, raccontano, raccontate, racconti, racconto, narrare.
satisfactory: soddisfacente.

sentimental: sentimentale.
sequel: seguito.
singular: singolare, strano.
somewhat: piuttosto, alquanto.
surroundings: ambiente, dintorni.
vague: vago.
waive: rinunciare.
weep: piangere, piangete, piangi, piangiamo, piangono, piango, lacrimare.
youth: gioventù, giovinezza, adolescenza, giovane.

the easiest way of life is the best. Hence, though I belong to a profession **proverbially energetic** and nervous, even to **turbulence**, at times, yet nothing of that sort have I ever suffered to **invade** my peace. I am one of those unambitious lawyers who never addresses a jury, or in any way draws down public **applause**; but, in the cool tranquillity of a **snug** retreat, do a snug business among rich men's bonds, and mortgages, and title-deeds. All who know me, consider me an **eminently** *safe* man. The late John Jacob Astor, a **personage** little given to poetic enthusiasm, had no **hesitation** in **pronouncing** my first grand point to be prudence; my next, method. I do not speak it in **vanity**, but simply record the fact, that I was not unemployed in my profession by the late John Jacob Astor; a name which, I admit, I love to repeat; for it hath a rounded and orbicular sound to it, and rings like **unto bullion**. I will freely add, that I was not **insensible** to the late John Jacob Astor's good opinion.

Some time prior to the period at which this little history begins, my avocations had been largely increased. The good old office, now **extinct** in the State of New York, of a Master in Chancery, had been **conferred** upon me. It was not a very **arduous** office, but very **pleasantly remunerative**. I seldom lose my temper; much more seldom **indulge** in dangerous **indignation** at wrongs and outrages; but, I must be permitted to be **rash** here, and declare, that I consider the sudden and violent **abrogation** of the office of Master in Chancery, by the new Constitution, as a— —premature act; **inasmuch** as I had counted upon a life-lease of the profits, whereas I only received those of a few short years. But this is by the way.

My chambers were up stairs, at No.— —Wall street. At one end, they looked upon the white wall of the interior of a **spacious skylight** shaft, **penetrating** the building from top to bottom.

This view might have been considered rather **tame** than otherwise, **deficient** in what landscape painters call "life." But, if so, the view from the other end of my chambers offered, at least, a contrast, if nothing more. In that direction, my windows commanded an **unobstructed** view of a **lofty** brick wall, black by age and **everlasting** shade; which wall required no spy-glass to bring out its lurking

Italian

abrogation: abrogazione, abolizione.
applause: applauso.
arduous: arduo.
bullion: lingotto.
conferred: conferito.
deficient: deficiente, carente, difettoso, insufficiente.
eminently: eminentemente.
energetic: energico, energetico.
everlasting: eterno.
extinct: estinto.
hesitation: esitazione, tentennamento.

inasmuch: in quanto.
indignation: indignazione, sdegno.
indulge: indulgere.
insensible: insensibile.
invade: invadere, invadi, invadiamo, invado, invadono, invadete.
lofty: alto, elevato.
penetrating: penetrando, penetrante.
personage: personaggio.
pleasantly: piacevolmente.
pronouncing: pronunciando.
proverbially: proverbialmente.

rash: eruzione, avventato, eruzione cutanea.
remunerative: rimunerativo.
skylight: lucernario.
snug: accogliente, comodo, raccolto.
spacious: ampio, spazioso.
tame: addomesticare, domestico, domare.
turbulence: turbolenza.
unobstructed: non ostruito.
unto: a.
vanity: vanità.

beauties, but, for the benefit of all **near**-sighted spectators, was pushed up to within ten feet of my window panes. **Owing** to the great height of the surrounding buildings, and my chambers being on the second floor, the interval between this wall and mine not a little **resembled** a huge square cistern.

At the period just **preceding** the **advent** of Bartleby, I had two persons as copyists in my employment, and a **promising** lad as an office-boy. First, Turkey; second, Nippers; third, Ginger Nut. These may seem names, the like of which are not usually found in the Directory. In truth, they were nicknames, **mutually** conferred upon each other by my three clerks, and were **deemed expressive** of their respective persons or characters. Turkey was a short, pursy Englishman, of about my own age—that is, somewhere not far from sixty. In the morning, one might say, his face was of a fine **florid** hue, but after twelve o'clock, **meridian**—his dinner hour—it **blazed** like a **grate** full of Christmas coals; and continued blazing—but, as it were, with a **gradual** wane—till six o'clock, P.M., or thereabouts; after which, I saw no more of the **proprietor** of the face, which, gaining its meridian with the sun, seemed to set with it, to rise, **culminate**, and decline the following day, with the like **regularity** and undiminished glory. There are many singular coincidences I have known in the course of my life, not the least among which was the fact, that, exactly when Turkey displayed his fullest beams from his red and **radiant countenance**, just then, too, at that critical moment, began the daily period when I considered his business capacities as seriously disturbed for the remainder of the twenty-four hours. Not that he was absolutely **idle**, or **averse** to business, then; far from it. The difficulty was, he was **apt** to be altogether too energetic. There was a strange, **inflamed**, flurried, **flighty recklessness** of activity about him. He would be **incautious** in dipping his pen into his **inkstand**. All his blots upon my documents were dropped there after twelve o'clock, meridian. Indeed, not only would he be reckless, and sadly given to making blots in the afternoon, but, some days, he went further, and was rather **noisy**. At such times, too, his face flamed with **augmented** blazonry, as if cannel coal had been heaped on **anthracite**. He made an unpleasant **racket** with his chair; spilled his sand-box; in **mending** his pens, **impatiently** split them all to pieces, and threw them on the floor in a sudden passion; stood up, and leaned

Italian

advent: avvento.
anthracite: antracite.
apt: adatto.
augmented: ingrandito, aumentato.
averse: avverso.
blazed: arso.
countenance: approvare, viso.
culminate: culminare, culmini, culminiamo, culminate, culminano, culmina, culmino.
deemed: creduto.
expressive: espressivo.

flighty: capriccioso.
florid: florido.
gradual: graduale.
grate: griglia, grattugiare, graticola, grata, grattare.
idle: ozioso, pigro, folle, inattivo.
impatiently: impazientemente.
incautious: imprudente, incauto.
inflamed: infiammato.
inkstand: calamaio.
mending: riparazione.
meridian: meridiano.

mutually: reciprocamente.
near-sighted: miope.
noisy: rumoroso, chiassoso.
owing: dovere.
preceding: precedendo, precedente.
promising: promettendo, promettente.
proprietor: proprietario.
racket: baccano.
radiant: radiante, raggiante.
reckless: spericolato.
regularity: regolarità.
resembled: rassomigliato.

over his table, **boxing** his papers about in a most **indecorous** manner, very sad
to behold in an elderly man like him. Nevertheless, as he was in many ways a
most valuable person to me, and all the time before twelve o'clock, meridian,
was the quickest, steadiest creature, too, **accomplishing** a great deal of work in a
style not easily to be matched—for these reasons, I was willing to **overlook** his
eccentricities, though, indeed, occasionally, I remonstrated with him. I did this
very gently, however, because, though the civilest, **nay**, the blandest and most
reverential of men in the morning, yet, in the afternoon, he was **disposed**, upon
provocation, to be slightly rash with his tongue—in fact, **insolent**. Now, valuing
his morning services as I did, and **resolved** not to lose them—yet, at the same
time, made **uncomfortable** by his inflamed ways after twelve o'clock—and being
a man of peace, **unwilling** by my admonitions to call **forth unseemly retorts**
from him, I took upon me, one Saturday noon (he was always worse on
Saturdays) to **hint** to him, very **kindly**, that, perhaps, now that he was growing
old, it might be well to **abridge** his labors; in short, he need not come to my
chambers after twelve o'clock, but, dinner over, had best go home to his lodgings,
and rest himself till tea-time. But no; he insisted upon his afternoon devotions.
His countenance became **intolerably fervid**, as he oratorically assured me—
gesticulating with a long **ruler** at the other end of the room—that if his services
in the morning were useful, how indispensable, then, in the afternoon?

"With **submission**, sir," said Turkey, on this occasion, "I consider myself
your right-hand man. In the morning I but **marshal** and **deploy** my columns; but
in the afternoon I put myself at their head, and **gallantly** charge the **foe**, thus"—
and he made a violent thrust with the ruler.

"But the **blots**, Turkey," intimated I.

"True; but, with submission, sir, behold these **hairs**! I am getting old. Surely,
sir, a blot or two of a warm afternoon is not to be **severely** urged against gray
hairs. Old age—even if it blot the page—is **honorable**. With submission, sir, we
both are getting old."

This appeal to my fellow-feeling was hardly to be **resisted**. At all events, I
saw that go he would not. So, I made up my mind to let him stay, resolving,

Italian

abridge: abbreviare, abbreviate, abbrevi, abbrevia, abbreviamo, abbreviano, abbrevio, limitare, accorciare, compendiare, ridurre.	**gallantly**: galantemente.	**overlook**: trascurare.
	hairs: capelli, peli.	**provocation**: provocazione.
	hint: alludere, suggerimento, allusione, cenno.	**resisted**: resistito.
		resolved: risolto.
accomplishing: compiendo.	**honorable**: onorevole.	**retorts**: replica.
blot: macchia.	**indecorous**: indecoroso.	**reverential**: reverenziale.
boxing: pugilato.	**insolent**: insolente.	**ruler**: righello, dominatore, sovrano.
deploy: schierare.	**intolerably**: intollerabilmente, intollerabile.	**severely**: severamente.
disposed: disposto.		**submission**: presentazione.
fervid: fervido.	**kindly**: gentilmente, gentile.	**uncomfortable**: scomodo, disagiato.
foe: nemico.	**marshal**: schierare, maresciallo.	**unseemly**: sconveniente, indecoroso.
forth: avanti.	**nay**: anzi.	**unwilling**: riluttante, restio.

nevertheless, to see to it that, during the afternoon, he had to do with my less important papers.

Nippers, the second on my list, was a whiskered, **sallow**, and, upon the whole, rather piratical-looking young man, of about five and twenty. I always deemed him the victim of two **evil** powers — ambition and **indigestion**. The ambition was **evinced** by a certain **impatience** of the duties of a mere **copyist**, an unwarrantable **usurpation** of strictly professional affairs, such as the original drawing up of legal documents. The indigestion seemed betokened in an occasional nervous testiness and grinning **irritability**, causing the teeth to **audibly grind** together over mistakes committed in **copying**; unnecessary maledictions, hissed, rather than spoken, in the heat of business; and especially by a **continual discontent** with the height of the table where he worked. Though of a very **ingenious** mechanical turn, Nippers could never get this table to suit him. He put chips under it, blocks of various sorts, bits of **pasteboard**, and at last went so far as to attempt an **exquisite adjustment**, by final pieces of **folded** blotting-paper. But no **invention** would answer. If, for the sake of easing his back, he brought the table **lid** at a sharp angle well up towards his **chin**, and wrote, there like a man using the steep roof of a Dutch house for his desk, then he declared that it stopped the **circulation** in his arms. If now he **lowered** the table to his waistbands, and stooped over it in writing, then there was a **sore aching** in his back. In short, the, truth of the matter was, Nippers knew not what he wanted. Or, if he wanted anything, it was to be rid of a scrivener's table altogether. Among the manifestations of his **diseased** ambition was a **fondness** he had for receiving visits from certain ambiguous-looking fellows in **seedy** coats, whom he called his clients. Indeed, I was aware that not only was he, at times, considerable of a ward-politician, but he occasionally did a little business at the Justices' courts, and was not unknown on the steps of the Tombs. I have good reason to believe, however, that one individual who called upon him at my chambers, and who, with a grand air, he insisted was his client, was no other than a dun, and the alleged title-deed, a bill. But, with all his failings, and the annoyances he caused me, Nippers, like his **compatriot** Turkey, was a very useful man to me; wrote a neat, **swift** hand; and, when he chose, was not

Italian

aching: dolorante, dolente.
adjustment: accomodamento, adattamento, adeguamento, regolazione, aggiustamento.
ambition: ambizione.
audibly: udibilmente.
chin: mento, il mento.
circulation: circolazione, diffusione.
compatriot: compatriota.
continual: continuo, costante.
copying: copia, copiatura, riproduzione.

copyist: copista.
discontent: malcontento.
diseased: malato.
evil: male, cattivo, malvagio.
evinced: manifestato.
exquisite: squisito.
folded: piegato.
fondness: affezione, passione.
grind: macinare, molare, triturare, rettificare.
impatience: impazienza.
indigestion: indigestione, cattiva

digestione.
ingenious: ingegnoso.
invention: invenzione.
irritability: irritabilità.
lid: coperchio, coperta, palpebra.
lowered: abbassato.
pasteboard: cartone.
sallow: pallido.
seedy: pieno di semi.
sore: piaga, dolente.
swift: rondone, veloce, rapido, celere.
usurpation: usurpazione.

deficient in a **gentlemanly** sort of **deportment**. Added to this, he always dressed in a gentlemanly sort of way; and so, incidentally, reflected credit upon my chambers. Whereas, with respect to Turkey, I had much **ado** to keep him from being a **reproach** to me. His clothes were apt to look **oily**, and smell of eating-houses. He wore his **pantaloons** very loose and **baggy** in summer. His **coats** were **execrable**; his hat not to be handled. But while the hat was a thing of indifference to me, inasmuch as his natural **civility** and **deference**, as a dependent Englishman, always led him to doff it the moment he entered the room, yet his coat was another matter. Concerning his coats, I reasoned with him; but with no effect. The truth was, I suppose, that a man with so small an income could not afford to sport such a **lustrous** face and a lustrous coat at one and the same time. As Nippers once observed, Turkey's money went chiefly for red ink. One winter day, I presented Turkey with a highly respectable-looking coat of my own—a padded gray coat, of a most comfortable warmth, and which **buttoned** straight up from the knee to the neck. I thought Turkey would appreciate the **favor**, and **abate** his **rashness** and obstreperousness of afternoons. But no; I **verily** believe that **buttoning** himself up in so **downy** and blanket-like a coat had a **pernicious** effect upon him—upon the same principle that too much oats are bad for horses. In fact, precisely as a rash, **restive** horse is said to feel his oats, so Turkey felt his coat. It made him insolent. He was a man whom prosperity **harmed**.

Though, concerning the self-indulgent habits of Turkey, I had my own private surmises, yet, touching Nippers, I was well persuaded that, whatever might be his faults in other respects, he was, at least, a temperate young man. But, indeed, nature herself seemed to have been his **vintner**, and, at his birth, charged him so thoroughly with an **irritable**, brandy-like disposition, that all subsequent potations were needless. When I consider how, amid the stillness of my chambers, Nippers would sometimes impatiently rise from his seat, and stooping over his table, spread his arms wide apart, seize the whole desk, and move it, and **jerk** it, with a grim, **grinding** motion on the floor, as if the table were a perverse voluntary agent, intent on **thwarting** and **vexing** him, I plainly perceive that, for Nippers, brandy-and-water were altogether **superfluous**.

Italian

abate: diminuire, diminuisci, diminuisco, diminuite, diminuiscono, diminuiamo, ridurre.
ado: rumore.
baggy: cascante, gonfio, rigonfio.
buttoned: abbottonato.
buttoning: abbottonare.
civility: civiltà, cortesia.
deference: deferenza.
deportment: condotta, comportamento.
downy: lanuginoso.

execrable: esecrabile.
favor: favore, favorire, cortesia.
gentlemanly: signorile, da gentiluomo.
grinding: rettifica, macinazione, molitura.
harmed: nociuto.
irritable: irritabile.
jerk: scossa, sobbalzo, scossone.
lustrous: lustro.
oats: avena.
oily: oleoso, untuoso, unto.

pantaloons: pantaloni.
pernicious: pernicioso.
rashness: avventatezza.
reproach: rimprovero, rimproverare, riprendere.
restive: restio.
superfluous: superfluo.
thwarting: contrastando, ostacolando.
verily: molto.
vexing: irritando, vessando, contrariando, indispettendo.
vintner: vinaio.

It was fortunate for me that, owing to its peculiar cause — indigestion — the irritability and **consequent nervousness** of Nippers were mainly **observable** in the morning, while in the afternoon he was **comparatively** mild. So that, Turkey's paroxysms only coming on about twelve o'clock, I never had to do with their eccentricities at one time. Their fits **relieved** each other, like guards. When Nippers's was on, Turkey's was off; and *vice versa*. This was a good natural arrangement, under the circumstances.

Ginger Nut, the third on my list, was a lad, some twelve years old. His, father was a carman, ambitious of seeing his son on the bench instead of a **cart**, before he died. So he sent him to my office, as student at law, errand-boy, **cleaner** and **sweeper**, at the rate of one dollar a week. He had a little desk to himself, but he did not use it much. Upon inspection, the **drawer exhibited** a great **array** of the shells of various sorts of **nuts**. Indeed, to this quick-witted youth, the whole noble science of the law was contained in a nut-shell. Not the least among the employments of Ginger Nut, as well as one which he **discharged** with the most **alacrity**, was his duty as cake and apple **purveyor** for Turkey and Nippers. Copying law-papers being proverbially a dry, **husky** sort of business, my two scriveners were fain to **moisten** their mouths very often with Spitzenbergs, to be had at the numerous **stalls** nigh the Custom House and Post Office. Also, they sent Ginger Nut very frequently for that peculiar cake — small, flat, round, and very spicy — after which he had been named by them. Of a cold morning, when business was but dull, Turkey would **gobble** up scores of these **cakes**, as if they were mere wafers — indeed, they sell them at the rate of six or eight for a penny — the **scrape** of his pen **blending** with the **crunching** of the **crisp** particles in his mouth. Of all the **fiery** afternoon blunders and flurried rashnesses of Turkey, was his once **moistening** a ginger-cake between his lips, and **clapping** it on to a mortgage, for a **seal**. I came within an ace of **dismissing** him then. But he **mollified** me by making an **oriental** bow, and saying —

"With submission, sir, it was generous of me to find you in **stationery** on my own account."

Italian

alacrity: entusiasmo, alacrità.
array: matrice, schiera, ordine, array.
blending: mescolanza, miscela.
cakes: dolci.
cart: carretta, carrello, carretto.
clapping: applaudire.
cleaner: pulitore.
comparatively: comparativamente.
consequent: conseguente.
crisp: croccante, crespo.
crunching: sgranocchiando.
discharged: scaricato.

dismissing: licenziando.
drawer: cassetto, tiretto, disegnatore.
exhibited: esibito.
fiery: infuocato.
gobble: ingurgitare, ingozzare, ingollare, ingoiare, tranguggiare.
husky: rauco, pieno di bucce.
moisten: umettare, inumidire.
moistening: inumidendo, umettando.
mollified: addolcito, ammollito, ammorbidito.
nervousness: nervosismo, nervosità.

nuts: matto.
observable: osservabile, visibile.
oriental: orientale.
purveyor: fornitore.
relieved: alleviato.
scrape: raschiare, scrostare.
seal: foca, sigillo, la foca, sigillare.
stalls: platea, stalle.
stationery: cancelleria, articoli di cancelleria.
sweeper: spazzatrice, spazzino.
vice: morsa, vizio, virtù.

Now my original business—that of a conveyancer and title **hunter**, and drawer-up of **recondite** documents of all sorts—was considerably increased by receiving the master's office. There was now great work for scriveners. Not only must I push the clerks already with me, but I must have additional help.

In answer to my **advertisement**, a **motionless** young man one morning stood upon my office threshold, the door being open, for it was summer. I can see that figure now—pallidly neat, **pitiably respectable**, incurably **forlorn**! It was Bartleby.

After a few words **touching** his qualifications, I engaged him, glad to have among my **corps** of copyists a man of so **singularly sedate** an aspect, which I thought might operate beneficially upon the flighty **temper** of Turkey, and the fiery one of Nippers.

I should have stated before that ground glass **folding**-doors divided my premises into two parts, one of which was occupied by my scriveners, the other by myself. According to my **humor**, I threw open these doors, or closed them. I resolved to **assign** Bartleby a corner by the folding-doors, but on my side of them, so as to have this quiet man within easy call, in case any **trifling** thing was to be done. I placed his desk close up to a small side-window in that part of the room, a window which originally had **afforded** a **lateral** view of certain **grimy** backyards and **bricks**, but which, owing to subsequent erections, **commanded** at present no view at all, though it gave some light. Within three feet of the panes was a wall, and the light came down from far above, between two lofty buildings, as from a very small opening in a **dome**. Still further to a satisfactory arrangement, I **procured** a high green folding screen, which might entirely **isolate** Bartleby from my sight, though not remove him from my voice. And thus, in a manner, **privacy** and society were **conjoined**.

At first, Bartleby did an extraordinary quantity of writing. As if long famishing for something to copy, he seemed to **gorge** himself on my documents. There was no pause for **digestion**. He ran a day and night line, copying by sunlight and by candle-light. I should have been quite delighted with his application,

Italian

advertisement: inserzione, annuncio, avviso, pubblicità, annuncio pubblicitario.
afforded: permesso.
assign: assegnare, assegnate, assegni, assegnano, assegna, assegniamo, assegno.
bricks: mattoni.
commanded: comandato.
conjoined: congiunto.
corps: corpo.
digestion: digestione.

dome: cupola.
folding: pieghevole, piegamento, piegatura.
forlorn: derelitto, abbandonato, misero.
gorge: burrone, gola, forra.
grimy: sudicio.
humor: umore, umorismo.
hunter: cacciatore.
isolate: isolare, isolate, isolo, isoli, isoliamo, isola, isolano.
lateral: laterale.

motionless: immobile.
pitiably: pietosamente.
privacy: vita privata, riserbo, intimità.
procured: procurato.
recondite: recondito.
respectable: rispettabile, onorevole.
sedate: calmo.
singularly: singolarmente.
temper: umore, temperamento, tempra.
touching: commovente.
trifling: insignificante.

had he been **cheerfully industrious**. But he wrote on **silently**, palely, **mechanically**.

It is, of course, an indispensable part of a scrivener's business to **verify** the accuracy of his copy, word by word. Where there are two or more scriveners in an office, they assist each other in this examination, one reading from the copy, the other holding the original. It is a very dull, **wearisome**, and **lethargic** affair. I can readily imagine that, to some **sanguine** temperaments, it would be altogether **intolerable**. For example, I cannot credit that the mettlesome poet, Byron, would have contentedly sat down with Bartleby to examine a law document of, say five hundred pages, closely written in a crimpy hand.

Now and then, in the **haste** of business, it had been my habit to assist in **comparing** some brief document myself, calling Turkey or Nippers for this purpose. One object I had, in placing Bartleby so **handy** to me behind the screen, was, to **avail** myself of his services on such **trivial** occasions. It was on the third day, I think, of his being with me, and before any necessity had **arisen** for having his own writing examined, that, being much **hurried** to complete a small affair I had in hand, I **abruptly** called to Bartleby. In my haste and natural **expectancy** of **instant** compliance, I sat with my head bent over the original on my desk, and my right hand **sideways**, and somewhat **nervously** extended with the copy, so that, immediately upon **emerging** from his **retreat**, Bartleby might **snatch** it and proceed to business without the least delay.

In this very attitude did I sit when I called to him, rapidly **stating** what it was I wanted him to do—namely, to examine a small paper with me. Imagine my surprise, nay, my **consternation**, when, without moving from his privacy, Bartleby, in a singularly mild, firm voice, replied, "I would prefer not to."

I sat awhile in perfect silence, rallying my **stunned** faculties. Immediately it occurred to me that my ears had **deceived** me, or Bartleby had entirely **misunderstood** my meaning. I repeated my request in the clearest tone I could assume; but in quite as clear a one came the previous reply, "I would prefer not to."

Italian

abruptly: improvvisamente.
arisen: nato, sorto.
avail: giovare, essere utile, servire, utilizzare.
cheerfully: allegramente.
comparing: confrontando, paragonando.
consternation: sbigottimento, costernazione.
deceived: ingannato, truffato.
emerging: apparendo.
expectancy: aspettativa.

handy: destro.
haste: fretta, furia.
hurried: affrettato, frettoloso.
industrious: diligente.
instant: istante, momento, immediato.
intolerable: intollerabile.
lethargic: letargico.
mechanically: meccanicamente.
misunderstood: incompreso, frainteso.
nervously: nervosamente.
retreat: ritirarsi.
sanguine: rubicondo, sanguigno.

sideways: lateralmente.
silently: silenziosamente.
snatch: afferrare, presa.
stating: dichiarare.
stunned: sbalordito, intontito, stordito, assordato, rintronato, tramortito.
trivial: banale, insignificante.
verify: verificare, verifica, verifico, verifichiamo, verifichi, verificate, verificano, controllare, controllo, controlla, controllano.
wearisome: faticoso, tedioso.

"Prefer not to," echoed I, rising in high excitement, and **crossing** the room with a **stride**. "What do you mean? Are you moon-struck? I want you to help me **compare** this sheet here—take it," and I **thrust** it towards him.

"I would prefer not to," said he.

I looked at him steadfastly. His face was **leanly composed**; his gray eye **dimly calm**. Not a **wrinkle** of **agitation** rippled him. Had there been the least **uneasiness**, anger, impatience or **impertinence** in his manner; in other words, had there been any thing **ordinarily** human about him, doubtless I should have **violently dismissed** him from the premises. But as it was, I should have as soon thought of turning my pale plaster-of-paris **bust** of Cicero out of doors. I stood **gazing** at him awhile, as he went on with his own writing, and then reseated myself at my desk. This is very strange, thought I. What had one best do? But my business hurried me. I concluded to forget the matter for the present, reserving it for my future leisure. So calling Nippers from the other room, the paper was **speedily** examined.

A few days after this, Bartleby concluded four **lengthy** documents, being **quadruplicates** of a week's **testimony** taken before me in my High Court of Chancery. It became necessary to examine them. It was an important suit, and great **accuracy** was **imperative**. Having all things arranged, I called Turkey, Nippers and Ginger Nut, from the next room, meaning to place the four copies in the hands of my four clerks, while I should read from the original. **Accordingly**, Turkey, Nippers, and Ginger Nut had taken their seats in a row, each with his document in his hand, when I called to Bartleby to join this interesting group.

"Bartleby! quick, I am waiting."

I heard a slow scrape of his chair legs on the uncarpeted floor, and soon he appeared standing at the entrance of his **hermitage**.

"What is wanted?" said he, **mildly**.

"The copies, the copies," said I, **hurriedly**. "We are going to examine them. There"—and I held towards him the fourth quadruplicate.

"I would prefer not to," he said, and gently **disappeared** behind the screen.

Italian

accordingly: di conseguenza, quindi.	**crossing**: attraversamento, incrocio, traversata, passaggio.	**mildly**: dolcemente, gentilmente.
accuracy: accuratezza, esattezza, precisione.	**dimly**: pallidamente.	**ordinarily**: ordinariamente.
agitation: agitazione.	**disappeared**: scomparso.	**quadruplicate**: quadruplicare.
bust: busto.	**dismissed**: licenziato.	**quadruplicates**: quadruplica.
calm: calmo, calmare, tranquillo, calma, placare.	**gazing**: fissare.	**speedily**: rapidamente.
compare: confrontare, confronta, confrontiamo, confronti, confrontano, confrontate, confronto, paragonare, paragono, paragona, paragonate.	**hermitage**: eremitaggio, eremo.	**stride**: passo.
	hurriedly: affrettatamente.	**testimony**: certificato attestato, testimonianza.
	imperative: imperativo.	**thrust**: spingere, spinta.
	impertinence: impertinenza.	**uneasiness**: disagio.
composed: composto.	**leanly**: magramente.	**violently**: violentemente.
	lengthy: lungo.	**wrinkle**: ruga, grinza.

For a few moments I was turned into a **pillar** of salt, standing at the head of my **seated** column of clerks. Recovering myself, I advanced towards the screen, and demanded the reason for such extraordinary conduct.

"*Why* do you refuse?"

"I would prefer not to."

With any other man I should have flown **outright** into a **dreadful passion**, scorned all further words, and thrust him ignominiously from my presence. But there was something about Bartleby that not only **strangely disarmed** me, but, in a wonderful manner, touched and **disconcerted** me. I began to reason with him.

"These are your own copies we are about to examine. It is **labor saving** to you, because one examination will answer for your four papers. It is common **usage**. Every copyist is bound to help examine his copy. Is it not so? Will you not speak? Answer!"

"I prefer not to," he replied in a flutelike tone. It seemed to me that, while I had been **addressing** him, he carefully **revolved** every statement that I made; fully **comprehended** the meaning; could not **gainsay** the **irresistible** conclusion; but, at the same time, some **paramount** consideration **prevailed** with him to reply as he did.

"You are decided, then, not to **comply** with my request—a request made according to common usage and common sense?"

He briefly gave me to understand, that on that point my judgment was sound. Yes: his decision was **irreversible**.

It is not seldom the case that, when a man is **browbeaten** in some **unprecedented** and violently **unreasonable** way, he begins to **stagger** in his own plainest faith. He begins, as it were, vaguely to **surmise** that, wonderful as it may be, all the justice and all the reason is on the other side. Accordingly, if any **disinterested** persons are present, he turns to them for some **reinforcement** for his own **faltering** mind.

"Turkey," said I, "what do you think of this? Am I not right?"

Italian

addressing: indirizzamento.
browbeaten: intimidito.
comply: ottemperi, accondiscendiamo, ottemperiamo, ottempero, ottemperate, ottemperano, ottempera, accondiscendo, accondiscendi, accondiscendete, accondiscendono.
comprehended: compreso.
disarmed: disarmato.
disconcerted: sconcertato, turbato.
disinterested: disinteressato,

imparziale.
dreadful: terribile.
faltering: balbettando.
gainsay: nego, nega, negano, negate, neghi, neghiamo, negare.
irresistible: irresistibile.
irreversible: irreversibile.
labor: fatica, lavoro.
outright: diretto, completamente.
paramount: supremo.
passion: ardore, passione.
pillar: colonna, pilastro.

prevailed: prevalso.
reinforcement: rinforzo, armatura.
revolved: girato, ruotato.
saving: salvando, risparmio, risparmiando.
seated: seduto.
stagger: barcollare.
strangely: stranamente.
surmise: supporre, congetturare.
unprecedented: senza precedenti.
unreasonable: irragionevole.
usage: uso, costume.

"With submission, sir," said Turkey, in his blandest tone, "I think that you
are."

"Nippers," said I, "what do *you* think of it?"

"I think I should **kick** him out of the office."

(The reader, of nice perceptions, will here **perceive** that, it being morning,
Turkey's answer is couched in **polite** and **tranquil** terms, but Nippers replies in
ill-tempered ones. Or, to **repeat** a previous sentence, Nippers's **ugly mood** was
on duty, and Turkey's off.)

"Ginger Nut," said I, willing to **enlist** the smallest **suffrage** in my behalf,
"what do *you* think of it?"

"I think, sir, he's a little *luny*," replied Ginger Nut, with a grin.

"You hear what they say," said I, turning **towards** the screen, "come forth
and do your duty."

But he vouchsafed no reply. I **pondered** a moment in sore **perplexity**. But
once more business hurried me. I determined again to **postpone** the
consideration of this dilemma to my future **leisure**. With a little trouble we made
out to examine the papers without Bartleby, though at every page or two Turkey
deferentially dropped his opinion, that this **proceeding** was quite out of the
common; while Nippers, twitching in his chair with a dyspeptic nervousness,
ground out, between his set teeth, **occasional** hissing maledictions against the
stubborn oaf behind the screen. And for his (Nippers's) part, this was the first
and the last time he would do another man's business without pay.

Meanwhile Bartleby sat in his hermitage, **oblivious** to everything but his own
peculiar business there.

Some days passed, the scrivener being **employed** upon another lengthy work.
His late **remarkable** conduct led me to regard his ways narrowly. I **observed** that
he never went to dinner; indeed, that he never went anywhere. As yet I had
never, of my personal knowledge, known him to be outside of my office. He was
a **perpetual sentry** in the corner. At about **eleven** o'clock though, in the morning,
I noticed that Ginger Nut would advance toward the opening in Bartleby's

Italian

eleven: undici.	**perceive**: percepire, accorgersi,	**proceeding**: procedendo,
employed: impiegato.	scorgere, percepiamo, scorgo,	procedimento.
enlist: arruolare, arruoliamo, arruoli,	scorgiamo, scorgi, scorgete,	**remarkable**: notevole, eccezionale.
arruolo, arruolano, arruola, arruolate.	percepite, scorgono, percepiscono.	**repeat**: ripetere, ripetono, ripetete,
kick: calcio, pedata, calciare.	**perpetual**: perpetuo.	ripetiamo, ripeto, ripeti, ripetizione.
leisure: tempo libero, ozio, svago.	**perplexity**: perplessità.	**sentry**: sentinella.
mood: umore, atmosfera.	**polite**: cortese, educato.	**stubborn**: ostinato, testardo, cocciuto,
oaf: zoticone.	**pondered**: meditato, ponderato.	caparbio.
oblivious: immemore, dimentico.	**postpone**: rimandare, rimanda,	**suffrage**: suffragio.
observed: osservato.	rimandano, rimandate, rimandi,	**toward**: verso, a.
occasional: occasionale.	rimandiamo, rimando, rinviare,	**tranquil**: tranquillo, calmo.
peculiar: strano, peculiare, particolare.	posporre.	**ugly**: brutto.

screen, as if silently **beckoned thither** by a gesture invisible to me where I sat. The boy would then leave the office, jingling a few pence, and **reappear** with a handful of ginger-nuts, which he delivered in the hermitage, receiving two of the cakes for his trouble.

He lives, then, on ginger-nuts, thought I; never eats a dinner, properly speaking; he must be a **vegetarian**, then; but no; he never eats even vegetables, he eats nothing but ginger-nuts. My mind then ran on in reveries concerning the probable effects upon the human constitution of living entirely on ginger-nuts. Ginger-nuts are so called, because they contain ginger as one of their peculiar constituents, and the final **flavoring** one. Now, what was ginger? A hot, **spicy** thing. Was Bartleby hot and spicy? Not at all. Ginger, then, had no effect upon Bartleby. Probably, he preferred it should have none.

Nothing so **aggravates** an earnest person as a passive resistance. If the individual so resisted be of a not **inhumane** temper, and the **resisting** one perfectly harmless in his **passivity**, then, in the better moods of the former, he will **endeavor charitably** to **construe** to his imagination what proves impossible to be solved by his judgment. Even so, for the most part, I regarded Bartleby and his ways. Poor fellow! thought I, he means no mischief; it is plain he intends no **insolence**; his aspect sufficiently **evinces** that his eccentricities are involuntary. He is useful to me. I can get along with him. If I turn him away, the chances are he will fall in with some less-indulgent employer, and then he will be rudely treated, and perhaps driven forth **miserably** to **starve**. Yes. Here I can cheaply purchase a delicious self-approval. To **befriend** Bartleby; to humor him in his strange willfulness, will cost me little or nothing, while I lay up in my soul what will eventually prove a sweet **morsel** for my conscience. But this mood was not **invariable**, with me. The passiveness of Bartleby sometimes **irritated** me. I felt strangely goaded on to encounter him in new opposition—to **elicit** some angry spark from him **answerable** to my own. But, indeed, I might as well have **essayed** to strike fire with my knuckles against a bit of Windsor soap. But one afternoon the evil impulse in me mastered me, and the following little scene **ensued**:

"Bartleby," said I, "when those papers are all **copied**, I will compare them with you."

"I would **prefer** not to."

"How? Surely you do not mean to **persist** in that **mulish** vagary?"

No answer.

I threw open the folding-doors near by, and, turning upon **Turkey** and Nippers, **exclaimed**:

"Bartleby a second time says, he won't **examine** his papers. What do you think of it, Turkey?"

It was afternoon, be it remembered. Turkey sat **glowing** like a **brass boiler**; his **bald** head steaming; his hands reeling among his **blotted** papers.

"Think of it?" roared Turkey; "I think I'll just step behind his screen, and black his eyes for him!"

So saying, Turkey rose to his feet and threw his arms into a pugilistic position. He was hurrying away to make good his **promise**, when I **detained** him, **alarmed** at the effect of incautiously **rousing** Turkey's **combativeness** after dinner.

"Sit down, Turkey," said I, "and hear what Nippers has to say. What do you think of it, Nippers? Would I not be **justified** in immediately dismissing Bartleby?"

"Excuse me, that is for you to decide, sir. I think his **conduct** quite **unusual**, and, indeed, **unjust**, as **regards** Turkey and myself. But it may only be a **passing** whim."

"Ah," exclaimed I, "you have strangely changed your mind, then—you speak very **gently** of him now."

"All beer," cried Turkey; "**gentleness** is effects of beer—Nippers and I **dined** together to-day. You see how gentle *I* am, sir. Shall I go and black his eyes?"

"You refer to Bartleby, I suppose. No, not to-day, Turkey," I replied; "pray, put up your fists."

Italian

alarmed: allarmato.
bald: calvo, pelato.
blotted: macchiato.
boiler: caldaia, calderotto, bollitore.
brass: ottone.
combativeness: combattività.
conduct: condotta, condurre, guidare, comportamento.
copied: copiato.
detained: ritenuto.
dined: pranzato, cenato.
examine: esaminare, esaminate, esamino, esamini, esaminano, esamina, esaminiamo.
exclaimed: esclamato.
gentle: mite, gentile, dolce, delicato.
gently: delicatamente.
glowing: raggiante, ardente.
justified: giustificato.
mulish: testardo.
passing: passeggero, passare, passaggio.
persist: persistere, persistono, persisto, persistiamo, persisti, persistete.
prefer: preferire, preferisci, preferite, preferiscono, preferisco, preferiamo.
promise: promessa, promettere, promettono, promettete, prometti, promettiamo, prometto.
refer: riferire.
regards: considera, saluti.
rousing: incitando, spronando, stimolando.
turkey: tacchino, Turchia.
unjust: ingiusto.
unusual: insolito, inconsueto.

I closed the doors, and again **advanced** towards Bartleby. I felt additional incentives **tempting** me to my **fate**. I **burned** to be **rebelled** against again. I remembered **that** Bartleby never left the office.

"Bartleby," said I, "Ginger Nut is away; just step around to the Post Office, won't you? (it was but a three minutes' walk), and see if there is anything for me."

"I would prefer not to."

"You *will* not?"

"I *prefer* not."

I **staggered** to my desk, and sat there in a deep study. My **blind** inveteracy returned. Was there any other thing in which I could **procure** myself to be ignominiously repulsed by this **lean, penniless** wight? — my **hired clerk**? What added thing is there, perfectly reasonable, that he will be sure to **refuse** to do?

"Bartleby!"

No answer.

"Bartleby," in a louder **tone**.

No answer.

"Bartleby," I roared.

Like a very **ghost**, **agreeably** to the laws of **magical invocation**, at the third **summons**, he appeared at the **entrance** of his hermitage.

"Go to the next room, and tell Nippers to come to me."

"I prefer not to," he **respectfully** and slowly said, and mildly disappeared.

"Very good, Bartleby," said I, in a quiet sort of serenely-severe self-possessed tone, intimating the **unalterable** purpose of some terrible **retribution** very close at hand. At the moment I half intended something of the kind. But upon the whole, as it was **drawing** towards my dinner-hour, I thought it best to put on my hat and walk home for the day, **suffering** much from perplexity and **distress** of mind.

Italian

advanced: avanzato, progredito.
agreeably: piacevolmente.
blind: cieco, accecare, acceca, accechi, accechiamo, accecate, accecano, acceco.
burned: bruciato.
clerk: commesso, cancelliere, impiegato.
distress: pericolo.
drawing: disegno, disegnando, prelievo.
entrance: entrata, ingresso, accesso, l'entrata, adito.
fate: destino, fato, sorte.
ghost: fantasma, spettro.
hat: cappello.
hired: noleggiato.
invocation: invocazione.
lean: magro, sostenere, appoggiarsi, sottile, appoggiare.
magical: magico.
penniless: squattrinato.
procure: procurare, procurate, procuro, procuri, procurano, procuriamo, procacciare, procura.
rebelled: ribellato.
refuse: rifiutare, rifiutarsi, rifiuti.
respectfully: rispettosamente.
retribution: castigo.
staggered: sfalsato.
suffering: soffrendo, sofferenza, soffrire, patendo.
summons: citazione, ingiunzione.
tempting: allettante, tentando.
tone: tono.
unalterable: inalterabile.

Shall I acknowledge it? The conclusion of this whole business was, that it soon became a fixed fact of my chambers, that a pale young scrivener, by the name of Bartleby, had a desk there; that he copied for me at the usual rate of four cents a **folio** (one hundred words); but he was **permanently exempt** from **examining** the work done by him, that duty being transferred to Turkey and Nippers, out of **compliment**, doubtless, to their superior **acuteness**; moreover, said Bartleby was never, on any account, to be **dispatched** on the most trivial **errand** of any sort; and that even if **entreated** to take upon him such a matter, it was generally understood that he would "prefer not to" — in other words, that he would refuse point-blank.

As days passed on, I became considerably **reconciled** to Bartleby. His **steadiness**, his freedom from all **dissipation**, his **incessant** industry (except when he chose to throw himself into a standing revery behind his screen), his great stillness, his unalterableness of demeanor under all circumstances, made him a valuable acquisition. One prime thing was this — *he was always there* — first in the morning, **continually** through the day, and the last at night. I had a singular confidence in his **honesty**. I felt my most precious papers perfectly safe in his hands. Sometimes, to be sure, I could not, for the very soul of me, avoid falling into sudden **spasmodic** passions with him. For it was **exceeding** difficult to bear in mind all the time those strange peculiarities, privileges, and **unheard** of exemptions, **forming** the **tacit** stipulations on Bartleby's part under which he remained in my office. Now and then, in the **eagerness** of **dispatching** pressing business, I would **inadvertently summon** Bartleby, in a short, rapid tone, to put his finger, say, on the **incipient** tie of a bit of red tape with which I was about compressing some papers. Of course, from behind the screen the usual answer, "I prefer not to," was sure to come; and then, how could a human creature, with the common infirmities of our nature, **refrain** from **bitterly exclaiming** upon such perverseness — such **unreasonableness**. However, every added **repulse** of this sort which I received only tended to **lessen** the probability of my **repeating** the **inadvertence**.

Italian

acuteness: acutezza.	**exclaiming**: esclamando.	**permanently**: permanentemente.
bitterly: amaramente.	**exempt**: esente.	**reconciled**: conciliato, riconciliato.
compliment: complimento.	**folio**: foglio.	**refrain**: ritornello, astenersi.
continually: continuamente.	**forming**: formazione.	**repeating**: ripetendo.
dispatched: spedito.	**honesty**: onestà.	**repulse**: rifiuto, respingere.
dispatching: spedire.	**inadvertence**: inavvertenza.	**spasmodic**: spasmodico.
dissipation: dispersione, dissipazione.	**inadvertently**: inavvertitamente.	**steadiness**: costanza, fermezza.
eagerness: impazienza.	**incessant**: incessante.	**summon**: convocare, chiamare,
entreated: supplicato.	**incipient**: incipiente.	intimare, citare.
errand: messaggio, commissione.	**lessen**: diminuire, diminuiamo,	**tacit**: tacito.
examining: esaminando, esaminare.	diminuisci, diminuisco,	**unheard**: non sentito.
exceeding: eccedendo.	diminuiscono, diminuite.	**unreasonableness**: irragionevolezza.

Here it must be said, that according to the **custom** of most legal gentlemen **occupying** chambers in densely-populated law buildings, there were several keys to my door. One was kept by a woman **residing** in the **attic**, which person weekly scrubbed and daily swept and dusted my apartments. Another was kept by Turkey for convenience sake. The third I sometimes carried in my own pocket. The fourth I knew not who had.

Now, one Sunday morning I happened to go to Trinity Church, to hear a **celebrated preacher**, and finding myself rather early on the ground I thought I would walk round to my chambers for a while. **Luckily** I had my key with me; but upon applying it to the lock, I found it resisted by something **inserted** from the inside. Quite surprised, I called out; when to my consternation a key was turned from within; and thrusting his lean **visage** at me, and holding the door **ajar**, the **apparition** of Bartleby appeared, in his shirt **sleeves**, and otherwise in a strangely tattered deshabille, saying quietly that he was sorry, but he was deeply **engaged** just then, and—preferred not **admitting** me at present. In a brief word or two, he moreover added, that perhaps I had better walk round the block two or three times, and by that time he would probably have concluded his affairs.

Now, the **utterly** unsurmised appearance of Bartleby, tenanting my law-chambers of a Sunday morning, with his **cadaverously** gentlemanly *nonchalance*, yet withal firm and self-possessed, had such a strange effect upon me, that **incontinently** I **slunk** away from my own door, and did as **desired**. But not without **sundry** twinges of **impotent rebellion** against the **mild effrontery** of this **unaccountable** scrivener. Indeed, it was his wonderful **mildness chiefly**, which not only disarmed me, but unmanned me as it were. For I consider that one, for the time, is a sort of unmanned when he tranquilly permits his hired clerk to **dictate** to him, and order him away from his own premises. Furthermore, I was full of uneasiness as to what Bartleby could possibly be doing in my office in his shirt sleeves, and in an otherwise dismantled condition of a Sunday morning. Was anything **amiss** going on? Nay, that was out of the question. It was not to be thought of for a moment that Bartleby was an **immoral** person. But what could he be doing there?—copying? Nay again, whatever might be his

Italian

admitting: confessando, ammettendo.
ajar: socchiuso.
amiss: male, inopportuno.
apparition: apparizione.
attic: soffitta, attico.
cadaverously: cadavericamente.
celebrated: celebrato, festeggiato, famoso.
chiefly: principalmente, soprattutto.
custom: costume, usanza, uso, abitudine, consuetudine.
desired: desiderato.

dictate: dettare, dettano, dettate, detti, dettiamo, detta, detto.
effrontery: sfrontatezza.
engaged: occupato, innestato, impegnato.
immoral: immorale.
impotent: impotente.
incontinently: incontinentemente.
inserted: inserito.
luckily: fortunatamente.
mild: mite, dolce.
mildness: mitezza.

nonchalance: noncuranza.
occupying: occupando.
preacher: predicatore, pastore.
rebellion: ribellione.
residing: risiedendo.
sleeves: manicotti.
slunk: sgattaiolato.
sundry: diversi.
unaccountable: inesplicabile, irresponsabile.
utterly: totalmente.
visage: viso, volto.

eccentricities, Bartleby was an eminently **decorous** person. He would be the last man to sit down to his desk in any state approaching to **nudity**. Besides, it was Sunday; and there was something about Bartleby that forbade the **supposition** that he would by any **secular** occupation **violate** the proprieties of the day.

Nevertheless, my mind was not **pacified**; and full of a restless curiosity, at last I returned to the door. Without **hindrance** I inserted my key, opened it, and entered.   Bartleby was not to be seen. I looked round **anxiously**, peeped behind his screen; but it was very plain that he was gone. Upon more closely examining the place, I surmised that for an **indefinite** period Bartleby must have ate, dressed, and slept in my office, and that, too without plate, mirror, or bed. The cushioned seat of a ricketty old sofa in one corner bore the faint **impress** of a lean, reclining form. Rolled away under his desk, I found a blanket; under the empty grate, a **blacking** box and brush; on a chair, a tin basin, with soap and a ragged **towel**; in a newspaper a few crumbs of ginger-nuts and a morsel of cheese. Yes, thought I, it is evident enough that Bartleby has been making his home here, keeping bachelor's hall all by himself. Immediately then the thought came sweeping across me, what miserable friendlessness and **loneliness** are here revealed! His poverty is great; but his solitude, how horrible! Think of it. Of a Sunday, Wall-street is **deserted** as Petra; and every night of every day it is an **emptiness**. This building, too, which of week-days hums with industry and life, at **nightfall** echoes with sheer **vacancy**, and all through Sunday is forlorn. And here Bartleby makes his home; sole **spectator**, of a solitude which he has seen all populous — a sort of innocent and transformed Marius brooding among the **ruins** of Carthage!

For the first time in my life a feeling of **overpowering stinging melancholy** seized me. Before, I had never experienced aught but a not unpleasing **sadness**. The bond of a common humanity now drew me **irresistibly** to **gloom**. A **fraternal** melancholy! For both I and Bartleby were sons of Adam. I remembered the bright silks and **sparkling** faces I had seen that day, in **gala trim**, swan-like sailing down the Mississippi of Broadway; and I contrasted them with the **pallid** copyist, and thought to myself, Ah, happiness courts the light, so we **deem** the

Italian

anxiously: ansiosamente.
blacking: nero, annerire, lucido nero.
decorous: decente, decoroso.
deem: credere, crediamo, credete, credi, credo, credono, ritenere, giudicare, guardare.
deserted: abbandonato, deserto.
emptiness: vuoto.
fraternal: fraterno.
gala: gala.
gloom: malinconia, tristezza.
hindrance: impaccio, ostacolo.

impress: impressionare, imprimere.
indefinite: indefinito.
irresistibly: irresistibilmente.
loneliness: solitudine.
melancholy: malinconia, malinconico.
nightfall: imbrunire, crepuscolo.
nudity: nudità.
overpowering: sopraffacendo, opprimente, prepotente, schiacciante.
pacified: pacificato.
pallid: pallido.
ruins: rovina, rovine.

sadness: tristezza, malinconia.
secular: secolare, laico.
sparkling: sfavillante.
spectator: spettatore.
stinging: pungente.
supposition: supposizione.
towel: asciugamano, l'asciugamano.
trim: rifilare.
vacancy: posto vacante.
violate: violare, violo, violiamo, violate, violano, violi, viola, assalire, aggredire, aggredite, assalite.

world is gay; but **misery hides aloof**, so we deem that misery there is none. These sad fancyings—chimeras, doubtless, of a sick and silly brain—led on to other and more special thoughts, concerning the eccentricities of Bartleby. Presentiments of strange discoveries **hovered** round me. The scriveners pale form appeared to me laid out, among uncaring strangers, in its **shivering winding** sheet.

Suddenly I was attracted by Bartleby's closed desk, the key in open sight left in the lock.

I mean no **mischief**, seek the **gratification** of no **heartless curiosity**, thought I; besides, the desk is mine, and its contents, too, so I will make **bold** to look within. Everything was **methodically** arranged, the papers **smoothly** placed. The **pigeon** holes were deep, and **removing** the files of documents, I **groped** into their recesses. **Presently** I felt something there, and **dragged** it out. It was an old bandanna **handkerchief**, heavy and **knotted**. I opened it, and saw it was a savings' bank.

I now recalled all the quiet **mysteries** which I had noted in the man. I remembered that he never spoke but to answer; that, though at intervals he had considerable time to himself, yet I had never seen him reading—no, not even a newspaper; that for long periods he would stand looking out, at his pale window behind the screen, upon the dead brick wall; I was quite sure he never visited any **refectory** or eating house; while his pale face clearly indicated that he never drank beer like Turkey, or tea and coffee even, like other men; that he never went anywhere in particular that I could learn; never went out for a walk, unless, indeed, that was the case at present; that he had declined telling who he was, or whence he came, or whether he had any relatives in the world; that though so thin and pale, he never **complained** of ill health. And more than all, I remembered a certain **unconscious** air of pallid—how shall I call it?—of pallid **haughtiness**, say, or rather an **austere** reserve about him, which had **positively** awed me into my tame **compliance** with his eccentricities, when I had **feared** to ask him to do the slightest **incidental** thing for me, even though I might know,

Italian

aloof: appartato, in disparte, alla larga, a distanza, distante.
austere: austero.
bold: grassetto, spesso, grosso, audace.
complained: reclamato, si lamentato.
compliance: conformità, compliance, cedevolezza.
curiosity: curiosità.
dragged: trascinato.
feared: temuto.
gratification: gratificazione,

soddisfazione.
groped: brancolato.
handkerchief: fazzoletto.
haughtiness: alterigia.
heartless: insensibile.
hides: nasconde.
hovered: gironzolato.
incidental: fortuito, incidentale.
knotted: nodo.
methodically: metodicamente.
mischief: birichinata.
misery: miseria.

mysteries: misteri.
pigeon: piccione, colombo.
positively: positivamente.
presently: attualmente.
refectory: refettorio, mensa.
removing: togliendo, asportando, rimuovendo.
shivering: rabbrividire.
smoothly: facilmente, agevolmente.
unconscious: svenuto, inconscio, privo di sensi, inconsapevole.
winding: tortuoso, avvolgimento.

from his long-continued motionlessness, that behind his screen he must be
standing in one of those dead-wall reveries of his.

Revolving all these things, and **coupling** them with the recently discovered
fact, that he made my office his constant **abiding** place and home, and not
forgetful of his **morbid moodiness**; revolving all these things, a **prudential**
feeling began to **steal** over me. My first emotions had been those of pure
melancholy and sincerest pity; but just in proportion as the forlornness of
Bartleby grew and grew to my imagination, did that same melancholy **merge**
into fear, that pity into **repulsion**. So true it is, and so **terrible**, too, that up to a
certain point the thought or sight of misery **enlists** our best affections; but, in
certain special cases, beyond that point it does not. They err who would assert
that invariably this is owing to the inherent **selfishness** of the human heart. It
rather **proceeds** from a certain hopelessness of remedying excessive and organic
ill. To a sensitive being, pity is not seldom pain. And when at last it is perceived
that such pity cannot lead to **effectual succor**, common sense bids the soul be rid
of it. What I saw that morning persuaded me that the scrivener was the victim of
innate and **incurable** disorder. I might give **alms** to his body; but his body did
not pain him; it was his soul that suffered, and his soul I could not reach.

I did not **accomplish** the purpose of going to Trinity Church that morning.
Somehow, the things I had seen **disqualified** me for the time from church-going.
I walked **homeward**, thinking what I would do with Bartleby. Finally, I resolved
upon this—I would put certain calm questions to him the next morning,
touching his history, etc., and if he declined to answer them openly and
unreservedly (and I supposed he would prefer not), then to give him a twenty
dollar bill over and above whatever I might owe him, and tell him his services
were no longer required; but that if in any other way I could assist him, I would
be happy to do so, especially if he desired to return to his native place, wherever
that might be, I would **willingly** help to **defray** the expenses. Moreover, if, after
reaching home, he found himself at any time in want of aid, a letter from him
would be sure of a reply.

The next morning came.

Italian

abiding: durevole, permanente, continuo, aspettando.
accomplish: compiere, compiamo, compio, compiono, compite, compi, eseguire, arrivare.
alms: elemosina.
coupling: accoppiamento, innesto, giunto, manicotto.
defray: risarcite, risarciscono, risarcisco, risarcisci, risarciamo, risarcire.
disqualified: squalificato.

effectual: efficace.
enlists: arruola.
err: errare, errano, errate, erri, erriamo, erro, erra, sbagliarsi.
forgetful: dimentico, smemorato.
homeward: verso casa.
incurable: incurabile, inguaribile, insanabile.
innate: innato, congenito.
merge: incorporiamo, uniscono, unisco, fondiamo, unisci, unite, uniamo, incorporo, incorpori,

incorporate, incorporano.
moodiness: broncio, malumore.
morbid: morboso.
proceeds: procede.
prudential: prudenziale.
repulsion: repulsione.
revolving: ruotando, girando, girevole.
selfishness: egoismo.
steal: rubare.
succor: soccorrere, soccorso, aiutare.
willingly: volentieri.

"Bartleby," said I, gently **calling** to him behind his screen.

No reply.

"Bartleby," said I, in a still gentler tone, "come here; I am not going to ask you to do anything you would prefer not to do—I simply wish to speak to you."

Upon this he **noiselessly** slid into view.

"Will you tell me, Bartleby, where you were born?"

"I would prefer not to."

"Will you tell me *anything* about yourself?"

"I would prefer not to."

"But what reasonable **objection** can you have to speak to me? I feel friendly towards you."

He did not look at me while I spoke, but kept his **glance** fixed upon my bust of Cicero, which, as I then sat, was directly behind me, some six inches above my head.

"What is your answer, Bartleby," said I, after waiting a considerable time for a reply, during which his countenance remained **immovable**, only there was the faintest **conceivable tremor** of the white **attenuated** mouth.

"At present I prefer to give no answer," he said, and **retired** into his hermitage.

It was rather **weak** in me I **confess**, but his manner, on this occasion, **nettled** me. Not only did there seem to **lurk** in it a certain calm **disdain**, but his perverseness seemed **ungrateful**, **considering** the **undeniable** good usage and **indulgence** he had received from me.

Again I sat **ruminating** what I should do. **Mortified** as I was at his **behavior**, and resolved as I had been to **dismiss** him when I entered my office, nevertheless I strangely felt something **superstitious** knocking at my heart, and forbidding me to carry out my purpose, and **denouncing** me for a **villain** if I **dared** to **breathe** one **bitter** word against this forlornest of **mankind**. At last, **familiarly** drawing my chair behind his screen, I sat down and said: "Bartleby, never mind, then,

Italian

attenuated: assottigliato, attenuato.
behavior: condotta, comportamento.
bitter: amaro.
breathe: respirare, respirate, respirano, respiri, respira, respiriamo, respiro, fiatare.
calling: chiamando, chiamata.
conceivable: concepibile.
confess: confessare, confessa, confessano, confessate, confessi, confessiamo, confesso.
considering: considerando.

dared: osato.
denouncing: denunciando.
disdain: sdegno, sdegnare.
dismiss: licenziare, licenzi, licenziate, licenziano, licenziamo, licenzio, licenzia, congedare.
familiarly: familiarmente.
glance: occhiata, sguardo.
immovable: immobile.
indulgence: indulgenza.
lurk: nascondersi.
mankind: umanità.

mortified: mortificato.
nettled: irritato.
noiselessly: tranquillamente.
objection: obiezione, opposizione.
retired: pensionato, ritirato, a riposo.
ruminating: ruminando.
superstitious: superstizioso.
tremor: tremore, tremito.
undeniable: innegabile.
ungrateful: ingrato.
villain: furfante.
weak: debole, fiacco.

about **revealing** your history; but let me **entreat** you, as a friend, to comply as far as may be with the usages of this office. Say now, you will help to examine papers to-morrow or next day: in short, say now, that in a day or two you will begin to be a little reasonable: — say so, Bartleby."

"At present I would prefer not to be a little reasonable," was his mildly **cadaverous** reply.

Just then the folding-doors opened, and Nippers approached. He seemed suffering from an **unusually** bad night's rest, **induced** by severer indigestion than common. He **overheard** those final words of Bartleby.

"*Prefer not*, eh?" gritted Nippers—"I'd *prefer* him, if I were you, sir," addressing me—"I'd *prefer* him; I'd give him **preferences**, the stubborn **mule**! What is it, sir, pray, that he *prefers* not to do now?"

Bartleby moved not a limb.

"Mr. Nippers," said I, "I'd prefer that you would **withdraw** for the present."

Somehow, of late, I had got into the way of **involuntarily** using this word "prefer" upon all sorts of not exactly suitable **occasions**. And I **trembled** to think that my contact with the scrivener had already and seriously affected me in a mental way. And what further and deeper **aberration** might it not yet produce? This **apprehension** had not been without **efficacy** in **determining** me to summary measures.

As Nippers, looking very **sour** and **sulky**, was **departing**, Turkey **blandly** and deferentially approached.

"With submission, sir," said he, "yesterday I was thinking about Bartleby here, and I think that if he would but prefer to take a **quart** of good **ale** every day, it would do much towards mending him, and **enabling** him to assist in examining his papers."

"So you have got the word, too," said I, slightly **excited**.

"With submission, what word, sir," asked Turkey, respectfully **crowding** himself into the **contracted** space behind the screen, and by so doing, making me **jostle** the scrivener. "What word, sir?"

Italian

aberration: aberrazione, errore, sbaglio.
ale: birra.
apprehension: apprensione, arresto.
blandly: blandamente.
cadaverous: cadaverico.
contracted: contratto.
crowding: folla, affollamento.
departing: partendo.
determining: definendo, fissando, definito, fissato, determinato, determinando.

efficacy: efficacia.
enabling: abilitando.
entreat: supplicare.
excited: eccitato, concitato, emozionato.
induced: indotto, concluso, dedotto.
involuntarily: involontariamente.
jostle: spingere, spintone.
mule: mulo.
occasions: occasioni.
overheard: origliato.
preferences: preferenze.

prefers: preferisce.
quart: quarto, quarto di gallone.
revealing: pubblicando, rivelando.
sour: acido, agro, brusco, rude, acerbo, aspro.
sulky: imbronciato.
trembled: tremato.
unusually: insolitamente.
withdraw: ritirare, ritiro, ritira, ritiriamo, ritiri, ritirate, ritirano, prelevare, ritirarsi, preleva, prelevano.

"I would prefer to be left **alone** here," said Bartleby, as if **offended** at being mobbed in his privacy.

"*That's* the word, Turkey," said I—"*that's* it."

"Oh, *prefer*? oh yes—queer wood. I never use it myself. But, sir, as I was saying, if he would but prefer—"

"Turkey," **interrupted** I, "you will please withdraw."

"Oh certainly, sir, if you prefer that I should."

As he opened the folding-door to **retire**, Nippers at his **desk** caught a **glimpse** of me, and asked whether I would prefer to have a certain paper copied on blue paper or white. He did not in the **least** roguishly **accent** the word prefer. It was **plain** that it involuntarily **rolled** from his **tongue**. I thought to myself, surely I must get **rid** of a **demented** man, who already has in some degree turned the tongues, if not the heads of myself and clerks. But I thought it **prudent** not to break the dismission at once.

The next day I noticed that Bartleby did nothing but stand at his window in his dead-wall revery. Upon asking him why he did not write, he said that he had decided upon doing no more writing.

"Why, how now? what next?" exclaimed I, "do no more writing?"

"No more."

"And what is the reason?"

"Do you not see the reason for yourself," he **indifferently** replied.

I looked steadfastly at him, and **perceived** that his eyes looked dull and glazed. **Instantly** it **occurred** to me, that his **unexampled diligence** in copying by his dim window for the first few weeks of his stay with me might have **temporarily** impared his **vision**.

I was **touched**. I said something in **condolence** with him. I **hinted** that of course he did **wisely** in abstaining from writing for a while; and urged him to **embrace** that opportunity of taking **wholesome** exercise in the open air. This, however, he did not do. A few days after this, my other clerks being absent, and

Italian

accent: accento, accentare, accentano, accentate, accenti, accentiamo, accenta.
alone: solo, da solo, solamente.
condolence: condoglianza.
demented: demente.
desk: scrivania, banco.
diligence: diligenza.
embrace: abbracciare, abbraccio.
glimpse: intravedere, occhiata, rapido sguardo.
hinted: suggerito.

indifferently: indifferentemente.
instantly: direttamente, istantaneamente, immediatamente.
interrupted: interrotto, sospeso.
least: minimo, meno.
occurred: successo, accaduto.
offended: offeso, insultato, oltraggiato.
perceived: scorto, percepito, intravisto.
plain: piano, pianura, evidente, distinto, chiaro.

prudent: prudente, sensato.
retire: ritirare, ritira, ritirano, ritirate, ritiri, ritiriamo, ritiro.
rid: sbarazzare.
rolled: laminato.
temporarily: temporaneamente.
tongue: lingua, linguetta, la lingua.
touched: toccato.
unexampled: singolare.
vision: visione, vista.
wholesome: sano, salubre.
wisely: saggiamente.

being in a great **hurry** to **dispatch** certain letters by the **mail**, I thought that, having nothing else **earthly** to do, Bartleby would surely be less **inflexible** than usual, and carry these letters to the post-office. But he blankly declined. So, much to my **inconvenience**, I went myself.

Still added days went by. Whether Bartleby's eyes improved or not, I could not say. To all appearance, I thought they did. But when I asked him if they did, he vouchsafed no answer. At all events, he would do no copying. At last, in reply to my urgings, he **informed** me that he had permanently given up copying.

"What!" exclaimed I; "suppose your eyes should get entirely well — better than ever before — would you not copy then?"

"I have given up copying," he answered, and slid aside.

He remained as ever, a **fixture** in my **chamber**. Nay — if that were possible — he became still more of a fixture than before. What was to be done? He would do nothing in the office; why should he stay there? In plain fact, he had now become a **millstone** to me, not only **useless** as a **necklace**, but afflictive to bear. Yet I was sorry for him. I speak less than truth when I say that, on his own account, he occasioned me uneasiness. If he would but have **named** a single relative or friend, I would instantly have written, and urged their taking the poor fellow away to some **convenient** retreat. But he seemed alone, absolutely alone in the **universe**. A bit of **wreck** in the **mid** Atlantic. At length, necessities **connected** with my business **tyrannized** over all other considerations. **Decently** as I could, I told Bartleby that in six days time he must unconditionally leave the office. I warned him to take measures, in the **interval**, for **procuring** some other abode. I offered to **assist** him in this endeavor, if he himself would but take the first step towards a **removal**. "And when you finally **quit** me, Bartleby," added I, "I shall see that you go not away entirely **unprovided**. Six days from this hour, remember."

At the **expiration** of that period, I peeped behind the screen, and lo! Bartleby was there.

I buttoned up my coat, **balanced** myself; advanced slowly towards him, touched his shoulder, and said, "The time has come; you must quit this place; I am sorry for you; here is money; but you must go."

Italian

assist: assistere, assistono, assistiamo, assistete, assisti, assisto, aiutare, aiuti, aiuta, aiutano, aiutate.
balanced: equilibrato, bilanciato.
chamber: camera.
connected: collegato, legato, connesso.
convenient: conveniente.
decently: decentemente.
dispatch: dispaccio, invio, spedizione.
earthly: terrestre, terreno, mondano.
expiration: scadenza, espirazione.
fixture: attrezzatura, apparecchiatura, attrezzo.
hurry: affrettarsi, fretta.
inconvenience: inconvenienza, disagio, disturbo.
inflexible: inflessibile, rigido.
informed: informato.
interval: intervallo.
mail: posta, corrispondenza.
mid: mezzo.
millstone: mola.
named: nome.
necklace: collana.
procuring: procurando.
quit: abbandonare, abbandonato, abbandono, abbandoni, abbandonate, abbandonano, abbandona, abbandoniamo, smettere.
removal: rimozione, asportazione, eliminazione.
tyrannized: tiranneggiato.
universe: universo.
unprovided: sprovvisto.
useless: inutile, inservibile.
wreck: naufragio, relitto, distruggere.

"I would prefer not," he replied, with his back still towards me.

"You *must.*"

He remained silent.

Now I had an **unbounded** confidence in this man's common honesty. He had frequently **restored** to me sixpences and shillings **carelessly** dropped upon the floor, for I am apt to be very reckless in such shirt-button affairs. The proceeding, then, which **followed** will not be deemed extraordinary.

"Bartleby," said I, "I owe you twelve **dollars** on account; here are thirty-two; the odd twenty are yours—Will you take it?" and I handed the bills towards him.

But he made no motion.

"I will leave them here, then," putting them under a weight on the table. Then taking my hat and **cane** and going to the door, I tranquilly turned and added—"After you have removed your things from these offices, Bartleby, you will of course lock the door—since every one is now gone for the day but you—and if you please, slip your key **underneath** the **mat**, so that I may have it in the morning. I shall not see you again; so good-by to you. If, **hereafter**, in your new place of abode, I can be of any service to you, do not fail to **advise** me by letter. Good-by, Bartleby, and **fare** you well."

But he answered not a word; like the last column of some **ruined temple**, he remained standing mute and **solitary** in the middle of the otherwise deserted room.

As I walked home in a **pensive** mood, my vanity got the better of my **pity**. I could not but highly **plume** myself on my **masterly** management in getting rid of Bartleby. Masterly I call it, and such it must appear to any **dispassionate thinker**. The beauty of my procedure seemed to **consist** in its perfect **quietness**. There was no **vulgar** bullying, no **bravado** of any sort, no **choleric** hectoring, and striding to and fro across the **apartment**, jerking out **vehement** commands for Bartleby to **bundle** himself off with his beggarly traps. Nothing of the kind. Without **loudly bidding** Bartleby depart—as an **inferior genius** might have

Italian

advise: consigliare, consigliano, consigli, consiglia, consigliamo, consigliate, consiglio, raccomandare.
apartment: appartamento.
bidding: offerta, licitazione, comando.
bravado: bravata.
bundle: fascio, fastello, pacco.
cane: bastone, canna, canna da zucchero.
carelessly: negligentemente.
choleric: collerico.
consist: consistere.

dispassionate: spassionato.
dollars: dollari.
fare: tariffa.
genius: genio.
hereafter: in futuro.
inferior: inferiore.
loudly: forte, ad alta voce.
masterly: magistrale.
mat: stuoia.
owe: dovere.
pensive: pensoso, pensieroso.
pity: compassione, pietà.

plume: penna, pennacchio, piuma.
quietness: quiete, calma.
restored: ripristinato, restaurato.
ruined: rovinato.
solitary: solo, solitario.
temple: tempia, tempio.
thinker: pensatore.
unbounded: illimitato.
underneath: sotto, dabbasso, giù, disotto.
vehement: veemente.
vulgar: volgare, triviale.

done—I *assumed* the ground that **depart** he must; and upon that assumption built all I had to say. The more I thought over my procedure, the more I was charmed with it. Nevertheless, next morning, upon **awakening**, I had my doubts—I had somehow **slept** off the **fumes** of vanity. One of the coolest and wisest hours a man has, is just after he awakes in the morning. My procedure seemed as **sagacious** as ever—but only in theory. How it would prove in practice—there was the **rub**. It was truly a beautiful thought to have assumed Bartleby's **departure**; but, after all, that assumption was simply my own, and none of Bartleby's. The great point was, not whether I had assumed that he would quit me, but whether he would prefer so to do. He was more a man of preferences than assumptions.

After breakfast, I walked down town, **arguing** the probabilities *pro* and *con*. One moment I thought it would prove a **miserable** failure, and Bartleby would be found all alive at my office as usual; the next moment it seemed certain that I should find his chair empty. And so I kept **veering** about. At the corner of Broadway and Canal street, I saw quite an excited group of people standing in **earnest** conversation.

"I'll take **odds** he doesn't," said a voice as I passed.

"Doesn't go?—done!" said I, "put up your money."

I was **instinctively** putting my hand in my pocket to produce my own, when I remembered that this was an election day. The words I had overheard **bore** no reference to Bartleby, but to the success or non-success of some candidate for the mayoralty. In my **intent** frame of mind, I had, as it were, **imagined** that all Broadway shared in my **excitement**, and were **debating** the same question with me. I passed on, very **thankful** that the **uproar** of the street **screened** my **momentary** absent-mindedness.

As I had intended, I was earlier than usual at my office door. I stood listening for a moment. All was still. He must be gone. I tried the **knob**. The door was **locked**. Yes, my procedure had worked to a charm; he indeed must be **vanished**. Yet a certain melancholy mixed with this: I was almost sorry for my brilliant success. I was **fumbling** under the door mat for the key, which Bartleby was to

Italian

arguing: argomentando, discutendo, disputando.	**excitement**: eccitazione, eccitamento.	miserando.
awakening: risveglio.	**fumbling**: armeggiando, brancolando, annaspando, frugando.	**momentary**: momentaneo.
bore: annoiare, alesaggio, foro, forare, succiello, seccare, alesare, perforare, trivellare.	**fumes**: vapore, esalazione, fumi.	**odds**: probabilità, disuguaglianza, differenza.
con: contro.	**imagined**: immaginato.	**rub**: fregare, strofinare.
debating: dibattere.	**instinctively**: istintivamente.	**sagacious**: saggio, sagace.
depart: partire, partite, partiamo, parti, partono, parto, andarsene.	**intent**: intento, intenzione.	**screened**: schermato.
departure: partenza.	**knob**: manopola, tenaglie, bottone, pomo, pomello.	**slept**: dormito.
earnest: serio, caparra.	**locked**: bloccato.	**thankful**: riconoscente, grato.
	miserable: miserabile, misero, afflitto, cattivo, triste, povero, miserevole,	**uproar**: baccano.
		vanished: sparito.
		veering: girando, virando.

have left there for me, when **accidentally** my **knee** knocked against a panel, **producing** a **summoning** sound, and in response a voice came to me from within—"Not yet; I am occupied."

It was Bartleby.

I was thunderstruck. For an instant I stood like the man who, **pipe** in mouth, was killed one **cloudless** afternoon long ago in Virginia, by summer lightning; at his own warm open window he was killed, and remained **leaning** out there upon the **dreamy** afternoon till some one touched him, when he fell.

"Not gone!" I murmured at last. But again **obeying** that **wondrous ascendancy** which the **inscrutable** scrivener had over me, and from which ascendancy, for all my chafing, I could not completely escape, I slowly went down stairs and out into the street, and while walking round the block, considered what I should next do in this unheard-of perplexity. Turn the man out by an actual thrusting I could not; to drive him away by calling him hard names would not do; calling in the police was an **unpleasant** idea; and yet, **permit** him to enjoy his cadaverous **triumph** over me—this, too, I could not think of. What was to be done? or, if nothing could be done, was there anything further that I could *assume* in the matter? Yes, as before I had **prospectively assumed** that Bartleby would depart, so now I might **retrospectively** assume that **departed** he was. In the **legitimate** carrying out of this **assumption**, I might enter my office in a great hurry, and **pretending** not to see Bartleby at all, walk straight against him as if he were air. Such a proceeding would in a singular degree have the appearance of a home-thrust. It was hardly possible that Bartleby could **withstand** such an application of the **doctrine** of assumptions. But upon second thoughts the success of the plan seemed rather **dubious**. I resolved to argue the matter over with him again.

"Bartleby," said I, **entering** the office, with a quietly severe expression, "I am seriously **displeased**. I am **pained**, Bartleby. I had thought better of you. I had imagined you of such a gentlemanly organization, that in any **delicate** dilemma a **slight** hint would suffice—in short, an assumption. But it appears I am deceived.

Italian

accidentally: accidentalmente.
ascendancy: predominio, ascendente.
assumed: presunto, supposto.
assumption: assunzione, supposizione, presupposto.
cloudless: sereno.
delicate: delicato.
departed: partito.
displeased: scontentato, scontento.
doctrine: dottrina.
dreamy: sognante.
dubious: equivoco.

entering: entrando, entrare.
inscrutable: inscrutabile.
knee: ginocchio, il ginocchio.
leaning: sporgente, propensione, pendente.
legitimate: legittimo.
obeying: ubbidendo, obbedendo.
pained: addolorato, afflitto, dolore.
permit: permettere, permesso, autorizzazione.
pipe: tubo, condotto, pipa.
pretending: fingendo.

producing: producendo, produrre.
prospectively: eventualmente.
retrospectively: retrospettivamente.
slight: leggero, lieve.
summoning: convocare.
triumph: vittoria, trionfo.
unpleasant: rude, spiacevole, brusco, sgradevole, scostante.
withstand: opporsi a, far fronte a, resistere, resisto, resistono, resistiamo, resisti, resistete.
wondrous: meraviglioso.

Why," I added, unaffectedly starting, "you have not even touched that money yet," pointing to it, just where I had left it the evening previous.

He answered nothing.

"Will you, or will you not, quit me?" I now **demanded** in a **sudden** passion, advancing close to him.

"I would prefer *not* to quit you," he replied gently **emphasizing** the *not*.

"What earthly right have you to stay here? Do you pay any **rent**? Do you pay my **taxes**? Or is this property yours?"

He answered nothing.

"Are you ready to go on and write now? Are your eyes **recovered**? Could you copy a small paper for me this morning? or help examine a few lines? or step round to the post-office? In a word, will you do anything at all, to give a **coloring** to your **refusal** to depart the premises?"

He silently retired into his hermitage.

I was now in such a state of **nervous resentment** that I thought it but prudent to check myself at present from further demonstrations. Bartleby and I were alone. I remembered the **tragedy** of the **unfortunate** Adams and the still more unfortunate Colt in the solitary office of the latter; and how poor Colt, being dreadfully **incensed** by Adams, and **imprudently** permitting himself to get **wildly** excited, was at **unawares** hurried into his **fatal** act—an act which certainly no man could possibly **deplore** more than the **actor** himself. Often it had occurred to me in my ponderings upon the subject, that had that **altercation** taken place in the public street, or at a private **residence**, it would not have **terminated** as it did. It was the **circumstance** of being alone in a solitary office, up **stairs**, of a building entirely unhallowed by **humanizing** domestic associations—an uncarpeted office, doubtless, of a **dusty**, **haggard** sort of appearance—this it must have been, which **greatly** helped to **enhance** the irritable **desperation** of the **hapless** Colt.

But when this old Adam of resentment rose in me and **tempted** me **concerning** Bartleby, I grappled him and threw him. How? Why, simply by

Italian

actor: attore.	**fatal**: fatale, mortale.	**resentment**: risentimento, astio.
altercation: lite, alterco.	**greatly**: molto, grandemente.	**residence**: residenza, alloggio,
circumstance: circostanza.	**haggard**: sparuto.	appartamento.
coloring: coloritura, colorante.	**hapless**: sfortunato, disgraziato.	**stairs**: scala, scale.
concerning: concernere.	**humanizing**: umanizzando.	**sudden**: subitaneo, improvviso.
demanded: richiesto.	**imprudently**: imprudentemente.	**taxes**: imposte.
deplore: deplorare.	**incensed**: incenso.	**tempted**: tentato.
desperation: disperazione.	**nervous**: nervoso.	**terminated**: terminato.
dusty: polveroso.	**recovered**: ricuperato.	**tragedy**: tragedia.
emphasizing: accentuando,	**refusal**: rifiuto.	**unawares**: inavvertitamente.
enfatizzando.	**rent**: affitto, affittare, canone,	**unfortunate**: sfortunato, sventurato.
enhance: accrescere, aumentare.	noleggiare, pigione.	**wildly**: selvaggiamente.

recalling the divine **injunction**: "A new **commandment** give I unto you, that ye love one another." Yes, this it was that saved me. Aside from higher considerations, charity often operates as a **vastly** wise and prudent principle — a great **safeguard** to its **possessor**. Men have committed murder for jealousy's sake, and anger's sake, and hatred's sake, and selfishness' sake, and spiritual pride's sake; but no man, that ever I heard of, ever committed a **diabolical** murder for sweet charity's sake. Mere self-interest, then, if no better motive can be **enlisted**, should, especially with high-tempered men, **prompt** all beings to charity and **philanthropy**. At any rate, upon the occasion in question, I strove to **drown** my **exasperated** feelings towards the scrivener by benevolently **construing** his conduct. — Poor fellow, poor fellow! thought I, he don't mean anything; and besides, he has seen hard times, and ought to be indulged.

I endeavored, also, immediately to occupy myself, and at the same time to comfort my despondency. I tried to fancy, that in the course of the morning, at such time as might prove **agreeable** to him, Bartleby, of his own free accord, would emerge from his hermitage and take up some decided line of march in the direction of the door. But no. Half-past twelve o'clock came; Turkey began to glow in the face, **overturn** his inkstand, and become generally obstreperous; Nippers **abated** down into **quietude** and courtesy; Ginger Nut **munched** his noon apple; and Bartleby remained standing at his window in one of his profoundest dead-wall reveries. Will it be **credited**? Ought I to acknowledge it? That afternoon I left the office without saying one further word to him.

Some days now passed, during which, at leisure intervals I looked a little into "Edwards on the Will," and "Priestley on Necessity." Under the circumstances, those books induced a **salutary** feeling. Gradually I slid into the **persuasion** that these troubles of mine, touching the scrivener, had been all predestinated from **eternity**, and Bartleby was billeted upon me for some mysterious purpose of an allwise Providence, which it was not for a mere mortal like me to **fathom**. Yes, Bartleby, stay there behind your screen, thought I; I shall **persecute** you no more; you are **harmless** and noiseless as any of these old chairs; in short, I never feel so private as when I know you are here. At last I see it, I feel it; I **penetrate** to the

Italian

abated: diminuito, ridotto.
agreeable: gradevole, piacevole, amabile.
commandment: comandamento.
construing: analizzando, interpretando.
credited: accreditato.
diabolical: diabolico.
drown: annegare, annega, annego, anneghiamo, anneghi, annegate, annegano, annegarsi, affogare.
enlisted: arruolato.

eternity: eternità.
exasperated: esasperato.
fathom: scandagliare.
harmless: innocuo, inoffensivo.
injunction: ingiunzione.
munched: sgranocchiato.
overturn: capovolgere, rovesciare.
penetrate: penetrare, penetri, penetriamo, penetrate, penetrano, penetra, penetro.
persecute: perseguitare, perseguito, perseguita, perseguitano,

perseguitate, perseguiti, perseguitiamo, perseguire.
persuasion: persuasione.
philanthropy: filantropia.
possessor: possessore.
prompt: preciso, esatto, sollecito, pronto.
quietude: calma, quiete.
safeguard: salvaguardia, salvaguardare.
salutary: salutare.
vastly: vastamente.

predestinated purpose of my life. I am content. Others may have loftier parts to **enact**; but my **mission** in this world, Bartleby, is to **furnish** you with office-room for such period as you may see fit to remain.

I believe that this **wise** and blessed frame of mind would have continued with me, had it not been for the **unsolicited** and **uncharitable remarks obtruded** upon me by my professional friends who visited the rooms. But thus it often is, that the constant **friction** of **illiberal** minds wears out at last the best resolves of the more **generous**. Though to be sure, when I reflected upon it, it was not strange that people entering my office should be struck by the peculiar aspect of the unaccountable Bartleby, and so be tempted to throw out some **sinister observations** concerning him. Sometimes an **attorney**, having business with me, and calling at my office, and finding no one but the scrivener there, would **undertake** to obtain some sort of precise information from him touching my **whereabouts**; but without heeding his idle talk, Bartleby would remain standing immovable in the middle of the room. So after **contemplating** him in that position for a time, the attorney would depart, no wiser than he came.

Also, when a reference was going on, and the room full of **lawyers** and witnesses, and business driving fast, some deeply-occupied legal gentleman present, seeing Bartleby **wholly** unemployed, would request him to run round to his (the legal gentleman's) office and **fetch** some papers for him. **Thereupon**, Bartleby would tranquilly decline, and yet remain idle as before. Then the lawyer would give a great **stare**, and turn to me. And what could I say? At last I was made aware that all through the circle of my professional **acquaintance**, a **whisper** of wonder was running round, having reference to the strange **creature** I kept at my office. This worried me very much. And as the idea came upon me of his possibly turning out a long-lived man, and keep occupying my chambers, and **denying** my authority; and perplexing my visitors; and **scandalizing** my professional reputation; and casting a general gloom over the premises; keeping soul and body together to the last upon his savings (for doubtless he spent but half a dime a day), and in the end perhaps **outlive** me, and claim possession of my office by right of his perpetual occupancy: as all these dark anticipations

Italian

acquaintance: conoscenza, conoscente.
attorney: procuratore, avvocato.
contemplating: contemplando.
creature: creatura.
denying: negando.
enact: decretare, decreto, decretiamo, decreti, decretate, decreta, decretano.
fetch: portare, portiamo, porto, porti, portate, portano, porta, ottenere, andare a prendere.
friction: attrito, frizione, sfregamento.
furnish: fornire, fornite, forniscono,

fornisco, fornisci, forniamo, arredare.
generous: generoso, liberale, munifico.
illiberal: illiberale.
lawyer: avvocato, legale, giurista.
mission: missione.
observations: osservazioni.
obtruded: imposto.
outlive: sopravvivere a.
remarks: osservazioni.
scandalizing: scandalizzando.
sinister: sinistro.
stare: fissare, sguardo fisso.

thereupon: in merito.
uncharitable: aspro.
undertake: intraprendere, intraprendete, intraprendono, intraprendo, intraprendi, intraprendiamo.
unsolicited: non richiesto.
whereabouts: dove.
whisper: sussurrare, bisbigliare, bisbiglio.
wholly: interamente, completamente.
wise: saggio, assennato.

crowded upon me more and more, and my friends continually **intruded** their **relentless** remarks upon the apparition in my room; a great change was **wrought** in me. I resolved to gather all my faculties together, and forever rid me of this intolerable **incubus**.

Ere revolving any **complicated** project, however, **adapted** to this end, I first simply suggested to Bartleby the **propriety** of his permanent departure. In a calm and serious tone, I commanded the idea to his careful and mature consideration. But, having taken three days to **meditate** upon it, he **apprised** me, that his original determination remained the same; in short, that he still preferred to **abide** with me.

What shall I do? I now said to myself, buttoning up my coat to the last button. What shall I do? what ought I to do? what does **conscience** say I *should* do with this man, or, rather, ghost. Rid myself of him, I must; go, he shall. But how? You will not thrust him, the poor, pale, **passive** mortal — you will not thrust such a **helpless** creature out of your door? you will not **dishonor** yourself by such **cruelty**? No, I will not, I cannot do that. Rather would I let him live and die here, and then **mason** up his remains in the wall. What, then, will you do? For all your **coaxing**, he will not **budge**. Bribes he leaves under your own paper-weight on your table; in short, it is quite plain that he prefers to **cling** to you.

Then something severe, something unusual must be done. What! surely you will not have him collared by a constable, and **commit** his innocent **pallor** to the common **jail**? And upon what ground could you procure such a thing to be done? — a vagrant, is he? What! he a vagrant, a **wanderer**, who refuses to budge? It is because he will *not* be a vagrant, then, that you seek to count him *as* a vagrant. That is too **absurd**. No visible means of support: there I have him. Wrong again: for indubitably he *does* support himself, and that is the only **unanswerable** proof that any man can show of his **possessing** the means so to do. No more, then. Since he will not quit me, I must quit him. I will change my offices; I will move elsewhere, and give him fair notice, that if I find him on my new premises I will then proceed against him as a common **trespasser**.

Italian

abide: aspettare, aspettiamo, aspetta, aspettano, aspetti, aspetto, aspettate, restare, sopportare.
absurd: assurdo.
adapted: adattato.
apprised: informato, avvisato, avvertito.
budge: spostarsi, muoversi.
cling: aderite, aderiscono, aderiamo, aderisco, aderisci, aggrapparsi, aderire.
coaxing: blandendo, persuadendo.

commit: commettere.
complicated: complicato.
conscience: coscienza.
cruelty: crudeltà.
dishonor: disonorare, disonore.
helpless: indifeso.
incubus: incubo.
intruded: imposto.
jail: prigione, carcere, incarcerare, imprigionare, galera.
mason: muratore.
meditate: meditare, mediti,

meditiamo, meditate, meditano, medita, medito.
pallor: pallore.
passive: passivo.
possessing: possedendo.
propriety: convenienza.
relentless: inflessibile.
trespasser: trasgressore.
unanswerable: incontestabile, irrefutabile.
wanderer: vagabondo.
wrought: battuto, lavorato.

Acting accordingly, next day I thus **addressed** him: "I find these chambers too far from the City Hall; the air is **unwholesome**. In a word, I **propose** to **remove** my offices next week, and shall no longer require your services. I tell you this now, in order that you may seek another place."

He made no **reply**, and nothing more was said.

On the appointed day I engaged carts and men, **proceeded** to my chambers, and, having but little **furniture**, everything was removed in a few hours. Throughout, the scrivener remained standing behind the screen, which I **directed** to be removed the last thing. It was **withdrawn**; and, being folded up like a huge folio, left him the motionless **occupant** of a **naked** room. I stood in the entry watching him a moment, while something from within me **upbraided** me.

I re-entered, with my hand in my pocket—and—and my heart in my mouth.

"Good-by, Bartleby; I am going—good-by, and God some way **bless** you; and take that," **slipping** something in his hand. But it dropped upon the floor, and then—strange to say—I tore myself from him whom I had so longed to be rid of.

Established in my new quarters, for a day or two I kept the door locked, and started at every footfall in the passages. When I returned to my rooms, after any little absence, I would **pause** at the threshold for an instant, and **attentively** listen, ere **applying** my key. But these fears were **needless**. Bartleby never came nigh me.

I thought all was going well, when a perturbed-looking **stranger visited** me, **inquiring** whether I was the person who had recently **occupied** rooms at No.——Wall street.

Full of forebodings, I replied that I was.

"Then, sir," said the stranger, who proved a lawyer, "you are responsible for the man you left there. He refuses to do any copying; he refuses to do anything; he says he prefers not to; and he refuses to quit the premises."

"I am very sorry, sir," said I, with assumed tranquillity, but an **inward** tremor, "but, really, the man you **allude** to is nothing to me—he is no **relation** or **apprentice** of mine, that you should hold me responsible for him."

Italian

addressed: rivolto.
allude: alludere, alludi, alludiamo, alludo, alludono, alludete.
applying: applicando.
apprentice: apprendista.
attentively: attentamente.
bless: benedire, benedi', benedite, benedicono, benedico, benedici, benediciamo.
directed: diretto.
furniture: mobili, mobilia.
inquiring: domandando, domandare.

inward: interno.
naked: nudo.
needless: inutile.
occupant: occupante.
occupied: occupato.
pause: pausa, sosta.
proceeded: proceduto.
propose: proporre, proponiamo, proponi, propongono, proponete, propongo.
relation: relazione, rapporto.
remove: togliere, togliamo, togli, tolgo,

tolgono, togliete, asportare, rimuovere, asporti, rimuovete, rimuovi.
reply: risposta, rispondere, replicare, replica.
slipping: slittamento.
stranger: sconosciuto, estraneo, forestiero.
unwholesome: malsano.
upbraided: rimproverato.
visited: visitato.
withdrawn: ritirato, prelevato.

"In mercy's name, who is he?"

"I certainly cannot inform you. I know nothing about him. **Formerly** I employed him as a copyist; but he has done nothing for me now for some time past."

"I shall **settle** him, then—good morning, sir."

Several days passed, and I heard nothing more; and, though I often felt a **charitable prompting** to call at the place and see poor Bartleby, yet a certain **squeamishness**, of I know not what, **withheld** me.

All is over with him, by this time, thought I, at last, when, through another week, no further **intelligence** reached me. But, coming to my room the day after, I found several persons **waiting** at my door in a high state of nervous excitement.

"That's the man—here he comes," cried the **foremost** one, whom I recognized as the lawyer who had **previously** called upon me alone.

"You must take him away, sir, at once," cried a **portly** person among them, advancing upon me, and whom I knew to be the **landlord** of No.——Wall street. "These gentlemen, my tenants, cannot stand it any longer; Mr. B——," pointing to the lawyer, "has turned him out of his room, and he now **persists** in **haunting** the building generally, sitting upon the **banisters** of the stairs by day, and sleeping in the **entry** by night. **Everybody** is concerned; clients are leaving the **offices**; some fears are **entertained** of a **mob**; something you must do, and that without delay."

Aghast at this **torrent**, I fell back before it, and would fain have locked myself in my new quarters. In vain I **persisted** that Bartleby was nothing to me—no more than to any one else. In vain—I was the last person known to have anything to do with him, and they held me to the **terrible** account. **Fearful**, then, of being **exposed** in the **papers** (as one person present **obscurely** threatened), I considered the matter, and, at **length**, said, that if the lawyer would give me a **confidential interview** with the scrivener, in his (the lawyer's) own room, I would, that afternoon, **strive** my best to rid them of the **nuisance** they complained of.

Italian

banisters: parapetto, ringhiera.
charitable: caritatevole, misericordioso.
confidential: confidenziale.
entertained: intrattenuto.
entry: entrata, ingresso, voce, immissione, partita, posta.
everybody: ognuno, tutti, ogni, tutto.
exposed: esposto.
fearful: spaventoso, pauroso.
foremost: primo.
formerly: precedentemente, davanti,
in passato, un tempo.
haunting: ossessionante.
intelligence: intelligenza.
interview: intervista, colloquio.
landlord: proprietario, locatore, affittacamere.
length: lunghezza, durata.
mob: folla, plebaglia, gentaglia.
nuisance: seccatura.
obscurely: oscuramente.
offices: uffici.
papers: documenti.
persisted: persistito.
persists: persiste.
portly: corpulento.
previously: precedentemente, davanti.
prompting: suggerimento.
settle: sistemare, regolare, saldare.
squeamishness: schizzinosità.
strive: sforzarsi.
terrible: terribile, tremendo.
torrent: torrente.
waiting: aspettando, attesa, servizio.
withheld: trattenuto.

Going up stairs to my old **haunt**, there was Bartleby silently **sitting** upon the **banister** at the **landing**.

"What are you doing here, Bartleby?" said I.

"Sitting upon the banister," he mildly replied.

I motioned him into the lawyer's room, who then left us.

"Bartleby" said I, "are you **aware** that you are the **cause** of great **tribulation** to me, by **persisting** in occupying the entry after being dismissed from the office?"

No answer.

"Now one of two things must take place. Either you must do something, or something must be done to you. Now what sort of business would you like to **engage** in? Would you like to re-engage in **copying** for some one?"

"No; I would prefer not to make any change."

"Would you like a clerkship in a dry-goods store?"

"There is too much **confinement** about that. No, I would not like a clerkship; but I am not particular."

"Too much confinement," I cried, "why you keep **yourself confined** all the time!"

"I would prefer not to take a clerkship," he **rejoined**, as if to settle that little **item** at once.

"How would a bar-tender's business **suit** you? There is no **trying** of the eye-sight in that."

"I would not like it at all; though, as I said before, I am not particular."

His unwonted **wordiness** inspirited me. I **returned** to the charge.

"Well, then, would you like to **travel** through the country **collecting bills** for the merchants? That would **improve** your health."

"No, I would prefer to be doing something else."

Italian

aware: cosciente, consapevole.
banister: ringhiera.
bills: effetti, banconote.
cause: causa, causare, provocare.
collecting: raccogliendo.
confined: limitato.
confinement: reclusione, prigionia, confinamento.
copying: copia, copiatura, riproduzione.
engage: innestare, innestiamo, innesta, innestano, innestate, innesti,

ingaggiare, ingranare, impegnare, assumere, innesto.
haunt: frequentare.
improve: migliorare, miglioro, miglioriamo, migliori, migliorate, migliora, migliorano, perfezionare, perfezioni, perfeziono, perfezioniamo.
item: articolo, elemento, voce.
landing: pianerottolo, sbarco, approdo, atterraggio.
persisting: persistendo.

rejoined: riunito.
returned: ritornato.
sitting: sedendo, covando, seduta.
suit: abito, costume, vestito, tailleur, completo.
travel: viaggiare, viaggi, viaggio, viaggiamo, viaggiano, viaggia, viaggiate, camminare.
tribulation: tribolazione.
trying: duro, difficile, tentare.
wordiness: verbosità.
yourself: ti.

"How, then, would going as a **companion** to Europe, to **entertain** some young gentleman with your conversation—how would that suit you?"

"Not at all. It does not strike me that there is anything **definite** about that. I like to be **stationary**. But I am not particular."

"Stationary you shall be, then," I cried, now losing all patience, and, for the first time in all my **exasperating** connection with him, fairly flying into a passion. "If you do not go away from these premises before night, I shall feel bound— indeed, I *am* bound—to—to—to quit the premises myself!" I rather **absurdly concluded**, knowing not with what possible threat to try to **frighten** his **immobility** into compliance. **Despairing** of all further efforts, I was precipitately leaving him, when a final thought occurred to me—one which had not been wholly unindulged before.

"Bartleby," said I, in the kindest tone I could assume under such exciting circumstances, "will you go home with me now—not to my office, but my dwelling—and remain there till we can conclude upon some convenient arrangement for you at our leisure? Come, let us start now, right away."

"No: at present I would prefer not to make any change at all."

I answered nothing; but, effectually **dodging** every one by the **suddenness** and **rapidity** of my flight, rushed from the building, ran up Wall street towards Broadway, and, **jumping** into the first **omnibus**, was soon removed from **pursuit**. As soon as tranquillity returned, I **distinctly** perceived that I had now done all that I possibly could, both in respect to the demands of the landlord and his tenants, and with regard to my own desire and sense of duty, to benefit Bartleby, and **shield** him from **rude persecution**, I now strove to be entirely care-free and **quiescent**; and my conscience justified me in the attempt; though, indeed, it was not so successful as I could have wished. So fearful was I of being again **hunted** out by the incensed landlord and his exasperated tenants, that, surrendering my business to Nippers, for a few days, I drove about the upper part of the town and through the **suburbs**, in my rockaway; **crossed** over to Jersey City and Hoboken, and paid **fugitive visits** to Manhattanville and Astoria. In fact, I almost lived in my rockaway for the time.

Italian

absurdly: assurdamente.
companion: compagno, accompagnatore.
conclude: concludere, concludo, concludono, concludiamo, concludi, concludete.
crossed: attraversato.
definite: definitivo, definito.
despairing: disperare.
distinctly: distintamente.
dodging: mascheratura in stampa.
entertain: intrattenere, intrattenete, intrattieni, intratteniamo, intrattengo, intrattengono, ricevere.
exasperating: esasperando.
frighten: spaventare, spaventiamo, spaventi, spaventate, spaventano, spaventa, spavento, impaurire, intimorire.
fugitive: fuggitivo.
hunted: cacciato.
immobility: immobilità.
jumping: saltare.
omnibus: autobus.
persecution: inseguimento, persecuzione.
pursuit: inseguimento, ricerca.
quiescent: quiescente.
rapidity: rapidità, velocità.
rude: scortese, rozzo, maleducato.
shield: scudo, riparo, proteggere, schermo, schermare.
stationary: fisso, stazionario, fermo.
suburbs: sobborgo, periferia.
suddenness: subitaneità.
visits: visita.

When again I entered my office, lo, a note from the landlord lay upon the desk. I opened it with **trembling** hands. It informed me that the writer had sent to the police, and had Bartleby removed to the Tombs as a vagrant. Moreover, since I knew more about him than any one else, he wished me to appear at that place, and make a suitable statement of the facts. These tidings had a **conflicting** effect upon me. At first I was **indignant**; but, at last, almost approved. The landlord's energetic, **summary disposition**, had led him to adopt a procedure which I do not think I would have decided upon myself; and yet, as a last **resort**, under such peculiar circumstances, it seemed the only plan.

As I afterwards learned, the poor scrivener, when told that he must be **conducted** to the Tombs, offered not the slightest **obstacle**, but, in his pale, unmoving way, silently **acquiesced**.

Some of the **compassionate** and **curious** bystanders joined the party; and **headed** by one of the constables arm in arm with Bartleby, the silent **procession** filed its way through all the noise, and heat, and joy of the roaring thoroughfares at noon.

The same day I received the note, I went to the Tombs, or, to speak more properly, the Halls of Justice. Seeking the right officer, I stated the purpose of my call, and was informed that the individual I described was, indeed, within. I then **assured** the **functionary** that Bartleby was a perfectly honest man, and greatly to be compassionated, however unaccountably **eccentric**. I **narrated** all I knew and closed by suggesting the idea of **letting** him remain in as **indulgent** confinement as possible, till something less **harsh** might be done—though, indeed, I hardly knew what. At all events, if nothing else could be decided upon, the alms-house must receive him. I then **begged** to have an interview.

Being under no **disgraceful** charge, and quite **serene** and harmless in all his ways, they had **permitted** him **freely** to **wander** about the prison, and, especially, in the inclosed grass-platted yards thereof. And so I found him there, standing all alone in the quietest of the yards, his face towards a high wall, while all around, from the narrow slits of the jail windows, I thought I saw peering out upon him the eyes of murderers and **thieves**.

Italian

acquiesced: acconsentito.
assured: assicurato, certo.
begged: mendicato.
compassionate: compassionevole.
conducted: condotto.
conflicting: conflitto.
curious: curioso.
disgraceful: disgraziata, vergognoso, disonorevole.
disposition: disposizione, predisposizione, ingegno, talento.
eccentric: eccentrico, stravagante.

freely: liberamente.
functionary: funzionario.
harsh: duro, brusco, rude, aspro, ruvido.
headed: diretto.
indignant: indignato.
indulgent: indulgente.
letting: affittando.
narrated: raccontato, narrato.
obstacle: ostacolo.
permitted: permesso.
procession: processione.

resort: ricorso, ricorrere, complesso turistico.
serene: sereno.
summary: riassunto, sommario, compendio, riepilogo.
thieves: ruba, ladri.
trembling: tremolante, tremulo, tremolio, tremito, tremante, tremore, tremare.
wander: vagare, vago, errare, vaghiamo, vaga, vagano, vaghi, vagate, vagabondare.

"Bartleby!"

"I know you," he said, without looking round—"and I want nothing to say to you."

"It was not I that brought you here, Bartleby," said I, keenly pained at his **implied suspicion**. "And to you, this should not be so **vile** a place. Nothing **reproachful attaches** to you by being here. And see, it is not so **sad** a place as one might think. Look, there is the **sky**, and here is the grass."

"I know where I am," he replied, but would say nothing more, and so I left him.

As I **entered** the **corridor** again, a broad meat-like man, in an apron, **accosted** me, and, jerking his **thumb** over his **shoulder**, said—"Is that your friend?"

"Yes."

"Does he want to starve? If he does, let him live on the **prison** fare, that's all."

"Who are you?" asked I, not **knowing** what to make of such an **unofficially speaking** person in such a place.

"I am the grub-man. Such gentlemen as have friends here, **hire** me to provide them with something good to eat."

"Is this so?" said I, **turning** to the **turnkey**.

He said it was.

"Well, then," said I, slipping some **silver** into the grub-man's hands (for so they called him), "I want you to give particular attention to my friend there; let him have the best **dinner** you can get. And you must be as polite to him as possible."

"Introduce me, will you?" said the grub-man, looking at me with an expression which seem to say he was all impatience for an opportunity to give a **specimen** of his **breeding**.

Thinking it would **prove** of benefit to the scrivener, I acquiesced; and, **asking** the grub-man his name, went up with him to Bartleby.

"Bartleby, this is a friend; you will find him very useful to you."

Italian

accosted: abbordato, accostato, avvicinato.
asking: chiedendo, domandando.
attaches: attacca, fissa, allega.
breeding: allevamento, riproduzione.
corridor: corridoio.
dinner: pranzo, colazione, cena, desinare.
entered: entrato.
hire: prendere in affitto, noleggio, noleggiare, noleggiate, noleggiano, noleggiamo, noleggia, noleggi,

affitto, assumere.
implied: significato, implicito, implicato.
knowing: conoscendo, sapendo.
prison: prigione, carcere.
prove: provare, proviamo, provi, provate, provano, provo, prova, comprovare, dimostrare.
reproachful: di rimprovero.
sad: triste, afflitto.
shoulder: spalla, la spalla, spallamento, bordo.

silver: argento.
sky: cielo.
speaking: parlando, parlare.
specimen: campione, esemplare, provino, saggio.
suspicion: sospetto.
thumb: pollice, il pollice.
turning: girando, svoltando, svolta, cambiando.
turnkey: carceriere.
unofficially: ufficiosamente.
vile: abietto.

"Your sarvant, sir, your sarvant," said the grub-man, making a low **salutation** behind his apron. "Hope you find it pleasant here, sir; nice grounds — cool apartments — hope you'll stay with us some time — try to make it agreeable. What will you have for dinner to-day?"

"I prefer not to **dine** to-day," said Bartleby, turning away. "It would **disagree** with me; I am **unused** to dinners." So saying, he slowly moved to the other side of the inclosure, and took up a position fronting the dead-wall.

"How's this?" said the grub-man, addressing me with a stare of **astonishment**. "He's odd, ain't he?"

"I think he is a little deranged," said I, **sadly**.

"**Deranged**? deranged is it? Well, now, upon my word, I thought that friend of yourn was a gentleman **forger**; they are always **pale**, and genteel-like, them forgers. I can't help pity 'em — can't help it, sir. Did you know Monroe Edwards?" he added, touchingly, and paused. Then, **laying** his hand piteously on my shoulder, sighed, "he died of **consumption** at Sing-Sing. So you weren't **acquainted** with Monroe?"

"No, I was never **socially** acquainted with any forgers. But I cannot stop longer. Look to my friend yonder. You will not lose by it. I will see you again."

Some few days after this, I again obtained **admission** to the Tombs, and went through the corridors in **quest** of Bartleby; but without finding him.

"I saw him coming from his cell not long ago," said a turnkey, "may be he's gone to **loiter** in the yards."

So I went in that direction.

"Are you looking for the **silent** man?" said another turnkey, passing me. "Yonder he lies — sleeping in the yard there. 'Tis not twenty minutes since I saw him lie down."

The yard was entirely quiet. It was not **accessible** to the common prisoners. The **surrounding** walls, of **amazing thickness**, kept off all sounds behind them. The Egyptian character of the **masonry weighed** upon me with its gloom. But a soft **imprisoned turf** grew under foot. The heart of the **eternal** pyramids, it

Italian

accessible: accessibile.
acquainted: informato.
admission: ammissione, confessione, immissione, accoglimento, accoglienza, ingresso.
amazing: sbalordendo, stupefacente, stupendosi, sorprendente, strabiliante.
astonishment: stupore, meraviglia, sorpresa.
consumption: consumo.
deranged: squilibrato.

dine: cenare.
disagree: dissentire, discordare.
eternal: eterno.
forger: falsificatore, falsario.
imprisoned: imprigionato.
laying: posando, posa.
loiter: bighelloniamo, gironzolo, gironzoliamo, gironzoli, gironzolate, gironzolano, gironzola, bighelloni, bighellonate, bighellonano, bighellona.
masonry: muratura.

pale: pallido, smorto, impallidire.
quest: ricerca.
sadly: tristemente.
salutation: saluto.
silent: silenzioso, zitto.
socially: socialmente.
surrounding: circondando, circostante.
thickness: spessore, grossezza.
turf: tappeto erboso, zolla erbosa.
unused: non usato, inutilizzato.
weighed: pesato.

seemed, **wherein**, by some strange **magic**, through the clefts, grass-seed, dropped by birds, had sprung.

Strangely huddled at the base of the wall, his knees drawn up, and lying on his side, his head touching the cold stones, I saw the **wasted** Bartleby. But nothing stirred. I paused; then went close up to him; stooped over, and saw that his dim eyes were open; otherwise he seemed **profoundly** sleeping. Something prompted me to touch him. I felt his hand, when a **tingling shiver** ran up my arm and down my **spine** to my, feet.

The round face of the grub-man peered upon me now. "His dinner is ready. Won't he dine to-day, either? Or does he live without dining?"

"Lives without dining," said I, and closed the eyes.

"Eh!—He's **asleep**, ain't he?"

"With kings and counselors," murmured I.

* * * * *

There would seem little need for proceeding further in this history. **Imagination** will **readily** supply the **meagre recital** of poor Bartleby's **interment**. But, ere **parting** with the reader, let me say, that if this little **narrative** has **sufficiently interested** him, to **awaken** curiosity as to who Bartleby was, and what manner of life he led **prior** to the present narrator's making his acquaintance, I can only reply, that in such curiosity I fully share, but am wholly unable to gratify it. Yet here I hardly know whether I should **divulge** one little item of rumor, which came to my **ear** a few months after the scrivener's **decease**. Upon what basis it rested, I could never **ascertain**; and hence, how true it is I cannot now tell. But, inasmuch as this vague report has not been without a certain **suggestive** interest to me, however sad, it may prove the same with some others; and so I will **briefly** mention it. The report was this: that Bartleby had been a **subordinate** clerk in the Dead Letter Office at Washington, from which he

Italian

ascertain: constatare, constatiamo, constati, constatate, constato, constatano, constata, accertare, accerto, accertiamo, accerti.
asleep: addormentato.
awaken: svegliamo, svegliano, svegli, risvegliate, risvegliano, risvegliamo, risvegli, svegliate, risveglia, sveglia, risveglio.
briefly: brevemente.
decease: decedere, decesso.
divulge: divulgare.

ear: orecchio, spiga, l'orecchio, pannocchia.
imagination: immagine, immaginazione, fantasia.
interment: inumazione.
magic: magia, magico.
meagre: scarso.
narrative: descrizione, narrativo.
parting: separazione, divisione.
prior: anteriore, precedente.
profoundly: profondamente.
readily: prontamente.

recital: concerto, recital, dizione.
rested: riposato.
shiver: tremare, brivido, rabbrividire.
spine: spina dorsale, spina, dorso.
subordinate: subordinato, subalterno.
sufficiently: abbastanza, sufficientemente.
suggestive: provocante, suggestivo, indicativo.
tingling: formicolio.
wasted: sprecato.
wherein: dove.

had been suddenly **removed** by a change in the **administration**. When I think over this rumor, hardly can I **express** the emotions which **seize** me. Dead letters! does it not sound like dead men? **Conceive** a man by nature and **misfortune prone** to a pallid hopelessness, can any business seem more **fitted** to **heighten** it than that of continually **handling** these dead letters, and **assorting** them for the flames? For by the cart-load they are **annually** burned. Sometimes from out the folded paper the pale clerk takes a ring—the **finger** it was meant for, perhaps, moulders in the grave; a bank-note sent in swiftest charity—he whom it would **relieve**, nor **eats** nor hungers any more; **pardon** for those who died despairing; hope for those who died unhoping; good tidings for those who died **stifled** by unrelieved **calamities**. On errands of life, these letters speed to death.

Ah, Bartleby! Ah, **humanity**!

Italian

administration: amministrazione, gestione, somministrazione, direzione, governo.
annually: annualmente.
assorting: assortendo.
calamities: calamità.
conceive: concepire, concepiamo, concepisci, concepisco, concepiscono, concepite.
eats: mangia.
express: espresso, esprimere, esprimete, esprimi, esprimiamo, esprimo, esprimono, direttissimo.
finger: dito, il dito.
fitted: aderente, adatto, attrezzato.
handling: movimentazione, maneggio, manipolazione.
heighten: innalzare.
humanity: umanità.
misfortune: sfortuna, traversia, disgrazia.
pardon: grazia, perdono, perdonare, scusare, scusa.
prone: prono, incline.
relieve: alleviare, allevio, allevi, allevia, alleviamo, alleviano, alleviate, rilevare.
removed: tolto, asportato, rimosso.
seize: afferrare, afferro, afferra, afferrano, afferrate, afferri, afferriamo, acciuffare, acchiappare, confiscare, prendere.
stifled: soffocato.

BENITO CERENO

In the year 1799, Captain Amasa Delano, of Duxbury, in Massachusetts, **commanding** a large **sealer** and general **trader**, lay at **anchor** with a **valuable cargo**, in the **harbor** of St. Maria — a small, **desert**, **uninhabited** island toward the southern **extremity** of the long coast of Chili. There he had touched for water.

On the second day, not long after dawn, while lying in his **berth**, his **mate** came below, **informing** him that a strange sail was coming into the **bay**. **Ships** were then not so plenty in those waters as now. He rose, **dressed**, and went on deck.

The morning was one peculiar to that coast. Everything was mute and calm; everything gray. The sea, though **undulated** into long roods of swells, seemed fixed, and was sleeked at the surface like waved lead that has **cooled** and set in the smelter's **mould**. The sky seemed a gray surtout. Flights of **troubled** gray **fowl**, **kith** and **kin** with flights of troubled gray vapors among which they were **mixed**, **skimmed** low and **fitfully** over the waters, as swallows over meadows before storms. Shadows present, **foreshadowing** deeper shadows to come.

To Captain Delano's surprise, the stranger, viewed through the glass, showed no **colors**; though to do so upon entering a **haven**, however uninhabited in its shores, where but a single other ship might be lying, was the custom among **peaceful seamen** of all nations. Considering the lawlessness and loneliness of the spot, and the sort of stories, at that day, associated with those seas, Captain

Italian

anchor: ancora, ancorare, ancoraggio, àncora, l'ancora.
bay: baia, campata, baio, abbaiare, latrare.
berth: cuccetta, ancoraggio, attraccare.
cargo: carico.
colors: colori.
commanding: comandare.
cooled: raffreddato.
desert: deserto, abbandonare.
dressed: vestito.
extremity: estremità.

fitfully: irregolarmente.
foreshadowing: prefigurando.
fowl: pollo, gallina, pollame.
haven: porto.
informing: informando.
kin: stirpe.
kith: amici.
mate: accoppiare, compagno, accoppiarsi.
mixed: misto, mescolato.
mould: forma, stampo, muffa,

plasmare, formare.
peaceful: pacifico, tranquillo.
sealer: isolante, sigillatore.
seamen: marinai.
ships: spedisce.
skimmed: scremato, schiumato.
trader: commerciante.
troubled: disturbato, preoccupato, agitato.
undulated: ondulatorio.
uninhabited: disabitato.
valuable: costoso, caro, prezioso.

Delano's surprise might have **deepened** into some uneasiness had he not been a person of a singularly undistrustful good-nature, not **liable**, except on extraordinary and repeated incentives, and hardly then, to indulge in personal alarms, any way involving the **imputation** of **malign** evil in man. Whether, in view of what humanity is capable, such a **trait implies**, along with a **benevolent** heart, more than ordinary **quickness** and accuracy of **intellectual perception**, may be left to the wise to determine.

But whatever **misgivings** might have obtruded on first seeing the stranger, would almost, in any seaman's mind, have been **dissipated** by **observing** that, the ship, in **navigating** into the harbor, was drawing too near the land; a sunken **reef** making out off her **bow**. This seemed to prove her a stranger, indeed, not only to the sealer, but the island; consequently, she could be no **wonted freebooter** on that **ocean**. With no small interest, Captain Delano continued to watch her—a proceeding not much **facilitated** by the vapors partly mantling the **hull**, through which the far matin light from her **cabin** streamed **equivocally** enough; much like the sun—by this time hemisphered on the **rim** of the **horizon**, and, apparently, in company with the strange ship entering the harbor—which, wimpled by the same low, **creeping** clouds, showed not unlike a Lima intriguante's one sinister eye peering across the Plaza from the Indian loop-hole of her dusk *saya-y-manta*.

It might have been but a **deception** of the vapors, but, the longer the stranger was watched the more singular appeared her manoeuvres. Ere long it seemed hard to decide whether she meant to come in or no—what she wanted, or what she was about. The wind, which had breezed up a little during the night, was now extremely light and **baffling**, which the more increased the apparent **uncertainty** of her movements. Surmising, at last, that it might be a ship in distress, Captain Delano ordered his whale-boat to be dropped, and, much to the **wary** opposition of his mate, prepared to board her, and, at the least, pilot her in. On the night previous, a fishing-party of the seamen had gone a long distance to some **detached** rocks out of sight from the sealer, and, an hour or two before **daybreak**, had returned, having met with no small success. **Presuming** that the

Italian

baffling: sconcertante.
benevolent: benevolo.
bow: arco, prua, fiocco, inchino, inchinarsi, curva, archetto.
cabin: cabina, capanna, abitacolo.
creeping: strisciando, strisciante.
daybreak: alba.
deception: inganno.
deepened: approfondito.
detached: isolato, staccato, distaccato.
dissipated: dissipato.
equivocally: equivocamente.

facilitated: facilitato, agevolato.
freebooter: pirata.
horizon: orizzonte.
hull: scafo, carena, baccello.
implies: significa, implica.
imputation: imputazione.
intellectual: intellettuale.
liable: responsabile.
malign: maligno.
misgivings: dubbi.
navigating: navigando.
observing: osservando.

ocean: oceano.
perception: percezione.
presuming: supponendo, presumendo, presumere.
quickness: prontezza, rapidità, lestezza.
reef: scogliera, terzarolare.
rim: orlo, cerchione, bordo, cerchio.
trait: caratteristica, tratto.
uncertainty: incertezza.
wary: cauto, guardingo.
wonted: usuale, consueto, solito.

stranger might have been long off soundings, the good captain put several baskets of the fish, for presents, into his boat, and so pulled away. From her continuing too near the sunken reef, **deeming** her in danger, calling to his men, he made all haste to **apprise** those on board of their situation. But, some time ere the boat came up, the wind, light though it was, having **shifted**, had headed the vessel off, as well as partly broken the vapors from about her.

Upon gaining a less remote view, the ship, when made **signally** visible on the **verge** of the leaden-hued swells, with the **shreds** of **fog** here and there **raggedly** furring her, appeared like a white-washed monastery after a thunder-storm, seen perched upon some dun cliff among the Pyrenees. But it was no purely **fanciful resemblance** which now, for a moment, almost led Captain Delano to think that nothing less than a ship-load of monks was before him. Peering over the bulwarks were what really seemed, in the **hazy** distance, throngs of dark cowls; while, fitfully revealed through the open port-holes, other dark moving figures were dimly **descried**, as of Black Friars **pacing** the cloisters.

Upon a still nigher approach, this appearance was modified, and the true character of the vessel was plain—a Spanish **merchantman** of the first class, carrying **negro slaves**, amongst other valuable **freight**, from one colonial port to another. A very large, and, in its time, a very fine vessel, such as in those days were at intervals encountered along that main; sometimes **superseded** Acapulco treasure-ships, or retired **frigates** of the Spanish king's navy, which, like superannuated Italian **palaces**, still, under a decline of masters, preserved signs of former state.

As the whale-boat drew more and more nigh, the cause of the peculiar pipe-clayed aspect of the stranger was seen in the **slovenly** neglect **pervading** her. The **spars**, ropes, and great part of the bulwarks, looked **woolly**, from long unacquaintance with the **scraper**, **tar**, and the brush. Her **keel** seemed laid, her ribs put together, and she launched, from Ezekiel's Valley of Dry Bones.

In the present business in which she was engaged, the ship's general model and rig appeared to have **undergone** no material change from their original **warlike** and Froissart pattern. However, no guns were seen.

Italian

apprise: avvertono, informo, informiamo, informi, informate, informano, informa, avviso, avvisiamo, avvisi, avvisate.
deeming: credendo.
descried: scorto, intravisto.
fanciful: fantasioso, fantastico.
fog: nebbia, annebbiare.
freight: carico, nolo.
hazy: nebbioso.
keel: chiglia.
merchantman: mercantile.

negro: negro.
pacing: pacing.
palaces: palazzi.
pervading: pervadendo.
raggedly: logoramente.
resemblance: somiglianza, rassomiglianza.
rig: attrezzatura.
scraper: raschietto, raschiatore, rastrello.
shifted: spostato.
shreds: straccia, tagliuzza.

signally: segnale.
slaves: schiavi.
slovenly: sciatto, trascurato.
spars: litiga.
superseded: sostituito, soppiantato, rimpiazzato.
tar: catrame, catramare.
undergone: subito.
verge: orlo, margine, bordo.
warlike: guerriero, bellicoso, battagliero.
woolly: lanoso, lanuto.

The tops were large, and were railed about with what had once been **octagonal** net-work, all now in sad **disrepair**. These tops hung overhead like three **ruinous** aviaries, in one of which was seen, perched, on a ratlin, a white noddy, a strange fowl, so called from its lethargic, somnambulistic character, being frequently caught by hand at sea. Battered and **mouldy**, the castellated **forecastle** seemed some ancient **turret**, long ago taken by assault, and then left to decay. Toward the stern, two high-raised quarter galleries—the **balustrades** here and there covered with dry, tindery sea-moss—opening out from the **unoccupied** state-cabin, whose dead-lights, for all the mild weather, were **hermetically** closed and calked—these tenantless **balconies** hung over the sea as if it were the grand Venetian canal. But the principal **relic** of faded **grandeur** was the ample **oval** of the shield-like stern-piece, **intricately** carved with the arms of Castile and Leon, medallioned about by groups of **mythological** or **symbolical** devices; uppermost and central of which was a dark **satyr** in a mask, holding his foot on the **prostrate** neck of a **writhing** figure, likewise masked.

Whether the ship had a figure-head, or only a plain **beak**, was not quite certain, owing to canvas wrapped about that part, either to protect it while **undergoing** a re-furbishing, or else decently to hide its decay. Rudely painted or chalked, as in a **sailor freak**, along the forward side of a sort of **pedestal** below the canvas, was the sentence, "*Seguid vuestro jefe*" (follow your leader); while upon the tarnished headboards, near by, appeared, in **stately** capitals, once **gilt**, the ship's name, "SAN DOMINICK," each letter streakingly **corroded** with tricklings of copper-spike **rust**; while, like **mourning** weeds, dark festoons of sea-grass slimily swept to and fro over the name, with every hearse-like roll of the hull.

As, at last, the boat was hooked from the bow along toward the **gangway** amidship, its keel, while yet some inches separated from the hull, **harshly grated** as on a sunken **coral** reef. It proved a huge bunch of conglobated barnacles **adhering** below the water to the side like a wen—a token of baffling airs and long calms passed somewhere in those seas.

Italian

adhering: aderendo.
balconies: balconi.
balustrades: balaustrate.
beak: becco, rostro.
coral: corallo.
corroded: corroso.
disrepair: rovina, sfacelo.
forecastle: castello di prua.
freak: capriccio.
gangway: passerella, passaggio, corsia.
gilt: doratura.

grandeur: grandiosità.
grated: grattuggiato.
harshly: duramente.
hermetically: ermeticamente.
intricately: complicato, intricatamente.
mouldy: ammuffito, muffito.
mourning: lutto, piangendo.
mythological: mitologico.
octagonal: ottagonale.
oval: ovale.
pedestal: piedistallo.
prostrate: prostrato.

relic: reliquia.
ruinous: rovinoso.
rust: ruggine, arrugginire, arrugginirsi, corrodere.
sailor: marinaio, navigatore.
satyr: satiro.
stately: imponente.
symbolical: simbolico.
turret: torretta.
undergoing: subendo.
unoccupied: vacante, libero.
writhing: storcendo, torcendo.

Climbing the side, the visitor was at once surrounded by a **clamorous throng** of whites and blacks, but the latter outnumbering the former more than could have been expected, negro transportation-ship as the stranger in port was. But, in one language, and as with one voice, all poured out a common tale of suffering; in which the negresses, of whom there were not a few, **exceeded** the others in their **dolorous vehemence**. The **scurvy**, together with the **fever**, had swept off a great part of their number, more especially the Spaniards. Off Cape Horn they had narrowly escaped **shipwreck**; then, for days together, they had lain tranced without wind; their provisions were low; their water next to none; their lips that moment were baked.

While Captain Delano was thus made the mark of all **eager** tongues, his one eager glance took in all faces, with every other object about him.

Always upon first **boarding** a large and **populous** ship at sea, especially a foreign one, with a nondescript crew such as Lascars or Manilla men, the impression **varies** in a peculiar way from that produced by first entering a strange house with strange inmates in a strange land. Both house and ship—the one by its walls and blinds, the other by its high bulwarks like ramparts—hoard from view their **interiors** till the last moment: but in the case of the ship there is this addition; that the living **spectacle** it contains, upon its sudden and complete **disclosure**, has, in contrast with the **blank** ocean which zones it, something of the effect of **enchantment**. The ship seems **unreal**; these strange **costumes**, gestures, and faces, but a **shadowy** tableau just emerged from the deep, which directly must receive back what it gave.

Perhaps it was some such influence, as above is attempted to be described, which, in Captain Delano's mind, **heightened** whatever, upon a **staid scrutiny**, might have seemed unusual; especially the **conspicuous** figures of four elderly **grizzled** negroes, their heads like black, **doddered willow** tops, who, in **venerable** contrast to the **tumult** below them, were couched, sphinx-like, one on the **starboard** cat-head, another on the **larboard**, and the remaining pair face to face on the opposite bulwarks above the main-chains. They each had bits of unstranded old **junk** in their hands, and, with a sort of **stoical** self-content, were

Italian

blank: bianco, vuoto, spazio, in bianco.
boarding: abbordaggio, tavolato, imbarco.
clamorous: clamoroso.
conspicuous: cospicuo.
costumes: costumi.
disclosure: rivelazione, scoperta.
doddered: tremato.
dolorous: doloroso.
eager: avido, desideroso, bramoso, impaziente.

enchantment: incantesimo, incanto.
exceeded: ecceduto.
fever: febbre.
grizzled: brizzolato.
heightened: innalzato.
interiors: interno.
junk: giunca.
larboard: babordo.
populous: popoloso.
scrutiny: esame minuzioso, scrutinio.
scurvy: scorbuto.
shadowy: ombroso.

shipwreck: naufragio.
spectacle: spettacolo.
staid: serio.
starboard: dritta, tribordo.
stoical: stoico.
throng: calca.
tumult: tumulto.
unreal: irreale.
varies: varia.
vehemence: veemenza.
venerable: venerabile.
willow: salice.

picking the junk into oakum, a small **heap** of which lay by their sides. They accompanied the task with a continuous, low, **monotonous**, chant; droning and **drilling** away like so many gray-headed bag-pipers playing a funeral march.

The quarter-deck rose into an ample **elevated poop**, upon the forward verge of which, lifted, like the oakum-pickers, some eight feet above the general throng, sat along in a row, separated by regular spaces, the cross-legged figures of six other blacks; each with a **rusty hatchet** in his hand, which, with a bit of brick and a **rag**, he was engaged like a scullion in **scouring**; while between each two was a small **stack** of hatchets, their rusted edges turned forward **awaiting** a like operation. Though occasionally the four oakum-pickers would briefly address some person or persons in the crowd below, yet the six hatchet-polishers neither spoke to others, nor **breathed** a whisper among themselves, but sat intent upon their task, except at intervals, when, with the peculiar love in negroes of **uniting** industry with **pastime**, two and two they sideways clashed their hatchets together,' like cymbals, with a **barbarous din**. All six, unlike the **generality**, had the raw aspect of **unsophisticated** Africans.

But that first comprehensive glance which took in those ten figures, with scores less conspicuous, rested but an instant upon them, as, **impatient** of the **hubbub** of voices, the visitor turned in quest of whomsoever it might be that commanded the ship.

But as if not unwilling to let nature make known her own case among his suffering charge, or else in despair of **restraining** it for the time, the Spanish captain, a gentlemanly, reserved-looking, and rather young man to a stranger's eye, dressed with singular **richness**, but bearing plain traces of recent **sleepless** cares and disquietudes, stood **passively** by, leaning against the main-mast, at one moment casting a **dreary**, **spiritless** look upon his excited people, at the next an unhappy glance toward his visitor. By his side stood a black of small **stature**, in whose rude face, as occasionally, like a shepherd's dog, he mutely turned it up into the Spaniard's, **sorrow** and affection were equally blended.

Struggling through the throng, the American advanced to the Spaniard, **assuring** him of his sympathies, and offering to **render** whatever assistance

Italian

assuring: assicurando.
awaiting: aspettando, attendendo.
barbarous: barbaro.
breathed: respirato.
din: rumore.
dreary: triste, scuro, afflitto, schifoso, sgradevole, mostruoso, spiacevole, buio, abominevole.
drilling: trapanazione, perforazione, trivellazione.
elevated: elevato.
generality: generalità.

hatchet: accetta, ascia.
heap: folla, mucchio, gruppo.
hubbub: fracasso, chiasso, baraonda, baccano.
impatient: impaziente.
monotonous: monotono, uniforme.
passively: passivamente.
pastime: passatempo.
poop: poppa.
rag: straccio, cencio.
render: rendere, rendono, rendete, rendi, rendiamo, rendo.

restraining: dominando.
richness: opulenza.
rusty: arrugginito, rugginoso.
scouring: sfregando, lavatura.
sleepless: insonne.
sorrow: tristezza, cordoglio.
spiritless: avvilito.
stack: accatastare, pila, catasta, camino, ammucchiare, bica.
stature: statura.
uniting: unendo.
unsophisticated: non sofisticato.

might be in his power. To which the Spaniard returned for the present but grave and **ceremonious** acknowledgments, his national **formality** dusked by the **saturnine** mood of ill-health.

But losing no time in mere **compliments**, Captain Delano, returning to the gangway, had his **basket** of fish brought up; and as the wind still continued light, so that some hours at least must **elapse** ere the ship could be brought to the **anchorage**, he bade his men return to the sealer, and fetch back as much water as the whale-boat could carry, with whatever soft bread the **steward** might have, all the remaining pumpkins on board, with a box of sugar, and a dozen of his private bottles of **cider**.

Not many minutes after the boat's pushing off, to the **vexation** of all, the wind entirely died away, and the tide turning, began drifting back the ship helplessly seaward. But **trusting** this would not long last, Captain Delano sought, with good hopes, to **cheer** up the strangers, feeling no small satisfaction that, with persons in their condition, he could — thanks to his frequent **voyages** along the Spanish main — converse with some freedom in their **native** tongue.

While left alone with them, he was not long in observing some things **tending** to heighten his first impressions; but surprise was lost in pity, both for the Spaniards and blacks, **alike evidently** reduced from **scarcity** of water and provisions; while long-continued suffering seemed to have brought out the less good-natured qualities of the negroes, besides, at the same time, **impairing** the Spaniard's authority over them. But, under the circumstances, precisely this condition of things was to have been **anticipated**. In armies, navies, cities, or families, in nature herself, nothing more **relaxes** good order than misery. Still, Captain Delano was not without the idea, that had Benito Cereno been a man of greater energy, misrule would hardly have come to the present pass. But the **debility**, constitutional or induced by hardships, **bodily** and mental, of the Spanish captain, was too obvious to be overlooked. A **prey** to settled **dejection**, as if long **mocked** with hope he would not now indulge it, even when it had **ceased** to be a mock, the prospect of that day, or evening at furthest, lying at anchor, with plenty of water for his people, and a brother captain to **counsel** and

Italian

alike: simile, similmente.
anchorage: ancoraggio.
anticipated: anticipato.
basket: cesto, canestro, cestino, cesta, paniere, cestello.
bodily: corporale, fisico.
ceased: cessato.
ceremonious: cerimonioso.
cheer: rallegrare.
cider: sidro.
compliments: complimenti.
counsel: consiglio, avvocato,

consigliare, raccomandare, avviso.
debility: debolezza.
dejection: deiezione, abbattimento, scoraggiamento, depressione.
elapse: trascorrere, trascorriamo, trascorro, trascorri, trascorrete, trascorrono, decorrere.
evidently: evidentemente.
formality: formalità.
impairing: danneggiando.
mock: deridere, deridono, derido, deridiamo, deridi, deridete, finto,

beffare.
mocked: deriso.
native: nativo, natio, indigeno, natale.
prey: preda.
relaxes: rilassa.
saturnine: saturnino, malinconico.
scarcity: scarsità.
steward: maggiordomo, dispensiere.
tending: tendendo.
trusting: fiducioso.
vexation: irritazione.
voyages: viaggia.

befriend, seemed in no **perceptible** degree to encourage him. His mind appeared unstrung, if not still more seriously affected. Shut up in these **oaken** walls, **chained** to one dull round of command, whose unconditionality **cloyed** him, like some **hypochondriac abbot** he moved slowly about, at times suddenly pausing, starting, or staring, **biting** his lip, biting his finger-nail, **flushing**, **paling**, twitching his beard, with other symptoms of an absent or **moody** mind. This distempered spirit was lodged, as before hinted, in as distempered a frame. He was rather tall, but seemed never to have been robust, and now with nervous suffering was almost worn to a **skeleton**. A tendency to some **pulmonary** complaint appeared to have been lately confirmed. His voice was like that of one with lungs half gone—hoarsely **suppressed**, a husky whisper. No wonder that, as in this state he **tottered** about, his private servant **apprehensively** followed him. Sometimes the negro gave his master his arm, or took his handkerchief out of his pocket for him; performing these and similar offices with that **affectionate zeal** which transmutes into something **filial** or fraternal acts in themselves but **menial**; and which has gained for the negro the **repute** of making the most **pleasing** body-servant in the world; one, too, whom a master need be on no **stiffly** superior terms with, but may treat with familiar trust; less a servant than a devoted companion.

Marking the noisy **indocility** of the blacks in general, as well as what seemed the **sullen inefficiency** of the whites it was not without **humane** satisfaction that Captain Delano witnessed the steady good conduct of Babo.

But the good conduct of Babo, hardly more than the ill-behavior of others, seemed to withdraw the half-lunatic Don Benito from his **cloudy languor**. Not that such precisely was the impression made by the Spaniard on the mind of his visitor. The Spaniard's individual unrest was, for the present, but noted as a conspicuous feature in the ship's general **affliction**. Still, Captain Delano was not a little concerned at what he could not help taking for the time to be Don Benito's **unfriendly indifference** towards himself. The Spaniard's manner, too, **conveyed** a sort of sour and gloomy disdain, which he seemed at no pains to disguise. But this the American in charity **ascribed** to the **harassing** effects of sickness, since, in

Italian

abbot: abate.	**flushing**: flussaggio, lavaggio.	**paling**: palizzata.
affectionate: affettuoso.	**harassing**: molestando, tormentando, assillante.	**perceptible**: percettibile.
affliction: afflizione.	**humane**: umano.	**pleasing**: piacevole.
apprehensively: timorosamente, apprensivamente.	**hypochondriac**: ipocondriaco.	**pulmonary**: polmonare.
ascribed: attribuito.	**indifference**: indifferenza.	**repute**: giudicare, reputazione.
biting: pungente, mordace.	**indocility**: indocilità.	**skeleton**: scheletro.
chained: incatenato.	**inefficiency**: inefficienza.	**stiffly**: rigidamente.
cloudy: nuvoloso, torbido.	**languor**: languore.	**sullen**: triste.
cloyed: saziato.	**menial**: umile.	**suppressed**: soffocato, soppresso.
conveyed: trasportato.	**moody**: triste.	**tottered**: traballato, barcollato.
filial: filiale.	**oaken**: di quercia.	**unfriendly**: scortese, ostile.
		zeal: zelo, ardore.

former instances, he had noted that there are peculiar natures on whom prolonged physical suffering seems to cancel every social instinct of **kindness**; as if, forced to black bread themselves, they deemed it but equity that each person coming nigh them should, indirectly, by some slight or **affront**, be made to **partake** of their fare.

But ere long Captain Delano bethought him that, indulgent as he was at the first, in judging the Spaniard, he might not, after all, have exercised charity enough. At bottom it was Don Benito's reserve which displeased him; but the same reserve was shown towards all but his faithful personal **attendant**. Even the formal reports which, according to sea-usage, were, at stated times, made to him by some **petty underling**, either a white, **mulatto** or black, he hardly had patience enough to listen to, without **betraying contemptuous aversion**. His manner upon such occasions was, in its degree, not unlike that which might be supposed to have been his imperial countryman's, Charles V., just previous to the anchoritish retirement of that **monarch** from the throne.

This splenetic disrelish of his place was evinced in almost every function **pertaining** to it. Proud as he was moody, he **condescended** to no personal **mandate**. Whatever special orders were necessary, their delivery was **delegated** to his body-servant, who in turn transferred them to their ultimate destination, through runners, alert Spanish boys or slave boys, like pages or pilot-fish within easy call continually **hovering** round Don Benito. So that to have **beheld** this undemonstrative **invalid** gliding about, **apathetic** and mute, no landsman could have **dreamed** that in him was lodged a **dictatorship** beyond which, while at sea, there was no earthly appeal.

Thus, the Spaniard, regarded in his reserve, seemed the **involuntary** victim of mental disorder. But, in fact, his reserve might, in some degree, have proceeded from design. If so, then here was evinced the **unhealthy climax** of that **icy** though **conscientious** policy, more or less adopted by all commanders of large ships, which, except in signal emergencies, **obliterates** alike the **manifestation** of **sway** with every trace of sociality; **transforming** the man into a block, or rather into a loaded **cannon**, which, until there is call for thunder, has nothing to say.

Italian

affront: affronto, insulto, insultare.
apathetic: apatico.
attendant: custode, compagno, inserviente.
aversion: avversione, ripugnanza.
beheld: guardato.
betraying: tradendo.
cannon: cannone.
climax: punto culminante.
condescended: degnato.
conscientious: coscienzioso.
contemptuous: sprezzante.
delegated: delegato.
dictatorship: dittatura.
dreamed: sognato.
hovering: librarsi.
icy: ghiacciato, gelato.
invalid: non valido, invalido.
involuntary: involontario.
kindness: gentilezza, bontà, cortesia.
mandate: mandato.
manifestation: manifestazione.
monarch: monarca.
mulatto: mulatto.
obliterates: cancella.
partake: partecipo, partecipa, partecipano, partecipate, partecipi, partecipiamo, partecipare.
pertaining: concernendo, riguardando, spettando.
petty: insignificante, piccolo.
sway: oscillare, ondeggiare, barcollare, oscillazione.
transforming: trasformando.
underling: subalterno.
unhealthy: malsano, malaticcio.

Viewing him in this light, it seemed but a natural **token** of the **perverse** habit induced by a long course of such hard self-restraint, that, **notwithstanding** the present condition of his ship, the Spaniard should still persist in a demeanor, which, however harmless, or, it may be, appropriate, in a well-appointed **vessel**, such as the San Dominick might have been at the **outset** of the voyage, was anything but **judicious** now. But the Spaniard, perhaps, thought that it was with **captains** as with **gods**: reserve, under all events, must still be their **cue**. But probably this appearance of slumbering **dominion** might have been but an attempted **disguise** to conscious imbecility — not deep policy, but **shallow** device. But be all this as it might, whether Don Benito's manner was designed or not, the more Captain Delano noted its pervading reserve, the less he felt uneasiness at any particular manifestation of that reserve towards himself.

Neither were his thoughts taken up by the captain alone. Wonted to the quiet **orderliness** of the sealer's comfortable family of a crew, the noisy confusion of the San Dominick's suffering host **repeatedly challenged** his eye. Some **prominent** breaches, not only of discipline but of **decency**, were observed. These Captain Delano could not but **ascribe**, in the main, to the absence of those subordinate deck-officers to whom, along with higher duties, is intrusted what may be styled the police department of a populous ship. True, the old oakum-pickers appeared at times to act the part of monitorial constables to their countrymen, the blacks; but though occasionally **succeeding** in **allaying** trifling outbreaks now and then between man and man, they could do little or nothing toward **establishing** general quiet. The San Dominick was in the condition of a **transatlantic emigrant** ship, among whose **multitude** of living freight are some individuals, doubtless, as little **troublesome** as crates and bales; but the friendly remonstrances of such with their ruder companions are of not so much avail as the unfriendly arm of the mate. What the San Dominick wanted was, what the emigrant ship has, **stern** superior officers. But on these **decks** not so much as a fourth-mate was to be seen.

The visitor's curiosity was **roused** to learn the **particulars** of those mishaps which had brought about such **absenteeism**, with its consequences; because,

Italian

absenteeism: assenteismo.
allaying: alleviando.
ascribe: attribuire, attribuite, attribuiscono, attribuisci, attribuiamo, attribuisco.
captains: capitani.
challenged: sfidato.
cue: stecca.
decency: decenza.
decks: adorna.
disguise: travestimento, travestire.
dominion: dominio.

emigrant: emigrante.
establishing: fondendo, stabilendo, constatando.
gods: dei.
judicious: giudizioso, assennato.
multitude: affluenza, folla, moltitudine.
notwithstanding: nonostante.
orderliness: ordine, regolarità.
outset: principio, esordio, inizio.
particulars: particolari.
perverse: perverso.

prominent: prominente.
repeatedly: ripetutamente.
roused: incitato, spronato, stimolato.
shallow: basso, poco profondo, superficiale.
stern: poppa, severo.
succeeding: riuscendo, successivo.
token: segno, gettone, prova.
transatlantic: transatlantico.
troublesome: fastidioso, noioso.
vessel: vaso, recipiente, vascello, cassa, tinozza, nave.

though **deriving** some **inkling** of the voyage from the wails which at the first moment had **greeted** him, yet of the details no clear understanding had been had. The best account would, doubtless, be given by the captain. Yet at first the **visitor** was **loth** to ask it, unwilling to **provoke** some distant **rebuff**. But plucking up **courage**, he at last **accosted** Don Benito, **renewing** the expression of his benevolent interest, adding, that did he (Captain Delano) but know the particulars of the ship's misfortunes, he would, perhaps, be better able in the end to relieve them. Would Don Benito favor him with the whole story.

Don Benito **faltered**; then, like some **somnambulist** suddenly **interfered** with, **vacantly** stared at his visitor, and ended by looking down on the deck. He maintained this **posture** so long, that Captain Delano, almost equally disconcerted, and involuntarily almost as rude, turned suddenly from him, walking forward to accost one of the Spanish seamen for the desired information. But he had hardly gone five **paces**, when, with a sort of eagerness, Don Benito invited him back, regretting his momentary absence of mind, and **professing** **readiness** to gratify him.

While most part of the story was being given, the two captains stood on the after part of the main-deck, a **privileged** spot, no one being near but the **servant**.

"It is now a hundred and ninety days," began the Spaniard, in his husky whisper, "that this ship, well officered and well manned, with several cabin passengers—some fifty Spaniards in all—sailed from Buenos Ayres bound to Lima, with a general cargo, **hardware**, Paraguay tea and the like—and," pointing forward, "that **parcel** of negroes, now not more than a hundred and fifty, as you see, but then **numbering** over three hundred souls. Off Cape Horn we had heavy gales. In one moment, by night, three of my best officers, with fifteen **sailors**, were lost, with the main-yard; the **spar** snapping under them in the **slings**, as they sought, with heavers, to beat down the icy sail. To **lighten** the hull, the **heavier sacks** of mata were thrown into the sea, with most of the water-pipes lashed on deck at the time. And this last necessity it was, combined with the **prolonged** detections afterwards experienced, which eventually brought about our chief causes of suffering. When—"

Italian

accost: abbordare, avvicinare.
courage: coraggio.
deriving: derivando.
faltered: balbettato.
greeted: salutato.
hardware: ferramenta, hardware.
heavier: più pesante.
inkling: accenno.
interfered: interferito.
lighten: alleggerire, alleggerisci, alleggerite, alleggerisco, alleggeriamo, alleggeriscono,

illuminare.
loth: riluttante.
numbering: numerazione.
paces: pace.
parcel: pacco, pacchetto, collo.
posture: postura, posizione, atteggiamento.
privileged: privilegiato.
professing: dichiarando, professando.
prolonged: prolungato.
provoke: spronare, provocare, incitare, provochi, sproniamo, sprono, sproni,

spronate, spronano, sprona, provoco.
readiness: prontezza.
rebuff: secco rifiuto.
renewing: rinnovando.
sacks: sacchi.
sailors: marinai.
servant: servire, servo, servitore.
slings: fasce a tracolla.
somnambulist: sonnambulo.
spar: longherone.
vacantly: vacantemente.
visitor: visitatore, ospite.

Here there was a sudden **fainting** attack of his **cough**, brought on, no doubt, by his mental distress. His servant sustained him, and drawing a **cordial** from his pocket placed it to his lips. He a little **revived**. But unwilling to leave him **unsupported** while yet **imperfectly** restored, the black with one arm still **encircled** his master, at the same time keeping his eye fixed on his face, as if to watch for the first sign of complete restoration, or **relapse**, as the event might prove.

The Spaniard proceeded, but brokenly and obscurely, as one in a dream.

—"Oh, my God! rather than pass through what I have, with joy I would have **hailed** the most terrible gales; but—"

His cough returned and with increased violence; this **subsiding**; with **reddened** lips and closed eyes he fell heavily against his **supporter**.

"His mind **wanders**. He was thinking of the **plague** that followed the gales," plaintively sighed the servant; "my poor, poor master!" **wringing** one hand, and with the other **wiping** the mouth. "But be patient, Señor," again turning to Captain Delano, "these fits do not last long; master will soon be himself."

Don Benito **reviving**, went on; but as this **portion** of the story was very brokenly delivered, the substance only will here be set down.

It appeared that after the ship had been many days tossed in storms off the Cape, the scurvy broke out, carrying off numbers of the whites and blacks. When at last they had worked round into the Pacific, their spars and sails were so damaged, and so **inadequately handled** by the **surviving** mariners, most of whom were become invalids, that, unable to lay her **northerly** course by the wind, which was powerful, the unmanageable ship, for successive days and nights, was blown northwestward, where the **breeze** suddenly deserted her, in unknown waters, to sultry calms. The absence of the water-pipes now proved as fatal to life as before their presence had **menaced** it. Induced, or at least **aggravated**, by the more than **scanty** allowance of water, a **malignant** fever followed the scurvy; with the **excessive** heat of the **lengthened** calm, making such short work of it as to **sweep** away, as by billows, whole families of the Africans, and a yet larger number, proportionably, of the Spaniards, including,

Italian

aggravated: aggravato.	**lengthened**: allungato.	cessando.
breeze: brezza.	**malignant**: maligno.	**supporter**: membro, sostenitore.
cordial: cordiale.	**menaced**: minacciato.	**surviving**: sopravvivendo,
cough: tossire, tosse.	**northerly**: settentrionale.	sopravvivere.
encircled: circondato.	**plague**: peste.	**sweep**: spazzare, scopare, spazzata.
excessive: eccessivo.	**portion**: parte, porzione.	**unsupported**: non confermato, non
fainting: svenendo.	**reddened**: arrossato, arrossito.	eseguibile, senza sostegno, non
hailed: grandinato.	**relapse**: ricaduta.	permesso.
handled: maneggiato.	**revived**: rianimato.	**wanders**: vaga.
imperfectly: imperfettamente.	**reviving**: rianimando.	**wiping**: asciugando, pulendo,
inadequately: inadeguatamente,	**scanty**: scarso.	strofinando.
insufficientemente.	**subsiding**: calando, sprofondando,	**wringing**: estorcendo.

by a **luckless fatality**, every remaining officer on board. **Consequently**, in the **smart** west winds eventually following the calm, the already rent sails, having to be simply dropped, not furled, at need, had been gradually reduced to the beggars' **rags** they were now. To procure substitutes for his lost sailors, as well as **supplies** of water and sails, the captain, at the earliest opportunity, had made for Baldivia, the southernmost **civilized** port of Chili and South America; but upon nearing the coast the **thick** weather had **prevented** him from so much as **sighting** that harbor. Since which period, almost without a **crew**, and almost without **canvas** and almost without water, and, at intervals giving its added dead to the sea, the San Dominick had been battle-dored about by **contrary** winds, inveigled by currents, or grown **weedy** in calms. Like a man lost in woods, more than once she had **doubled** upon her own track.

"But throughout these calamities," huskily continued Don Benito, **painfully** turning in the half embrace of his servant, "I have to thank those negroes you see, who, though to your **inexperienced** eyes **appearing unruly**, have, indeed, conducted themselves with less of **restlessness** than even their owner could have thought possible under such circumstances."

Here he again fell **faintly** back. Again his mind **wandered**; but he rallied, and less obscurely proceeded.

"Yes, their owner was quite right in assuring me that no fetters would be needed with his blacks; so that while, as is **wont** in this **transportation**, those negroes have always remained upon deck—not thrust below, as in the Guinea-men—they have, also, from the beginning, been freely permitted to range within given bounds at their pleasure."

Once more the **faintness** returned—his mind roved—but, recovering, he resumed:

"But it is Babo here to whom, under God, I owe not only my own **preservation**, but **likewise** to him, chiefly, the **merit** is due, of **pacifying** his more **ignorant brethren**, when at intervals tempted to murmurings."

"Ah, master," sighed the black, **bowing** his face, "don't speak of me; Babo is nothing; what Babo has done was but duty."

Italian

appearing: apparendo.
bowing: archeggio.
brethren: fratelli, confratelli.
canvas: tela, canovaccio.
civilized: civilizzato.
consequently: conseguentemente.
contrary: contrario.
crew: equipaggio, squadra.
doubled: raddoppiato.
faintly: debolmente.
faintness: debolezza.
fatality: fatalità.

ignorant: ignorante.
inexperienced: inesperto.
likewise: anche, altrettanto.
luckless: sfortunato.
merit: meritare, merito, benemerenza, pregio.
pacifying: pacificando.
painfully: dolorosamente.
preservation: conservazione, preservazione.
prevented: impedito, prevenuto.
rags: stracci.

restlessness: inquietudine, irrequietezza.
sighting: avvistamento.
smart: intelligente.
supplies: approvvigionamento, fornitura.
thick: spesso, grosso, denso.
transportation: trasporto.
unruly: indisciplinato.
wandered: vagato.
weedy: allampanato.
wont: avvezzo, abitudine.

"Faithful fellow!" cried Captain Delano. "Don Benito, I **envy** you such a friend; **slave** I cannot call him."

As master and man stood before him, the black **upholding** the white, Captain Delano could not but bethink him of the beauty of that relationship which could present such a spectacle of **fidelity** on the one hand and confidence on the other. The scene was heightened by, the contrast in dress, **denoting** their relative positions. The Spaniard wore a loose Chili jacket of dark velvet; white small-clothes and stockings, with silver buckles at the knee and **instep**; a high-crowned sombrero, of fine grass; a **slender** sword, silver mounted, hung from a **knot** in his sash — the last being an almost invariable **adjunct**, more for utility than **ornament**, of a South American gentleman's dress to this hour. **Excepting** when his occasional nervous contortions brought about **disarray**, there was a certain precision in his **attire curiously** at **variance** with the **unsightly** disorder around; especially in the belittered Ghetto, forward of the main-mast, wholly occupied by the blacks.

The servant wore nothing but wide trowsers, apparently, from their **coarseness** and **patches**, made out of some old **topsail**; they were clean, and confined at the waist by a bit of unstranded rope, which, with his composed, deprecatory air at times, made him look something like a **begging friar** of St. Francis.

However **unsuitable** for the time and place, at least in the blunt-thinking American's eyes, and however strangely surviving in the **midst** of all his afflictions, the toilette of Don Benito might not, in fashion at least, have gone beyond the style of the day among South Americans of his class. Though on the present voyage sailing from Buenos Ayres, he had **avowed** himself a native and resident of Chili, whose inhabitants had not so generally adopted the plain coat and once **plebeian** pantaloons; but, with a becoming modification, **adhered** to their provincial **costume**, **picturesque** as any in the world. Still, relatively to the pale history of the voyage, and his own pale face, there seemed something so **incongruous** in the Spaniard's **apparel**, as almost to suggest the image of an invalid **courtier tottering** about London streets in the time of the plague.

Italian

adhered: aderito.
adjunct: aggiunta.
apparel: vestimento, abito.
attire: abbigliare, abbigliamento.
avowed: dichiarato.
begging: mendicando.
coarseness: grossolanità, ruvidezza.
costume: costume, abito.
courtier: cortigiano.
curiously: curiosamente.
denoting: denotando.
disarray: scompiglio.

envy: invidia, invidiare, invidio, invidiate, invidiano, invidi, invidiamo.
excepting: salvo.
fidelity: fedeltà.
incongruous: incongruo.
instep: collo del piede.
knot: nodo, annodare, piovanello maggiore.
midst: mezzo.
ornament: ornamento, decorare,

soprammobile.
patches: toppe.
picturesque: pittoresco.
plebeian: plebeo.
slave: schiavo, sgobbare.
slender: sottile, snello, esile.
topsail: vela di gabbia.
tottering: barcollando, traballando.
unsightly: brutto.
unsuitable: disadatto.
upholding: sostenendo.
variance: varietà, disaccordo.

The portion of the narrative which, perhaps, most excited interest, as well as some surprise, considering the latitudes in question, was the long calms spoken of, and more particularly the ship's so long drifting about. Without **communicating** the opinion, of course, the American could not but **impute** at least part of the detentions both to **clumsy** seamanship and **faulty navigation**. Eying Don Benito's small, yellow hands, he easily **inferred** that the young captain had not got into command at the hawse-hole, but the cabin-window; and if so, why wonder at **incompetence**, in youth, sickness, and **gentility** united?

But **drowning** criticism in **compassion**, after a fresh **repetition** of his sympathies, Captain Delano, having heard out his story, not only engaged, as in the first place, to see Don Benito and his people supplied in their immediate bodily needs, but, also, now **farther** promised to assist him in procuring a large permanent supply of water, as well as some sails and **rigging**; and, though it would involve no small embarrassment to himself, yet he would spare three of his best seamen for temporary deck officers; so that without delay the ship might proceed to Conception, there fully to refit for Lima, her **destined** port.

Such **generosity** was not without its effect, even upon the invalid. His face **lighted** up; eager and **hectic**, he met the honest glance of his visitor. With **gratitude** he seemed overcome.

"This excitement is bad for master," whispered the servant, taking his arm, and with **soothing** words gently drawing him aside.

When Don Benito returned, the American was pained to observe that his hopefulness, like the sudden **kindling** in his cheek, was but **febrile** and **transient**.

Ere long, with a **joyless mien**, looking up towards the poop, the host invited his guest to **accompany** him there, for the benefit of what little breath of wind might be **stirring**.

As, during the telling of the story, Captain Delano had once or twice started at the occasional cymballing of the hatchet-polishers, wondering why such an **interruption** should be allowed, especially in that part of the ship, and in the ears of an invalid; and moreover, as the hatchets had anything but an attractive look, and the handlers of them still less so, it was, therefore, to tell the truth, not

Italian

accompany: accompagnare, accompagna, accompagniamo, accompagno, accompagni, accompagnate, accompagnano.
clumsy: goffo, maldestro, impacciato.
communicating: comunicando.
compassion: compassione.
destined: destinato.
drowning: annegando, annegamento, annegare.
farther: più lontano.
faulty: difettoso.

febrile: febbrile.
generosity: generosità.
gentility: raffinatezza, nascita elevata.
gratitude: gratitudine, riconoscenza, grazie.
hectic: frenetico, etico.
impute: attribuire.
incompetence: incompetenza, insufficienza.
inferred: dedotto, concluso.
interruption: interruzione.
joyless: senza gioia, mesto.

kindling: accendendo, accensione.
lighted: illuminato.
mien: aspetto.
navigation: navigazione.
repetition: ripetizione, replica.
rigging: attrezzatura, manovra, sartiame.
soothing: calmando, calmante, calmare.
stirring: mescolare, eccitante, agitazione.
transient: transitorio.

without some lurking **reluctance**, or even **shrinking**, it may be, that Captain Delano, with apparent **complaisance**, acquiesced in his host's invitation. The more so, since, with an **untimely caprice** of punctilio, **rendered distressing** by his cadaverous aspect, Don Benito, with Castilian **bows**, **solemnly** insisted upon his guest's preceding him up the **ladder** leading to the **elevation**; where, one on each side of the last step, sat for **armorial** supporters and sentries two of the ominous file. **Gingerly** enough stepped good Captain Delano between them, and in the instant of leaving them behind, like one running the **gauntlet**, he felt an **apprehensive twitch** in the **calves** of his legs.

But when, facing about, he saw the whole file, like so many organ-grinders, still **stupidly** intent on their work, **unmindful** of everything beside, he could not but smile at his late **fidgety** panic.

Presently, while standing with his host, looking forward upon the decks below, he was struck by one of those instances of **insubordination** previously **alluded** to. Three black boys, with two Spanish boys, were sitting together on the hatches, **scraping** a rude wooden **platter**, in which some scanty mess had recently been **cooked**. Suddenly, one of the black boys, **enraged** at a word dropped by one of his white companions, seized a knife, and, though called to **forbear** by one of the oakum-pickers, struck the lad over the head, **inflicting** a **gash** from which blood flowed.

In **amazement**, Captain Delano **inquired** what this meant. To which the pale Don Benito dully muttered, that it was merely the sport of the lad.

"Pretty serious sport, truly," rejoined Captain Delano. "Had such a thing happened on board the Bachelor's Delight, instant punishment would have followed."

At these words the Spaniard turned upon the American one of his sudden, staring, half-lunatic looks; then, relapsing into his **torpor**, answered, "Doubtless, doubtless, Señor."

Is it, thought Captain Delano, that this hapless man is one of those paper captains I've known, who by policy **wink** at what by power they cannot put

Italian

alluded: alluso.
amazement: stupore, meraviglia.
apprehensive: apprensivo.
armorial: araldico.
bows: archetti.
calves: figlia, partorisce, vitelli.
caprice: capriccio.
complaisance: compiacenza.
cooked: cotto.
distressing: doloroso, penoso, angoscioso.
elevation: elevazione, altezza,

prospetto.
enraged: irritato, arrabbiato, incollerito, adirato.
fidgety: agitato, irrequieto.
forbear: antenato, astenersi.
gash: sfregiare, taglio.
gauntlet: guanto.
gingerly: cauto.
inflicting: infliggendo.
inquired: domandato.
insubordination: insubordinazione.
ladder: scala, la scala, smagliare.

platter: piatto.
reluctance: riluttanza.
rendered: reso.
scraping: raschiatura.
shrinking: restringere, contrazione.
solemnly: solennemente.
stupidly: stupidamente.
torpor: torpore.
twitch: ticchio, contrarsi.
unmindful: immemore.
untimely: prematuro.
wink: ammiccare.

down? I know no sadder sight than a **commander** who has little of command but the name.

"I should think, Don Benito," he now said, glancing towards the oakum-picker who had **sought** to **interfere** with the boys, "that you would find it **advantageous** to keep all your blacks employed, especially the **younger** ones, no matter at what useless task, and no matter what happens to the **ship**. Why, even with my little band, I find such a course indispensable. I once kept a crew on my quarter-deck thrumming mats for my cabin, when, for three days, I had given up my ship—mats, men, and all—for a **speedy** loss, owing to the **violence** of a **gale**, in which we could do nothing but helplessly drive before it."

"Doubtless, doubtless," muttered Don Benito.

"But," continued Captain Delano, again glancing upon the oakum-pickers and then at the hatchet-polishers, near by, "I see you keep some, at least, of your **host** employed."

"Yes," was again the vacant response.

"Those old men there, **shaking** their pows from their pulpits," continued Captain Delano, pointing to the oakum-pickers, "seem to act the part of old dominies to the rest, little heeded as their admonitions are at times. Is this **voluntary** on their part, Don Benito, or have you **appointed** them shepherds to your flock of black sheep?"

"What posts they **fill**, I appointed them," rejoined the Spaniard, in an **acrid** tone, as if resenting some supposed **satiric reflection**.

"And these others, these Ashantee conjurors here," continued Captain Delano, rather **uneasily** eying the brandished **steel** of the hatchet-polishers, where, in spots, it had been brought to a **shine**, "this seems a curious business they are at, Don Benito?"

"In the gales we met," answered the Spaniard, "what of our general cargo was not **thrown overboard** was much **damaged** by the **brine**. Since coming into calm weather, I have had several cases of knives and hatchets daily brought up for **overhauling** and cleaning."

Italian

acrid: acre, aspro, pungente.
advantageous: vantaggioso, utile.
appointed: nominato.
brine: salamoia, acqua salata.
command: comando, ordine, comandare, padronanza.
commander: comandante.
damaged: danneggiato, guasto.
fill: riempire, riempimento.
gale: burrasca.
host: ospite, folla, ostia.
interfere: interferire, interferiamo, interferite, interferiscono, interferisco, interferisci.
overboard: in mare, fuoribordo, fuori bordo.
overhauling: aggiustando, revisionando, riparando, sorpassando, verificando.
reflection: riflesso, riflessione.
satiric: satirico.
shaking: scuotendo.
shine: risplendere, brillare, lustro, splendere.
ship: nave, spedire, bastimento, spedite, spediscono, spedisci, spediamo, spedisco, vascello.
sought: cercato.
speedy: rapido.
steel: acciaio, osso di balena, acciaiare, d'acciaio.
thrown: gettato.
uneasily: inquietamente.
violence: violenza.
voluntary: volontario.
younger: più giovane.

"A prudent idea, Don Benito. You are part owner of ship and cargo, I **presume**; but none of the slaves, perhaps?"

"I am owner of all you see," impatiently returned Don Benito, "except the main company of blacks, who **belonged** to my late friend, Alexandro Aranda."

As he **mentioned** this name, his air was heart-broken; his knees shook; his servant **supported** him.

Thinking he divined the cause of such unusual **emotion**, to **confirm** his surmise, Captain Delano, after a pause, said: "And may I ask, Don Benito, whether—since awhile ago you spoke of some cabin passengers—the friend, whose loss so **afflicts** you, at the outset of the voyage **accompanied** his blacks?"

"Yes."

"But died of the fever?"

"Died of the fever. Oh, could I but—"

Again quivering, the Spaniard paused.

"Pardon me," said Captain Delano, **lowly**, "but I think that, by a **sympathetic** experience, I **conjecture**, Don Benito, what it is that gives the keener edge to your **grief**. It was once my hard fortune to lose, at sea, a dear friend, my own brother, then supercargo. Assured of the welfare of his spirit, its departure I could have borne like a man; but that **honest** eye, that honest hand—both of which had so often met mine—and that warm heart; all, all—like scraps to the dogs—to **throw** all to the sharks! It was then I vowed never to have for fellow-voyager a man I **loved**, unless, unbeknown to him, I had provided every **requisite**, in case of a fatality, for **embalming** his mortal part for interment on **shore**. Were your friend's remains now on board this ship, Don Benito, not thus strangely would the mention of his name affect you."

"On board this ship?" echoed the Spaniard. Then, with **horrified** gestures, as directed against some **spectre**, he **unconsciously** fell into the ready arms of his attendant, who, with a silent appeal toward Captain Delano, seemed **beseeching** him not again to **broach** a **theme** so **unspeakably** distressing to his master.

Italian

accompanied: accompagnato.
afflicts: affligge.
belonged: appartenuto.
beseeching: implorando, scongiurando, supplicando, supplichevole, implorante.
broach: spiedo, spillare, broccia.
confirm: confermare, confermiamo, confermo, confermano, confermate, confermi, conferma.
conjecture: congettura.
embalming: imbalsamando,
imbalsamare.
emotion: emozione, commozione.
grief: dolore, pena.
honest: onesto.
horrified: impressionato, inorridito, atterrito, far inorridire.
loved: benvoluto.
lowly: umile.
mentioned: menzionato.
presume: supporre, supponiamo, supponi, suppongono, suppongo, supponete, presumere, presumiamo,
presumo, presumi, presumete.
requisite: requisito.
shore: costa, riva, sponda, puntello, puntellare.
spectre: spettro.
supported: sostenuto.
sympathetic: simpatico, comprensivo.
theme: tema.
throw: gettare, lanciare, lancio, tiro, alzata.
unconsciously: inconsciamente.
unspeakably: inesprimibilmente.

This poor fellow now, thought the pained American, is the victim of that sad **superstition** which associates goblins with the deserted body of man, as ghosts with an abandoned house. How unlike are we made! What to me, in like case, would have been a solemn satisfaction, the bare suggestion, even, **terrifies** the Spaniard into this trance. Poor Alexandro Aranda! what would you say could you here see your friend — who, on former voyages, when you, for months, were left behind, has, I dare say, often longed, and longed, for one peep at you — now **transported** with **terror** at the least thought of having you anyway nigh him.

At this moment, with a dreary grave-yard **toll**, betokening a **flaw**, the ship's forecastle bell, smote by one of the grizzled oakum-pickers, **proclaimed** ten o'clock, through the **leaden** calm; when Captain Delano's attention was caught by the moving figure of a gigantic black, emerging from the general crowd below, and slowly advancing towards the elevated poop. An iron **collar** was about his neck, from which **depended** a chain, **thrice** wound round his body; the **terminating** links padlocked together at a broad band of iron, his **girdle**.

"How like a mute Atufal moves," murmured the servant.

The black **mounted** the steps of the poop, and, like a **brave prisoner**, brought up to receive sentence, stood in unquailing **muteness** before Don Benito, now recovered from his attack.

At the first glimpse of his approach, Don Benito had started, a **resentful** shadow swept over his face; and, as with the sudden memory of bootless **rage**, his white lips **glued** together.

This is some mulish **mutineer**, thought Captain Delano, **surveying**, not without a mixture of **admiration**, the **colossal** form of the negro.

"See, he **waits** your question, master," said the servant.

Thus **reminded**, Don Benito, nervously **averting** his glance, as if **shunning**, by **anticipation**, some **rebellious** response, in a disconcerted voice, thus spoke: —

"Atufal, will you ask my pardon, now?"

The black was silent.

Italian

admiration: ammirazione.
anticipation: anticipazione, previsione.
averting: distogliendo, evitando, allontanando.
brave: coraggioso, valoroso, strenuo, affrontare.
collar: colletto, collare, collo, bavero.
colossal: colossale.
depended: dipeso.
flaw: difetto, screpolatura, fessura, crepa, imperfezione, incrinatura.

girdle: cintura.
glued: incollato.
leaden: di piombo.
mounted: montato.
muteness: mutismo, mutezza.
mutineer: ammutinato.
prisoner: detenuto, prigioniero, arrestato, carcerato.
proclaimed: proclamato.
rage: furore, ira, furia, collera.
rebellious: ribelle.
reminded: ricordato.

resentful: risentito, astioso.
shunning: evitando.
superstition: superstizione.
surveying: agrimensura.
terminating: terminando.
terrifies: terrifica, terrorizza, atterrisce, spaventa.
terror: terrore.
thrice: tre volte.
toll: pedaggio.
transported: trasportato.
waits: aspetta.

"Again, **master**," murmured the servant, with bitter **upbraiding** eyeing his **countryman**, "Again, master; he will **bend** to master yet."

"Answer," said Don Benito, still averting his glance, "say but the one word, *pardon*, and your **chains** shall be off."

Upon this, the black, **slowly raising** both **arms**, let them lifelessly **fall**, his **links clanking**, his head **bowed**; as much as to say, "no, I am content."

"Go," said Don Benito, with inkept and **unknown** emotion.

Deliberately as he had come, the black **obeyed**.

"**Excuse** me, Don Benito," said Captain Delano, "but this **scene** surprises me; what means it, pray?"

"It means that that negro alone, of all the **band**, has given me peculiar cause of **offense**. I have put him in chains; I—"

Here he paused; his hand to his head, as if there were a **swimming** there, or a sudden **bewilderment** of **memory** had come over him; but meeting his servant's kindly glance seemed **reassured**, and proceeded:—

"I could not **scourge** such a form. But I told him he must ask my pardon. As yet he has not. At my command, every two hours he stands before me."

"And how long has this been?"

"Some **sixty** days."

"And **obedient** in all else? And respectful?"

"Yes."

"Upon my conscience, then," exclaimed Captain Delano, impulsively, "he has a **royal spirit** in him, this fellow."

"He may have some right to it," bitterly returned Don Benito, "he says he was king in his own land."

"Yes," said the servant, entering a word, "those slits in Atufal's **ears** once held wedges of **gold**; but **poor** Babo here, in his own land, was only a poor slave; a black man's slave was Babo, who now is the white's."

Italian

arms: bracci.	cado, cadiamo, cadi, cadete, diminuire, calo, piombare.	**raising**: sollevamento, allevamento, sopraelevazione, aumento.
band: banda, fascia, nastro.	**gold**: oro, d'oro.	**reassured**: rassicurato.
bend: curva, curvarsi, piegare, curvatura, chinare, curvare, flettere.	**king**: re.	**royal**: reale.
bewilderment: perplessità.	**links**: collegamenti.	**scene**: scena.
bowed: chino.	**master**: maestro, padrone, principale, master, dominare, anagrafica.	**scourge**: frustare.
chains: catene.	**memory**: memoria, ricordo.	**sixty**: sessanta.
countryman: compatriota.	**obedient**: ubbidiente, obbediente.	**slowly**: lentamente.
ears: orecchie.	**obeyed**: ubbidito, obbedito.	**spirit**: spirito, anima.
excuse: scusa, scusare, giustificazione, pretesto.	**offense**: offesa.	**swimming**: nuotando, nuoto.
fall: cadere, caduta, autunno, cadono,	**poor**: povero, cattivo.	**unknown**: sconosciuto, ignoto.
		upbraiding: rimproverando.

Somewhat **annoyed** by these **conversational** familiarities, Captain Delano turned curiously upon the attendant, then glanced **inquiringly** at his master; but, as if long wonted to these little informalities, neither master nor man seemed to understand him.

"What, pray, was Atufal's offense, Don Benito?" asked Captain Delano; "if it was not something very serious, take a fool's advice, and, in view of his general **docility**, as well as in some natural respect for his spirit, **remit** him his penalty."

"No, no, master never will do that," here murmured the servant to himself, "proud Atufal must first ask master's pardon. The slave there carries the **padlock**, but master here carries the key."

His attention thus directed, Captain Delano now noticed for the first, that, suspended by a slender **silken cord**, from Don Benito's neck, hung a key. At once, from the servant's muttered syllables, divining the key's purpose, he smiled, and said:—"So, Don Benito—padlock and key—significant symbols, truly."

Biting his lip, Don Benito faltered.

Though the remark of Captain Delano, a man of such native **simplicity** as to be **incapable** of **satire** or **irony**, had been dropped in **playful allusion** to the Spaniard's singularly evidenced **lordship** over the black; yet the hypochondriac seemed some way to have taken it as a **malicious** reflection upon his **confessed inability** thus far to break down, at least, on a **verbal** summons, the **entrenched** will of the slave. **Deploring** this supposed **misconception**, yet despairing of **correcting** it, Captain Delano shifted the subject; but finding his companion more than ever withdrawn, as if still sourly **digesting** the **lees** of the **presumed** affront above-mentioned, by-and-by Captain Delano likewise became less **talkative**, **oppressed**, against his own will, by what seemed the secret vindictiveness of the **morbidly** sensitive Spaniard. But the good sailor, himself of a quite contrary disposition, refrained, on his part, alike from the appearance as from the feeling of resentment, and if silent, was only so from **contagion**.

Presently the Spaniard, **assisted** by his servant somewhat discourteously crossed over from his guest; a procedure which, **sensibly** enough, might have been allowed to pass for idle caprice of ill-humor, had not master and man,

Italian

allusion: allusione.	**entrenched**: trincerato.	**padlock**: lucchetto.
annoyed: infastidito, irritato, seccato.	**inability**: inabilità, incapacità.	**playful**: giocoso.
assisted: assistito, aiutato.	**incapable**: incapace.	**presumed**: supposto, presunto.
confessed: confessato.	**inquiringly**: domandare.	**remit**: annullare, annullano, annullo,
contagion: contagio.	**irony**: ironia.	annulliamo, annullate, annulla,
conversational: conversazionale,	**lees**: sedimento, feccia.	annulli, condonare, rimettere.
loquace, colloquiale.	**lordship**: signoria, dominio.	**satire**: satira.
cord: corda, cordone, cavo, spago.	**malicious**: maligno, doloso, malizioso.	**sensibly**: assennatamente.
correcting: correggere.	**misconception**: idea sbagliata.	**silken**: di seta.
deploring: deplorando.	**morbidly**: morboso.	**simplicity**: semplicità.
digesting: digerire.	**oppressed**: premuto, oppresso,	**talkative**: loquace.
docility: docilità.	serrato, stretto.	**verbal**: verbale.

lingering round the corner of the elevated skylight, began **whispering** together in low voices. This was unpleasing. And more; the moody air of the Spaniard, which at times had not been without a sort of valetudinarian **stateliness**, now seemed anything but **dignified**; while the menial **familiarity** of the servant lost its original charm of simple-hearted attachment.

In his **embarrassment**, the visitor turned his face to the other side of the ship. By so doing, his glance accidentally fell on a young Spanish sailor, a **coil** of **rope** in his hand, just stepped from the deck to the first round of the mizzen-rigging. Perhaps the man would not have been particularly noticed, were it not that, during his **ascent** to one of the **yards**, he, with a sort of **covert** intentness, kept his eye fixed on Captain Delano, from whom, presently, it passed, as if by a natural sequence, to the two whisperers.

His own attention thus **redirected** to that quarter, Captain Delano gave a slight start. From something in Don Benito's manner just then, it seemed as if the visitor had, at least partly, been the subject of the withdrawn **consultation** going on—a conjecture as little agreeable to the **guest** as it was little **flattering** to the host.

The singular alternations of **courtesy** and ill-breeding in the Spanish captain were unaccountable, except on one of two suppositions—innocent **lunacy**, or **wicked imposture**.

But the first idea, though it might naturally have occurred to an **indifferent observer**, and, in some respect, had not **hitherto** been wholly a stranger to Captain Delano's mind, yet, now that, in an incipient way, he began to **regard** the stranger's conduct something in the light of an **intentional** affront, of course the idea of lunacy was virtually **vacated**. But if not a **lunatic**, what then? Under the circumstances, would a gentleman, nay, any honest **boor**, act the part now acted by his host? The man was an **impostor**. Some low-born **adventurer**, masquerading as an oceanic grandee; yet so ignorant of the first requisites of **mere** gentlemanhood as to be **betrayed** into the present remarkable indecorum. That strange ceremoniousness, too, at other times evinced, seemed not uncharacteristic of one playing a part above his real level. Benito Cereno—Don

Italian

adventurer: avventuriero.
ascent: ascesa, ascensione.
betrayed: tradito.
boor: cafone.
coil: bobina, rotolo.
consultation: consulto, consultazione.
courtesy: cortesia.
covert: nascosto, rifugio, riparo.
dignified: dignitoso.
embarrassment: imbarazzo.
familiarity: dimestichezza.
flattering: lusingando, adulatorio.

guest: ospite, invitato.
hitherto: finora.
impostor: impostore.
imposture: impostura, inganno.
indifferent: indifferente.
intentional: intenzionale.
lingering: indugiando, indugiare, prolungato.
lunacy: pazzia.
lunatic: pazzo, lunatico.
mere: mero, laghetto, semplice.
observer: osservatore.

redirected: reinstradato, riorientato.
regard: riguardo, considerazione, considerare, rispetto, considerano, consideriamo, considero, considera, consideri, considerate, stima.
rope: corda, fune, cavo, la corda.
stateliness: grandiosità.
vacated: evacuato, liberato, sgombrato.
whispering: sussurrio.
wicked: cattivo, malvagio.
yards: iarde.

Benito Cereno—a **sounding** name. One, too, at that period, not unknown, in the **surname**, to super-cargoes and sea captains trading along the Spanish Main, as belonging to one of the most **enterprising** and extensive mercantile families in all those provinces; several members of it having titles; a sort of Castilian Rothschild, with a noble brother, or cousin, in every great trading town of South America. The alleged Don Benito was in early **manhood**, about twenty-nine or thirty. To assume a sort of **roving** cadetship in the **maritime** affairs of such a house, what more likely scheme for a young **knave** of talent and spirit? But the Spaniard was a pale invalid. Never mind. For even to the degree of **simulating** mortal disease, the craft of some tricksters had been known to **attain**. To think that, under the aspect of **infantile** weakness, the most **savage** energies might be couched—those velvets of the Spaniard but the **silky paw** to his fangs.

From no train of thought did these fancies come; not from within, but from without; suddenly, too, and in one throng, like **hoar** frost; yet as soon to **vanish** as the mild sun of Captain Delano's good-nature **regained** its meridian.

Glancing over once more towards his host—whose side-face, revealed above the skylight, was now turned towards him—he was struck by the profile, whose **clearness** of cut was **refined** by the **thinness**, incident to ill-health, as well as **ennobled** about the chin by the beard. Away with suspicion. He was a true off-shoot of a true hidalgo Cereno.

Relieved by these and other better thoughts, the visitor, lightly **humming** a tune, now began indifferently pacing the poop, so as not to **betray** to Don Benito that he had at all **mistrusted** incivility, much less **duplicity**; for such mistrust would yet be proved **illusory**, and by the event; though, for the present, the circumstance which had provoked that **distrust** remained **unexplained**. But when that little mystery should have been cleared up, Captain Delano thought he might extremely regret it, did he allow Don Benito to become aware that he had **indulged** in ungenerous surmises. In short, to the Spaniard's black-letter text, it was best, for awhile, to leave open margin.

Presently, his pale face twitching and **overcast**, the Spaniard, still supported by his attendant, moved over towards his guest, when, with even more than his

Italian

attain: arrivare, arrivi, arriviamo, arrivate, arrivano, arriva, arrivo, ottenere, raggiungere, conseguire.
betray: tradire, tradisci, tradite, tradisco, tradiamo, tradiscono.
clearness: limpidezza, chiarezza.
distrust: diffidenza.
duplicity: duplicità.
ennobled: nobilitato.
enterprising: intraprendente.
hoar: canuto.
humming: ronzante, ronzio.

illusory: illusorio.
indulged: compiaciuto, indulto.
infantile: infantile.
knave: canaglia, farabutto, briccone, furfante.
manhood: virilità.
maritime: marittimo.
mistrust: diffidenza, sfiducia.
overcast: coperto.
paw: gamba, zampa, piede.
refined: raffinato, delicato.
regained: riacquistato, riconquistato,

ricuperato, riguadagnato, ripreso.
roving: stoppino.
savage: selvaggio, crudele.
silky: serico, di seta.
simulating: simulando.
sounding: sondaggio.
surname: cognome.
thinness: finezza, leggerezza, magrezza, sottigliezza.
unexplained: non spiegato.
vanish: sparire, spariscono, sparisco, sparisci, spariamo, sparite, svanire.

usual embarrassment, and a **strange** sort of **intriguing intonation** in his husky whisper, the following **conversation** began:—

"Señor, may I ask how long you have lain at this isle?"

"Oh, but a day or two, Don Benito."

"And from what **port** are you last?"

"Canton."

"And there, Señor, you **exchanged** your sealskins for teas and silks, I think you said?"

"Yes, Silks, mostly."

"And the **balance** you took in **specie**, perhaps?"

Captain Delano, fidgeting a little, answered—

"Yes; some silver; not a very great **deal**, though."

"Ah—well. May I ask how many men have you, Señor?"

Captain Delano **slightly started**, but answered—

"About five-and-twenty, all told."

"And at present, Señor, all on **board**, I suppose?"

"All on board, Don Benito," replied the Captain, now with **satisfaction**.

"And will be to-night, Señor?"

At this last question, following so many pertinacious ones, for the **soul** of him Captain Delano could not but look very **earnestly** at the **questioner**, who, **instead** of meeting the glance, with every token of **craven** discomposure dropped his eyes to the deck; presenting an **unworthy contrast** to his servant, who, just then, was kneeling at his feet, **adjusting** a **loose** shoe-buckle; his **disengaged** face **meantime**, with **humble** curiosity, turned openly up into his master's **downcast** one.

The Spaniard, still with a **guilty shuffle**, **repeated** his question:

"And—and will be to-night, Señor?"

Italian

adjusting: aggiustando, regolando.
balance: equilibrio, saldo, bilancio, bilanciamento, bilanciare, equilibrare, bilancia, quadrare, pareggio.
board: consiglio, asse, tavola, commissione, bordo, scheda, pannello.
contrast: contrasto.
conversation: conversazione, discorso.
craven: codardo.
deal: affare, trattare, accordo.
disengaged: disimpegnato, disinnestato.
downcast: abbattuto.
earnestly: seriamente.
exchanged: scambiato.
guilty: colpevole.
humble: umile, modesto.
instead: invece.
intonation: intonazione, cadenza.
intriguing: intrigante.
loose: sciolto, lasco, slegare, slacciare, sciogliere.
meantime: frattanto, nel frattempo, intanto.
port: porto, porta, portello.
questioner: interrogante.
repeated: ripetuto.
satisfaction: soddisfazione.
shuffle: mescolare.
slightly: leggermente, lievemente.
soul: anima.
specie: moneta metallica.
started: cominciato.
strange: strano.
unworthy: indegno.

"Yes, for aught I know," returned Captain Delano—"but nay," rallying himself into **fearless** truth, "some of them talked of going off on another **fishing** party about midnight."

"Your ships generally go—go more or less armed, I believe, Señor?"

"Oh, a six-pounder or two, in case of emergency," was the **intrepidly** indifferent reply, "with a small stock of muskets, sealing-spears, and cutlasses, you know."

As he thus **responded**, Captain Delano again glanced at Don Benito, but the latter's eyes were **averted**; while abruptly and awkwardly **shifting** the subject, he made some **peevish** allusion to the calm, and then, without **apology**, once more, with his attendant, withdrew to the opposite bulwarks, where the whispering was resumed.

At this moment, and ere Captain Delano could cast a **cool** thought upon what had just passed, the young Spanish sailor, before mentioned, was seen **descending** from the rigging. In act of stooping over to spring **inboard** to the deck, his **voluminous**, unconfined **frock**, or shirt, of **coarse woolen**, much **spotted** with tar, opened out far down the chest, revealing a **soiled** under **garment** of what seemed the finest **linen**, edged, about the neck, with a narrow blue **ribbon**, sadly **faded** and **worn**. At this moment the young sailor's eye was again fixed on the whisperers, and Captain Delano thought he observed a lurking significance in it, as if silent signs, of some Freemason sort, had that instant been interchanged.

This once more **impelled** his own glance in the direction of Don Benito, and, as before, he could not but **infer** that himself formed the subject of the conference. He paused. The sound of the hatchet-polishing fell on his ears. He cast another swift side-look at the two. They had the air of conspirators. In connection with the late questionings, and the incident of the young sailor, these things now begat such return of involuntary suspicion, that the singular guilelessness of the American could not **endure** it. Plucking up a **gay** and **humorous** expression, he crossed over to the two rapidly, saying:—"Ha, Don Benito, your black here seems high in your trust; a sort of privy-counselor, in fact."

Italian

apology: scusa, apologia.
averted: evitato, allontanato, distolto.
coarse: rozzo, grossolano.
cool: fresco, raffreddare, freddo.
descending: scendendo, discendendo.
endure: sopportare, sopporta, sopporto, sopportiamo, sopporti, sopportano, sopportate, tollerare, durare, duriamo, dura.
faded: sbiadito, svanito.
fearless: intrepido, impavido.
fishing: pesca, pescaggio.

frock: vestito, tonaca, abito.
garment: indumento, abito.
gay: allegro, gaio.
humorous: umoristico, divertente.
impelled: costretto, incitato.
inboard: entrobordo.
infer: dedurre, deducete, deduco, deduciamo, deducono, deduci, concludere, concludi, concludiamo, concludete, concludo.
intrepidly: intrepidamente.
linen: lino, biancheria.

peevish: permaloso, stizzoso.
responded: risposto, replicato.
ribbon: nastro, fettuccia.
shifting: spostare, spostamento.
soiled: sporca, sporcano, sporcate, sporchi, sporchiamo, sporco, sporcare.
spotted: maculato.
voluminous: voluminoso.
woolen: di lana.
worn: consumato, usato, esausto, portato, logoro.

Upon this, the servant looked up with a good-natured **grin**, but the master started as from a **venomous bite**. It was a moment or two before the Spaniard sufficiently recovered himself to reply; which he did, at last, with cold constraint: — "Yes, Señor, I have trust in Babo."

Here Babo, **changing** his previous grin of mere animal humor into an **intelligent** smile, not **ungratefully eyed** his master.

Finding that the Spaniard now stood silent and **reserved**, as if involuntarily, or **purposely** giving hint that his guest's **proximity** was **inconvenient** just then, Captain Delano, unwilling to appear **uncivil** even to incivility itself, made some trivial **remark** and moved off; again and again turning over in his mind the **mysterious** demeanor of Don Benito Cereno.

He had **descended** from the poop, and, **wrapped** in thought, was passing near a dark **hatchway**, leading down into the steerage, when, **perceiving** motion there, he looked to see what moved. The same instant there was a sparkle in the shadowy hatchway, and he saw one of the Spanish sailors, prowling there hurriedly **placing** his hand in the bosom of his frock, as if **hiding** something. Before the man could have been certain who it was that was passing, he slunk below out of sight. But enough was seen of him to make it sure that he was the same young sailor before noticed in the rigging.

What was that which so sparkled? thought Captain Delano. It was no lamp — no match — no live coal. Could it have been a **jewel**? But how come sailors with jewels? — or with silk-trimmed under-shirts either? Has he been **robbing** the trunks of the dead cabin-passengers? But if so, he would hardly wear one of the **stolen** articles on board ship here. Ah, ah — if, now, that was, indeed, a **secret** sign I saw passing between this **suspicious** fellow and his captain awhile since; if I could only be certain that, in my uneasiness, my **senses** did not **deceive** me, then —

Here, passing from one suspicious thing to another, his mind revolved the strange questions put to him concerning his ship.

By a curious **coincidence**, as each point was **recalled**, the black wizards of Ashantee would strike up with their hatchets, as in ominous comment on the

Italian

bite: mordere, morso, puntura, boccone, abboccare.
changing: cambiare.
coincidence: coincidenza.
deceive: ingannare, ingannano, inganniamo, ingannate, inganna, inganni, inganno, truffare, truffate, truffano, truffiamo.
descended: sceso, disceso.
eyed: occhio.
grin: sogghignare, sorriso.
hatchway: boccaporto.

hiding: nascondendo.
inconvenient: difficile, pesante, inconveniente, incomodo.
intelligent: intelligente.
jewel: gioiello, gemma, gioia.
mysterious: misterioso.
perceiving: percependo, scorgendo, intravedendo.
placing: collocamento.
proximity: prossimità.
purposely: intenzionalmente.
recalled: ricordato.

remark: commento, osservazione, nota.
reserved: riservato.
robbing: derubando.
secret: segreto.
senses: sensi.
stolen: rubato.
suspicious: sospettoso, sospetto.
uncivil: incivile.
ungratefully: ingrato.
venomous: velenoso.
wrapped: nella.

white stranger's thoughts. **Pressed** by such enigmas: and portents, it would have been almost against nature, had not, even into the least **distrustful** heart, some ugly misgivings obtruded.

Observing the ship, now helplessly fallen into a current, with enchanted sails, drifting with increased rapidity seaward; and noting that, from a **lately intercepted projection** of the land, the sealer was hidden, the **stout mariner** began to **quake** at thoughts which he **barely** durst confess to himself. Above all, he began to feel a **ghostly dread** of Don Benito. And yet, when he roused himself, **dilated** his chest, felt himself strong on his legs, and coolly considered it—what did all these phantoms amount to?

Had the Spaniard any sinister scheme, it must have reference not so much to him (Captain Delano) as to his ship (the Bachelor's Delight). Hence the present drifting away of the one ship from the other, instead of favoring any such possible scheme, was, for the time, at least, **opposed** to it. Clearly any suspicion, combining such contradictions, must need be **delusive**. Beside, was it not absurd to think of a vessel in distress—a vessel by **sickness** almost dismanned of her crew—a vessel whose inmates were **parched** for water—was it not a thousand times absurd that such a **craft** should, at present, be of a piratical character; or her commander, either for himself or those under him, **cherish** any desire but for speedy relief and **refreshment**? But then, might not general distress, and **thirst** in particular, be affected? And might not that same undiminished Spanish crew, **alleged** to have **perished** off to a **remnant**, be at that very moment lurking in the hold? On heart-broken **pretense** of **entreating** a cup of cold water, fiends in human form had got into **lonely** dwellings, nor retired until a dark **deed** had been done. And among the Malay pirates, it was no unusual thing to **lure** ships after them into their **treacherous** harbors, or **entice** boarders from a declared enemy at sea, by the spectacle of **thinly** manned or vacant decks, beneath which prowled a hundred spears with yellow arms ready to upthrust them through the mats. Not that Captain Delano had entirely credited such things. He had heard of them—and now, as stories, they **recurred**. The present **destination** of the ship was the anchorage. There she would be near his own vessel. Upon gaining that

Italian

alleged: presunto.
barely: appena, a mala pena.
cherish: adoriamo, adori, adorate, adorano, adora, adoro, adorare, curare teneramente.
craft: natante.
deed: atto, azione.
delusive: ingannevole, illusorio.
destination: destinazione.
dilated: dilatato.
distrustful: sospettoso, diffidente.
dread: temere.

entice: attirare.
entreating: supplicando, supplicare.
ghostly: spettrale.
intercepted: intercettato.
lately: ultimamente, recentemente.
lonely: solitario, solo.
lure: allettare.
mariner: marinaio.
opposed: opposto, contrapposto.
parched: disseccato.
perished: perito.
pressed: premuto.

pretense: pretesa, finta, finzione.
projection: proiezione, sporgenza.
quake: tremito, tremare.
recurred: ricorso, ritornato.
refreshment: rinfresco, ristoro.
remnant: scampolo, resto.
sickness: malattia.
stout: forte, corpulento, robusto, birra scura.
thinly: sottilmente, magramente.
thirst: sete.
treacherous: traditore.

vicinity,   might not the San Dominick, like a slumbering **volcano**, suddenly let loose **energies** now hid?

He recalled the Spaniard's manner while telling his story. There was a **gloomy hesitancy** and **subterfuge** about it. It was just the manner of one making up his **tale** for evil purposes, as he goes. But if that story was not true, what was the truth? That the ship had **unlawfully** come into the Spaniard's possession? But in many of its details, especially in reference to the more **calamitous** parts, such as the fatalities among the seamen, the consequent prolonged **beating** about, the past sufferings from **obstinate** calms, and **still** continued suffering from thirst; in all these points, as well as others, Don Benito's story had **corroborated** not only the **wailing** ejaculations of the **indiscriminate** multitude, white and black, but likewise—what seemed impossible to be counterfeit—by the very expression and play of every human feature, which Captain Delano saw. If Don Benito's story was, throughout, an invention, then every soul on board, down to the youngest negress, was his carefully drilled **recruit** in the plot: an **incredible inference**. And yet, if there was ground for mistrusting his **veracity**, that inference was a legitimate one.

But those questions of the Spaniard. There, indeed, one might pause. Did they not seem put with much the same object with which the **burglar** or **assassin**, by day-time, reconnoitres the walls of a house? But, with ill purposes, to **solicit** such information openly of the chief person **endangered**, and so, in effect, setting him on his guard; how unlikely a procedure was that? Absurd, then, to suppose that those questions had been prompted by evil designs. Thus, the same conduct, which, in this **instance**, had raised the **alarm**, served to **dispel** it. In short, **scarce** any suspicion or uneasiness, however apparently reasonable at the time, which was not now, with equal apparent reason, dismissed.

At last he began to laugh at his former forebodings; and laugh at the strange ship for, in its aspect, **someway siding** with them, as it were; and laugh, too, at the odd-looking blacks, particularly those old scissors-grinders, the Ashantees; and those bed-ridden old **knitting** women, the oakum-pickers; and almost at the dark Spaniard himself, the central **hobgoblin** of all.

Italian

alarm: allarme, sveglia, allarmare.
assassin: assassino.
beating: battito, battitura.
burglar: ladro, scassinatore.
calamitous: calamitoso.
corroborated: confermato, corroborato.
dispel: dissipare.
endangered: mettere in pericolo.
energies: energie.
gloomy: tetro, tenebroso, oscuro.
hesitancy: esitazione.

hobgoblin: spiritello maligno.
ill: malato, ammalato.
incredible: incredibile.
indiscriminate: indiscriminato.
inference: conclusione, illazione, inferenza, deduzione.
instance: istanza, esempio.
knitting: lavorazione a maglia, lavoro a maglia.
obstinate: ostinato.
recruit: arruolare, ingaggiare, reclutare, recluta, assoldare.

scarce: scarso, raro.
siding: parteggiare.
solicit: sollecito, sollecitare, sollecitate, solleciti, sollecitano, sollecita, sollecitiamo.
someway: in qualche modo.
subterfuge: sotterfugio.
tale: racconto, storia, novella, favola.
unlawfully: illegalmente.
veracity: veracità.
volcano: vulcano.
wailing: piagnisteo, gemere.

For the rest, whatever in a serious way seemed enigmatical, was now good-naturedly **explained** away by the thought that, for the most part, the poor invalid **scarcely** knew what he was about; either sulking in black vapors, or putting idle questions without sense or object. Evidently for the present, the man was not fit to be intrusted with the ship. On some benevolent **plea withdrawing** the command from him, **Captain** Delano would yet have to send her to Conception, in charge of his second mate, a **worthy** person and good navigator — a plan not more convenient for the San Dominick than for Don Benito; for, relieved from all **anxiety**, keeping wholly to his cabin, the **sick** man, under the good **nursing** of his servant, would, probably, by the end of the **passage**, be in a measure restored to health, and with that he should also be restored to authority.

Such were the American's thoughts. They were **tranquilizing**. There was a difference between the idea of Don Benito's darkly pre-ordaining Captain Delano's fate, and Captain Delano's **lightly arranging** Don Benito's. Nevertheless, it was not without something of relief that the good **seaman** presently perceived his whale-boat in the distance. Its absence had been prolonged by **unexpected detention** at the sealer's side, as well as its returning **trip** lengthened by the continual **recession** of the goal.

The advancing **speck** was observed by the blacks. Their shouts **attracted** the attention of Don Benito, who, with a return of courtesy, **approaching** Captain Delano, **expressed** satisfaction at the coming of some supplies, slight and **temporary** as they must necessarily prove.

Captain Delano responded; but while doing so, his attention was drawn to something passing on the deck below: among the **crowd** climbing the **landward** bulwarks, anxiously watching the coming boat, two blacks, to all appearances accidentally incommoded by one of the sailors, violently **pushed** him **aside**, which the sailor someway resenting, they **dashed** him to the deck, despite the earnest cries of the oakum-pickers.

"Don Benito," said Captain Delano quickly, "do you see what is going on there? Look!"

Italian

anxiety: ansia, ansietà, angoscia, inquietudine.
approaching: avvicinamento.
arranging: sistemando, predisponendo, ordinando.
aside: da parte, a parte.
attracted: attirato, attratto.
captain: capitano.
crowd: folla, affluenza, calca, affollarsi.
dashed: tratteggiato.
detention: arresto, detenzione.

explained: spiegato.
expressed: espresso.
landward: verso terra.
lightly: leggermente.
nursing: allattamento.
passage: passaggio, corridoio, brano, varco, corsia.
plea: argomento, appello.
pushed: spinto.
recession: recessione.
scarcely: appena, a stento.
seaman: marinaio.

sick: malato, ammalato.
speck: bruscolo, pagliuzza, macchiolina, puntino, granello, macchietta.
temporary: provvisorio, temporaneo, transitorio, interino, interinale.
tranquilizing: tranquillizzando.
trip: viaggio, escursione.
unexpected: inatteso, imprevisto, inaspettato.
withdrawing: ritirando, prelevando.
worthy: degno, meritevole.

But, **seized** by his cough, the Spaniard staggered, with both hands to his face, on the point of **falling**. Captain Delano would have supported him, but the servant was more **alert**, who, with one hand **sustaining** his master, with the other applied the cordial. Don Benito restored, the black withdrew his support, slipping aside a little, but dutifully **remaining** within call of a whisper. Such **discretion** was here evinced as quite wiped away, in the visitor's eyes, any **blemish** of **impropriety** which might have **attached** to the attendant, from the indecorous conferences before mentioned; showing, too, that if the servant were to **blame**, it might be more the master's **fault** than his own, since, when left to himself, he could conduct thus well.

His glance called away from the spectacle of **disorder** to the more pleasing one before him, Captain Delano could not avoid again **congratulating** his host upon possessing such a servant, who, though perhaps a little too forward now and then, must upon the whole be **invaluable** to one in the invalid's situation.

"Tell me, Don Benito," he added, with a smile—"I should like to have your man here, myself—what will you take for him? Would fifty doubloons be any object?"

"Master wouldn't part with Babo for a thousand doubloons," murmured the black, **overhearing** the offer, and taking it in earnest, and, with the strange vanity of a **faithful** slave, **appreciated** by his master, scorning to hear so **paltry** a **valuation** put upon him by a stranger. But Don Benito, apparently hardly yet completely restored, and again interrupted by his cough, made but some broken reply.

Soon his physical distress became so great, **affecting** his mind, too, apparently, that, as if to **screen** the sad spectacle, the servant gently conducted his master below.

Left to himself, the American, to while away the time **till** his boat should **arrive**, would have pleasantly accosted some one of the few Spanish seamen he saw; but recalling something that Don Benito had said touching their ill conduct, he refrained; as a shipmaster **indisposed** to countenance **cowardice** or **unfaithfulness** in seamen.

Italian

affecting: riguardando.
alert: allarme, sveglio.
appreciated: apprezzato.
arrive: arrivare, arrivano, arriva, arrivi, arriviamo, arrivate, arrivo, giungere.
attached: fissato, attaccato, allegato.
blame: colpa, biasimare, riprendere, incolpare, biasimo.
blemish: difetto.
congratulating: felicitando.
cowardice: codardia, vigliaccheria.

discretion: discrezione.
disorder: disordine, disturbo, disfunzione.
faithful: fedele, leale.
falling: cadendo.
fault: difetto, faglia, guasto, fallo.
impropriety: scorrettezza, improprietà.
indisposed: indisposto.
invaluable: inestimabile.
overhearing: origliando.
paltry: meschino.

remaining: rimanendo, restando, rimanente, restante.
screen: schermo, vaglio, retino, riparo, schermare, schermata, riparare, paravento.
seized: afferrato.
sustaining: sostenendo, poggiando, sostenere.
till: finchè, coltivare, cassa, fino, arare.
unfaithfulness: infedeltà.
valuation: valutazione, valorizzazione.

While, with these thoughts, standing with eye directed forward towards that **handful** of sailors, suddenly he thought that one or two of them returned the glance and with a sort of meaning. He rubbed his eyes, and looked again; but again seemed to see the same thing. Under a new form, but more **obscure** than any previous one, the old suspicions recurred, but, in the absence of Don Benito, with less of **panic** than before. Despite the bad account given of the sailors, Captain Delano resolved **forthwith** to accost one of them. Descending the poop, he made his way through the blacks, his movement drawing a **queer** cry from the oakum-pickers, prompted by whom, the negroes, twitching each other aside, divided before him; but, as if curious to see what was the object of this **deliberate** visit to their Ghetto, **closing** in behind, in **tolerable** order, followed the white stranger up. His progress thus proclaimed as by mounted kings-at-arms, and escorted as by a Caffre **guard** of **honor**, Captain Delano, **assuming** a good-humored, off-handed air, continued to advance; now and then saying a **blithe** word to the negroes, and his eye curiously surveying the white faces, here and there **sparsely** mixed in with the blacks, like **stray** white pawns venturously involved in the ranks of the chess-men opposed.

While thinking which of them to select for his purpose, he **chanced** to **observe** a sailor seated on the deck engaged in **tarring** the **strap** of a large block, a circle of blacks squatted round him **inquisitively** eying the process.

The mean employment of the man was in contrast with something **superior** in his figure. His hand, black with continually thrusting it into the tar-pot held for him by a negro, seemed not naturally **allied** to his face, a face which would have been a very fine one but for its haggardness. Whether this haggardness had aught to do with **criminality**, could not be determined; since, as **intense** heat and cold, though unlike, produce like sensations, so **innocence** and **guilt**, when, through **casual** association with mental pain, **stamping** any visible impress, use one seal — a **hacked** one.

Not again that this reflection occurred to Captain Delano at the time, charitable man as he was. Rather another idea. Because observing so singular a haggardness combined with a dark eye, averted as in trouble and **shame**, and

Italian

allied: alleato.	proteggere, guardia, carter, riparo,	osserva, osservi, eseguire, compiere.
assuming: presumendo, presuntuoso.	custodire, sorvegliare.	**panic**: panico.
blithe: allegro.	**guilt**: colpa.	**queer**: strano, omosessuale.
casual: casuale, accidentale.	**hacked**: tagliato.	**shame**: vergogna, pudore.
chanced: successo.	**handful**: manciata.	**sparsely**: scarsamente.
closing: chiudendo, chiusura.	**honor**: onore, onorare.	**stamping**: affrancatura, bollatura.
criminality: delinquenza.	**innocence**: innocenza.	**strap**: cinghia, correggia, cinghia a
deliberate: intenzionale, deliberare,	**inquisitively**: curiosamente.	tracolla, cinturino, strap.
riflettere, deliberato.	**intense**: intenso.	**stray**: randagio, deviare, smarrirsi.
forthwith: immediatamente.	**obscure**: oscuro, sconosciuto.	**superior**: superiore.
good-humored: di buon umore.	**observe**: osservare, osservano,	**tarring**: catramatura, incatramare.
guard: capotreno, protezione,	osservo, osserviamo, osservate,	**tolerable**: tollerabile.

then again recalling Don Benito's confessed ill opinion of his crew, insensibly he was **operated** upon by certain general notions which, while **disconnecting** pain and **abashment** from **virtue**, **invariably** link them with vice.

If, indeed, there be any **wickedness** on board this ship, thought Captain Delano, be sure that man there has fouled his hand in it, even as now he fouls it in the **pitch**. I don't like to accost him. I will speak to this other, this old Jack here on the **windlass**.

He advanced to an old Barcelona tar, in ragged red **breeches** and dirty night-cap, cheeks trenched and **bronzed**, **whiskers dense** as **thorn** hedges. Seated between two sleepy-looking Africans, this mariner, like his younger **shipmate**, was employed upon some rigging—splicing a cable—the sleepy-looking blacks **performing** the inferior function of holding the **outer** parts of the ropes for him.

Upon Captain Delano's approach, the man at once **hung** his head below its previous level; the one necessary for business. It appeared as if he desired to be thought **absorbed**, with more than common fidelity, in his task. Being addressed, he glanced up, but with what seemed a **furtive**, **diffident** air, which sat strangely enough on his weather-beaten visage, much as if a **grizzly** bear, instead of **growling** and biting, should simper and cast sheep's eyes. He was asked several questions concerning the voyage—questions purposely **referring** to several particulars in Don Benito's narrative, not previously corroborated by those **impulsive** cries **greeting** the visitor on first coming on board. The questions were briefly answered, **confirming** all that remained to be confirmed of the story. The negroes about the windlass joined in with the old sailor; but, as they became talkative, he by degrees became mute, and at length quite **glum**, seemed morosely unwilling to answer more questions, and yet, all the while, this ursine air was somehow mixed with his **sheepish** one.

Despairing of getting into unembarrassed talk with such a **centaur**, Captain Delano, after glancing round for a more promising countenance, but seeing none, spoke pleasantly to the blacks to make way for him; and so, **amid** various grins and grimaces, returned to the poop, feeling a little strange at first, he could hardly tell why, but upon the whole with regained confidence in Benito Cereno.

Italian

abashment: confusione.
absorbed: assorbito, assorto.
amid: tra, fra.
breeches: brache, calzoni alla zuava.
bronzed: bronzo.
centaur: centauro.
confirming: confermando.
dense: denso, fitto.
diffident: timido.
disconnecting: disinnestando, sconnettendo.
furtive: furtivo.

glum: accigliato.
greeting: salutando, saluto, accoglienza.
grizzly: grigio, brizzolato, grigiastro, orso grigio.
growling: ringhiare.
hung: appeso.
impulsive: impulsivo.
invariably: invariabilmente.
operated: operato, azionato.
outer: esterno, esterne, esteriore.
performing: eseguendo.

pitch: passo, beccheggio, pece, beccheggiare, intonazione, pendenza, inclinazione.
referring: deferendo, indirizzando, riferendo.
sheepish: timido, imbarazzato.
shipmate: compagno di bordo.
thorn: spina.
virtue: virtù.
whiskers: baffi.
wickedness: cattiveria.
windlass: argano, verricello.

How plainly, thought he, did that old whiskerando yonder betray a **consciousness** of ill desert. No doubt, when he saw me coming, he dreaded **lest** I, apprised by his Captain of the crew's general **misbehavior**, came with sharp words for him, and so down with his head. And yet—and yet, now that I think of it, that very old fellow, if I err not, was one of those who seemed so earnestly eying me here awhile since. Ah, these currents **spin** one's head round almost as much as they do the ship. Ha, there now's a pleasant sort of **sunny** sight; quite **sociable**, too.

His attention had been drawn to a slumbering negress, partly **disclosed** through the lacework of some rigging, lying, with **youthful** limbs carelessly disposed, under the lee of the bulwarks, like a doe in the **shade** of a **woodland** rock. **Sprawling** at her lapped **breasts**, was her wide-awake **fawn**, **stark** naked, its black little body half lifted from the deck, **crosswise** with its dam's; its hands, like two paws, clambering upon her; its mouth and nose ineffectually rooting to get at the mark; and meantime giving a **vexatious** half-grunt, blending with the composed **snore** of the negress.

The **uncommon vigor** of the child at length roused the mother. She started up, at a distance facing Captain Delano. But as if not, at all concerned at the attitude in which she had been caught, delightedly she caught the child up, with **maternal** transports, covering it with **kisses**.

There's naked nature, now; pure **tenderness** and love, thought Captain Delano, well **pleased**.

This incident prompted him to remark the other negresses more particularly than before. He was **gratified** with their **manners**: like most **uncivilized** women, they seemed at once tender of heart and **tough** of **constitution**; equally ready to die for their infants or fight for them. Unsophisticated as leopardesses; **loving** as doves. Ah! thought Captain Delano, these, perhaps, are some of the very women whom Ledyard saw in Africa, and gave such a **noble** account of.

These natural sights somehow insensibly deepened his confidence and ease. At last he looked to see how his boat was getting on; but it was still pretty **remote**. He turned to see if Don Benito had returned; but he had not.

Italian

breasts: seno.
consciousness: consapevolezza, coscienza.
constitution: costituzione.
crosswise: trasversalmente.
disclosed: dischiuso, svelato.
ease: agio, facilità.
fawn: cerbiatto.
gratified: gratificato.
kisses: baci.
lest: affinchè non, per paura che.
loving: affettuoso.

manners: educazione.
maternal: materno.
misbehavior: cattiva condotta.
noble: nobile, gentilizio, nobiliare.
remote: distante, lontano, remoto, isolato, a distanza, periferico.
shade: ombra, adombrare, tinta, ombreggiare, oscurità, sfumatura, sfumare.
snore: russare.
sociable: socievole.
spin: rotazione, filare.

sprawling: che si stravacca.
stark: rigido.
sunny: soleggiato, assolato.
tender: tenero, dolce, offerta, tender.
tenderness: tenerezza, affettuosità.
tough: duro, tenace.
uncivilized: incivile.
uncommon: insolito, raro.
vexatious: irritante.
vigor: vigore, vigoria.
woodland: boschivo.
youthful: giovane, giovanile.

To change the scene, as well as to please himself with a leisurely **observation** of the coming boat, stepping over into the mizzen-chains, he clambered his way into the starboard quarter-gallery—one of those **abandoned** Venetian-looking water-balconies previously mentioned—retreats cut off from the deck. As his foot pressed the half-damp, half-dry sea-mosses **matting** the place, and a chance **phantom** cats-paw—an **islet** of breeze, unheralded unfollowed—as this ghostly cats-paw came fanning his **cheek**; as his glance fell upon the row of small, round dead-lights—all closed like coppered eyes of the coffined—and the state-cabin door, once **connecting** with the gallery, even as the dead-lights had once looked out upon it, but now **calked** fast like a **sarcophagus** lid; and to a purple-black tarred-over, panel, threshold, and post; and he bethought him of the time, when that state-cabin and this state-balcony had heard the voices of the Spanish king's officers, and the forms of the Lima viceroy's **daughters** had perhaps leaned where he stood—as these and other images **flitted** through his mind, as the cats-paw through the calm, gradually he felt **rising** a dreamy **inquietude**, like that of one who alone on the **prairie feels unrest** from the **repose** of the noon.

He leaned against the **carved balustrade**, again looking off toward his boat; but found his eye falling upon the ribbon grass, **trailing** along the ship's water-line, straight as a border of green box; and parterres of sea-weed, broad ovals and crescents, floating nigh and far, with what seemed long formal alleys between, crossing the **terraces** of swells, and **sweeping** round as if leading to the grottoes below. And overhanging all was the balustrade by his arm, which, partly **stained** with pitch and partly **embossed** with **moss**, seemed the **charred ruin** of some summer-house in a grand garden long running to waste.

Trying to break one charm, he was but becharmed anew. Though upon the wide sea, he seemed in some far inland country; prisoner in some deserted château, left to stare at empty grounds, and **peer** out at vague roads, where never **wagon** or **wayfarer** passed.

But these enchantments were a little **disenchanted** as his eye fell on the corroded main-chains. Of an ancient style, massy and rusty in link, **shackle** and

Italian

abandoned: abbandonato.
balustrade: parapetto, balaustra, balaustrata.
calked: calafatato.
carved: intagliato, tagliato, scolpito.
charred: carbonizzato.
cheek: guancia, la guancia.
connecting: legando, collegando.
daughters: figlie.
disenchanted: disilluso, disincantato.
embossed: stampato in rilievo.
feels: sente, tasta, tocca, trova, prova.

flitted: aleggiato, svolazzato.
inquietude: inquietudine.
islet: isoletta, isolotto.
matting: stuoia.
moss: muschio.
observation: osservazione.
peer: fissare.
phantom: fantasma.
prairie: prateria.
repose: riposo, riposarsi.
rising: aumento, salita, sorgere, sorgente, levata, ascendente, ascesa,

nascente, sommossa, levante, crescita.
ruin: rovinare, rovina.
sarcophagus: sarcofago.
shackle: anello di trazione.
stained: macchiato.
sweeping: spazzatura, spazzare, vasto.
terraces: terrazze.
trailing: trascinare.
unrest: agitazione.
wagon: vagone.
wayfarer: viandante.

bolt, they seemed even more fit for the ship's present business than the one for which she had been built.

Presently he thought something moved nigh the chains. He rubbed his eyes, and looked hard. Groves of rigging were about the chains; and there, peering from behind a great stay, like an Indian from behind a **hemlock**, a Spanish sailor, a marlingspike in his hand, was seen, who made what seemed an **imperfect gesture** towards the **balcony**, but immediately as if alarmed by some advancing step along the deck within, vanished into the recesses of the **hempen** forest, like a **poacher**.

What meant this? Something the man had sought to communicate, unbeknown to any one, even to his captain. Did the secret involve aught unfavorable to his captain? Were those previous misgivings of Captain Delano's about to be **verified**? Or, in his haunted mood at the moment, had some **random**, **unintentional** motion of the man, while busy with the stay, as if **repairing** it, been **mistaken** for a significant **beckoning**?

Not unbewildered, again he gazed off for his boat. But it was temporarily hidden by a **rocky spur** of the **isle**. As with some eagerness he **bent** forward, watching for the first **shooting** view of its beak, the balustrade gave way before him like **charcoal**. Had he not clutched an outreaching rope he would have fallen into the sea. The crash, though feeble, and the fall, though hollow, of the **rotten** fragments, must have been overheard. He glanced up. With **sober** curiosity peering down upon him was one of the old oakum-pickers, slipped from his **perch** to an outside **boom**; while below the old negro, and, **invisible** to him, reconnoitering from a port-hole like a fox from the mouth of its den, **crouched** the Spanish sailor again. From something suddenly suggested by the man's air, the mad idea now darted into Captain Delano's mind, that Don Benito's plea of **indisposition**, in withdrawing below, was but a pretense: that he was engaged there **maturing** his plot, of which the sailor, by some means gaining an inkling, had a mind to **warn** the stranger against; **incited**, it may be, by gratitude for a kind word on first boarding the ship. Was it from **foreseeing** some possible **interference** like this, that Don Benito had, **beforehand**, given such a bad

Italian

balcony: balcone, terrazzo, balconata.
beckoning: accennando.
beforehand: in anticipo.
bent: curvo, piegato.
bolt: bullone, chiavistello, catenaccio.
boom: boom, giraffa, boma, rimbombare, braccio, asta.
charcoal: carbone di legna.
crouched: rannicchiato, accoccolato.
foreseeing: prevedendo.
gesture: gesto.
hemlock: cicuta.

hempen: di canapa.
imperfect: imperfetto.
incited: incitato, spronato.
indisposition: indisposizione.
interference: interferenza.
invisible: invisibile.
isle: isola.
maturing: maturando.
mistaken: sbagliato.
perch: persico, pesce persico, appollaiarsi.
poacher: bracconiere.

random: casuale, aleatorio.
repairing: riparazione, riparare.
rocky: roccioso.
rotten: marcio, putrido.
shooting: sparando, ripresa.
sober: sobrio.
spur: sperone, sprone, spronare.
unintentional: involontario.
verified: verificato, controllato.
warn: avvertire, avvertiamo, avvertono, avverti, avverto, avvertite, ammonire, avvisare.

character of his sailors, while **praising** the negroes; though, indeed, the former seemed as **docile** as the latter the contrary? The whites, too, by nature, were the shrewder race. A man with some evil design, would he not be likely to speak well of that **stupidity** which was blind to his **depravity**, and malign that intelligence from which it might not be **hidden**? Not **unlikely**, perhaps. But if the whites had dark secrets concerning Don Benito, could then Don Benito be any way in **complicity** with the blacks? But they were too stupid. Besides, who ever heard of a white so far a **renegade** as to **apostatize** from his very species almost, by leaguing in against it with negroes? These difficulties recalled former ones. Lost in their mazes, Captain Delano, who had now regained the deck, was uneasily advancing along it, when he observed a new face; an **aged** sailor seated cross-legged near the main hatchway. His skin was **shrunk** up with wrinkles like a pelican's **empty pouch**; his hair frosted; his countenance grave and composed. His hands were full of ropes, which he was working into a large knot. Some blacks were about him **obligingly** dipping the strands for him, here and there, as the exigencies of the operation demanded.

Captain Delano crossed over to him, and stood in silence surveying the knot; his mind, by a not uncongenial **transition**, passing from its own entanglements to those of the **hemp**. For **intricacy**, such a knot he had never seen in an American ship, nor indeed any other. The old man looked like an Egyptian **priest**, making Gordian **knots** for the temple of Ammon. The knot seemed a **combination** of double-bowline-knot, treble-crown-knot, back-handed-well-knot, knot-in-and-out-knot, and jamming-knot.

At last, puzzled to **comprehend** the meaning of such a knot, Captain Delano addressed the knotter: —

"What are you **knotting** there, my man?"

"The knot," was the **brief** reply, without looking up.

"So it seems; but what is it for?"

"For some one else to undo," muttered back the old man, **plying** his **fingers harder** than ever, the knot being now nearly **completed**.

Italian

aged: anziano.	comprendiamo, comprendi, comprendete.	**obligingly**: servizievole, cortesemente.
apostatize: apostatate, apostati, apostato, apostatiamo, apostatano, apostata, apostatare.	**depravity**: depravazione.	**plying**: maneggiando.
	docile: arrendevole, mansueto.	**pouch**: sacchetto, borsa.
brief: breve, corto, riassunto, conciso, memoria.	**empty**: vuoto, vuotare, vacuo.	**praising**: lodare.
	fingers: dito.	**priest**: prete, sacerdote, curato.
combination: combinazione.	**harder**: più duro.	**renegade**: rinnegato.
completed: finito, completato, terminato.	**hemp**: canapa.	**shrunk**: ristretto.
complicity: complicità.	**hidden**: nascosto.	**stupid**: stupido, sciocco, ignorante, balordo.
comprehend: comprendere, comprendo, comprendono,	**intricacy**: complessità, complicazione.	**stupidity**: stupidità.
	knots: nodi.	**transition**: transizione, passaggio.
	knotting: annodamento.	**unlikely**: improbabile.

While Captain Delano stood **watching** him, suddenly the old man threw the knot towards him, saying in broken English—the first heard in the ship—something to this effect: "Undo it, cut it, quick." It was said lowly, but with such **condensation** of rapidity, that the long, **slow** words in Spanish, which had **preceded** and followed, almost operated as covers to the brief English between.

For a moment, knot in hand, and knot in head, Captain Delano stood mute; while, without further heeding him, the old man was now intent upon other ropes. Presently there was a slight stir behind Captain Delano. Turning, he saw the chained negro, Atufal, **standing quietly** there. The next moment the old sailor rose, muttering, and, followed by his subordinate negroes, removed to the forward part of the ship, where in the crowd he disappeared.

An elderly negro, in a **clout** like an infant's, and with a **pepper** and **salt** head, and a kind of attorney air, now approached Captain Delano. In tolerable Spanish, and with a good-natured, knowing wink, he informed him that the old knotter was simple-witted, but harmless; often playing his **odd** tricks. The negro **concluded** by begging the knot, for of course the stranger would not care to be troubled with it. Unconsciously, it was handed to him. With a sort of congé, the negro received it, and, turning his back, ferreted into it like a **detective** custom-house officer after **smuggled** laces. Soon, with some African word, **equivalent** to pshaw, he tossed the knot overboard.

All this is very queer now, thought Captain Delano, with a qualmish sort of emotion; but, as one feeling incipient sea-sickness, he strove, by **ignoring** the **symptoms**, to get rid of the **malady**. Once more he looked off for his **boat**. To his **delight**, it was now again in view, leaving the rocky spur **astern**.

The **sensation** here **experienced**, after at first **relieving** his uneasiness, with **unforeseen** efficacy soon began to remove it. The less **distant** sight of that well-known boat—showing it, not as before, half blended with the haze, but with **outline defined**, so that its **individuality**, like a man's, was **manifest**; that boat, Rover by name, which, though now in strange seas, had often pressed the **beach** of Captain Delano's home, and, brought to its threshold for **repairs**, had familiarly lain there, as a Newfoundland dog; the sight of that **household**, boat

Italian

astern: indietro, a poppa.
beach: spiaggia, lido, la spiaggia.
boat: barca, battello, imbarcazione, la barca, natante, nave.
clout: colpire, colpo.
concluded: concluso.
condensation: condensazione.
defined: definito.
delight: delizia, deliziare, dilettare, diletto, godimento, rallegrare, gioia.
detective: investigatore.
distant: distante, lontano.

equivalent: equivalente.
experienced: esperto.
household: famiglia.
ignoring: ignorando.
individuality: individualità.
malady: malattia.
manifest: manifesto, manifestare, palese.
odd: strano, dispari.
outline: contorno, profilo, schema, progetto, abbozzo.
pepper: pepe, peperone.

preceded: preceduto.
quietly: tranquillamente.
relieving: alleviando.
repairs: riparazioni.
salt: sale, salare, salato, il sale.
sensation: sensazione.
slow: lento.
smuggled: contrabbandato.
standing: in piedi.
symptoms: sintomi.
unforeseen: imprevisto.
watching: guardare.

evoked a thousand **trustful associations**, which, contrasted with previous suspicions, filled him not only with lightsome confidence, but **somehow** with half humorous self-reproaches at his former lack of it.

"What, I, Amasa Delano—Jack of the Beach, as they called me when a lad—I, Amasa; the same that, duck-satchel in hand, used to **paddle** along the water-side to the school-house made from the old hulk—I, little Jack of the Beach, that used to go berrying with **cousin** Nat and the rest; I to be **murdered** here at the ends of the earth, on board a haunted pirate-ship by a **horrible** Spaniard? Too **nonsensical** to think of! Who would murder Amasa Delano? His conscience is clean. There is some one above. Fie, fie, Jack of the Beach! you are a child indeed; a child of the second **childhood**, old boy; you are beginning to **dote** and drule, I'm afraid."

Light of heart and foot, he stepped **aft**, and there was met by Don Benito's servant, who, with a pleasing expression, **responsive** to his own present feelings, informed him that his master had recovered from the effects of his **coughing** fit, and had just **ordered** him to go present his compliments to his good guest, Don Amasa, and say that he (Don Benito) would soon have the **happiness** to **rejoin** him.

There now, do you mark that? again thought Captain Delano, walking the poop. What a **donkey** I was. This kind **gentleman** who here **sends** me his kind compliments, he, but ten minutes ago, dark-lantern in had, was dodging round some old grind-stone in the hold, **sharpening** a hatchet for me, I thought. Well, well; these long calms have a morbid effect on the mind, I've often heard, though I never believed it before. Ha! glancing towards the boat; there's Rover; good dog; a white **bone** in her mouth. A **pretty** big bone though, seems to me.—What? Yes, she has **fallen** afoul of the **bubbling** tide-rip there. It sets her the other way, too, for the time. Patience.

It was now about noon, though, from the **grayness** of everything, it seemed to be getting towards dusk.

The calm was **confirmed**. In the far distance, away from the influence of land, the leaden ocean seemed **laid** out and leaded up, it's course finished, soul gone,

Italian

aft: a poppa.
associations: associazioni.
bone: osso, l'osso, disossare, spina.
bubbling: gorgogliare, gorgoglio, ribollimento, bolla.
childhood: infanzia, fanciullezza.
confirmed: confermato.
coughing: tosse, tossire.
cousin: cugino, cugina.
donkey: asino, ciuco.
dote: essere rimbambito.
evoked: evocato.

fallen: caduto.
gentleman: signore, galantuomo, gentiluomo.
grayness: grigiore.
happiness: felicità.
horrible: orribile, orrendo, mostruoso, schifoso, terribile, sgradevole, spiacevole.
laid: posato.
murder: omicidio, assassinare, assassinio.
murdered: assassinato.

nonsensical: assurdo, privo di senso.
ordered: ordinato, disposto.
paddle: pala, pagaia, remo.
pretty: grazioso, bellino, carino, bello.
rejoin: riuniamo, riunite, riuniscono, riunisco, riunisci, riunire, ricongiungersi.
responsive: sensibile.
sends: manda, spedisce.
sharpening: affilando, acuendo.
somehow: in qualche modo.
trustful: fiducioso.

defunct. But the current from landward, where the ship was, increased; silently sweeping her further and further towards the tranced waters beyond.

Still, from his knowledge of those latitudes, **cherishing hopes** of a breeze, and a fair and fresh one, at any moment, Captain Delano, **despite** present prospects, buoyantly **counted** upon **bringing** the San Dominick **safely** to anchor ere night. The distance swept over was nothing; since, with a good wind, ten minutes' **sailing** would retrace more than sixty minutes, drifting. Meantime, one moment turning to mark "Rover" fighting the tide-rip, and the next to see Don Benito approaching, he continued walking the poop.

Gradually he felt a vexation **arising** from the **delay** of his boat; this soon **merged** into uneasiness; and at last—his eye falling continually, as from a stage-box into the pit, upon the strange crowd before and below him, and, by-and-by, **recognizing** there the face—now composed to indifference—of the Spanish sailor who had seemed to **beckon** from the main-chains—something of his old trepidations returned.

Ah, thought he—gravely enough—this is like the **ague**: because it went off, it follows not that it won't come back.

Though **ashamed** of the relapse, he could not **altogether subdue** it; and so, **exerting** his good-nature to the **utmost**, insensibly he came to a **compromise**.

Yes, this is a strange craft; a strange history, too, and strange **folks** on board. But—nothing more.

By way of keeping his mind out of mischief till the boat should arrive, he tried to occupy it with turning over and over, in a **purely speculative** sort of way, some lesser peculiarities of the captain and crew. Among others, four curious points recurred:

First, the **affair** of the Spanish **lad assailed** with a **knife** by the slave boy; an act winked at by Don Benito. Second, the **tyranny** in Don Benito's treatment of Atufal, the black; as if a child should lead a **bull** of the Nile by the ring in his **nose**. Third, the trampling of the sailor by the two negroes; a piece of insolence passed over without so much as a **reprimand**. Fourth, the cringing submission to

Italian

affair: affare, faccenda, caso.
ague: febbre.
altogether: tutto, complessivamente.
arising: nascendo, sorgendo.
ashamed: vergognoso.
assailed: assalito.
beckon: accenna, accennano, accennate, accenni, accenniamo, accenno, accennare.
bringing: portando.
bull: toro, rialzista.
cherishing: adorando.
compromise: compromesso.
counted: contato.
defunct: defunto.
delay: ritardo, tardare, ritardare, indugio, indugiare.
exerting: esercitando, praticando.
folks: gente.
gradually: gradualmente, poco a poco.
hopes: spera.
knife: coltello, accoltellare.
lad: ragazzo.
merged: incorporato, unito, fuso.
nose: naso, il naso, fiuto.
pit: fossa.
purely: puramente.
recognizing: riconoscendo.
reprimand: rimprovero, rabbuffo.
safely: al sicuro, sicuramente.
sailing: veleggiare, vela, navigazione, navigare.
speculative: speculativo.
subdue: sottomettere, assoggettare.
tyranny: tirannia.
utmost: massimo.

their master, of all the ship's underlings, mostly blacks; as if by the least inadvertence they feared to draw down his **despotic** displeasure.

Coupling these points, they seemed somewhat **contradictory**. But what then, thought Captain Delano, glancing towards his now nearing boat—what then? Why, Don Benito is a very **capricious** commander. But he is not the first of the sort I have seen; though it's true he rather **exceeds** any other. But as a nation— continued he in his reveries—these Spaniards are all an odd set; the very word Spaniard has a curious, **conspirator**, Guy-Fawkish **twang** to it. And yet, I **dare** say, Spaniards in the main are as good folks as any in Duxbury, Massachusetts. Ah good! last "Rover" has come.

As, with its welcome freight, the boat touched the side, the oakum-pickers, with venerable gestures, sought to **restrain** the blacks, who, at the sight of three gurried water-casks in its bottom, and a **pile** of **wilted** pumpkins in its bow, hung over the bulwarks in **disorderly** raptured.

Don Benito, with his servant, now appeared; his coming, perhaps, **hastened** by hearing the noise. Of him Captain Delano sought **permission** to serve out the water, so that all might share alike, and none **injure** themselves by **unfair excess**. But **sensible**, and, on Don Benito's account, kind as this offer was, it was received with what seemed impatience; as if aware that he **lacked** energy as a commander, Don Benito, with the true **jealousy** of **weakness**, resented as an affront any interference. So, at least, Captain Delano inferred.

In another moment the casks were being hoisted in, when some of the eager negroes accidentally jostled Captain Delano, where he stood by the gangway; so, that, unmindful of Don Benito, **yielding** to the **impulse** of the moment, with good-natured authority he bade the blacks stand back; to **enforce** his words making use of a half-mirthful, half-menacing gesture. Instantly the blacks paused, just where they were, each negro and negress **suspended** in his or her posture, exactly as the word had found them—for a few seconds continuing so—while, as between the responsive posts of a **telegraph**, an unknown **syllable** ran from man to man among the perched oakum-pickers. While the visitor's attention was

Italian

capricious: capriccioso.
conspirator: cospiratore.
contradictory: contraddittorio.
dare: osare, oso, osiamo, osi, osate, osano, osa, sfida.
despotic: dispotico.
disorderly: disordinato.
enforce: imporre.
exceeds: eccede.
excess: eccesso, eccedenza, franchigia.
hastened: affrettato, sollecitato.
impulse: impulso.

injure: danneggiare, danneggia, danneggiamo, danneggiano, danneggiate, danneggio, danneggi, ferire, ferisco, feriscono, feriamo.
jealousy: gelosia.
lacked: mancato.
permission: permesso, accordo, autorizzazione, nullaosta, licenza.
pile: mucchio, folla, pelo, palo, accatastare.
restrain: dominare, domina, domino, dominiamo, dominano, dominate,

domini, reprimere, governare.
sensible: sensato, ragionevole, sensibile.
suspended: sospeso.
syllable: sillaba.
telegraph: telegrafo.
twang: vibrazione, dare un suono metallico.
unfair: ingiusto.
weakness: debolezza.
wilted: appassito.
yielding: cedendo.

fixed by this scene, suddenly the hatchet-polishers half rose, and a **rapid cry** came from Don Benito.

Thinking that at the **signal** of the Spaniard he was about to be massacred, Captain Delano would have sprung for his boat, but paused, as the oakum-pickers, **dropping** down into the crowd with earnest exclamations, forced every white and every negro back, at the same moment, with gestures **friendly** and familiar, almost **jocose**, bidding him, in **substance**, not be a **fool**. **Simultaneously** the hatchet-polishers resumed their seats, quietly as so many tailors, and at once, as if nothing had happened, the work of **hoisting** in the casks was resumed, whites and blacks **singing** at the **tackle**.

Captain Delano glanced towards Don Benito. As he saw his meagre form in the act of recovering itself from reclining in the servant's arms, into which the **agitated** invalid had fallen, he could not but **marvel** at the panic by which himself had been **surprised**, on the darting supposition that such a commander, who, upon a legitimate occasion, so trivial, too, as it now appeared, could lose all self-command, was, with energetic **iniquity**, going to bring about his murder.

The casks being on deck, Captain Delano was handed a number of jars and **cups** by one of the steward's aids, who, in the name of his captain, entreated him to do as he had proposed—dole out the water. He **complied**, with **republican impartiality** as to this republican element, which always **seeks** one level, **serving** the oldest white no better than the youngest black; excepting, indeed, poor Don Benito, whose condition, if not **rank**, demanded an extra **allowance**. To him, in the first place, Captain Delano presented a fair **pitcher** of the **fluid**; but, thirsting as he was for it, the Spaniard quaffed not a drop until after several grave bows and salutes. A reciprocation of courtesies which the sight-loving Africans hailed with clapping of hands.

Two of the less wilted pumpkins being reserved for the cabin table, the **residue** were **minced** up on the spot for the general regalement. But the soft **bread**, **sugar**, and bottled cider, Captain Delano would have given the whites alone, and in chief Don Benito; but the latter objected; which **disinterestedness** not a little pleased the American; and so mouthfuls all around were given alike

Italian

agitated: agitato.
allowance: indennità, assegno, tolleranza, abbuono, detrazione, sconto, permesso.
bread: pane, impanare, il pane.
complied: accondisceso, ottemperato.
cry: piangere, grido, gridare, urlare.
cups: tazza.
disinterestedness: disinteresse.
dropping: gocciolamento.
fluid: fluido, liquido.
fool: babbeo, sciocco, allocco,

ingannare.
friendly: amichevole, cortese, amicale, gradevole, benevole, carino, grazioso.
hoisting: sollevamento.
impartiality: imparzialità.
iniquity: iniquità.
jocose: giocoso.
marvel: meraviglia, stupirsi.
minced: tritato.
pitcher: brocca, lanciatore.
rank: rango, ordine, classificare.
rapid: rapido.

republican: repubblicano.
residue: residuo, residui.
seeks: cerca.
serving: servendo.
signal: segnale, segno.
simultaneously: simultaneamente.
singing: cantando, canto.
substance: sostanza, materia.
sugar: zucchero, zuccherare, lo zucchero.
surprised: sorpreso, sorpresa.
tackle: paranco, attrezzatura.

to whites and blacks; excepting one **bottle** of cider, which Babo **insisted** upon setting aside for his master.

Here it may be observed that as, on the first visit of the boat, the American had not permitted his men to board the ship, neither did he now; being unwilling to **add** to the **confusion** of the decks.

Not uninfluenced by the peculiar good-humor at present **prevailing**, and for the time oblivious of any but benevolent thoughts, Captain Delano, who, from recent indications, counted upon a breeze within an hour or two at furthest, dispatched the boat back to the sealer, with **orders** for all the hands that could be **spared** immediately to set about rafting casks to the watering-place and **filling** them. Likewise he bade word be carried to his **chief officer**, that if, against present **expectation**, the ship was not brought to anchor by sunset, he need be under no concern; for as there was to be a full **moon** that night, he (Captain Delano) would remain on board ready to play the **pilot**, come the **wind** soon or late.

As the two Captains stood together, observing the departing boat—the servant, as it happened, having just spied a **spot** on his master's velvet **sleeve**, and silently engaged **rubbing** it out—the American expressed his regrets that the San Dominick had no boats; none, at least, but the unseaworthy old **hulk** of the long-boat, which, **warped** as a camel's skeleton in the desert, and almost as bleached, lay pot-wise **inverted amidships**, one side a little tipped, **furnishing** a subterranean sort of den for family groups of the blacks, mostly women and small children; who, squatting on old mats below, or perched above in the **dark** dome, on the elevated seats, were descried, some **distance** within, like a social circle of bats, sheltering in some friendly cave; at intervals, ebon flights of naked boys and girls, three or four years old, darting in and out of the den's mouth.

"Had you three or four boats now, Don Benito," said Captain Delano, "I think that, by tugging at the **oars**, your negroes here might help along matters some. Did you sail from port without boats, Don Benito?"

"They were **stove** in the gales, Señor."

Italian

add: aggiungere, aggiungiamo, aggiungete, aggiungi, aggiungo, aggiungono, addizionare, addizioniamo, addizioni, addizionate, addizionano.
amidships: a mezza nave.
bottle: bottiglia, imbottigliare, la bottiglia.
chief: capo, principale.
confusion: confusione.
dark: scuro, oscuro, buio, oscurità, tenebroso.

distance: distanza.
expectation: attesa, aspettativa.
filling: otturazione, ripieno, riempimento.
furnishing: fornendo, arredamento.
hulk: carcassa.
insisted: insistito.
inverted: invertito.
moon: luna, la luna.
oars: remo, remi.
officer: funzionario, ufficiale, impiegato.

orders: ordine, comande ai tavoli.
pilot: pilota, pilotare, dirigere, guidare.
prevailing: prevalente, prevalendo.
rubbing: sfregamento.
sleeve: manicotto, manica.
spared: risparmiato.
spot: luogo, macchia, punto, posto, spot, macchiare.
stove: stufa, fornello.
warped: deformato.
wind: vento, flatulenza, avvolgere.

"That was bad. Many men, too, you lost then. Boats and men. Those must have been hard gales, Don Benito."

"Past all speech," cringed the Spaniard.

"Tell me, Don Benito," **continued** his companion with increased interest, "tell me, were these gales immediately off the pitch of Cape Horn?"

"Cape Horn?—who spoke of Cape Horn?"

"Yourself did, when giving me an account of your voyage," answered Captain Delano, with almost **equal** astonishment at this **eating** of his own words, even as he ever seemed eating his own heart, on the part of the Spaniard. "You yourself, Don Benito, spoke of Cape Horn," he **emphatically** repeated.

The Spaniard turned, in a sort of stooping posture, pausing an instant, as one about to make a plunging exchange of **elements**, as from air to water.

At this moment a messenger-boy, a white, hurried by, in the **regular** performance of his function **carrying** the last **expired** half hour forward to the forecastle, from the cabin time-piece, to have it struck at the ship's large **bell**.

"Master," said the servant, **discontinuing** his work on the **coat** sleeve, and addressing the **rapt** Spaniard with a sort of **timid** apprehensiveness, as one **charged** with a duty, the **discharge** of which, it was **foreseen**, would prove **irksome** to the very person who had **imposed** it, and for whose benefit it was **intended**, "master told me never mind where he was, or how engaged, always to **remind** him to a **minute**, when shaving-time comes. Miguel has gone to **strike** the half-hour **afternoon**. It is *now*, master. Will master go into the cuddy?"

"Ah—yes," answered the Spaniard, **starting**, as from dreams into realities; then turning upon Captain Delano, he said that ere long he would **resume** the conversation.

"Then if master means to talk more to Don Amasa," said the servant, "why not let Don Amasa sit by master in the cuddy, and master can talk, and Don Amasa can **listen**, while Babo here lathers and strops."

"Yes," said Captain Delano, not unpleased with this sociable plan, "yes, Don Benito, unless you had rather not, I will go with you."

Italian

afternoon: pomeriggio.
bell: campana, campanello.
carrying: portando, trasportando.
charged: caricato.
coat: cappotto, rivestire.
continued: continuato, durato.
discharge: scarico, scarica, portata, scaricare.
discontinuing: interrompendo.
eating: mangiando.
elements: elementi, alfabeto.
emphatically: enfatico, enfaticamente.

equal: eguale, uguale, pari.
expired: morto, scaduto.
foreseen: previsto.
imposed: imposto.
intended: inteso.
irksome: seccante.
listen: ascoltare, ascolti, ascoltiamo, ascoltate, ascoltano, ascolta, ascolto.
minute: minuto, il minuto, minuscolo, momento.
rapt: rapito.
regular: regolare, normale.

remind: ricordare, ricorda, ricordo, ricordiamo, ricordi, ricordate, ricordano.
resume: riprendere, riprendete, riprendiamo, riprendo, riprendono, riprendi.
starting: avviamento, cominciare, avvio.
strike: picchiare, colpire, battere, sciopero, scioperare, fare sciopero.
timid: pauroso, angoscioso, timido, timoroso.

"Be it so, Señor."

As the three passed aft, the American could not but think it another strange instance of his host's capriciousness, this being **shaved** with such uncommon **punctuality** in the middle of the day. But he deemed it more than likely that the servant's anxious fidelity had something to do with the matter; inasmuch as the **timely** interruption served to **rally** his master from the mood which had evidently been coming upon him.

The place called the cuddy was a light deck-cabin formed by the poop, a sort of attic to the large cabin below. Part of it had formerly been the quarters of the officers; but since their death all the **partitioning** had been thrown down, and the whole interior **converted** into one spacious and **airy marine** hall; for absence of fine furniture and picturesque disarray of odd appurtenances, somewhat **answering** to the wide, cluttered hall of some eccentric bachelor-squire in the country, who hangs his shooting-jacket and tobacco-pouch on **deer** antlers, and keeps his fishing-rod, **tongs**, and walking-stick in the same corner.

The similitude was heightened, if not originally suggested, by glimpses of the surrounding sea; since, in one aspect, the country and the ocean seem cousins-german.

The floor of the cuddy was matted. **Overhead**, four or five old muskets were stuck into **horizontal** holes along the beams. On one side was a claw-footed old table lashed to the deck; a thumbed **missal** on it, and over it a small, meagre **crucifix** attached to the bulk-head. Under the table lay a **dented** cutlass or two, with a hacked **harpoon**, among some; melancholy old rigging, like a heap of poor friars' girdles. There were also two long, sharp-ribbed settees of Malacca cane, black with age, and uncomfortable to look at as inquisitors' racks, with a large, **misshapen** arm-chair, which, **furnished** with a rude barber's **crotch** at the back, working with a **screw**, seemed some **grotesque** engine of **torment**. A **flag locker** was in one corner, open, **exposing** various **colored bunting**, some rolled up, others half **unrolled**, still others **tumbled**. Opposite was a cumbrous washstand, of black **mahogany**, all of one block, with a pedestal, like a **font**, and over it a railed **shelf**, containing combs, brushes, and other implements of the

Italian

airy: arioso.
answering: risposta, rispondere.
bunting: pavese.
colored: colorato.
converted: convertito.
crotch: forca.
crucifix: crocifisso.
deer: cervo, capriolo.
dented: ammaccato.
exposing: esponendo.
flag: bandiera, stendardo, bandiera taglialuce, la bandiera.

font: fonte battesimale, carattere, tipo di carattere.
furnished: ammobiliato, fornito.
grotesque: grottesco.
harpoon: arpione, fiocina.
horizontal: orizzontale.
locker: armadietto.
mahogany: mogano.
marine: marino.
missal: messale.
misshapen: deforme.
overhead: di sopra.

partitioning: partizione.
punctuality: puntualità.
rally: riunione, rally, raccogliere, raduno.
screw: vite, la vite, avvitare.
shaved: raso.
shelf: scaffale, mensola, asse, ripiano.
timely: tempestivo, opportuno.
tongs: pinzette.
torment: tormento.
tumbled: caduto.
unrolled: si srotolato, svolto.

toilet. A **torn hammock** of stained grass swung near; the **sheets** tossed, and the pillow **wrinkled** up like a **brow**, as if who ever slept here slept but **illy**, with **alternate** visitations of sad thoughts and bad dreams.

The further extremity of the cuddy, overhanging the ship's stern, was **pierced** with three openings, windows or port-holes, according as men or cannon might peer, socially or unsocially, out of them. At present neither men nor cannon were seen, though huge ring-bolts and other rusty iron fixtures of the wood-work hinted of twenty-four-pounders.

Glancing towards the hammock as he entered, Captain Delano said, "You sleep here, Don Benito?"

"Yes, Señor, since we got into mild weather."

"This seems a sort of **dormitory**, sitting-room, sail-loft, **chapel**, **armory**, and private **closet** all together, Don Benito," added Captain Delano, looking round.

"Yes, Señor; events have not been favorable to much order in my arrangements."

Here the servant, **napkin** on arm, made a motion as if waiting his master's good pleasure. Don Benito **signified** his readiness, when, **seating** him in the Malacca arm-chair, and for the guest's convenience drawing opposite one of the settees, the servant **commenced** operations by **throwing** back his master's collar and **loosening** his cravat.

There is something in the negro which, in a peculiar way, fits him for avocations about one's person. Most negroes are natural valets and hair-dressers; taking to the **comb** and **brush congenially** as to the castinets, and **flourishing** them apparently with almost equal satisfaction. There is, too, a smooth **tact** about them in this employment, with a **marvelous**, noiseless, gliding **briskness**, not **ungraceful** in its way, singularly pleasing to behold, and still more so to be the **manipulated** subject of. And above all is the great gift of good-humor. Not the mere grin or **laugh** is here meant. Those were unsuitable. But a certain easy **cheerfulness**, **harmonious** in every glance and gesture; as though God had set the whole negro to some pleasant **tune**.

Italian

alternate: alternare, alterno, alternato.
armory: arsenale, armeria.
briskness: vivacità.
brow: sopracciglio, fronte.
brush: spazzola, spazzolare, pennello.
chapel: cappella.
cheerfulness: contentezza, allegria.
closet: armadio.
comb: pettine, pettinare, favo.
commenced: cominciato.
congenially: congenialmente.
dormitory: dormitorio.
flourishing: fiorendo, fiorente.
hammock: amaca.
harmonious: armonioso, armonico.
illy: malatamente.
laugh: ridere, riso, risata.
loosening: allentando, allentamento, sciogliendo.
manipulated: manipolato.
marvelous: meraviglioso.
napkin: tovagliolo, salvietta, pannolino.
pierced: perforato.
seating: posto, corretto posizionamento, stabilizzazione.
sheets: fogli, le lenzuola.
signified: significato.
tact: tatto.
throwing: lancio.
toilet: gabinetto, cesso, ritirata.
torn: strappato, lacero.
tune: melodia, sintonizzare, aggiustare, adattare.
ungraceful: sgraziato.
wrinkled: spiegazzato.

When to this is added the docility arising from the unaspiring **contentment** of a limited mind and that **susceptibility** of blind **attachment** sometimes inhering in **indisputable** inferiors, one readily **perceives** why those hypochondriacs, Johnson and Byron — it may be, something like the hypochondriac Benito Cereno — took to their **hearts**, almost to the **exclusion** of the entire white race, their serving men, the negroes, Barber and Fletcher. But if there be that in the negro which exempts him from the **inflicted sourness** of the morbid or **cynical** mind, how, in his most **prepossessing** aspects, must he appear to a benevolent one? When at ease with respect to **exterior** things, Captain Delano's nature was not only **benign**, but familiarly and humorously so. At home, he had often taken rare satisfaction in sitting in his door, watching some free man of **color** at his work or play. If on a voyage he chanced to have a black sailor, invariably he was on **chatty** and half-gamesome terms with him. In fact, like most men of a good, blithe heart, Captain Delano took to negroes, not **philanthropically**, but **genially**, just as other men to Newfoundland dogs.

Hitherto, the circumstances in which he found the San Dominick had **repressed** the **tendency**. But in the cuddy, relieved from his former uneasiness, and, for various reasons, more **sociably inclined** than at any previous period of the day, and seeing the colored servant, napkin on arm, so **debonair** about his master, in a business so familiar as that of **shaving**, too, all his old weakness for negroes returned.

Among other things, he was **amused** with an odd instance of the African love of bright colors and fine shows, in the black's **informally** taking from the flag-locker a great piece of bunting of all hues, and **lavishly** tucking it under his master's chin for an apron.

The **mode** of shaving among the Spaniards is a little different from what it is with other **nations**. They have a basin, **specifically** called a barber's basin, which on one side is scooped out, so as **accurately** to receive the chin, against which it is closely held in lathering; which is done, not with a brush, but with **soap** dipped in the water of the basin and rubbed on the face.

Italian

accurately: con precisione.
amused: divertito.
attachment: accessorio, allegato, attaccamento.
benign: benigno, benevolo.
chatty: chiacchierino.
color: colore, colorare.
contentment: soddisfazione.
cynical: cinico.
debonair: affabile.
exclusion: esclusione.
exterior: esteriore, esterno.

genially: genialmente.
hearts: cuori.
inclined: disposto, inclinato, propenso.
indisputable: indiscutibile.
inflicted: inflitto.
informally: senza formalità, informalmente.
lavishly: generosamente.
mode: modo, moda, maniera.
nations: nazioni.
perceives: percepisce, scorge,

intravede.
philanthropically: filantropicamente.
prepossessing: affascinante, attraente.
repressed: represso.
shaving: rasatura, truciolo, radere.
soap: sapone.
sociably: socievole.
sourness: acidità, asprezza.
specifically: specificatamente, specificamente.
susceptibility: suscettibilità.
tendency: tendenza.

In the present instance salt-water was used for lack of better; and the parts **lathered** were only the upper **lip**, and low down under the throat, all the rest being **cultivated** beard.

The **preliminaries** being somewhat novel to Captain Delano, he sat curiously eying them, so that no conversation took place, nor, for the present, did Don Benito appear disposed to **renew** any.

Setting down his basin, the negro searched among the **razors**, as for the sharpest, and having found it, gave it an additional edge by **expertly strapping** it on the firm, smooth, oily skin of his open **palm**; he then made a gesture as if to begin, but **midway** stood suspended for an instant, one hand **elevating** the razor, the other professionally **dabbling** among the bubbling **suds** on the Spaniard's lank neck. Not **unaffected** by the close sight of the gleaming steel, Don Benito nervously shuddered; his usual ghastliness was heightened by the lather, which lather, again, was **intensified** in its hue by the **contrasting** sootiness of the negro's body. Altogether the scene was somewhat peculiar, at least to Captain Delano, nor, as he saw the two thus postured, could he **resist** the vagary, that in the black he saw a **headsman**, and in the white a man at the block. But this was one of those **antic** conceits, appearing and **vanishing** in a breath, from which, perhaps, the best **regulated** mind is not always free.

Meantime the agitation of the Spaniard had a little **loosened** the bunting from around him, so that one broad **fold** swept curtain-like over, the chair-arm to the floor, revealing, amid a **profusion** of armorial **bars** and ground-colors—black, blue, and yellow—a closed castle in a blood red field **diagonal** with a lion **rampant** in a white.

"The castle and the lion," exclaimed Captain Delano—"why, Don Benito, this is the flag of Spain you use here. It's well it's only I, and not the King, that sees this," he added, with a smile, "but"—turning towards the black—"it's all one, I suppose, so the colors be gay;" which playful remark did not fail somewhat to **tickle** the negro.

Italian

antic: bizzarro, grottesco.
bars: sbarra.
contrasting: contrastante.
cultivated: coltivato.
dabbling: bagnando, sguazzando.
diagonal: diagonale.
elevating: elevando.
expertly: espertamente.
fold: piegare, piega, plica, ovile, grinza, stabbio.
headsman: carnefice.
intensified: intensificato.

lather: schiuma, insaponare.
lip: labbro, il labbro.
loosened: allentato, sciolto.
midway: a metà strada.
palm: palma, palmo.
preliminaries: preliminare, preliminari.
profusion: profusione.
rampant: rampante, violento, dilagante.
razor: rasoio.
regulated: regolato.

renew: rinnovare, rinnova, rinnovano, rinnovate, rinnovi, rinnoviamo, rinnovo.
resist: resistere, resistete, resistono, resisto, resistiamo, resisti.
strapping: reggiatura.
suds: saponata.
tickle: stimolare, stuzzicare, solleticare, solletico.
unaffected: spontaneo, non affettato, semplice.
vanishing: sparendo.

"Now, master," he said, **readjusting** the flag, and **pressing** the head gently further back into the crotch of the **chair**; "now, master," and the steel glanced nigh the **throat**.

Again Don Benito faintly shuddered.

"You must not **shake** so, master. See, Don Amasa, master always **shakes** when I **shave** him. And yet master **knows** I never yet have **drawn blood**, though it's true, if master will shake so, I may some of these times. Now master," he continued. "And now, Don Amasa, please go on with your talk about the gale, and all that; master can hear, and, between times, master can answer."

"Ah yes, these gales," said Captain Delano; "but the more I think of your voyage, Don Benito, the more I **wonder**, not at the gales, terrible as they must have been, but at the **disastrous** interval following them. For here, by your account, have you been these two months and more getting from Cape Horn to St. Maria, a distance which I **myself**, with a good wind, have sailed in a few days. True, you had calms, and long ones, but to be becalmed for two months, that is, at least, unusual. Why, Don Benito, had almost any other gentleman told me such a story, I should have been half disposed to a little incredulity."

Here an involuntary **expression** came over the Spaniard, similar to that just before on the deck, and whether it was the start he gave, or a sudden **gawky roll** of the hull in the calm, or a momentary unsteadiness of the servant's hand, however it was, just then the razor drew blood, spots of which stained the **creamy** lather under the throat: immediately the black **barber** drew back his steel, and, remaining in his **professional attitude**, back to Captain Delano, and face to Don Benito, held up the trickling razor, saying, with a sort of half humorous sorrow, "See, master—you shook so—here's Babo's first blood."

No **sword** drawn before James the First of England, no **assassination** in that timid King's **presence**, could have **produced** a more **terrified** aspect than was now presented by Don Benito.

Poor fellow, thought Captain Delano, so nervous he can't even **bear** the sight of barber's blood; and this unstrung, sick man, is it **credible** that I should have imagined he **meant** to **spill** all my blood, who can't endure the sight of one little

Italian

assassination: assassinio.	locuzione.	rullio, rollio, cilindrare.
attitude: atteggiamento, assetto.	**gawky**: goffo.	**shake**: scuotere, scuotono, scuoto,
barber: barbiere, parrucchiere.	**knows**: conosce, sa.	scuotiamo, scuoti, scuotete, scossa.
bear: orso, produrre, ribassista,	**meant**: significato.	**shakes**: scuote.
partorire, l'orso, portare.	**myself**: mi, me stesso, io stesso.	**shave**: far la barba, rasare, radere.
blood: sangue.	**presence**: presenza.	**spill**: versare, rovesciare.
chair: sedia, la sedia.	**pressing**: pressatura, urgente.	**sword**: spada.
creamy: cremoso.	**produced**: prodotto.	**terrified**: atterrito, spaventato,
credible: credibile.	**professional**: professionista,	terrificato, terrorizzato.
disastrous: disastroso.	professionale.	**throat**: gola, la gola.
drawn: disegnato.	**readjusting**: riaggiustando.	**wonder**: stupirsi, stupore, meraviglia,
expression: espressione, aria,	**roll**: rullo, panino, rotolare, rotolo,	domandarsi, meravigliarsi.

drop of his own? Surely, Amasa Delano, you have been **beside** yourself this day. Tell it not when you get home, **sappy** Amasa. Well, well, he looks like a **murderer**, doesn't he? More like as if himself were to be done for. Well, well, this day's experience shall be a good lesson.

Meantime, while these things were running through the honest seaman's mind, the servant had taken the napkin from his arm, and to Don Benito had said—"But answer Don Amasa, please, master, while I **wipe** this ugly stuff off the razor, and **strop** it again."

As he said the words, his face was turned half round, so as to be alike **visible** to the Spaniard and the American, and seemed, by its expression, to hint, that he was **desirous**, by getting his master to go on with the conversation, **considerately** to withdraw his attention from the recent **annoying** accident. As if **glad** to snatch the offered relief, Don Benito resumed, **rehearsing** to Captain Delano, that not only were the calms of **unusual duration**, but the ship had fallen in with obstinate currents; and other things he added, some of which were but repetitions of former statements, to explain how it came to pass that the passage from Cape Horn to St. Maria had been so **exceedingly** long; now and then, **mingling** with his words, incidental praises, less **qualified** than before, to the blacks, for their general good conduct. These particulars were not given **consecutively**, the servant, at convenient times, using his razor, and so, between the intervals of shaving, the story and **panegyric** went on with more than usual huskiness.

To Captain Delano's imagination, now again not wholly at rest, there was something so hollow in the Spaniard's **manner**, with **apparently** some **reciprocal hollowness** in the servant's **dusky comment** of **silence**, that the idea flashed across him, that possibly master and man, for some unknown purpose, were **acting** out, both in word and deed, nay, to the very tremor of Don Benito's limbs, some juggling play before him. Neither did the suspicion of **collusion** lack apparent support, from the fact of those **whispered** conferences before mentioned. But then, what could be the **object** of **enacting** this play of the barber before him? At last, **regarding** the **notion** as a **whimsy**, insensibly suggested,

Italian

acting: recitazione, rappresentazione.
annoying: irritante.
apparent: apparente, evidente.
beside: accanto, su, a.
collusion: collusione.
comment: commento.
consecutively: successivamente.
considerately: premurosamente.
desirous: desideroso.
drop: goccia, diminuire, abbassamento, abbassare, caduta.
duration: durata.

dusky: tetro.
enacting: decretando.
exceedingly: estremamente.
glad: contento, felice, lieto.
hollowness: falsità, cavità.
manner: maniera, modo.
mingling: mescolando, mischiando.
murderer: assassino.
notion: nozione, idea.
object: oggetto, cosa, scopo.
panegyric: panegirico.
qualified: qualificato, abilitato.

reciprocal: reciproco.
regarding: considerando.
rehearsing: provando.
sappy: succoso.
silence: silenzio.
strop: coramella, stroppo.
usual: usuale, consueto, solito, generale, abituale.
visible: visibile.
whimsy: capriccio.
whispered: bisbigliato.
wipe: asciugare, pulire, strofinare.

perhaps, by the **theatrical** aspect of Don Benito in his **harlequin ensign**, Captain Delano speedily **banished** it.

The shaving over, the servant bestirred himself with a small bottle of **scented** waters, **pouring** a few drops on the head, and then diligently rubbing; the vehemence of the exercise **causing** the **muscles** of his face to twitch rather strangely.

His next operation was with comb, **scissors**, and brush; going round and round, **smoothing** a **curl** here, **clipping** an unruly whisker-hair there, giving a **graceful** sweep to the temple-lock, with other **impromptu touches evincing** the hand of a master; while, like any **resigned** gentleman in barber's hands, Don Benito bore all, much less uneasily, at least than he had done the razoring; indeed, he sat so pale and **rigid** now, that the negro seemed a Nubian **sculptor finishing** off a white statue-head.

All being over at last, the standard of Spain removed, tumbled up, and tossed back into the flag-locker, the negro's warm breath **blowing** away any stray hair, which might have lodged down his master's neck; collar and cravat **readjusted**; a speck of **lint** whisked off the velvet **lapel**; all this being done; **backing** off a little space, and pausing with an expression of **subdued** self-complacency, the servant for a moment **surveyed** his master, as, in toilet at least, the creature of his own **tasteful** hands.

Captain Delano playfully complimented him upon his **achievement**; at the same time congratulating Don Benito.

But neither **sweet** waters, nor shampooing, nor fidelity, nor sociality, **delighted** the Spaniard. Seeing him relapsing into forbidding gloom, and still remaining seated, Captain Delano, thinking that his presence was undesired just then, withdrew, on pretense of seeing whether, as he had **prophesied**, any signs of a breeze were visible.

Walking forward to the main-mast, he stood awhile thinking over the scene, and not without some **undefined** misgivings, when he heard a noise near the cuddy, and turning, saw the negro, his hand to his cheek. Advancing, Captain

Italian

achievement: successo, realizzazione, azione.
backing: sostegno, appoggio, avallo.
banished: bandito.
blowing: soffiatura.
causing: causare.
clipping: tosatura, taglio.
curl: arricciare, ricciolo, riccio.
delighted: lietissimo.
ensign: insegna, alfiere.
evincing: manifestando.
finishing: finendo, finitura, finire,

finissaggio, ultimando, rifinitura.
graceful: grazioso, aggraziato.
harlequin: arlecchino.
impromptu: improvvisato, estemporaneo.
lapel: risvolto.
lint: garza.
muscles: muscolatura.
pouring: versare, torrenziale, colata.
prophesied: predetto.
readjusted: riaggiustato.
resigned: rassegnato.

rigid: rigido, inflessibile.
scented: profumato.
scissors: forbici, le forbici.
sculptor: scultore.
smoothing: spianatura, lisciatura.
subdued: sottomesso.
surveyed: esaminato.
sweet: dolce, soave, caramella.
tasteful: raffinato.
theatrical: teatrale.
touches: tocca.
undefined: indefinito.

Delano perceived that the cheek was **bleeding**. He was about to ask the cause, when the negro's wailing **soliloquy enlightened** him.

"Ah, when will master get better from his sickness; only the sour heart that sour sickness breeds made him serve Babo so; **cutting** Babo with the razor, because, only by accident, Babo had given master one little **scratch**; and for the first time in so many a day, too. Ah, ah, ah," holding his hand to his face.

Is it possible, thought Captain Delano; was it to **wreak** in private his Spanish **spite** against this poor friend of his, that Don Benito, by his sullen manner, impelled me to withdraw? Ah this **slavery** breeds ugly passions in man. — Poor fellow!

He was about to speak in **sympathy** to the negro, but with a timid reluctance he now re-entered the cuddy.

Presently master and man came forth; Don Benito leaning on his servant as if nothing had happened.

But a sort of love-quarrel, after all, thought Captain Delano.

He accosted Don Benito, and they slowly walked together. They had gone but a few paces, when the steward — a **tall**, rajah-looking mulatto, **orientally** set off with a **pagoda turban formed** by three or four Madras handkerchiefs wound about his head, **tier** on tier — approaching with a saalam, announced **lunch** in the cabin.

On their way thither, the two captains were preceded by the mulatto, who, turning round as he advanced, with continual smiles and bows, ushered them on, a display of **elegance** which quite completed the **insignificance** of the small bare-headed Babo, who, as if not unconscious of **inferiority**, eyed **askance** the graceful steward. But in part, Captain Delano **imputed** his **jealous watchfulness** to that peculiar feeling which the full-blooded African **entertains** for the **adulterated** one. As for the steward, his manner, if not **bespeaking** much **dignity** of self-respect, yet evidenced his **extreme desire** to please; which is **doubly meritorious**, as at once Christian and Chesterfieldian.

Italian

adulterated: adulterato.
askance: di traverso, sospettosamente, obliquamente.
bespeaking: prenotando.
bleeding: sanguinando, salasso, emorragia, spurgo.
cutting: taglio, tagliente, talea, affilato.
desire: desiderio, desiderare, bramare.
dignity: dignità, decoro.
doubly: doppiamente.
elegance: eleganza.
enlightened: illuminato.

entertains: intrattiene.
extreme: estremo.
formed: formato.
imputed: attribuito, imputato.
inferiority: inferiorità.
insignificance: banalità, futilità.
jealous: geloso.
lunch: pranzo, pranzare, colazione.
meritorious: meritorio, benemerito.
orientally: orientale.
pagoda: pagoda.
scratch: graffiare, graffio, grattare,

raschiare, graffiatura, scalfire, unghiata.
slavery: schiavitù.
soliloquy: monologo, soliloquio.
spite: dispetto.
sympathy: compassione.
tall: alto, grande, elevato.
tier: fila.
turban: turbante.
watchfulness: vigilanza.
wreak: sfogare, sfogano, sfogate, sfoghi, sfoghiamo, sfogo, sfoga.

Captain Delano observed with interest that while the **complexion** of the mulatto was **hybrid**, his **physiognomy** was European—classically so.

"Don Benito," whispered he, "I am glad to see this usher-of-the-golden-rod of **yours**; the sight **refutes** an ugly remark once made to me by a Barbadoes **planter**; that when a mulatto has a regular European face, look out for him; he is a **devil**. But see, your steward here has **features** more regular than King George's of England; and yet there he nods, and bows, and smiles; a king, indeed—the king of kind hearts and polite fellows. What a pleasant voice he has, too?"

"He has, Señor."

"But tell me, has he not, so far as you have known him, always **proved** a good, worthy fellow?" said Captain Delano, pausing, while with a final genuflexion the steward disappeared into the cabin; "come, for the reason just mentioned, I am curious to know."

"Francesco is a good man," a sort of **sluggishly** responded Don Benito, like a **phlegmatic** appreciator, who would **neither** find fault **nor flatter**.

"Ah, I thought so. For it were strange, indeed, and not very **creditable** to us white-skins, if a little of our blood mixed with the African's, should, far from **improving** the latter's quality, have the sad effect of pouring vitriolic **acid** into black **broth**; improving the hue, perhaps, but not the wholesomeness."

"Doubtless, doubtless, Señor, but"—glancing at Babo—"not to **speak** of negroes, your planter's remark I have heard **applied** to the Spanish and Indian intermixtures in our **provinces**. But I know nothing about the matter," he listlessly **added**.

And here they entered the cabin.

The lunch was a **frugal** one. Some of Captain Delano's **fresh fish** and pumpkins, **biscuit** and salt **beef**, the reserved bottle of cider, and the San Dominick's last bottle of Canary.

As they entered, Francesco, with two or three colored aids, was hovering over the table **giving** the last **adjustments**. Upon perceiving their master they withdrew, Francesco making a **smiling** congé, and the Spaniard, without

Italian

acid: acido, agro, aspro.
added: aggiunto, addizionato.
adjustments: conguagli.
applied: applicato.
beef: manzo, carne di manzo.
biscuit: biscotto.
broth: brodo.
complexion: carnagione.
creditable: lodevole.
devil: diavolo, demonio.
features: caratteristiche, fattezze.
fish: pesce, pescare, il pesce.

flatter: lusingare, lusingate, lusingo, lusinghi, lusingano, lusinghiamo, lusinga, adulare.
fresh: fresco.
frugal: frugale.
giving: dando, regalando.
hybrid: ibrido.
improving: migliorando, perfezionando.
neither: ne, neanche, nemmeno, neppure.
nor: ne.

phlegmatic: flemmatico.
physiognomy: fisionomia.
planter: fioriera, piantatore, seminatrice.
proved: provato.
provinces: province.
refutes: confuta.
sluggishly: lentamente.
smiling: sorridere.
speak: parlare, parla, parlo, parliamo, parli, parlate, parlano, favellare.
yours: il vostro, vostro.

condescending to notice it, fastidiously remarking to his companion that he relished not superfluous attendance.

Without companions, host and guest sat down, like a childless married couple, at opposite ends of the table, Don Benito waving Captain Delano to his place, and, weak as he was, insisting upon that gentleman being seated before himself.

The negro placed a rug under Don Benito's feet, and a cushion behind his back, and then stood behind, not his master's chair, but Captain Delano's. At first, this a little surprised the latter. But it was soon evident that, in taking his position, the black was still true to his master; since by facing him he could the more readily anticipate his slightest want.

"This is an uncommonly intelligent fellow of yours, Don Benito," whispered Captain Delano across the table.

"You say true, Señor."

During the repast, the guest again reverted to parts of Don Benito's story, begging further particulars here and there. He inquired how it was that the scurvy and fever should have committed such wholesale havoc upon the whites, while destroying less than half of the blacks. As if this question reproduced the whole scene of plague before the Spaniard's eyes, miserably reminding him of his solitude in a cabin where before he had had so many friends and officers round him, his hand shook, his face became hueless, broken words escaped; but directly the sane memory of the past seemed replaced by insane terrors of the present. With starting eyes he stared before him at vacancy. For nothing was to be seen but the hand of his servant pushing the Canary over towards him. At length a few sips served partially to restore him. He made random reference to the different constitution of races, enabling one to offer more resistance to certain maladies than another. The thought was new to his companion.

Presently Captain Delano, intending to say something to his host concerning the pecuniary part of the business he had undertaken for him, especially—since he was strictly accountable to his owners—with reference to the new suit of sails, and other things of that sort; and naturally preferring to conduct such affairs in

Italian

accountable: responsabile.
anticipate: anticipare, anticipiamo, anticipi, anticipate, anticipa, anticipano, anticipo, prevedere, prevenire.
childless: senza figli.
condescending: degnando, condiscendente.
cushion: cuscino.
destroying: distruggendo.
evident: evidente, chiaro, palese, lampante.
havoc: rovina, devastazione.
insane: matto, insano, demente, folle.
insisting: insistendo.
intending: intendendo.
partially: parzialmente, in parte.
pecuniary: pecuniario.
preferring: preferendo.
pushing: spingere.
races: corse.
remarking: osservare.
reminding: ricordando.
reproduced: riprodotto.
restore: ripristinare, ripristiniamo, ripristini, ripristinano, ripristinate, ripristina, restaurare, ripristino, restaura, restauriamo, restauri.
reverted: ritornato.
rug: tappeto.
sane: sensato, sano di mente.
strictly: rigorosamente, strettamente.
uncommonly: insolitamente.
undertaken: intrapreso.
waving: ondeggiare.
wholesale: all'ingrosso, ingrosso.

private, was desirous that the servant should **withdraw**; **imagining** that Don Benito for a few minutes could **dispense** with his **attendance**. He, however, **waited** awhile; thinking that, as the conversation proceeded, Don Benito, without being prompted, would perceive the propriety of the step.

But it was **otherwise**. At last catching his host's eye, Captain Delano, with a slight **backward** gesture of his thumb, whispered, "Don Benito, pardon me, but there is an interference with the full expression of what I have to say to you."

Upon this the Spaniard changed countenance; which was imputed to his resenting the hint, as in some way a reflection upon his servant. After a moment's pause, he assured his guest that the black's remaining with them could be of no **disservice**; because since **losing** his officers he had made Babo (whose original office, it now **appeared**, had been captain of the slaves) not only his **constant** attendant and companion, but in all things his **confidant**.

After this, nothing more could be said; though, indeed, Captain Delano could hardly **avoid** some little **tinge** of **irritation** upon being left ungratified in so inconsiderable a wish, by one, too, for whom he intended such **solid** services. But it is only his querulousness, thought he; and so filling his glass he proceeded to business.

The price of the sails and other matters was **fixed** upon. But while this was being done, the American observed that, though his original offer of **assistance** had been hailed with hectic **animation**, yet now when it was **reduced** to a business **transaction**, indifference and **apathy** were betrayed. Don Benito, in fact, appeared to **submit** to hearing the details more out of regard to common propriety, than from any **impression** that **weighty** benefit to himself and his voyage was involved.

Soon, his manner became still more reserved. The **effort** was vain to **seek** to draw him into social talk. **Gnawed** by his splenetic mood, he sat twitching his beard, while to little purpose the hand of his servant, mute as that on the wall, slowly pushed over the Canary.

Italian

animation: animazione, vivacità.
apathy: apatia.
appeared: apparso.
assistance: assistenza, aiuto.
attendance: servizio, presenza.
avoid: evitare, evitano, evito, evitiamo, evitate, evita, eviti.
backward: indietro, a rovescio, supino, deficiente.
confidant: confidente.
constant: costante, fedele.
dispense: distribuire, distribuiamo,
distribuiscono, distribuite, distribuisci, distribuisco, dispensare.
disservice: danno, disservizio.
draw: disegnare, disegna, disegniamo, disegni, disegnate, disegnano, disegno, tirare, attrarre, sorteggio, eguaglianza.
effort: sforzo, fatica.
fixed: fissato, riparato, fisso, fermo.
gnawed: rosicchiato, roso.
imagining: immaginando.
impression: impressione, impronta.
irritation: irritazione.
losing: perdendo.
otherwise: altrimenti.
reduced: ridotto.
seek: cercare, cercano, cerchiamo, cercate, cerchi, cerco, cerca.
solid: solido, massiccio, compatto.
submit: sottomettere, sottoporre.
tinge: tingere, sfumare, tinta.
transaction: transazione, operazione.
waited: aspettato.
weighty: pesante.

Lunch being over, they sat down on the cushioned transom; the servant placing a pillow behind his master. The long continuance of the calm had now **affected** the **atmosphere**. Don Benito sighed **heavily**, as if for breath.

"Why not **adjourn** to the cuddy," said Captain Delano; "there is more air there." But the host sat silent and motionless.

Meantime his servant knelt before him, with a large **fan** of feathers. And Francesco coming in on tiptoes, handed the negro a little cup of **aromatic** waters, with which at intervals he chafed his master's brow; smoothing the hair along the temples as a **nurse** does a child's. He spoke no word. He only rested his eye on his master's, as if, amid all Don Benito's distress, a little to **refresh** his spirit by the silent sight of fidelity.

Presently the ship's bell sounded two o'clock; and through the cabin **windows** a slight **rippling** of the sea was **discerned**; and from the desired **direction**.

"There," exclaimed Captain Delano, "I told you so, Don Benito, look!"

He had **risen** to his feet, speaking in a very **animated** tone, with a view the more to **rouse** his companion. But though the **crimson** curtain of the stern-window near him that moment fluttered against his pale cheek, Don Benito seemed to have even less **welcome** for the breeze than the calm.

Poor fellow, thought Captain Delano, bitter experience has **taught** him that one ripple does not make a wind, any more than one **swallow** a summer. But he is mistaken for once. I will get his ship in for him, and prove it.

Briefly **alluding** to his weak **condition**, he urged his host to remain quietly where he was, since he (Captain Delano) would with **pleasure** take upon himself the responsibility of making the best use of the wind.

Upon gaining the deck, Captain Delano started at the unexpected figure of Atufal, **monumentally** fixed at the threshold, like one of those **sculptured** porters of black marble **guarding** the porches of Egyptian tombs.

But this time the start was, perhaps, purely physical. Atufal's presence, singularly **attesting** docility even in sullenness, was contrasted with that of the

Italian

adjourn: aggiornare, rimandare.
affected: riguardato.
alluding: alludendo.
animated: animato.
aromatic: aromatico.
atmosphere: atmosfera.
attesting: attestando.
condition: condizione, condizionare.
crimson: cremisi.
direction: direzione, senso.
discerned: distinto, discernuto, percepito.

fan: ventilatore, ventola, tifoso, ventaglio, ammiratore.
guarding: guardia.
heavily: pesante, assai, molto, pesantemente.
monumentally: monumentalmente.
nurse: infermiera, balia, curare, badare, allattare, infermiere, asciutta, nutrice.
pleasure: piacere, gradimento.
refresh: ristorare, rinfrescare.
rippling: increspatura.

risen: sorto.
rouse: stimolare, incitare, spronare, stimoli, spronate, sproni, sproniamo, sprono, stimola, stimolate, stimoliamo.
sculptured: scolpito.
swallow: rondine, inghiottire, deglutire.
taught: insegnato.
welcome: benvenuto, bene arrivate, accoglienza, gradito, accogliere.
windows: finestre.

hatchet-polishers, who in patience evinced their industry; while both **spectacles** showed, that **lax** as Don Benito's general authority might be, still, **whenever** he chose to **exert** it, no man so savage or colossal but must, more or less, bow.

Snatching a **trumpet** which hung from the bulwarks, with a free **step** Captain Delano advanced to the forward **edge** of the poop, **issuing** his orders in his best Spanish. The few sailors and many negroes, all **equally** pleased, **obediently** set about **heading** the ship towards the harbor.

While giving some **directions** about setting a lower stu'n'-sail, suddenly Captain Delano heard a voice **faithfully** repeating his orders. Turning, he saw Babo, now for the time acting, under the pilot, his original part of captain of the slaves. This assistance proved valuable. Tattered sails and warped yards were soon brought into some trim. And no **brace** or **halyard** was **pulled** but to the blithe songs of the inspirited negroes.

Good fellows, thought Captain Delano, a little training would make fine sailors of them. Why see, the very women pull and **sing** too. These must be some of those Ashantee negresses that make such capital soldiers, I've heard. But who's at the **helm**. I must have a good hand there.

He went to see.

The San Dominick steered with a cumbrous **tiller**, with large horizontal pullies attached. At each pully-end stood a subordinate black, and between them, at the tiller-head, the **responsible** post, a Spanish seaman, whose countenance evinced his **due** share in the general hopefulness and **confidence** at the coming of the breeze.

He proved the same man who had **behaved** with so shame-faced an air on the windlass.

"Ah, — it is you, my man," exclaimed Captain Delano — "well, no more sheep's-eyes now; — look straight forward and keep the ship so. Good hand, I trust? And want to get into the harbor, don't you?"

The man assented with an inward **chuckle**, **grasping** the tiller-head **firmly**. Upon this, unperceived by the American, the two blacks eyed the sailor **intently**.

Italian

behaved: agito, comportato.
brace: parentesi graffa, sostegno.
chuckle: riso soffocato, ridacchiare.
confidence: fiducia, confidenza, affidamento.
directions: avvertenze.
due: dovuto.
edge: orlo, bordo, spigolo, margine, lembo.
equally: ugualmente.
exert: praticare, esercitare, eserciti, pratico, pratichiamo, pratichi, praticate, praticano, pratica, esercitiamo, esercitate.
faithfully: fedelmente.
firmly: fermamente.
grasping: avido.
halyard: drizza.
heading: intestazione, titolo.
helm: timone, remo.
intently: intensamente.
issuing: emittente, emettere, emanazione, di emissione, emissione.
lax: molle.
obediently: ubbidientemente.
pull: tirare, tirano, tiriamo, tirate, tira, tiri, tiro, trarre, tirata.
pulled: tirato.
responsible: responsabile.
sing: cantare, canta, cantano, cantate, canti, cantiamo, canto.
spectacles: occhiali.
step: passo, gradino, scalino.
tiller: sbarra, barra, barra del timone.
trumpet: tromba, barrire.
whenever: ogni volta che, quando.

Finding all right at the helm, the pilot went forward to the forecastle, to see how matters stood there.

The ship now had way enough to **breast** the current. With the approach of evening, the breeze would be sure to **freshen**.

Having done all that was needed for the present, Captain Delano, giving his last orders to the sailors, turned aft to report affairs to Don Benito in the cabin; perhaps **additionally** incited to rejoin him by the hope of **snatching** a moment's private **chat** while the servant was engaged upon deck.

From **opposite** sides, there were, **beneath** the poop, two approaches to the cabin; one further forward than the other, and consequently communicating with a longer passage. **Marking** the servant still above, Captain Delano, taking the nighest entrance — the one last named, and at whose **porch** Atufal still stood — hurried on his way, till, arrived at the cabin threshold, he paused an instant, a little to **recover** from his eagerness. Then, with the words of his intended business upon his lips, he entered. As he advanced toward the seated Spaniard, he heard another **footstep**, keeping time with his. From the opposite door, a **salver** in hand, the servant was likewise advancing.

"**Confound** the faithful fellow," thought Captain Delano; "what a vexatious coincidence."

Possibly, the vexation might have been something different, were it not for the **brisk** confidence **inspired** by the breeze. But even as it was, he felt a slight **twinge**, from a sudden indefinite association in his mind of Babo with Atufal.

"Don Benito," said he, "I give you **joy**; the breeze will hold, and will increase. By the way, your tall man and time-piece, Atufal, stands without. By your order, of course?"

Don Benito recoiled, as if at some **bland satirical** touch, **delivered** with such **adroit garnish** of apparent good breeding as to present no **handle** for **retort**.

He is like one **flayed alive**, thought Captain Delano; where may one touch him without causing a **shrink**?

Italian

additionally: inoltre.
adroit: abile, destro, sveglio, lesto.
alive: vivo.
beneath: sotto.
bland: dolce, blando.
breast: petto, seno, mammella.
brisk: vivace, attivo.
chat: chiacchierare, chiacchierata, pettegolezzo.
confound: confondere.
delivered: consegnato.
flayed: scuoiato, si scorticato.

footstep: passo.
freshen: rinfrescare.
garnish: guarnire.
handle: maniglia, manico, trattare, manopola, maneggiare, impugnatura, manovella, ansa, tenaglie.
inspired: ispirato.
joy: gioia.
marking: marcatura, contrassegno.
opposite: dirimpetto, opposto, contrario, contro, di fronte a, di

fronte.
porch: veranda, porticato.
recover: ricuperare, ricupera, ricuperi, ricuperiamo, ricuperano, ricuperate, ricupero, recuperare, guarire, riprendere.
retort: replica, storta.
salver: vassoio.
satirical: satirico.
shrink: restringere, restringersi.
snatching: afferrare.
twinge: dolore lancinante.

The servant **moved** before his master, adjusting a cushion; recalled to civility, the Spaniard stiffly replied: "you are right. The slave **appears** where you saw him, according to my command; which is, that if at the given **hour** I am below, he must take his **stand** and abide my coming."

"Ah now, pardon me, but that is **treating** the poor fellow like an ex-king indeed. Ah, Don Benito," smiling, "for all the **license** you permit in some things, I **fear** lest, at **bottom**, you are a bitter hard master."

Again Don Benito shrank; and this time, as the good sailor thought, from a **genuine** twinge of his conscience.

Again conversation became **constrained**. In vain Captain Delano called attention to the now perceptible **motion** of the keel gently **cleaving** the **sea**; with lack-lustre **eye**, Don Benito returned words few and reserved.

By-and-by, the wind having **steadily** risen, and still blowing right into the harbor bore the San Dominick **swiftly** on. Sounding a point of land, the sealer at distance came into open view.

Meantime Captain Delano had again **repaired** to the deck, remaining there some time. Having at last **altered** the ship's course, so as to give the reef a **wide** berth, he returned for a few moments below.

I will cheer up my poor friend, this time, thought he.

"Better and better," Don Benito, he cried as he blithely re-entered: "there will soon be an end to your cares, at least for awhile. For when, after a long, sad voyage, you know, the anchor drops into the haven, all its **vast weight** seems lifted from the captain's heart. We are getting on **famously**, Don Benito. My ship is in sight. Look through this side-light here; there she is; all a-taunt-o! The Bachelor's Delight, my good friend. Ah, how this wind **braces** one up. Come, you must take a **cup** of **coffee** with me this evening. My old steward will give you as fine a cup as ever any **sultan** tasted. What say you, Don Benito, will you?"

At first, the Spaniard glanced **feverishly** up, casting a **longing** look towards the sealer, while with mute **concern** his servant gazed into his face. Suddenly the old ague of **coldness** returned, and dropping back to his cushions he was silent.

Italian

altered: alterato.
appears: appare.
bottom: fondo, basso, carena.
braces: bretelle.
cleaving: spaccando, fendendo, spaccatura.
coffee: caffè.
coldness: freddezza.
concern: riguardare, concernere, cura, azienda, importanza, preoccupazione.
constrained: costretto.

cup: tazza, coppa, la tazza, calice.
eye: occhio, cruna.
famously: famosamente.
fear: paura, temere, angoscia, timore, aver timore.
feverishly: febbricitantemente.
genuine: genuino, autentico.
hour: ora, l'ora.
license: licenza.
longing: bramoso.
motion: movimento, mozione, moto.
moved: commosso.

repaired: riparato.
sea: mare.
stand: stare in piedi, granaio, alzarsi, bancarella.
steadily: costantemente, fermamente.
sultan: sultano.
swiftly: presto, rapidamente, velocemente.
treating: trattare.
vast: vasto.
weight: peso, carico.
wide: largo, vasto, ampio.

"You do not answer. Come, all day you have been my host; would you have **hospitality** all on one side?"

"I cannot go," was the response.

"What? it will not **fatigue** you. The ships will **lie** together as near as they can, without **swinging foul**. It will be little more than stepping from deck to deck; which is but as from room to room. Come, come, you must not refuse me."

"I cannot go," decisively and **repulsively** repeated Don Benito.

Renouncing all but the last appearance of courtesy, with a sort of cadaverous sullenness, and biting his **thin nails** to the **quick**, he glanced, almost glared, at his guest, as if impatient that a stranger's presence should interfere with the full indulgence of his morbid hour. Meantime the sound of the parted waters came more and more gurglingly and **merrily** in at the windows; as **reproaching** him for his dark **spleen**; as telling him that, **sulk** as he might, and go **mad** with it, nature cared not a **jot**; since, whose fault was it, **pray**?

But the foul mood was now at its **depth**, as the fair wind at its **height**.

There was something in the man so far beyond any mere unsociality or sourness previously evinced, that even the **forbearing** good-nature of his guest could no longer endure it. Wholly at a loss to account for such demeanor, and deeming sickness with **eccentricity**, however extreme, no adequate excuse, well **satisfied**, too, that nothing in his own conduct could **justify** it, Captain Delano's **pride** began to be roused. Himself became reserved. But all seemed one to the Spaniard. **Quitting** him, therefore, Captain Delano once more went to the deck.

The ship was now within less than two miles of the sealer. The whale-boat was seen darting over the interval.

To be brief, the two vessels, **thanks** to the pilot's **skill**, ere long **neighborly** style lay **anchored** together.

Before returning to his own vessel, Captain Delano had intended communicating to Don Benito the smaller details of the **proposed** services to be rendered. But, as it was, unwilling anew to subject himself to rebuffs, he resolved, now that he had seen the San Dominick safely moored, immediately to quit her,

Italian

anchored: ancorato.
depth: profondità.
eccentricity: eccentricità.
fatigue: fatica, affaticare, stancare, stanchezza, affaticamento.
forbearing: indulgente, paziente.
foul: fallo.
height: altezza, altitudine, altura.
hospitality: ospitalità.
jot: annotare in fretta.
justify: giustificare, giustificate, giustifico, giustifichiamo, giustificano,
giustifici, giustifica.
lie: mentire, bugia, giacere, menzogna.
mad: matto, pazzo, arrabbiato, rabbioso, folle.
merrily: allegramente.
nails: chiodi.
neighborly: da buon vicino.
pray: pregare, pregate, prego, preghi, prega, preghiamo, pregano.
pride: orgoglio, fierezza.
proposed: proposto.
quick: rapido, svelto, veloce.
quitting: abbandonando.
reproaching: rimproverare.
repulsively: ripulsivamente.
satisfied: soddisfatto, contento, accontentato.
skill: abilità, destrezza, maestria.
spleen: milza, malumore.
sulk: essere di cattivo umore, fare il broncio.
swinging: oscillazione.
thanks: grazie, ringrazia.
thin: magro, sottile.

without further allusion to hospitality or business. **Indefinitely postponing** his **ulterior** plans, he would **regulate** his future actions according to future circumstances. His boat was ready to receive him; but his host still **tarried** below. Well, thought Captain Delano, if he has little breeding, the more need to show mine. He descended to the cabin to bid a ceremonious, and, it may be, **tacitly** rebukeful **adieu**. But to his great satisfaction, Don Benito, as if he began to feel the weight of that treatment with which his slighted guest had, not **indecorously**, retaliated upon him, now supported by his servant, rose to his feet, and grasping Captain Delano's hand, stood **tremulous**; too much agitated to speak. But the good **augury** hence drawn was suddenly dashed, by his **resuming** all his previous reserve, with augmented gloom, as, with half-averted eyes, he silently reseated himself on his cushions. With a corresponding return of his own **chilled** feelings, Captain Delano bowed and withdrew.

He was hardly midway in the narrow corridor, dim as a tunnel, leading from the cabin to the stairs, when a sound, as of the tolling for execution in some jail-yard, fell on his ears. It was the echo of the ship's flawed bell, striking the hour, **drearily reverberated** in this subterranean **vault**. Instantly, by a fatality not to be **withstood**, his mind, responsive to the **portent**, swarmed with superstitious suspicions. He paused. In images far swifter than these sentences, the minutest details of all his former distrusts swept through him.

Hitherto, **credulous** good-nature had been too ready to furnish excuses for reasonable fears. Why was the Spaniard, so **superfluously** punctilious at times, now **heedless** of common propriety in not **accompanying** to the side his departing guest? Did indisposition **forbid**? Indisposition had not forbidden more irksome **exertion** that day. His last **equivocal** demeanor recurred. He had risen to his feet, **grasped** his guest's hand, motioned toward his hat; then, in an instant, all was eclipsed in sinister muteness and gloom. Did this imply one brief, **repentant relenting** at the final moment, from some **iniquitous** plot, followed by **remorseless** return to it? His last glance seemed to express a calamitous, yet **acquiescent farewell** to Captain Delano forever. Why decline the invitation to visit the sealer that evening? Or was the Spaniard less **hardened** than the Jew,

Italian

accompanying: accompagnando.
acquiescent: acquiescente.
adieu: addio.
augury: presagio, augurio.
chilled: raffreddato.
credulous: credulo.
drearily: tristemente.
equivocal: ambiguo, equivoco.
exertion: sforzo.
farewell: addio, congedo.
forbid: vietare, vieti, vietate, vietano, vietiamo, vieta, vieto, proibire,

proibite, proibiamo, proibisci.
grasped: afferrato.
hardened: indurito, temprato.
heedless: sbadato, disattento.
indecorously: indecorosamente.
indefinitely: indefinitamente.
iniquitous: iniquo.
portent: augurio.
postponing: rimandando.
regulate: regolare, regolano, regolate, regoli, regoliamo, regolo, regola.
relenting: cedendo.

remorseless: spietato.
repentant: pentito.
resuming: riprendendo.
reverberated: riecheggiato, rimbombato, riverberato.
superfluously: superfluamente.
tacitly: tacitamente.
tarried: rimasto.
tremulous: tremante.
ulterior: ulteriore.
vault: volta.
withstood: resistito.

who refrained not from **supping** at the board of him whom the same night he meant to betray? What **imported** all those day-long enigmas and contradictions, except they were intended to **mystify, preliminary** to some **stealthy** blow? Atufal, the **pretended rebel**, but **punctual** shadow, that moment lurked by the threshold without. He seemed a sentry, and more. Who, by his own **confession**, had stationed him there? Was the negro now lying in wait?

The Spaniard behind — his creature before: to rush from darkness to light was the involuntary choice.

The next moment, with **clenched jaw** and hand, he passed Atufal, and stood **unharmed** in the light. As he saw his trim ship lying **peacefully** at anchor, and almost within ordinary call; as he saw his household boat, with familiar faces in it, **patiently** rising and falling, on the short waves by the San Dominick's side; and then, glancing about the decks where he stood, saw the oakum-pickers still **gravely** plying their fingers; and heard the low, **buzzing whistle** and industrious **hum** of the hatchet-polishers, still bestirring themselves over their **endless** occupation; and more than all, as he saw the benign aspect of nature, taking her innocent repose in the evening; the screened sun in the quiet camp of the west **shining** out like the mild light from Abraham's **tent**; as charmed eye and ear took in all these, with the chained figure of the black, clenched jaw and hand **relaxed**. Once again he smiled at the phantoms which had mocked him, and felt something like a tinge of **remorse**, that, by harboring them even for a moment, he should, by **implication**, have betrayed an **atheist** doubt of the ever-watchful Providence above.

There was a few minutes' delay, while, in **obedience** to his orders, the boat was being **hooked** along to the gangway. During this interval, a sort of **saddened** satisfaction stole over Captain Delano, at thinking of the kindly offices he had that day discharged for a stranger. Ah, thought he, after good actions one's conscience is never ungrateful, however much so the benefited party may be.

Presently, his foot, in the first act of **descent** into the boat, pressed the first round of the side-ladder, his face presented inward upon the deck. In the same moment, he heard his name **courteously** sounded; and, to his pleased surprise,

Italian

atheist: ateo.
buzzing: ronzio.
clenched: serrato.
confession: confessione.
courteously: cortesemente.
descent: discesa, discendenza.
endless: senza fine, infinito, interminabile.
gravely: tomba, seriamente.
hooked: gancio, adunco, agganciato.
hum: ronzio.
implication: implicazione, coinvolgimento.
imported: importato.
jaw: mascella, mandibola, ganascia.
mystify: mistificare, mistifichi, mistifichiamo, mistificano, mistifica, mistifico, mistificate.
obedience: ubbidienza, obbedienza.
patiently: pazientemente.
peacefully: pacificamente.
preliminary: preliminare.
pretended: finto.
punctual: esatto, puntuale, preciso.
rebel: ribelle.
relaxed: rilassato.
remorse: rimorso.
saddened: rattristato.
shining: lucente, brillante.
stealthy: nascosto, furtivo, clandestino.
supping: cenando.
tent: tenda.
unharmed: illeso.
whistle: fischiare, fischio, fischietto, zufolare, fischiettare, sibilo.

saw Don Benito advancing—an unwonted energy in his air, as if, at the last moment, intent upon making **amends** for his recent **discourtesy**. With **instinctive** good feeling, Captain Delano, withdrawing his foot, turned and **reciprocally** advanced. As he did so, the Spaniard's nervous eagerness increased, but his **vital** energy **failed**; so that, the better to support him, the servant, placing his master's hand on his naked shoulder, and gently **holding** it there, formed himself into a sort of **crutch**.

When the two captains met, the Spaniard again fervently took the hand of the American, at the same time casting an earnest glance into his eyes, but, as before, too much **overcome** to speak.

I have done him wrong, self-reproachfully thought Captain Delano; his apparent coldness has deceived me: in no instance has he meant to **offend**.

Meantime, as if fearful that the continuance of the scene might too much unstring his master, the servant seemed **anxious** to **terminate** it. And so, still presenting himself as a crutch, and **walking** between the two captains, he advanced with them towards the gangway; while still, as if full of kindly **contrition**, Don Benito would not let go the hand of Captain Delano, but **retained** it in his, across the black's body.

Soon they were standing by the side, looking over into the boat, whose crew turned up their curious eyes. Waiting a moment for the Spaniard to **relinquish** his hold, the now **embarrassed** Captain Delano lifted his foot, to **overstep** the threshold of the open gangway; but still Don Benito would not let go his hand. And yet, with an agitated tone, he said, "I can go no further; here I must **bid** you adieu. Adieu, my **dear**, dear Don Amasa. Go—go!" suddenly **tearing** his hand loose, "go, and God guard you better than me, my best friend."

Not unaffected, Captain Delano would now have **lingered**; but catching the **meekly admonitory** eye of the servant, with a **hasty** farewell he descended into his boat, followed by the continual adieus of Don Benito, standing **rooted** in the gangway.

Seating himself in the stern, Captain Delano, making a last **salute**, ordered the boat **shoved** off. The crew had their oars on end. The bowsmen pushed the

Italian

admonitory: ammonitorio.
amends: emenda, ammenda.
anxious: ansioso.
bid: offerta, offrire, chiedere.
contrition: contrizione.
crutch: stampella, gruccia.
dear: caro, costoso, egregio.
discourtesy: scortesia.
embarrassed: imbarazzato.
failed: fallito, non riuscito.
hasty: affrettato, frettoloso.
holding: tenere, tenuta, detenzione,
podere, presa.
instinctive: istintivo.
lingered: indugiato.
meekly: umilmente.
offend: offendere, offendiamo, offendo, offendi, offendete, offendono, insultare, insulto, insulti, insultate, insultano.
overcome: superare.
overstep: oltrepassare.
reciprocally: reciprocamente.
relinquish: cedere, cedete, cedono,
cedo, cedi, cediamo, abbandonare.
retained: ritenuto, trattenuto.
rooted: radicato.
salute: salutare, saluto.
shoved: spinto.
tearing: strappo, lacerazione, stracciare.
terminate: terminare, termino, terminiamo, termini, terminate, termina, terminano, finire.
vital: vitale.
walking: camminando, camminare.

boat a sufficient distance for the oars to be **lengthwise** dropped. The instant that was done, Don Benito sprang over the bulwarks, falling at the feet of Captain Delano; at the same time calling towards his ship, but in tones so **frenzied**, that none in the boat could understand him. But, as if not equally **obtuse**, three sailors, from three different and distant parts of the ship, splashed into the sea, swimming after their captain, as if intent upon his rescue.

The **dismayed** officer of the boat **eagerly** asked what this meant. To which, Captain Delano, turning a **disdainful** smile upon the unaccountable Spaniard, answered that, for his part, he neither knew nor cared; but it seemed as if Don Benito had taken it into his head to produce the impression among his people that the boat wanted to **kidnap** him. "Or else—give way for your lives," he wildly added, starting at a clattering hubbub in the ship, above which rang the tocsin of the hatchet-polishers; and **seizing** Don Benito by the throat he added, "this plotting **pirate** means murder!" Here, in apparent **verification** of the words, the servant, a **dagger** in his hand, was seen on the rail overhead, poised, in the act of **leaping**, as if with **desperate** fidelity to befriend his master to the last; while, **seemingly** to aid the black, the three white sailors were trying to **clamber** into the hampered bow. Meantime, the whole host of negroes, as if inflamed at the sight of their **jeopardized** captain, **impended** in one **sooty avalanche** over the bulwarks.

All this, with what preceded, and what followed, occurred with such involutions of rapidity, that past, present, and future seemed one.

Seeing the negro coming, Captain Delano had flung the Spaniard aside, almost in the very act of clutching him, and, by the unconscious **recoil**, shifting his place, with arms thrown up, so **promptly** grappled the servant in his descent, that with dagger presented at Captain Delano's heart, the black seemed of purpose to have **leaped** there as to his mark. But the **weapon** was wrenched away, and the **assailant** dashed down into the bottom of the boat, which now, with **disentangled** oars, began to speed through the sea.

At this **juncture**, the left hand of Captain Delano, on one side, again clutched the half-reclined Don Benito, heedless that he was in a **speechless faint**, while his

Italian

assailant: assalitore, aggressore.
avalanche: valanga.
clamber: arrampicarsi.
dagger: pugnale, daga.
desperate: disperato.
disdainful: sdegnoso, sprezzante.
disentangled: districato.
dismayed: costernato.
eagerly: ardentemente.
faint: debole, svenire, svengo, svengono, sveniamo, svenite, svieni, svenimento, vago.
frenzied: delirante, frenetico.
impended: incombito.
jeopardized: arrischiato, compromesso, pregiudicato, messo a repentaglio.
juncture: giuntura.
kidnap: rapire, rapiamo, rapisci, rapisco, rapiscono, rapite.
leaped: saltato.
leaping: saltare.
lengthwise: longitudinalmente, per il lungo.
obtuse: ottuso, spuntato, smussato.
pirate: pirata.
promptly: sollecitamente, prontamente.
recoil: balzo indietro, rinculare, contraccolpo, indietreggiare, rinculo.
seemingly: apparentemente.
seizing: afferrando, grippaggio.
sooty: fuligginoso.
speechless: muto.
verification: verifica, accertamento.
weapon: arma.

right-foot, on the other side, ground the prostrate negro; and his right arm pressed for added speed on the after **oar**, his eye bent forward, **encouraging** his men to their utmost.

But here, the officer of the boat, who had at last **succeeded** in beating off the **towing** sailors, and was now, with face turned aft, **assisting** the bowsman at his oar, suddenly called to Captain Delano, to see what the black was about; while a Portuguese **oarsman** shouted to him to give **heed** to what the Spaniard was saying.

Glancing down at his feet, Captain Delano saw the **freed** hand of the servant **aiming** with a second dagger — a small one, before **concealed** in his wool — with this he was snakishly writhing up from the boat's bottom, at the heart of his master, his countenance **lividly vindictive**, **expressing** the centred purpose of his soul; while the Spaniard, half-choked, was **vainly** shrinking away, with husky words, **incoherent** to all but the Portuguese.

That moment, across the long-benighted mind of Captain Delano, a **flash** of **revelation** swept, **illuminating**, in unanticipated clearness, his host's whole mysterious demeanor, with every **enigmatic** event of the day, as well as the entire past voyage of the San Dominick. He smote Babo's hand down, but his own heart smote him harder. With **infinite** pity he withdrew his hold from Don Benito. Not Captain Delano, but Don Benito, the black, in leaping into the boat, had intended to **stab**.

Both the black's hands were held, as, glancing up towards the San Dominick, Captain Delano, now with **scales** dropped from his eyes, saw the negroes, not in misrule, not in tumult, not as if **frantically** concerned for Don Benito, but with **mask** torn away, flourishing hatchets and knives, in **ferocious** piratical **revolt**. Like **delirious** black dervishes, the six Ashantees danced on the poop. Prevented by their foes from **springing** into the water, the Spanish boys were hurrying up to the topmost spars, while such of the few Spanish sailors, not already in the sea, less alert, were descried, helplessly mixed in, on deck, with the blacks.

Meantime Captain Delano hailed his own vessel, **ordering** the ports up, and the guns run out. But by this time the **cable** of the San Dominick had been cut;

Italian

aiming: mirando, puntando, punteria.	baleno.	**oarsman**: rematore, vogatore.
assisting: assistendo, aiutando.	**frantically**: freneticamente.	**ordering**: ordinare.
cable: cavo, fune.	**freed**: liberato.	**revelation**: rivelazione.
concealed: nascosto.	**heed**: cura, attenzione.	**revolt**: rivolta, ribellarsi.
delirious: delirante.	**illuminating**: illuminando,	**scales**: bilancia.
encouraging: incoraggiando,	accendendo.	**springing**: saltare, correzione.
incoraggiante.	**incoherent**: incoerente.	**stab**: pungere, coltellata, pugnalare,
enigmatic: enigmatico.	**infinite**: infinito.	pugnalata.
expressing: esprimendo.	**lividly**: lividamente.	**succeeded**: riuscito.
ferocious: feroce.	**mask**: maschera, mascherare,	**towing**: traino, alaggio, rimorchio.
flash: lampo, lampeggiatore, flash,	mascherina.	**vainly**: vanamente.
lampeggiare, scintillare, balenare,	**oar**: remo.	**vindictive**: vendicativo.

and the fag-end, in **lashing** out, whipped away the canvas **shroud** about the beak, suddenly revealing, as the bleached hull swung round towards the open ocean, death for the figure-head, in a human skeleton; **chalky** comment on the chalked words below, "*Follow your leader.*"

At the sight, Don Benito, **covering** his face, wailed out: " 'Tis he, Aranda! my murdered, unburied friend!"

Upon reaching the sealer, calling for ropes, Captain Delano **bound** the negro, who made no **resistance**, and had him hoisted to the deck. He would then have assisted the now almost helpless Don Benito up the side; but Don Benito, **wan** as he was, **refused** to move, or be moved, until the negro should have been first put below out of view. When, presently assured that it was done, he no more shrank from the ascent.

The boat was immediately dispatched back to pick up the three swimming sailors. Meantime, the guns were in readiness, though, owing to the San Dominick having glided somewhat astern of the sealer, only the aftermost one could be brought to bear. With this, they **fired** six times; thinking to **cripple** the fugitive ship by bringing down her spars. But only a few inconsiderable ropes were **shot** away. Soon the ship was beyond the gun's range, **steering** broad out of the bay; the blacks **thickly** clustering round the **bowsprit**, one moment with **taunting** cries towards the whites, the next with upthrown gestures hailing the now dusky moors of ocean—cawing crows escaped from the hand of the **fowler**.

The first impulse was to **slip** the **cables** and give **chase**. But, upon second thoughts, to **pursue** with whale-boat and yawl seemed more promising.

Upon inquiring of Don Benito what firearms they had on board the San Dominick, Captain Delano was answered that they had none that could be used; because, in the earlier stages of the **mutiny**, a cabin-passenger, since dead, had **secretly** put out of order the locks of what few muskets there were. But with all his remaining strength, Don Benito entreated the American not to give chase, either with ship or boat; for the negroes had already proved themselves such desperadoes, that, in case of a present **assault**, nothing but a total **massacre** of the whites could be looked for. But, regarding this **warning** as coming from one

Italian

assault: aggredire, assalire, assalto, attaccare, attentato, aggressione.
bound: limite, confine.
bowsprit: bompresso.
cables: cavi.
chalky: gessoso.
chase: cacciare, inseguimento, perseguire, perseguitare, inseguire, caccia.
covering: copertura, rivestimento, coprire, monta.
cripple: storpio, storpiare.

fired: licenziato, forno a rullo a gas.
fowler: uccellatore.
lashing: frustatura, rizza, frustata, fustigazione.
massacre: massacro, strage, carneficina, massacrare.
mutiny: ammutinamento, ammutinarsi.
pursue: perseguire, persegui, perseguite, perseguo, perseguiamo, perseguono, perseguitare, inseguire.
refused: rifiutato.

resistance: resistenza.
secretly: segretamente.
shot: sparato, sparo, tiro, colpo, scatto.
shroud: protezione, sudario.
slip: scivolare, slittamento, sottoveste, slittare, frana, ingobbio.
steering: direzione, sterzo.
taunting: rinfacciando, schernendo.
thickly: spesso, spessamente.
wan: pallido, smunto.
warning: avvertendo, avviso, avvertimento, diffida, avvertenza.

whose spirit had been **crushed** by misery the American did not give up his design.

The boats were got ready and **armed**. Captain Delano ordered his men into them. He was going himself when Don Benito grasped his arm.

"What! have you **saved** my life, Señor, and are you now going to throw away your own?"

The officers also, for reasons connected with their interests and those of the voyage, and a duty owing to the owners, **strongly** objected against their commander's going. **Weighing** their remonstrances a moment, Captain Delano felt bound to remain; **appointing** his chief mate — an **athletic** and **resolute** man, who had been a privateer's-man — to head the party. The more to **encourage** the sailors, they were told, that the Spanish captain considered his ship good as lost; that she and her cargo, including some gold and silver, were worth more than a thousand doubloons. Take her, and no small part should be **theirs**. The sailors replied with a **shout**.

The fugitives had now almost **gained** an **offing**. It was nearly night; but the moon was rising. After hard, prolonged **pulling**, the boats came up on the ship's quarters, at a suitable distance laying upon their oars to discharge their muskets. Having no bullets to return, the negroes sent their yells. But, upon the second **volley**, Indian-like, they hurtled their hatchets. One took off a sailor's fingers. Another struck the whale-boat's bow, cutting off the rope there, and remaining **stuck** in the gunwale like a woodman's axe. Snatching it, quivering from its lodgment, the mate hurled it back. The returned gauntlet now stuck in the ship's broken quarter-gallery, and so remained.

The negroes giving too hot a **reception**, the whites kept a more **respectful** distance. Hovering now just out of reach of the hurtling hatchets, they, with a view to the close **encounter** which must soon come, sought to **decoy** the blacks into entirely **disarming** themselves of their most **murderous weapons** in a hand-to-hand fight, by **foolishly** flinging them, as missiles, short of the mark, into the sea. But, ere long, perceiving the **stratagem**, the negroes **desisted**, though not before many of them had to **replace** their lost hatchets with handspikes; an

---

Italian

appointing: nominando.	incoraggiano, incoraggiate.	**resolute**: risoluto, deciso.
armed: armato.	**foolishly**: scioccamente.	**respectful**: rispettoso.
athletic: atletico.	**gained**: guadagnato.	**saved**: salvato, risparmiato.
crushed: schiacciato.	**murderous**: omicida.	**shout**: gridare, grido, urlo, sbraitare,
decoy: esca.	**offing**: mare al largo.	urlare.
desisted: desistito.	**pulling**: tirando.	**stratagem**: stratagemma.
disarming: disarmando.	**reception**: ricezione, ricevimento,	**strongly**: fortemente.
encounter: incontro, incontrare,	accettazione, reception, portineria.	**stuck**: bloccato.
incontra, incontriamo, incontri,	**replace**: sostituire, sostituiamo,	**theirs**: loro.
incontrano, incontrate.	sostituiscono, sostituisco, sostituite,	**volley**: volata, raffica.
encourage: incoraggiare, incoraggio,	sostituisci, rimpiazzare, rimpiazza,	**weapons**: armi.
incoraggi, incoraggia, incoraggiamo,	rimpiazzano, rimpiazzate, rimpiazzi.	**weighing**: pesando, pesatura.

exchange which, as counted upon, proved, in the end, favorable to the assailants.

Meantime, with a strong wind, the ship still clove the water; the boats **alternately** falling behind, and pulling up, to discharge fresh volleys.

The fire was mostly directed towards the stern, since there, chiefly, the negroes, at present, were clustering. But to **kill** or **maim** the negroes was not the object. To take them, with the ship, was the object. To do it, the ship must be **boarded**; which could not be done by boats while she was sailing so fast.

A thought now struck the mate. Observing the Spanish boys still **aloft**, high as they could get, he called to them to **descend** to the yards, and cut **adrift** the sails. It was done. About this time, owing to **causes** hereafter to be shown, two Spaniards, in the **dress** of sailors, and **conspicuously showing** themselves, were killed; not by volleys, but by deliberate marksman's shots; while, as it afterwards appeared, by one of the general discharges, Atufal, the black, and the Spaniard at the helm likewise were killed. What now, with the loss of the sails, and loss of leaders, the ship became unmanageable to the negroes.

With **creaking** masts, she came heavily round to the wind; the **prow** slowly swinging into view of the boats, its skeleton gleaming in the horizontal **moonlight**, and casting a gigantic ribbed shadow upon the water. One **extended** arm of the ghost seemed beckoning the whites to **avenge** it.

"Follow your leader!" cried the mate; and, one on each bow, the boats **boarded**. Sealing-spears and cutlasses crossed hatchets and hand-spikes. Huddled upon the long-boat amidships, the negresses raised a wailing chant, whose **chorus** was the **clash** of the steel.

For a time, the attack **wavered**; the negroes **wedging** themselves to beat it back; the half-repelled sailors, as yet unable to gain a **footing**, fighting as troopers in the **saddle**, one leg sideways flung over the bulwarks, and one without, plying their cutlasses like carters' whips. But in vain. They were almost overborne, when, rallying themselves into a **squad** as one man, with a huzza, they sprang inboard, where, **entangled**, they involuntarily **separated** again. For a few breaths' space, there was a vague, muffled, **inner** sound, as of submerged

Italian

adrift: alla deriva.
aloft: in alto.
alternately: alternativamente, alternatamente.
avenge: vendicare, vendico, vendica, vendicano, vendicate, vendichi, vendichiamo.
boarded: imbarcato.
causes: causa.
chorus: coro.
clash: scontro.
conspicuously: cospicuamente.

creaking: cigolando, stridendo, cigolio, scricchiolio.
descend: scendere, scendiamo, scendono, scendi, scendete, scendo, discendere, discendono, discendo, discendiamo, discendi.
dress: vestire, vestito, vestirsi, abito, abbigliare.
entangled: intrappolato, ingarbugliato, impigliato, imbrogliato, aggrovigliato.
extended: esteso.

footing: punto d'appoggio.
inner: interno.
kill: uccidere, ammazzare.
maim: mutilare.
moonlight: chiaro di luna.
prow: prua.
saddle: sella.
separated: separato.
showing: mostrando.
squad: squadra, compagnia.
wavered: esitato.
wedging: cassa da morto.

sword-fish rushing hither and thither through shoals of black-fish. Soon, in a **reunited** band, and joined by the Spanish seamen, the whites came to the surface, irresistibly driving the negroes toward the stern. But a **barricade** of casks and sacks, from side to side, had been thrown up by the main-mast. Here the negroes faced about, and though scorning peace or **truce**, yet fain would have had **respite**. But, without pause, overleaping the **barrier**, the **unflagging** sailors again closed. **Exhausted**, the blacks now fought in **despair**. Their red tongues lolled, wolf-like, from their black mouths. But the pale sailors' teeth were set; not a word was spoken; and, in five minutes more, the ship was won.

Nearly a score of the negroes were killed. Exclusive of those by the **balls**, many were mangled; their wounds — mostly inflicted by the long-edged sealing-spears, **resembling** those **shaven** ones of the English at Preston Pans, made by the poled **scythes** of the Highlanders. On the other side, none were killed, though several were **wounded**; some severely, including the mate. The surviving negroes were temporarily **secured**, and the ship, towed back into the harbor at **midnight**, once more lay anchored.

Omitting the incidents and arrangements **ensuing**, **suffice** it that, after two days spent in refitting, the ships sailed in company for Conception, in Chili, and **thence** for Lima, in Peru; where, before the vice-regal courts, the whole affair, from the beginning, underwent investigation.

Though, midway on the passage, the ill-fated Spaniard, relaxed from **constraint**, showed some signs of **regaining** health with free-will; yet, agreeably to his own foreboding, shortly before **arriving** at Lima, he relapsed, finally becoming so reduced as to be carried **ashore** in arms. Hearing of his story and **plight**, one of the many religious institutions of the City of Kings opened an **hospitable refuge** to him, where both **physician** and priest were his nurses, and a member of the order volunteered to be his one special **guardian** and consoler, by night and by day.

The following extracts, **translated** from one of the official Spanish documents, will, it is hoped, **shed** light on the preceding narrative, as well as, in the first

Italian

arriving: arrivando.
ashore: a terra.
balls: sfere, palla, balli.
barricade: barricata, barricare.
barrier: barriera, sbarramento, imballo barriera.
constraint: costrizione, vincolo.
despair: disperazione, disperare.
ensuing: seguendo.
exhausted: esausto, sfinito, esaurito.
guardian: guardiano, tutore.
hospitable: ospitale.

midnight: mezzanotte.
omitting: omettendo.
physician: medico, dottore.
plight: situazione critica.
refuge: rifugio.
regaining: riacquistando, riprendendo, riguadagnando, riconquistando, ricuperando.
resembling: rassomigliando.
respite: tregua.
reunited: riunito.
scythes: falci.

secured: fissato.
shaven: sbarbato, raso, rasato.
shed: baracca, versare, versate, verso, versiamo, versato, versano, versa, versi, capannone, tettoia.
suffice: bastare, basta, bastano, bastate, basti, bastiamo, basto.
thence: di là.
translated: tradotto.
truce: tregua.
unflagging: instancabile, infaticabile.
wounded: ferito.

place, **reveal** the true port of departure and true history of the San Dominick's voyage, down to the time of her touching at the **island** of St. Maria.

But, ere the extracts come, it may be well to **preface** them with a remark.

The document **selected**, from among many others, for **partial translation**, **contains** the **deposition** of Benito Cereno; the first taken in the case. Some disclosures **therein** were, at the time, held dubious for both **learned** and natural reasons. The **tribunal** inclined to the opinion that the **deponent**, not **undisturbed** in his mind by recent events, **raved** of some things which could never have happened. But **subsequent** depositions of the surviving sailors, **bearing** out the revelations of their captain in several of the strangest particulars, gave **credence** to the rest. So that the tribunal, in its final decision, rested its capital sentences upon statements which, had they lacked **confirmation**, it would have deemed it but duty to **reject**.

* * * * *

I, DON JOSE DE ABOS AND PADILLA, His Majesty's Notary for the Royal Revenue, and Register of this Province, and Notary Public of the Holy Crusade of this Bishopric, **etc.**

Do **certify** and **declare**, as much as is requisite in law, that, in the **criminal** cause commenced the twenty-fourth of the month of September, in the year **seventeen** hundred and ninety-nine, against the negroes of the ship San Dominick, the following **declaration** before me was made:

Declaration of the first witness, DON BENITO CERENO.

The same day, and month, and year, His Honor, Doctor Juan Martinez de Rozas, Councilor of the Royal Audience of this Kingdom, and learned in the law of this Intendency, ordered the captain of the ship San Dominick, Don Benito

Italian

bearing: cuscinetto, rapporto.
certify: certificare, certifichiamo, certifico, certifichi, certificano, certifica, certificate.
confirmation: conferma.
contains: contiene.
credence: credenza.
criminal: criminale, malfattore.
declaration: dichiarazione.
declare: dichiarare, dichiara, dichiaro, dichiariamo, dichiari, dichiarano, dichiarate.

deponent: deponente.
deposition: deposizione.
etc: ecc.
island: isola, l'isola.
learned: imparato, erudito, colto, dotto, istruito.
partial: parziale.
preface: prefazione.
raved: delirato, farneticato, vaneggiato.
reject: rifiutare, respingere, scarto, rigettare, rifiutarsi, bocciare, scartare.

reveal: pubblicare, rivelare, pubblicano, pubblicate, pubblichi, pubblichiamo, pubblico, rivela, rivelano, rivelate, riveli.
selected: selezionato, scelto.
seventeen: diciassette.
subsequent: successivo, seguente.
therein: in ciò.
translation: traduzione, traslazione.
tribunal: tribunale.
undisturbed: indisturbato.
witness: testimone, testimoniare.

Cereno, to appear; which he did, in his **litter**, **attended** by the **monk** Infelez; of whom he received the **oath**, which he took by God, our Lord, and a **sign** of the Cross; under which he **promised** to tell the truth of whatever he should know and should be asked;—and being **interrogated** agreeably to the **tenor** of the act **commencing** the process, he said, that on the **twentieth** of May last, he set sail with his ship from the port of Valparaiso, bound to that of Callao; **loaded** with the produce of the country beside thirty cases of hardware and one hundred and sixty blacks, of both sexes, mostly **belonging** to Don Alexandro Aranda, gentleman, of the city of Mendoza; that the crew of the ship **consisted** of thirty-six men, beside the persons who went as **passengers**; that the negroes were in part as follows:

[*Here, in the original, follows a list of some fifty* **names***, descriptions, and ages,* **compiled** *from certain recovered* **documents** *of Aranda's, and also from recollections of the deponent, from which portions only are extracted.*]

—One, from about **eighteen** to **nineteen** years, named José, and this was the man that waited upon his master, Don Alexandro, and who **speaks** well the Spanish, having **served** him four or five years; * * * a mulatto, named Francesco, the cabin steward, of a good person and voice, having **sung** in the Valparaiso **churches**, native of the **province** of Buenos Ayres, aged about thirty-five years. * * * A smart negro, named Dago, who had been for many years a grave-digger among the Spaniards, aged forty-six years. * * * Four old negroes, **born** in Africa, from sixty to seventy, but sound, calkers by trade, whose names are as follows:— the first was named Muri, and he was **killed** (as was also his son named Diamelo); the second, Nacta; the third, Yola, likewise killed; the **fourth**, Ghofan; and six full-grown negroes, aged from thirty to forty-five, all **raw**, and born among the Ashantees—Matiluqui, Yan, Leche, Mapenda, Yambaio, Akim; four of whom were killed; * * * a **powerful** negro named Atufal, who being **supposed** to have been a chief in Africa, his **owner** set great **store** by him. * * * And a small negro of Senegal, but some years among the Spaniards, aged about thirty, which negro's name was Babo; * * * that he does not remember the names of the others,

Italian

attended: visitato, curato, assistito.	**killed**: ucciso.	**province**: provincia.
belonging: appartenendo.	**litter**: rifiuti, figliata, barella.	**raw**: crudo, grezzo, greggio.
born: nato.	**loaded**: caricato.	**served**: servito.
churches: chiese.	**monk**: monaco.	**sign**: firmare, segno, segnale, prova,
commencing: cominciando.	**names**: nomi.	augurio.
compiled: compilato.	**nineteen**: diciannove.	**speaks**: parla.
consisted: consistito, constato.	**oath**: giuramento, imprecazione.	**store**: negozio, magazzino, deposito,
documents: documenti,	**owner**: proprietario, titolare,	immagazzinare, memorizzare.
documentazione.	possessore.	**sung**: cantato.
eighteen: diciotto.	**passengers**: viaggiatori, passeggeri.	**supposed**: supposto.
fourth: quarto, quarta.	**powerful**: potente.	**tenor**: tenore.
interrogated: interrogato.	**promised**: promesso.	**twentieth**: ventesimo.

but that still **expecting** the residue of Don Alexandra's papers will be found, will then take due account of them all, and remit to the court; * * * and thirty-nine women and children of all ages.

[*The* **catalogue** *over, the deposition goes on:*]

* * * That all the negroes slept upon deck, as is **customary** in this navigation, and none wore fetters, because the owner, his friend Aranda, told him that they were all **tractable**; * * * that on the **seventh** day after leaving port, at three o'clock in the morning, all the Spaniards being asleep **except** the two officers on the watch, who were the **boatswain**, Juan Robles, and the **carpenter**, Juan Bautista Gayete, and the **helmsman** and his boy, the Negroes **revolted** suddenly, wounded **dangerously** the boatswain and the carpenter, and **successively** killed eighteen men of those who were sleeping upon deck, some with hand-spikes and hatchets, and others by throwing them alive overboard, after tying them; that of the Spaniards upon deck, they left about seven, as he **thinks**, alive and tied, to **manoeuvre** the ship, and three or four more, who hid themselves, remained also alive. Although in the act of revolt the negroes made themselves masters of the hatchway, six or seven wounded went through it to the **cockpit**, without any hindrance on their part; that during the act of revolt, the mate and another person, whose name he does not **recollect**, **attempted** to come up through the hatchway, but being quickly wounded, were **obliged** to return to the cabin; that the deponent resolved at break of day to come up the companion-way, where the negro Babo was, being the **ringleader**, and Atufal, who assisted him, and having **spoken** to them, **exhorted** them to **cease committing** such atrocities, asking them, at the same time, what they wanted and intended to do, **offering**, himself, to **obey** their commands; that notwithstanding this, they threw, in his presence, three men, alive and tied, overboard; that they told the deponent to come up, and that they would not kill him; which having done, the negro Babo asked him whether there were in those seas any negro countries where they might be carried, and he answered them, No; that the negro Babo **afterwards** told him to

Italian

afterwards: dopo, dietro, in seguito, successivamente.
attempted: provato.
boatswain: nostromo.
carpenter: falegname, carpentiere.
catalogue: catalogo, catalogare, cataloghi, cataloghiamo, catalogano, cataloga, catalogate.
cease: cessare.
cockpit: abitacolo, cabina di guida.
committing: commettendo.
customary: consueto, usuale, abituale.

dangerously: pericolosamente.
except: eccetto, salvo, tranne, eccettuare.
exhorted: esortato.
expecting: aspettando.
helmsman: timoniere.
manoeuvre: manovra, manovrare.
obey: ubbidire, ubbidiamo, ubbidite, ubbidiscono, ubbidisci, ubbidisco, obbedire, obbediamo, obbediscono, obbedisco, obbedisci.
obliged: obbligato.

offering: offerta.
recollect: rammenta, rammentano, rammentate, rammenti, rammentiamo, rammento, rammentare, ricordarsi.
revolted: rivoltato.
ringleader: capobanda, caporione.
seventh: settimo.
spoken: parlato.
successively: successivamente.
thinks: pensa.
tractable: docile, trattabile.

carry them to Senegal,   or to the neighboring islands of St. Nicholas; and he answered, that this was **impossible**, on account of the great distance, the necessity involved of **rounding** Cape Horn, the bad condition of the vessel, the want of **provisions**, sails, and water; but that the negro Babo replied to him he must carry them in any way; that they would do and **conform** themselves to everything the deponent should require as to eating and drinking; that after a long conference, being **absolutely compelled** to please them, for they **threatened** to kill all the whites if they were not, at all events, carried to Senegal, he told them that what was most **wanting** for the voyage was water; that they would go near the **coast** to take it, and thence they would **proceed** on their course; that the negro Babo agreed to it; and the deponent steered towards the **intermediate** ports, **hoping** to meet some Spanish, or foreign vessel that would save them; that within ten or eleven days they saw the land, and continued their course by it in the vicinity of Nasca; that the deponent observed that the negroes were now restless and **mutinous**, because he did not effect the taking in of water, the negro Babo having required, with **threats**, that it should be done, without **fail**, the following day; he told him he saw plainly that the coast was steep, and the rivers **designated** in the maps were not to be found, with other reasons **suitable** to the circumstances; that the best way would be to go to the island of Santa Maria, where they might water easily, it being a solitary island, as the **foreigners** did; that the deponent did not go to Pisco, that was near, nor make any other port of the coast, because the negro Babo had intimated to him several times, that he would kill all the whites the very moment he should perceive any city, town, or **settlement** of any kind on the shores to which they should be carried: that having **determined** to go to the island of Santa Maria, as the deponent had **planned**, for the purpose of trying whether, on the passage or near the island itself, they could find any vessel that should favor them, or whether he could **escape** from it in a boat to the neighboring coast of Arruco, to **adopt** the necessary means he immediately changed his course, steering for the island; that the negroes Babo and Atufal held daily conferences, in which they **discussed** what was necessary for their design of returning to Senegal, whether they were to kill all the Spaniards, and particularly the deponent; that eight days after

Italian

absolutely: assolutamente, infatti, davvero, completamente.
adopt: adottare, adotta, adotto, adottiamo, adotti, adottano, adottate.
coast: costa, litorale.
compelled: costretto, forzato.
conform: conformarsi.
designated: designato.
determined: definito, fissato, determinato.
discussed: discusso.
escape: scarico, evasione, scappare,

sfuggire, evadere, fuoriuscire, fuga.
fail: fallire, morire, mancare.
foreigners: stranieri.
hoping: sperando.
impossible: impossibile.
intermediate: intermedio.
mutinous: ammutinato.
planned: progettato.
proceed: procedere, procedete, procedono, procedo, procediamo, procedi.
provisions: disposizioni,

accantonamenti.
rounding: arrotondamento.
settlement: liquidazione, pareggiamento dei conti, accordo, assestamento, composizione, definizione transattiva.
suitable: adatto, conveniente, idoneo, appropriato, utile, capace, decente, utilizzabile.
threatened: minacciato.
threats: minaccia.
wanting: volendo.

parting from the coast of Nasca, the deponent being   on the **watch** a little after day-break, and soon after the negroes had their meeting, the negro Babo came to the place where the deponent was, and told him that he had determined to kill his master, Don Alexandro Aranda, both because he and his companions could not otherwise be sure of their **liberty**, and that to keep the seamen in **subjection**, he wanted to **prepare** a warning of what road they should be made to take did they or any of them **oppose** him; and that, by means of the death of Don Alexandro, that warning would best be given; but, that what this last meant, the deponent did not at the time comprehend, nor could not, further than that the death of Don Alexandro was intended; and **moreover** the negro Babo proposed to the deponent to call the mate Raneds, who was sleeping in the cabin, before the thing was done, for fear, as the deponent **understood** it, that the mate, who was a good **navigator**, should be killed with Don Alexandro and the rest; that the deponent, who was the friend, from youth, of Don Alexandro, **prayed** and **conjured**, but all was useless; for the negro Babo answered him that the thing could not be prevented, and that all the Spaniards **risked** their death if they should **attempt** to **frustrate** his will in this matter, or any other; that, in this **conflict**, the deponent called the mate, Raneds, who was **forced** to go apart, and immediately the negro Babo commanded the Ashantee Martinqui and the Ashantee Lecbe to go and commit the murder; that those two went down with hatchets to the berth of Don Alexandro; that, yet half alive and mangled, they dragged him on deck; that they were going to throw him overboard in that state, but the negro Babo **stopped** them, bidding the murder be completed on the deck before him, which was done, when, by his orders, the body was **carried** below, forward; that nothing more was seen of it by the deponent for three days; * * * that Don Alonzo Sidonia, an old man, long **resident** at Valparaiso, and lately appointed to a **civil** office in Peru, **whither** he had taken passage, was at the time sleeping in the berth opposite Don Alexandro's; that awakening at his cries, surprised by them, and at the sight of the negroes with their **bloody** hatchets in their hands, he threw himself into the sea through a window which was near him, and was **drowned**, without it being in the power of the deponent to assist or take him up; * * * that a short time after **killing** Aranda, they brought upon deck

Italian

attempt: tentativo, provare, provate, provo, provi, provano, proviamo, prova, tentare, sforzo, attentato.
bloody: sanguinante, sanguinoso, maledetto, cruento.
carried: portato, trasportato.
civil: civile.
conflict: conflitto.
conjured: evocato.
drowned: annegato.
forced: forzato.
frustrate: frustrare, frustrano,

frustrate, frustri, frustriamo, frustro, frustra.
killing: uccisione.
liberty: libertà.
moreover: inoltre, d'altronde.
navigator: navigatore.
oppose: contrapporre, contrapponete, contrapponi, contrapponiamo, contrappongono, contrappongo, opporre.
prayed: pregato.
prepare: preparare, prepari,

prepariamo, preparate, preparano, prepara, preparo, allestire, allestiamo, allestisci, allestisco.
resident: residente.
risked: rischiato.
stopped: fermato, cessato, interrotto, smesso, arrestato.
subjection: sottomissione, soggezione.
understood: capito, compreso.
watch: orologio, guardare, sorvegliare, guardia, sentinella, osservare.
whither: dove.

his german-cousin, of middle-age, Don Francisco Masa, of Mendoza, and the young Don Joaquin, Marques de Aramboalaza, then lately from Spain, with his Spanish servant Ponce, and the three young clerks of Aranda, José Mozairi Lorenzo Bargas, and Hermenegildo Gandix, all of Cadiz; that Don Joaquin and Hermenegildo Gandix, the negro Babo, for purposes hereafter to **appear**, **preserved** alive; but Don Francisco Masa, José Mozairi, and Lorenzo Bargas, with Ponce the servant, beside the boatswain, Juan Robles, the boatswain's mates, Manuel Viscaya and Roderigo Hurta, and four of the sailors, the negro Babo ordered to be thrown alive into the sea, although they made no resistance, nor begged for anything else but **mercy**; that the boatswain, Juan Robles, who knew how to **swim**, **kept** the longest above water, making acts of contrition, and, in the last words he uttered, charged this deponent to cause **mass** to be said for his soul to our Lady of Succor: * * * that, during the three days which **followed**, the deponent, **uncertain** what fate had **befallen** the **remains** of Don Alexandro, **frequently** asked the negro Babo where they were, and, if still on board, whether they were to be preserved for interment ashore, entreating him so to order it; that the negro Babo answered nothing till the fourth day, when at sunrise, the deponent **coming** on deck, the negro Babo showed him a skeleton, which had been **substituted** for the ship's **proper** figure-head — the **image** of Christopher Colon, the **discoverer** of the New World; that the negro Babo asked him **whose** skeleton that was, and whether, from its **whiteness**, he should not think it a white's; that, upon **discovering** his face, the negro Babo, coming close, said words to this effect: "Keep **faith** with the blacks from here to Senegal, or you shall in spirit, as now in body, follow your leader," pointing to the prow; * * * that the same morning the negro Babo took by **succession** each Spaniard **forward**, and asked him whose skeleton that was, and whether, from its whiteness, he should not think it a white's; that each Spaniard **covered** his face; that then to each the negro Babo repeated the words in the first place said to the deponent; * * * that they (the Spaniards), being then **assembled** aft, the negro Babo **harangued** them, **saying** that he had now done all; that the deponent (as navigator for the negroes) might pursue his course, warning him and all of them that they should, soul and body, go the way of Don Alexandro, if he saw them

Italian

appear: apparire, apparite, appariamo, appari, appaiono, appaio, parere, comparire.
assembled: montato, assemblato.
befallen: successo.
coming: venendo.
covered: coperto.
discoverer: scopritore.
discovering: scoprendo.
faith: fede, fiducia.
follow: seguire, seguiamo, seguite, seguo, seguono, segui.

followed: seguito.
forward: avanti, spedire, attaccante, in avanti, inoltrare.
frequently: frequentemente, spesso, sovente.
harangued: arringato, concionato.
image: immagine, pittura, figura, illustrazione.
kept: conservato, osservato, trattenuto.
mass: massa, folla, affluenza, messa.
mercy: misericordia.
preserved: conservato.

proper: decente, proprio.
remains: rimane, resta, resti.
saying: dicendo, detto, proverbio.
substituted: sostituito.
succession: successione.
swim: nuotare, nuoto, nuotiamo, nuoti, nuotate, nuota, nuotano, nuotata.
uncertain: incerto, malsicuro.
whiteness: punto di bianco, bianchezza.
whose: di chi, il cui.

(the Spaniards) speak, or **plot** anything against them (the negroes)—a **threat** which was repeated every day; that, before the events last mentioned, they had tied the **cook** to throw him overboard, for it is not known what thing they **heard** him speak, but **finally** the negro Babo spared his life, at the **request** of the deponent; that a few days after, the deponent, endeavoring not to **omit** any means to **preserve** the lives of the remaining whites, spoke to the negroes **peace** and tranquillity, and **agreed** to draw up a paper, **signed** by the deponent and the sailors who could **write**, as also by the negro Babo, for himself and all the blacks, in which the deponent obliged himself to **carry** them to Senegal, and they not to kill any more, and he **formally** to make over to them the ship, with the cargo, with which they were for that time satisfied and quieted. * * * But the next day, the more **surely** to guard against the sailors' escape, the negro Babo commanded all the boats to be **destroyed** but the long-boat, which was unseaworthy, and another, a **cutter** in good condition, which knowing it would yet be wanted for towing the water casks, he had it lowered down into the hold.

*   *   *   *   *

[*Various particulars of the prolonged and **perplexed** navigation ensuing here follow, with incidents of a calamitous calm, from which portion one passage is **extracted**, to wit:*]

—That on the **fifth** day of the calm, all on board suffering much from the **heat**, and want of water, and five having **died** in fits, and mad, the negroes became irritable, and for a **chance** gesture, which they deemed suspicious— though it was harmless—made by the mate, Raneds, to the deponent in the act of handing a **quadrant**, they killed him; but that for this they afterwards were **sorry**, the mate being the only remaining navigator on board, except the deponent.

Italian

agreed: concordato, pattuito.

carry: portare, porti, portate, portiamo, portano, porto, porta, trasportare, trasporta, trasportano, trasportate.

chance: caso.

cook: cuoco, cuoca, cucinare, cuocere.

cutter: taglierina, fresa, tagliatore, coltello, taglierino.

destroyed: distrutto.

died: morto.

extracted: estratto.

fifth: quinto, quinta.

finally: finalmente, alla fine, infine.

formally: formalmente.

heard: udito, sentito.

heat: calore, riscaldare, ardore, caldo, scaldare.

omit: omettere, omettete, ometti, omettiamo, omettono, trascurare, ometto.

peace: pace.

perplexed: confuso, turbato, perplesso.

plot: complotto, trama, macchinare, complottare, appezzamento, intreccio, congiura, disegnare.

preserve: conservare, conserva.

quadrant: quadrante.

request: richiesta, richiedere, chiedere, domanda.

signed: firmato.

sorry: addolorato, spiacente.

surely: certamente, sicuramente.

threat: minaccia.

write: scrivere, scrivi, scrivono, scriviamo, scrivete, scrivo.

*　　*　　*　　*　　*

—That omitting other events, which **daily happened**, and which can only **serve uselessly** to **recall** past misfortunes and **conflicts**, after seventy-three days' navigation, **reckoned** from the time they sailed from Nasca, during which they **navigated** under a scanty allowance of water, and were **afflicted** with the calms before mentioned, they at last **arrived** at the island of Santa Maria, on the **seventeenth** of the month of August, at about six o'clock in the afternoon, at which hour they cast anchor very near the American ship, Bachelor's Delight, which lay in the same bay, commanded by the generous Captain Amasa Delano; but at six o'clock in the morning, they had already descried the port, and the negroes became **uneasy**, as soon as at distance they saw the ship, not having expected to see one there; that the negro Babo pacified them, assuring them that no fear need be had; that straightway he ordered the figure on the bow to be covered with canvas, as for repairs and had the decks a little set in order; that for a time the negro Babo and the negro Atufal conferred; that the negro Atufal was for sailing away, but the negro Babo would not, and, by himself, cast about what to do; that at last he came to the deponent, **proposing** to him to say and do all that the deponent **declares** to have said and done to the American captain; * * * * * * * that the negro Babo **warned** him that if he **varied** in the least, or uttered any word, or gave any look that should give the least **intimation** of the past events or present state, he would instantly kill him, with all his companions, showing a dagger, which he carried hid, saying something which, as he understood it, meant that that dagger would be alert as his eye; that the negro Babo then **announced** the plan to all his companions, which pleased them; that he then, the better to disguise the truth, devised many expedients, in some of them uniting **deceit** and **defense**; that of this sort was the **device** of the six Ashantees before named, who were his bravoes; that them he stationed on the **break** of the poop, as if to **clean** certain hatchets (in cases, which were part of the cargo), but in **reality** to use them, and **distribute** them at need, and at a given word he told

Italian

afflicted: afflitto.
announced: annunciato, annunziato.
arrived: arrivato.
break: rompere, rottura, spezzare, rompersi, frattura, pausa, schiantare, infrangere, sosta, spaccare.
clean: pulito, pulire, puliamo, pulite, puliscono, pulisco, pulisci, puro, netto, lindo.
conflicts: scontri.
daily: quotidiano, giornaliero, quotidianamente, ogni giorno,

giornalmente.
deceit: frode.
declares: dichiara.
defense: difesa.
device: dispositivo, apparecchio, congegno.
distribute: distribuire, distribuite, distribuiscono, distribuiamo, distribuisco, distribuisci.
happened: successo, avvenuto.
intimation: accenno.
navigated: navigato.

proposing: proponendo.
reality: realtà, verità.
recall: richiamo, ricordare, richiamare.
reckoned: contato, calcolato, computato.
serve: servire, serviamo, servi, servono, servite, servo.
seventeenth: diciassettesimo.
uneasy: inquieto.
uselessly: inutilmente.
varied: variato, vario.
warned: avvertito.

them; that, among other **devices**, was the device of presenting Atufal, his right hand man, as chained, though in a moment the chains could be dropped; that in every particular he informed the **deponent** what part he was **expected** to **enact** in every device, and what **story** he was to tell on every **occasion**, always **threatening** him with instant death if he varied in the least: that, **conscious** that many of the negroes would be **turbulent**, the negro Babo appointed the four aged negroes, who were calkers, to keep what **domestic** order they could on the decks; that again and again he **harangued** the Spaniards and his companions, informing them of his intent, and of his devices, and of the invented story that this deponent was to tell; **charging** them lest any of them varied from that story; that these arrangements were made and **matured** during the interval of two or three **hours**, between their first **sighting** the ship and the **arrival** on board of Captain Amasa Delano; that this happened about half-past **seven** o'clock in the morning, Captain Amasa Delano coming in his boat, and all **gladly receiving** him; that the deponent, as well as he could **force** himself, acting then the part of **principal** owner, and a free captain of the ship, told Captain Amasa Delano, when called upon, that he came from Buenos Ayres, bound to Lima, with three **hundred** negroes; that off Cape Horn, and in a subsequent fever, many negroes had died; that also, by **similar casualties**, all the sea **officers** and the greatest part of the crew had died.

*   *   *   *   *

[*And so the deposition* **goes** *on, circumstantially recounting the* **fictitious** *story* **dictated** *to the deponent by Babo, and through the deponent imposed upon Captain Delano; and also recounting the friendly offers of Captain Delano, with other things, but all of which is here* **omitted**. *After the fictitious story, etc. the deposition proceeds:*]

—that the generous Captain Amasa Delano **remained** on board all the day, till he left the ship anchored at six o'clock in the **evening**, deponent speaking to

Italian

arrival: arrivo, venuta.
casualties: incidenti, morti e feriti.
charging: caricamento, carico, carica, addebitare.
conscious: cosciente.
deponent: deponente.
devices: dispositivi.
dictated: dettato.
domestic: domestico, nazionale.
enact: decretare, decreto, decretiamo, decreti, decretate, decreta, decretano.
evening: sera, la sera, serata.

expected: aspettato, atteso.
fictitious: fittizio.
force: forza, forzare, costringere, vigore.
gladly: volentieri, con piacere.
goes: va.
harangued: arringato, concionato.
hours: ore.
hundred: cento, centinaio.
matured: maturo, maturato.
occasion: occasione.
officers: ufficiali.

omitted: omesso.
principal: principale, committente, capitale, mandante.
receiving: ricevendo, accogliendo, ricezione, ricevere, ricevente.
remained: rimasto, restato.
seven: sette.
sighting: avvistamento.
similar: simile.
story: storia, piano, racconto.
threatening: minacciando, minaccioso.
turbulent: turbolento.

him always of his pretended misfortunes, under the fore-mentioned principles, without having had it in his power to tell a single word, or give him the least hint, that he might know the truth and state of things; because the negro Babo, performing   the office of an **officious** servant with all the **appearance** of submission of the humble slave, did not leave the deponent one moment; that this was in order to observe the deponent's actions and words, for the negro Babo **understands** well the Spanish; and besides, there were thereabout some others who were **constantly** on the watch, and likewise understood the Spanish; * * * that upon one occasion, while deponent was standing on the deck conversing with Amasa Delano, by a secret sign the negro Babo drew him (the deponent) aside, the act appearing as if **originating** with the deponent; that then, he being drawn aside, the negro Babo proposed to him to **gain** from Amasa Delano full particulars about his ship, and crew, and arms; that the deponent asked "For what?" that the negro Babo answered he might conceive; that, **grieved** at the **prospect** of what might **overtake** the generous Captain Amasa Delano, the deponent at first refused to ask the desired questions, and used every **argument** to **induce** the negro Babo to give up this new design; that the negro Babo showed the point of his dagger; that, after the information had been **obtained** the negro Babo again drew him aside, **telling** him that that very night he (the deponent) would be captain of two ships, instead of one, for that, great part of the American's ship's crew being to be absent fishing, the six Ashantees, without any one else, would **easily** take it; that at this time he said other things to the same **purpose**; that no entreaties **availed**; that, before Amasa Delano's coming on board, no hint had been given touching the **capture** of the American ship: that to **prevent** this project the deponent was **powerless**; * * *—that in some things his memory is **confused**, he cannot distinctly recall every event; * * *—that as soon as they had cast anchor at six of the **clock** in the evening, as has before been stated, the American Captain took leave, to return to his vessel; that upon a sudden impulse, which the deponent **believes** to have come from God and his angels, he, after the farewell had been said, followed the generous Captain Amasa Delano as far as the gunwale, where he **stayed**, under pretense of taking leave, until Amasa Delano should have been seated in his boat; that on shoving

Italian

appearance: apparenza, aspetto, aria, comparizione, comparsa.
argument: argomento.
availed: servito.
believes: crede.
capture: prendere, cattura, catturare.
clock: orologio.
confused: confuso.
constantly: costantemente.
easily: facilmente.
event: evento, avvenimento.
gain: guadagno, profitto, guadagnare,
vantaggio, beneficio.
grieved: accorato, addolorato.
induce: dedurre, concludere, indurre, induci, inducono, induciamo, inducete, deducono, deduco, deduciamo, deducete.
obtained: ottenuto.
officious: ufficioso, invadente.
originating: discendendo.
overtake: sorpassare, sorpassa, sorpassano, sorpassate, sorpassi, sorpassiamo, sorpasso.
powerless: impotente.
prevent: impedire, impediamo, impedisci, impedisco, impediscono, impedite, prevenire, prevenite, previeni, preveniamo, prevengono.
prospect: prospettiva, esplorare.
purpose: scopo, proposito, fine, intenzione.
stayed: stato, restato.
telling: dicendo, raccontando, narrando.
understands: capisce, comprende.

off, the **deponent** sprang from the gunwale into the boat, and **fell** into it, he knows not how, God guarding him; that—

* * * * *

[*Here, in the* **original**, **follows** *the* **account** *of what further happened at the escape, and how the San Dominick was retaken, and of the passage to the coast; including in the* **recital** *many* **expressions** *of "eternal gratitude" to the "generous Captain Amasa Delano." The deposition then proceeds with recapitulatory remarks, and a partial renumeration of the* **negroes**, *making* **record** *of their* **individual** *part in the past events, with a view to* **furnishing**, **according** *to command of the court, the* **data** *whereon to found the criminal sentences to be* **pronounced**. *From this portion is the following:*]

—That he believes that all the negroes, though not in the first place knowing to the **design** of revolt, when it was **accomplished**, **approved** it. * * * That the negro, José, eighteen years old, and in the **personal** service of Don Alexandro, was the one who **communicated** the information to the negro Babo, about the state of things in the cabin, before the revolt; that this is known, because, in the preceding midnight, he use to come from his **berth**, which was under his master's, in the cabin, to the deck where the **ringleader** and his associates were, and had secret conversations with the negro Babo, in which he was several times seen by the mate; that, one night, the mate **drove** him away **twice**; * * that this same negro José was the one who, without being commanded to do so by the negro Babo, as Lecbe and Martinqui were, stabbed his master, Don Alexandro, after be had been dragged half-lifeless to the deck; * * that the **mulatto** steward, Francesco, was of the first band of revolters, that he was, in all things, the creature and **tool** of the negro Babo; that, to make his court, he, just before a repast in the cabin, proposed, to the negro Babo, **poisoning** a dish for the generous Captain Amasa Delano; this is known and believed, because the negroes have said it; but that the negro Babo, having another design, forbade

---

Italian

accomplished: compiuto.
according: secondo.
account: conto, considerare, rendiconto, spiegazione, pareggiamento dei conti, credere, account.
approved: approvato, omologato.
berth: cuccetta, ancoraggio, attraccare.
communicated: comunicato.
data: dati, materiale, dato.
deponent: deponente.
design: disegno, progetto, disegnare, progettazione, design, progettare, piano, costruttive.
dish: piatto, pietanza.
drove: gregge.
expressions: espressioni.
fell: abbattere.
follows: segue.
furnishing: fornendo, arredamento.
individual: individuale, individuo, singolo.
mulatto: mulatto.
negro: negro.
original: originale.
personal: personale, proprio.
poisoning: avvelenamento, intossicazione, avvelenare.
pronounced: pronunciato.
recital: concerto, recital, dizione.
record: registrare, disco, record, registrazione, verbale, documento.
ringleader: capobanda, caporione.
tool: strumento, arnese, attrezzo, strumento di lavoro, utensile.
twice: due volte.

Francesco; * * that the Ashantee Lecbe was one of the **worst** of them; for that, on the day the ship was retaken, he assisted in the defense of her, with a hatchet in each hand, with one of which he wounded, in the breast, the chief mate of Amasa Delano,   in the first act of boarding; this all knew; that, in sight of the deponent, Lecbe struck, with a hatchet, Don Francisco Masa, when, by the negro Babo's orders, he was carrying him to throw him overboard, alive, beside **participating** in the murder, before mentioned, of Don Alexandro Aranda, and others of the cabin-passengers; that, owing to the **fury** with which the Ashantees fought in the engagement with the boats, but this Lecbe and Yan **survived**; that Yan was **bad** as Lecbe; that Yan was the man who, by Babo's command, willingly **prepared** the skeleton of Don Alexandro, in a way the negroes afterwards told the deponent, but which he, so long as **reason** is left him, can never divulge; that Yan and Lecbe were the two who, in a calm by night, riveted the skeleton to the bow; this also the negroes told him; that the negro Babo was he who traced the **inscription below** it; that the negro Babo was the **plotter** from first to last; he ordered every murder, and was the helm and keel of the revolt; that Atufal was his **lieutenant** in all; but Atufal, with his own hand, **committed** no murder; nor did the negro Babo; * * that Atufal was shot, being killed in the **fight** with the boats, ere boarding; * * that the negresses, of age, were knowing to the revolt, and **testified** themselves satisfied at the death of their master, Don Alexandro; that, had the negroes not **restrained** them, they would have **tortured** to death, instead of **simply** killing, the Spaniards **slain** by command of the negro Babo; that the negresses used their utmost **influence** to have the deponent made away with; that, in the **various** acts of murder, they sang songs and danced — not **gaily**, but solemnly; and before the engagement with the boats, as well as during the action, they sang melancholy songs to the negroes, and that this melancholy tone was more **inflaming** than a different one would have been, and was so intended; that all this is believed, because the negroes have said it. — that of the thirty-six men of the crew, **exclusive** of the passengers (all of **whom** are now dead), which the deponent had **knowledge** of, six only remained alive, with four cabin-boys and ship-boys, not **included** with the crew; * * — that the negroes **broke** an **arm** of one of the cabin-boys and gave him strokes with hatchets.

Italian

arm: armare, braccio, arma, il braccio, armi.
bad: cattivo, male.
below: sotto, giù, dabbasso.
broke: al verde, rovinato, scarti di fabbricazione.
committed: commesso.
exclusive: esclusivo.
fight: combattere, duellare, lotta, lottare, battaglia, picchiarsi, combattimento.
fury: furia, furore.

gaily: gaiamente.
included: incluso, contenuto.
inflaming: infiammando.
influence: influenza, influsso, influenzare, influire.
inscription: iscrizione.
knowledge: conoscenza, cognizione.
lieutenant: tenente.
participating: partecipando, spartendo.
plotter: plotter.
prepared: preparato, allestito,

apprestato.
reason: ragione, causa, intelletto, ragionare, argomentare, motivo.
restrained: dominato.
simply: semplicemente.
slain: ucciso, ammazzato.
survived: sopravvissuto.
testified: testimoniato.
tortured: torturato.
various: vario, differente.
whom: chi, cui.
worst: peggiore.

[*Then follow various random disclosures referring to various periods of time. The following are extracted:*]

—That during the presence of Captain Amasa Delano on board, some **attempts** were made by the sailors, and one by Hermenegildo Gandix, to **convey** hints to him of the true state of **affairs**; but that these attempts were **ineffectual**, owing to fear of **incurring** death, and, futhermore, owing to the devices which **offered** contradictions to the true state of affairs, as well as owing to the generosity and piety of Amasa Delano incapable of sounding such wickedness; * * * that Luys Galgo, a sailor about sixty years of age, and formerly of the king's **navy**, was one of those who sought to convey tokens to Captain Amasa Delano; but his intent, though undiscovered, being suspected, he was, on a pretense, made to retire out of sight, and at last into the **hold**, and there was made away with. This the negroes have since said; * * * that one of the ship-boys **feeling**, from Captain Amasa Delano's presence, some hopes of **release**, and not having enough prudence, dropped some chance-word **respecting** his **expectations**, which being overheard and understood by a slave-boy with whom he was eating at the time, the **latter** struck him on the head with a knife, inflicting a bad wound, but of which the **boy** is now **healing**; that likewise, not long before the ship was **brought** to anchor, one of the seamen, steering at the time, endangered himself by letting the blacks remark some expression in his countenance, arising from a cause similar to the above; but this sailor, by his **heedful** after conduct, escaped; * * * that these statements are made to show the court that from the **beginning** to the end of the revolt, it was impossible for the deponent and his men to act otherwise than they did; * * *—that the third clerk, Hermenegildo Gandix, who before had been forced to live among the seamen, **wearing** a seaman's **habit**, and in all respects appearing to be one for the time; he, Gandix, was killed by a **musket ball** fired through **mistake** from the boats before boarding; having in his **fright** run up the mizzen-rigging, calling to the boats—"don't board," lest upon their boarding the negroes should kill him; that this **inducing** the Americans to believe he some way **favored** the cause of the negroes, they fired two balls at him,

Italian

affairs: affari.
attempts: prova.
ball: palla, ballo, sfera, globo, pallone, la palla, gomitolo.
beginning: inizio, cominciando, principio, iniziando.
boy: ragazzo, servire.
brought: portato.
convey: trasportare.
expectations: aspettativa, aspettative.
favored: favorito.
feeling: sentimento, sensazione.

fright: paura, spavento, timore, angoscia.
habit: abitudine, costume, vizio, consuetudine.
healing: guarendo, guarigione, guarire.
heedful: attento, cauto.
hold: tenere, stiva, stretta, mantenere, ritenere.
incurring: incorrendo.
inducing: deducendo, inducendo, concludendo.

ineffectual: inefficace, vano.
latter: ultimo.
mistake: errore, sbaglio, sbagliare, confondere, fallo.
musket: moschetto.
navy: marina, marina militare, flotta.
offered: offerto, offerta.
release: liberare, rilasciare, rilascio, disinnesto, liberazione, svincolo, versione.
respecting: rispettare.
wearing: usura.

so that he fell wounded from the rigging, and was drowned in the sea; * * *—that the   young Don Joaquin, Marques de Aramboalaza, like Hermenegildo Gandix, the third clerk, was **degraded** to the office and appearance of a **common** seaman; that upon one occasion when Don Joaquin shrank, the negro Babo commanded the Ashantee Lecbe to take tar and heat it, and **pour** it upon Don Joaquin's **hands**; * * *—that Don Joaquin was killed owing to another mistake of the Americans, but one impossible to be **avoided**, as upon the **approach** of the boats, Don Joaquin, with a hatchet tied edge out and **upright** to his hand, was made by the negroes to appear on the bulwarks; **whereupon**, seen with arms in his hands and is a **questionable altitude**, he was shot for a renegade seaman; * * *—that on the person of Don Joaquin was found secreted a jewel, which, by papers that were **discovered**, proved to have been meant for the **shrine** of our Lady of Mercy in Lima; a votive offering, beforehand prepared and **guarded**, to **attest** his gratitude, when he should have **landed** in Peru, his last destination, for the **safe conclusion** of his entire voyage from Spain; * * *—that the jewel, with the other effects of the **late** Don Joaquin, is in the **custody** of the brethren of the Hospital de Sacerdotes, awaiting the disposition of the honorable court; * * *—that, owing to the condition of the deponent, as well as the haste in which the boats departed for the **attack**, the Americans were not **forewarned** that there were, among the apparent crew, a **passenger** and one of the clerks **disguised** by the negro Babo; * * *—that, beside the negroes killed in the action, some were killed after the capture and re-anchoring at night, when shackled to the ring-bolts on deck; that these deaths were committed by the sailors, ere they could be prevented. That so **soon** as informed of it, Captain Amasa Delano used all his **authority**, and, in particular with his own hand, struck down Martinez Gola, who, having found a razor in the **pocket** of an old **jacket** of his, which one of the shackled negroes had on, was aiming it at the negro's throat; that the noble Captain Amasa Delano also wrenched from the hand of Bartholomew Barlo a dagger, secreted at the time of the massacre of the whites, with which he was in the act of stabbing a shackled negro, who, the same day, with another negro, had thrown him down and **jumped** upon him; * * *—that, for all the events, **befalling** through so long a time, during which the ship was in the hands of the negro Babo, he cannot here give

Italian

altitude: altitudine, altezza, quota.
approach: accesso, approccio, avvicinare, avvicinamento, avvicinarsi, accostare.
attack: attacco, attaccare, assalto, aggredire, assalire, aggressione, accesso.
attest: attestare, attesto, attestiamo, attesti, attestate, attesta, attestano.
authority: autorità.
avoided: evitato.
befalling: succedendo.

common: comune, volgare, ordinario.
conclusion: conclusione, risultato.
custody: custodia.
degraded: degradato.
discovered: scoperto.
disguised: travestito.
forewarned: prevenuto, preavvertito, preavvisato.
guarded: guardingo, custodito.
hands: mani.
jacket: giacca, giacchetta, giubbotto, rivestimento.

jumped: saltato.
landed: fondiario, atterrato.
late: tardi, tardo, in ritardo, tardivo.
passenger: passeggero.
pocket: tasca, intascare, la tasca, sacca.
pour: versare.
questionable: discutibile, dubbio.
safe: sicuro, cassaforte.
shrine: santuario.
soon: fra poco, presto.
upright: montante, verticale, dritto.
whereupon: dopo di che.

account; but that, what he has said is the most **substantial** of what **occurs** to him at **present**, and is the truth under the oath which he has taken; which declaration he **affirmed** and **ratified**, after hearing it read to him.

He said that he is twenty-nine years of age, and **broken** in body and mind; that when finally dismissed by the court, he shall not return home to Chili, but **betake** himself to the monastery on Mount Agonia without; and signed with his honor, and crossed himself, and, for the time, departed as he came, in his litter, with the monk Infelez, to the Hospital de Sacerdotes.

BENITO CERENO.

DOCTOR ROZAS.

If the Deposition have served as the **key** to **fit** into the **lock** of the complications which **precede** it, then, as a vault whose door has been flung back, the San Dominick's hull lies open to-day.

Hitherto the nature of this narrative, besides **rendering** the intricacies in the beginning **unavoidable**, has more or less **required** that many things, instead of being set down in the order of **occurrence**, should be retrospectively, or **irregularly** given; this last is the case with the following passages, which will conclude the account:

During the long, mild voyage to Lima, there was, as before hinted, a period during which the sufferer a little recovered his health, or, at least in some **degree**, his tranquillity. Ere the **decided** relapse which came, the two captains had many cordial conversations—their fraternal unreserve in singular contrast with former withdrawments.

Again and again it was repeated, how hard it had been to enact the part forced on the Spaniard by Babo.

"Ah, my dear friend," Don Benito once said, "at those very times when you thought me so **morose** and ungrateful, nay, when, as you now **admit**, you half thought me plotting your murder, at those very times my **heart** was **frozen**; I could not look at you, **thinking** of what, both on board this ship and your own,

Italian

admit: confessare, confessa, confessiamo, confessi, confessate, confessano, confesso, ammettere, permettere, ammetto, ammettiamo.
affirmed: affermato.
betake: recarsi.
broken: rotto, spezzato.
decided: deciso.
degree: grado, laurea.
doctor: medico, dottore.
fit: adattare, aggiustare, apoplessia, in forma, adatto.

frozen: congelato, gelato, surgelato.
heart: cuore, il cuore.
irregularly: irregolarmente.
key: chiave, tasto, chiavetta, la chiave, pulsante.
lock: serratura, serrare a chiave, chiusa, bloccaggio, bloccare, blocco, fermo, ciocca.
morose: imbronciato, cupo.
occurrence: avvenimento, evento, fatto.
occurs: accade, succede.

precede: precedere, precedo, precedono, precediamo, precedi, precedete.
present: presente, regalo, dono, presentare, attuale.
ratified: ratificato.
rendering: rendering, rendendo, traduzione.
required: richiesto.
substantial: sostanziale, sostanzioso.
thinking: pensando.
unavoidable: inevitabile.

hung, from other hands, over my kind **benefactor**. And as God lives, Don Amasa, I know not whether desire for my own **safety** alone could have nerved me to that **leap** into your boat, had it not been for the thought that, did you, unenlightened, return to your ship, you, my best friend, with all who might be with you, stolen upon, that night, in your hammocks, would never in this world have **wakened** again. Do but think how you **walked** this deck, how you **sat** in this cabin, every **inch** of **ground mined** into honey-combs under you. Had I dropped the least hint, made the least **advance** towards an **understanding** between us, death, **explosive** death—yours as mine—would have ended the scene."

"True, true," cried Captain Delano, starting, "you have saved my life, Don Benito, more than I yours; saved it, too, against my knowledge and will."

"Nay, my friend," rejoined the Spaniard, **courteous** even to the point of **religion**, "God charmed your life, but you saved mine. To think of some things you did—those smilings and chattings, rash pointings and gesturings. For less than these, they slew my mate, Raneds; but you had the Prince of Heaven's safe-conduct through all ambuscades."

"Yes, all is owing to Providence, I know: but the temper of my mind that morning was more than **commonly** pleasant, while the sight of so much suffering, more apparent than real, added to my good-nature, compassion, and **charity**, **happily interweaving** the three. Had it been otherwise, doubtless, as you hint, some of my interferences might have ended **unhappily** enough. Besides, those feelings I spoke of **enabled** me to get the better of momentary distrust, at times when acuteness might have cost me my life, without saving another's. Only at the end did my suspicions get the better of me, and you know how wide of the mark they then proved."

"Wide, indeed," said Don Benito, sadly; "you were with me all day; stood with me, sat with me, **talked** with me, looked at me, ate with me, drank with me; and yet, your last act was to **clutch** for a **monster**, not only an **innocent** man, but the most **pitiable** of all men. To such degree may malign machinations and deceptions **impose**. So far may even the best man err, in **judging** the conduct of one with the recesses of whose condition he is not acquainted. But you were

Italian

advance: avanzare, anticipo, proporre, avvicinarsi, anticipazione, avanzamento, avanzata, acconto, progredire, prestito, progresso.
benefactor: benefattore.
charity: elemosina.
clutch: frizione, afferrare.
commonly: comunemente.
courteous: cortese.
enabled: abilitato.
explosive: esplosivo.
ground: suolo, fondo, terra, massa, terreno.
happily: felicemente.
impose: imporre, imponete, imponiamo, imponi, impongo, impongono.
inch: pollice.
innocent: innocente.
interweaving: intessendo, intrecciandosi, intreccio.
judging: giudicare.
leap: salto, saltare, balzo.
mine: miniera, mina, minare, estrarre.
monster: mostro.
pitiable: pietoso.
religion: religione.
safety: sicurezza.
sat: seduto, covato.
talked: parlato.
understanding: capendo, comprendendo, comprensione, intesa.
unhappily: infelicemente.
wakened: svegliato.
walked: camminato.

forced to it; and you were in time **undeceived**. Would that, in both respects, it was so ever, and with all men."

"You **generalize**, Don Benito; and mournfully enough. But the past is passed; why **moralize** upon it? Forget it. See, **yon bright** sun has **forgotten** it all, and the blue sea, and the blue sky; these have turned over new leaves."

"Because they have no memory," he dejectedly replied; "because they are not human."

"But these mild trades that now fan your cheek, do they not come with a human-like healing to you? Warm friends, **steadfast** friends are the trades."

"With their steadfastness they but **waft** me to my **tomb**, Señor," was the foreboding response.

"You are saved," cried Captain Delano, more and more astonished and pained; "you are saved: what has cast such a shadow upon you?"

"The negro."

There was silence, while the moody man sat, slowly and unconsciously **gathering** his **mantle** about him, as if it were a **pall**.

There was no more conversation that day.

But if the Spaniard's melancholy sometimes ended in muteness upon topics like the above, there were others upon which he never spoke at all; on which, indeed, all his old **reserves** were piled. Pass over the worst, and, only to **elucidate** let an item or two of these be **cited**. The dress, so **precise** and **costly**, worn by him on the day whose events have been narrated, had not willingly been put on. And that silver-mounted sword, apparent **symbol** of despotic command, was not, indeed, a sword, but the ghost of one. The **scabbard**, **artificially stiffened**, was empty.

As for the black—whose **brain**, not body, had **schemed** and led the revolt, with the plot—his slight **frame**, **inadequate** to that which it held, had at once **yielded** to the superior **muscular** strength of his captor, in the boat. **Seeing** all was over, he uttered no sound, and could not be forced to. His aspect seemed to say, since I cannot do **deeds**, I will not speak words. Put in irons in the hold, with

Italian

artificially: artificialmente.
brain: cervello.
bright: brillante, luminoso, splendente, chiaro.
cited: citato.
costly: costoso, caro.
deeds: gesta.
elucidate: delucidare.
forgotten: dimenticato.
frame: telaio, intelaiatura, cornice, fotogramma, incorniciare, struttura, inquadrare, immagine, incastellatura,

ordinata.
gathering: convegno, raccolta.
generalize: generalizzare, generalizziamo, generalizzo, generalizzi, generalizzate, generalizzano, generalizza.
inadequate: inadeguato, insufficiente.
mantle: mantello, manto.
moralize: moraleggiare, moralizzare.
muscular: muscolare, muscoloso.
pall: coltre, cappa.
precise: preciso, accurato.

reserves: riserve.
scabbard: fodero.
schemed: progettato.
seeing: vedendo, segando.
steadfast: risoluto, costante.
stiffened: indurito, irrigidito.
symbol: simbolo.
tomb: tomba, sepolcro.
undeceived: disingannato.
waft: spandersi, soffio, diffondere.
yielded: ceduto.
yon: laggiù, là, li.

the **rest**, he was carried to Lima. During the passage, Don Benito did not **visit** him. Nor then, nor at any time after, would he look at him. Before the **tribunal** he refused. When **pressed** by the judges he **fainted**. On the **testimony** of the **sailors** alone **rested** the **legal identity** of Babo.

Some months after, **dragged** to the **gibbet** at the **tail** of a **mule**, the black **met** his **voiceless** end. The body was **burned** to **ashes**; but for many days, the head, that **hive** of subtlety, fixed on a pole in the Plaza, met, unabashed, the **gaze** of the whites; and across the Plaza looked towards St. Bartholomew's church, in whose vaults **slept** then, as now, the **recovered bones** of Aranda: and across the Rimac **bridge** looked towards the **monastery**, on Mount Agonia without; where, three months after being **dismissed** by the court, Benito Cereno, borne on the **bier**, did, **indeed**, follow his **leader**.

Italian

ashes: cenere.
bier: bara.
bones: ossa.
bridge: ponte, ponte di comando, ponticello, plancia.
burned: bruciato.
dismissed: licenziato.
dragged: trascinato.
fainted: svenuto.
gaze: fissare, sguardo fisso.
gibbet: patibolo, condannare all'impiccagione, forca.

hive: alveare, arnia.
identity: identità.
indeed: davvero, infatti, di fatto, veramente.
leader: capo.
legal: legale, legittimo.
met: incontrato.
monastery: monastero.
mule: mulo.
pressed: premuto.
recovered: ricuperato.
rest: riposo, riposarsi, riposare, resto,

pausa.
rested: riposato.
sailors: marinai.
slept: dormito.
tail: coda, la coda.
testimony: certificato attestato, testimonianza.
tribunal: tribunale.
visit: visita, visitare, visitano, visitate, visiti, visitiamo, visito, andare a trovare.
voiceless: muto.

THE LIGHTNING-ROD MAN

What grand irregular thunder, thought I, standing on my hearth-stone among the Acroceraunian hills, as the **scattered bolts** boomed overhead, and crashed down among the valleys, every bolt **followed** by **zigzag** irradiations, and swift slants of **sharp** rain, which **audibly** rang, like a **charge** of spear-points, on my **low** shingled roof. I suppose, though, that the mountains hereabouts break and **churn** up the thunder, so that it is far more **glorious** here than on the plain. Hark!—someone at the door. Who is this that **chooses** a time of thunder for making **calls**? And why don't he, man-fashion, use the **knocker**, instead of making that doleful undertaker's **clatter** with his **fist** against the hollow **panel**? But let him in. Ah, here he **comes**. "Good day, sir:" an entire stranger. "Pray be seated." What is that strange-looking walking-stick he **carries**: "A fine thunder-storm, sir."

"Fine?—Awful!"

"You are **wet**. Stand here on the hearth before the fire."

"Not for worlds!"

The stranger still stood in the **exact middle** of the **cottage**, where he had first planted himself. His **singularity** impelled a closer scrutiny. A lean, gloomy **figure**. Hair dark and lank, mattedly **streaked** over his brow. His sunken pitfalls of eyes were ringed by **indigo** halos, and **played** with an **innocuous** sort of lightning: the gleam without the bolt. The whole man was **dripping**. He stood in

Italian

audibly: udibilmente.
bolts: bulloni.
calls: chiama.
carries: porta, trasporta.
charge: carica, carico, addebito, spese, onere, tassa, caricare, imputazione, accusa.
chooses: sceglie, elegge.
churn: zangola.
clatter: sferragliare, ticchettio, acciottolio, sferragliamento.
comes: viene.

cottage: casolare, villetta, casetta.
dripping: sgocciolatura, stillicidio, gocciolamento.
exact: esatto, preciso.
figure: figura, calcolare, cifra, numero.
fist: pugno.
glorious: glorioso.
indigo: indaco.
innocuous: innocuo.
knocker: battente.
low: basso.
middle: mezzo, medio, metà, di

mezzo.
panel: pannello.
played: giocato, suonato.
scattered: versato, sparso.
sharp: affilato, aguzzo, acuto, tagliente, appuntito, piccante, giusto, giustamente, aspro, diesis, nitido.
singularity: stranezza, singolarità.
streaked: striato.
wet: bagnato, bagnare, umido, inumidire.
zigzag: zigzagare, zigzag.

a **puddle** on the bare **oak** floor: his strange walking-stick **vertically** resting at his side.

It was a **polished copper rod**, four feet long, lengthwise attached to a **neat** wooden staff, by **insertion** into two balls of **greenish** glass, ringed with copper bands. The metal rod terminated at the top tripodwise, in three keen tines, **brightly** gilt. He held the thing by the wooden part alone.

"Sir," said I, bowing **politely**, "have I the honor of a visit from that **illustrious** god, **Jupiter** Tonans? So stood he in the Greek **statue** of old, grasping the lightning-bolt. If you be he, or his **viceroy**, I have to thank you for this noble storm you have **brewed** among our mountains. Listen: That was a glorious **peal**. Ah, to a **lover** of the **majestic**, it is a good thing to have the Thunderer himself in one's cottage. The thunder **grows** finer for that. But pray be seated. This old rush-bottomed arm-chair, I grant, is a poor **substitute** for your **evergreen throne** on Olympus; but, **condescend** to be seated."

While I thus pleasantly spoke, the stranger eyed me, half in wonder, and half in a strange sort of horror; but did not move a foot.

"Do, sir, be seated; you need to be **dried** ere going forth again."

I planted the chair **invitingly** on the broad hearth, where a little fire had been kindled that afternoon to **dissipate** the **dampness**, not the cold; for it was early in the month of September.

But without heeding my **solicitation**, and still standing in the middle of the floor, the stranger gazed at me portentously and spoke.

"Sir," said he, "excuse me; but instead of my **accepting** your **invitation** to be seated on the hearth there, I solemnly warn *you*, that you had best accept *mine*, and stand with me in the middle of the room. Good heavens!" he cried, starting—"there is another of those awful crashes. I warn you, sir, quit the hearth."

"Mr. Jupiter Tonans," said I, quietly **rolling** my body on the stone, "I stand very well here."

Italian

accepting: accettando.
brewed: fermentato.
brightly: luminosamente.
condescend: degna, degnano, degnate, degni, degniamo, degno, degnare.
copper: rame.
dampness: umidità.
dissipate: dissipare.
dried: secco.
evergreen: sempreverde.
greenish: verdognolo, verdastro.
grows: cresce, coltiva.

illustrious: illustre.
insertion: inserzione, inserimento.
invitation: invito.
invitingly: invitare.
jupiter: giove.
lover: amante.
majestic: maestoso.
neat: pulito, puro, ordinato.
oak: quercia.
peal: scampanio.
polished: lucidato.
politely: cortesemente.

puddle: pozzanghera.
rod: barra, verga, bacchetta, asta.
rolling: rotolamento, laminazione, cilindratura, rullatura, rollio.
solicitation: sollecitazione.
statue: statua.
substitute: sostituto, sostituire, supplente, rimpiazzare, succedaneo, surrogato.
throne: trono.
vertically: verticalmente.
viceroy: vicerè.

"Are you so horridly ignorant, then," he cried, "as not to know, that by far the most **dangerous** part of a house, during such a **terrific tempest** as this, is the fire-place?"

"Nay, I did not know that," involuntarily stepping upon the first board next to the stone.

The stranger now assumed such an unpleasant **air** of **successful admonition**, that—quite involuntarily again—I stepped back upon the hearth, and threw myself into the erectest, proudest posture I could command. But I said nothing.

"For Heaven's sake," he cried, with a strange **mixture** of alarm and intimidation—"for Heaven's sake, get off the hearth! Know you not, that the **heated** air and **soot** are conductors;—to say nothing of those **immense iron** fire-dogs? Quit the spot—I conjure—I command you."

"Mr. Jupiter Tonans, I am not **accustomed** to be commanded in my own house."

"Call me not by that **pagan** name. You are **profane** in this time of terror."

"Sir, will you be so good as to tell me your business? If you seek **shelter** from the **storm**, you are welcome, so long as you be civil; but if you come on business, open it forthwith. Who are you?"

"I am a **dealer** in lightning-rods," said the stranger, **softening** his tone; "my special business is—Merciful **heaven**! what a crash!—Have you ever been struck—your **premises**, I mean? No? It's best to be provided;"—significantly rattling his **metallic** staff on the floor;—"by **nature**, there are no **castles** in thunder-storms; yet, say but the word, and of this cottage I can make a Gibraltar by a few waves of this **wand. Hark**, what Himalayas of concussions!"

"You interrupted yourself; your special business you were about to speak of."

"My special business is to travel the country for orders for lightning-rods. This is my specimen-rod;" **tapping** his staff; "I have the best of references"—fumbling in his pockets. "In Criggan last **month**, I put up three-and-twenty rods on only five buildings."

Italian

accustomed: consueto, abituato, usuale, solito, avvezzo.
admonition: ammonimento, ammonizione, esortazione.
air: aria.
castles: castelli.
dangerous: pericoloso.
dealer: commerciante, negoziante.
hark: ascoltare.
heated: riscaldato.
heaven: cielo, paradiso.
immense: immenso, enorme.

iron: ferro, ferro da stiro, stirare.
metallic: metallico.
mixture: mistura, miscela, commistione, impasto, mescolanza, miscuglio.
month: mese, il mese.
nature: natura, indole, carattere.
pagan: pagano.
premises: locali, locale, premesse.
profane: profanare.
shelter: rifugio, riparo, ricovero, riparare.

softening: ammorbidimento, ritenitura, rammollimento, ammorbidendo.
soot: fuliggine.
storm: tempesta, burrasca, temporale, bufera.
successful: riuscito.
tapping: maschiatura, rubinetto, colata.
tempest: tempesta.
terrific: straordinario.
wand: bacchetta.

"Let me see. Was it not at Criggan last week, about midnight on Saturday, that the **steeple**, the big elm, and the assembly-room **cupola** were struck? Any of your rods there?"

"Not on the tree and cupola, but the steeple."

"Of what use is your rod, then?"

"Of life-and-death use. But my **workman** was heedless. In **fitting** the rod at top to the steeple, he allowed a part of the metal to **graze** the tin **sheeting**. Hence the accident. Not my fault, but his. Hark!"

"Never mind. That **clap burst** quite **loud** enough to be heard without finger-pointing. Did you hear of the event at Montreal last year? A servant girl struck at her bed-side with a **rosary** in her hand; the **beads** being metal. Does your beat extend into the Canadas?"

"No. And I hear that there, iron rods only are in use. They should have *mine*, which are copper. Iron is easily **fused**. Then they draw out the rod so slender, that it has not body enough to conduct the full electric current. The metal melts; the building is destroyed. My copper rods never act so. Those Canadians are fools. Some of them knob the rod at the top, which risks a **deadly explosion**, instead of **imperceptibly** carrying down the current into the earth, as this sort of rod does. *Mine* is the only true rod. Look at it. Only one **dollar** a foot."

"This abuse of your own calling in another might make one distrustful with respect to yourself."

"Hark! The thunder becomes less muttering. It is nearing us, and nearing the earth, too. Hark! One crammed **crash**! All the **vibrations** made one by **nearness**. Another flash. Hold!"

"What do you?" I said, seeing him now, **instantaneously relinquishing** his staff, lean intently forward towards the window, with his right **fore** and middle fingers on his left **wrist**. But ere the words had well escaped me, another **exclamation** escaped him.

"Crash! only three pulses — less than a third of a mile off — yonder, somewhere in that wood. I passed three **stricken oaks** there, **ripped** out new and

Italian

beads: rosario.	**exclamation**: esclamazione.	**oaks**: querce.
burst: scoppiare, scoppio, crepa, screpolatura, fessura, esplosione, crepare, irrompere, burst.	**explosion**: esplosione, scoppio.	**relinquishing**: cedendo.
	fitting: decente, prova, aggiustaggio, calzante.	**ripped**: strappato.
clap: applaudire, battere le mani, applauso.	**fore**: anteriore, parte anteriore.	**rosary**: rosario.
	fused: fuso.	**sheeting**: tela per lenzuola.
crash: crollare, collisione, precipitare, caduta, schianto, crollo, scontro, tracollo, fragore, fracasso, disastro.	**graze**: graffio, escoriazione, sfiorare, pascolare, pascere.	**steeple**: campanile.
	imperceptibly: impercettibilmente.	**stricken**: colpito.
cupola: cupola.	**instantaneously**: istantaneamente.	**tin**: stagno, latta, barattolo, lattina, scatola.
deadly: mortale.	**loud**: forte, alto, rumoroso.	**vibrations**: vibrazione, vibrazioni.
dollar: dollaro.	**nearness**: vicinanza.	**workman**: operaio.
		wrist: polso.

glittering. The oak **draws** lightning more than other **timber**, having iron in **solution** in its **sap**. Your **floor** here seems oak.

"Heart-of-oak. From the peculiar time of your call upon me, I suppose you purposely **select stormy weather** for your journeys. When the thunder is roaring, you deem it an hour **peculiarly** favorable for producing impressions favorable to your trade."

"Hark! — Awful!"

"For one who would arm others with fear you seem unbeseemingly **timorous** yourself. Common men **choose fair** weather for their **travels**: you choose thunder-storms; and yet—"

"That I travel in thunder-storms, I **grant**; but not without particular **precautions**, such as only a lightning-rod man may know. Hark! Quick—look at my specimen rod. Only one dollar a foot."

"A very fine rod, I dare say. But what are these particular precautions of yours? Yet first let me close yonder shutters; the slanting rain is beating through the **sash**. I will **bar** up."

"Are you mad? Know you not that yon iron bar is a swift **conductor**? Desist."

"I will simply close the shutters, then, and call my boy to bring me a **wooden** bar. Pray, **touch** the bell-pull there."

"Are you **frantic**? That bell-wire might **blast** you. Never touch bell-wire in a thunder-storm, nor ring a bell of any sort."

"Nor those in belfries? Pray, will you tell me where and how one may be safe in a time like this? Is there any part of my house I may touch with hopes of my life?"

"There is; but not where you now stand. Come away from the wall. The current will sometimes run down a wall, and—a man being a better conductor than a wall—it would leave the wall and run into him. **Swoop!** *That* must have fallen very nigh. That must have been **globular** lightning."

Italian

bar: bar, sbarrare, barra, sbarro, sbarriamo, sbarri, sbarrano, sbarrate, sbarra, eccetto, impedire.
blast: scoppio, esplosione.
choose: scegliere, scegli, scegliamo, scegliete, scelgo, scelgono, eleggere, eleggete, eleggi, eleggiamo, eleggo.
conductor: conduttore, bigliettaio, capotreno.
draws: disegna.
fair: biondo, fiera, giusto, bazar, correttamente, bello, equo.

floor: pavimento, piano.
frantic: frenetico.
glittering: scintillare, brillio, brillare, scintillio.
globular: globulare.
grant: concessione, accordare, sovvenzione.
peculiarly: particolarmente.
precautions: precauzioni.
ring: anello, circolo.
sap: linfa.
sash: fusciacca.

select: selezionare, selezionano, seleziono, selezioniamo, selezioni, selezionate, seleziona, scegliere.
solution: soluzione, risoluzione.
stormy: tempestoso, temporalesco.
swoop: piombare, avventarsi.
timber: legno, legname.
timorous: timoroso.
touch: toccare, tocco, tatto.
travels: viaggia.
weather: tempo.
wooden: di legno.

"Very probably. Tell me at once, which is, in your **opinion**, the **safest** part of this house?

"This room, and this one **spot** in it where I stand. Come **hither**."

"The reasons first."

"Hark!—after the **flash** the gust—the sashes shiver—the house, the house!— Come hither to me!"

"The reasons, if you please."

"Come hither to me!"

"Thank you again, I think I will try my old stand—the **hearth**. And now, Mr. Lightning-rod-man, in the pauses of the **thunder**, be so good as to tell me your reasons for esteeming this one room of the house the safest, and your own one stand-point there the safest spot in it."

There was now a little **cessation** of the **storm** for a while. The Lightning-rod man seemed **relieved**, and replied:—

"Your house is a one-storied house, with an **attic** and a **cellar**; this room is between. **Hence** its **comparative** safety. Because **lightning** sometimes passes from the clouds to the earth, and sometimes from the earth to the clouds. Do you comprehend?—and I **choose** the middle of the room, because if the lightning should **strike** the house at all, it would come down the **chimney** or walls; so, **obviously**, the further you are from them, the better. Come hither to me, now."

"Presently. Something you just said, instead of **alarming** me, has **strangely inspired** confidence."

"What have I said?"

"You said that sometimes lightning flashes from the earth to the clouds."

"Aye, the returning-stroke, as it is called; when the earth, being overcharged with the **fluid**, flashes its **surplus** upward."

"The returning-stroke; that is, from earth to **sky**. Better and better. But come here on the hearth and **dry** yourself."

"I am better here, and better wet."

Italian

alarming: allarmante.
attic: soffitta, attico.
cellar: cantina.
cessation: cessazione.
chimney: camino, fumaiolo.
choose: scegliere, scegli, scegliamo, scegliete, scelgo, scelgono, eleggere, eleggete, eleggi, eleggiamo, eleggo.
comparative: comparativo.
dry: secco, seccare, asciutto, essiccare, asciugare.
flash: lampo, lampeggiatore, flash,

lampeggiare, scintillare, balenare, baleno.
fluid: fluido, liquido.
hearth: focolare.
hence: da qui, quindi.
hither: qui, quà.
inspired: ispirato.
lightning: fulmine, baleno, lampo.
obviously: ovviamente, evidentemente.
opinion: parere, opinione, avviso.
relieved: alleviato.

safest: il più sicuro.
sky: cielo.
spot: luogo, macchia, punto, posto, spot, macchiare.
storm: tempesta, burrasca, temporale, bufera.
strangely: stranamente.
strike: picchiare, colpire, battere, sciopero, scioperare, fare sciopero.
surplus: eccedenza, surplus, eccedente, avanzo, eccesso.
thunder: tuono, tuonare.

"How?"

"It is the safest thing you can do—Hark, again!—to get yourself **thoroughly** drenched in a thunder-storm. Wet **clothes** are better conductors than the body; and so, if the lightning strike, it might pass down the wet clothes without touching the body. The storm **deepens** again. Have you a rug in the house? Rugs are non-conductors. Get one, that I may stand on it here, and you, too. The skies blacken—it is dusk at noon. Hark!—the rug, the rug!"

I gave him one; while the hooded mountains seemed closing and **tumbling** into the cottage.

"And now, since our being **dumb** will not help us," said I, resuming my place, "let me **hear** your precautions in **traveling** during thunder-storms."

"Wait till this one is passed."

"Nay, proceed with the precautions. You stand in the safest possible place according to your own account. Go on."

"Briefly, then. I avoid pine-trees, high **houses**, lonely barns, upland pastures, **running** water, flocks of **cattle** and **sheep**, a crowd of men. If I travel on foot—as to-day—I do not walk **fast**; if in my **buggy**, I touch not its back or sides; if on **horseback**, I **dismount** and lead the horse. But of all things, I avoid tall men."

"Do I dream? Man avoid man? and in danger-time, too."

"Tall men in a thunder-storm I avoid. Are you so grossly ignorant as not to know, that the height of a six-footer is **sufficient** to discharge an **electric** cloud upon him? Are not lonely Kentuckians, **ploughing**, smit in the **unfinished furrow**? Nay, if the six-footer stand by running water, the cloud will sometimes *select* him as its conductor to that running water. Hark! **Sure**, yon black **pinnacle** is **split**. Yes, a man is a good conductor. The lightning goes through and through a man, but only peels a tree. But **sir**, you have kept me so long answering your questions, that I have not yet come to business. Will you order one of my rods? Look at this specimen one? See: it is of the best of copper. Copper's the best conductor. Your house is low; but being upon the mountains, that **lowness** does not one **whit depress** it. You mountaineers are most exposed. In mountainous

Italian

buggy: carrozzino, calesse, carrello, calessino.
cattle: bovini, bestiame.
clothes: veste, vestiti.
deepens: approfondisce.
depress: deprimere.
dismount: scendere, scendete, scendi, scendiamo, scendo, scendono, smontare.
dumb: muto.
electric: elettrico.
fast: veloce, digiuno, velocemente,

presto, digiunare, rapido.
furrow: solco, solcare.
hear: udire, odono, odi, odo, udite, udiamo, sentire, sentono, sento, sentite, senti.
horse: cavallo, il cavallo.
horseback: groppa, dorso del cavallo.
houses: case.
lowness: bassezza.
pinnacle: pinnacolo.
ploughing: aratura.
running: correndo, funzionamento,

scorrendo, corsa, marcia, corrente.
sheep: pecora, la pecora.
sir: signore.
split: fendere, fessura, spaccato, dividere, spaccare.
sufficient: sufficiente.
sure: certo, sicuro.
thoroughly: completamente.
traveling: viaggiando, viaggiare.
tumbling: voltolamento, cadere.
unfinished: incompiuto.
whit: briciolo.

countries the lightning-rod man should have most business. Look at the specimen, sir. One rod will answer for a house so small as this. Look over these **recommendations**. Only one rod, sir; cost, only twenty dollars. Hark! There go all the **granite** Taconics and Hoosics dashed together like **pebbles**. By the sound, that must have struck something. An elevation of five feet above the house, will protect twenty feet **radius** all about the rod. Only twenty dollars, sir—a dollar a foot. Hark!—Dreadful!—Will you order? Will you buy? Shall I put down your name? Think of being a heap of charred **offal**, like a haltered horse **burnt** in his **stall**; and all in one flash!"

"You pretended **envoy** extraordinary and minister **plenipotentiary** to and from Jupiter Tonans," laughed I; "you mere man who come here to put you and your pipestem between **clay** and sky, do you think that because you can strike a bit of green light from the Leyden **jar**, that you can thoroughly **avert** the supernal bolt? Your rod **rusts**, or breaks, and where are you? Who has **empowered** you, you Tetzel, to **peddle** round your indulgences from **divine** ordinations? The hairs of our heads are **numbered**, and the days of our lives. In thunder as in sunshine, I stand at ease in the hands of my God. False **negotiator**, away! See, the **scroll** of the storm is rolled back; the house is unharmed; and in the blue heavens I read in the rainbow, that the Deity will not, of purpose, make war on man's earth."

"Impious wretch!" **foamed** the stranger, blackening in the face as the rainbow **beamed**, "I will **publish** your **infidel** notions."

The **scowl** grew blacker on his face; the indigo-circles **enlarged** round his eyes as the storm-rings round the midnight moon. He sprang upon me; his tri-forked thing at my heart.

I seized it; I snapped it; I dashed it; I trod it; and **dragging** the dark lightning-king out of my door, flung his elbowed, copper **sceptre** after him.

But spite of my treatment, and spite of my dissuasive talk of him to my neighbors, the Lightning-rod man still **dwells** in the land; still travels in storm-time, and **drives** a brave trade with the fears of man.

Italian

avert: evitate, eviti, distogli, distogliete, evitiamo, evitano, evita, evito, distolgo, distogliamo, allontaniamo.
beamed: irradiato.
burnt: bruciato.
clay: argilla, creta.
divine: divino.
dragging: trascinando.
drives: comanda, guida, sospinge, spinge.
dwells: abita, dimora.

empowered: autorizzato.
enlarged: ingrandito, ampliato.
envoy: inviato.
foamed: espanso.
granite: granito.
infidel: miscredente, infedele.
jar: giara, barattolo.
negotiator: negoziatore.
numbered: numerato.
offal: frattaglie.
pebbles: ciottoli.
peddle: vendere al minuto.

plenipotentiary: plenipotenziario.
publish: pubblicare, pubblicate, pubblichi, pubblichiamo, pubblica, pubblicano, pubblico.
radius: raggio, radio.
recommendations: raccomandazioni.
rusts: ruggine.
sceptre: scettro.
scowl: sguardo torvo, cipiglio, accigliarsi.
scroll: rotolo di pergamena, scorrere.
stall: stalla, bancarella.

THE ENCANTADAS, OR ENCHANTED ISLES
By Salvator R. Tarnmoor

SKETCH FIRST
THE ISLES AT LARGE

—"That may not be, said then the **ferryman**,
Least we unweeting hap to be fordonne;
For those same **islands seeming** now and than,
Are not firme land, **nor** any certein wonne,
But stragling plots which to and fro do ronne
In the **wide** waters; therefore are they hight
The Wandering Islands; therefore do them shonne;
For they have **oft** drawne many a wandring wight
Into most **deadly** daunger and **distressed plight**;
For whosoever once hath **fastened**
His **foot** thereon may never it **secure**
But wandreth **evermore** uncertein and unsure."

*   *   *   *   *

Italian

deadly: mortale.
distressed: afflitto.
evermore: sempre.
fastened: fissato.
ferryman: traghettatore.
foot: piede, base, il piede, zampa.
land: terra, atterrare, paese, terreno.
nor: ne.
oft: spesso.
plight: situazione critica.
secure: fissare, fissa, fissano, fissate,
  fissi, fissiamo, fisso, sicuro,

assicurare.
seeming: parendo, sembrando,
  sembrare.
wide: largo, vasto, ampio.

"Darke, dolefull, dreary, like a **greedy** grave,
  That still for **carrion** carcasses doth **crave**;
On top whereof ay dwelt the **ghastly owl**,
Shrieking his balefull note, which ever drave
Far from that haunt all other **cheerful** fowl,
And all about it wandring ghosts did wayle and howl."

Take five-and-twenty heaps of **cinders** dumped here and there in an outside city lot; imagine some of them **magnified** into mountains, and the vacant lot the sea; and you will have a fit idea of the general aspect of the Encantadas, or Enchanted Isles. A group rather of extinct volcanoes than of isles; looking much as the world at large might, after a **penal** conflagration.

It is to be doubted whether any spot of earth can, in desolateness, furnish a **parallel** to this group. Abandoned cemeteries of long ago, old **cities** by **piecemeal** tumbling to their ruin, these are melancholy enough; but, like all else which has but once been **associated** with humanity, they still awaken in us some thoughts of sympathy, however sad. Hence, even the Dead Sea, along with **whatever** other emotions it may at times **inspire**, does not fail to touch in the **pilgrim** some of his less unpleasurable feelings.

And as for solitariness; the great forests of the north, the expanses of unnavigated waters, the Greenland **ice**-fields, are the profoundest of solitudes to a human observer; still the magic of their **changeable tides** and seasons **mitigates** their terror; because, though unvisited by men, those forests are visited by the May; the remotest seas reflect familiar stars even as Lake Erie does; and in the clear air of a fine Polar day, the **irradiated**, azure ice shows **beautifully** as **malachite**.

But the special **curse**, as one may call it, of the Encantadas, that which **exalts** them in **desolation** above Idumea and the Pole, is, that to them change never comes; neither the change of seasons nor of sorrows. Cut by the Equator, they know not **autumn**, and they know not **spring**; while already reduced to the lees of fire, ruin itself can work little more upon them. The showers refresh the

Italian

associated: cointeressato.	imprecazione.	**malachite**: malachite.
autumn: autunno, l'autunno.	**desolation**: desolazione, devastazione.	**mitigates**: mitiga.
beautifully: bellamente,	**exalts**: esalta.	**owl**: gufo, civetta.
magnificamente.	**ghastly**: orribile, orrendo, sgradevole,	**parallel**: parallelo.
carrion: carogna.	spiacevole, abominevole.	**penal**: penale.
changeable: variabile, mutevole.	**greedy**: avido, bramoso, goloso,	**piecemeal**: frammentario.
cheerful: allegro.	ghiotto, ingordo.	**pilgrim**: pellegrino.
cinders: cenere.	**ice**: ghiaccio, glassare.	**spring**: molla, sorgente, primavera,
cities: città.	**inspire**: ispirare, ispira, ispirate, ispiri,	fonte, saltare, la primavera.
crave: bramare.	ispiro, ispirano, ispiriamo.	**tides**: marea.
curse: bestemmiare, maledire,	**irradiated**: irradiato.	**whatever**: qualunque, qualsiasi cosa,
imprecare, maledizione,	**magnified**: ingigantito, ingrandito.	qualunque cosa.

deserts; but in these isles, rain never falls. Like split Syrian gourds left **withering** in the sun, they are cracked by an everlasting drought beneath a **torrid** sky. "Have mercy upon me," the wailing spirit of the Encantadas seems to cry, "and send Lazarus that he may dip the tip of his finger in water and cool my tongue, for I am tormented in this flame."

Another feature in these isles is their **emphatic** uninhabitableness. It is deemed a fit type of all-forsaken overthrow, that the **jackal** should den in the **wastes** of weedy Babylon; but the Encantadas refuse to harbor even the outcasts of the beasts. Man and wolf alike **disown** them. Little but **reptile** life is here found: tortoises, **lizards**, immense spiders, snakes, and that strangest **anomaly** of **outlandish** nature, the *aguano*. No voice, no low, no **howl** is heard; the chief sound of life here is a hiss.

On most of the isles where vegetation is found at all, it is more ungrateful than the blankness of Aracama. **Tangled** thickets of **wiry** bushes, without fruit and without a name, springing up among deep fissures of **calcined** rock, and **treacherously masking** them; or a parched growth of distorted **cactus** trees.

In many places the coast is rock-bound, or, more properly, clinker-bound; tumbled masses of **blackish** or greenish stuff like the **dross** of an iron-furnace, forming dark clefts and caves here and there, into which a ceaseless sea pours a fury of foam; overhanging them with a **swirl** of gray, haggard mist, **amidst** which sail screaming flights of **unearthly** birds **heightening** the dismal din. However calm the sea without, there is no rest for these swells and those rocks; they **lash** and are lashed, even when the outer ocean is most at peace with, itself. On the **oppressive**, **clouded** days, such as are peculiar to this part of the **watery** Equator, the dark, vitrified masses, many of which raise themselves among white whirlpools and breakers in detached and perilous places off the shore, present a most Plutonian sight. In no world but a fallen one could such lands exist.

Those parts of the strand free from the marks of fire, stretch away in wide level beaches of **multitudinous** dead shells, with here and there **decayed** bits of sugar-cane, bamboos, and cocoanuts, washed upon this other and darker world from the charming palm isles to the westward and **southward**; all the way from

Italian

amidst: tra, fra.
anomaly: anomalia.
blackish: nerastro.
cactus: cactus.
calcined: calcinato.
clouded: annuvolato.
decayed: decrepito.
disown: rinnegano, ripudiate, ripudiano, ripudiamo, ripudia, ripudi, rinnego, rinneghiamo, rinnegate, rinnega, disconoscono.
dross: scoria.

emphatic: enfatico.
heightening: innalzando.
howl: muggire, ululare, ululato, urlare.
jackal: sciacallo.
lash: sferza, frusta.
lizards: lucertole.
masking: mascheramento.
multitudinous: innumerevole.
oppressive: oppressivo.
outlandish: inconsueto, esotico, straniero, strano, bizzarro.

reptile: rettile.
southward: verso sud.
swirl: vortice, turbinare, turbine.
tangled: aggrovigliato.
torrid: torrido.
treacherously: traditormente.
unearthly: misterioso, soprannaturale, non terreno.
wastes: spreca.
watery: acquoso.
wiry: di filo metallico.
withering: avvizzimento, appassendo.

Paradise to Tartarus; while mixed with the relics of distant **beauty** you will
sometimes see fragments of charred **wood** and mouldering ribs of wrecks.
Neither will any one be surprised at meeting these last, after observing the
conflicting **currents** which **eddy** throughout **nearly** all the wide **channels** of the
entire group. The capriciousness of the tides of air **sympathizes** with those of the
sea. **Nowhere** is the wind so light, baffling, and every way **unreliable**, and so
given to perplexing calms, as at the Encantadas. Nigh a month has been **spent** by
a ship going from one isle to another, though but **ninety** miles between; for
owing to the force of the current, the boats employed to **tow** barely suffice to
keep the craft from sweeping upon the cliffs, but do nothing towards
accelerating her voyage. Sometimes it is impossible for a vessel from **afar** to fetch
up with the group itself, **unless** large allowances for **prospective** lee-way have
been made ere its coming in sight. And yet, at other times, there is a mysterious
indraft, which irresistibly draws a passing vessel among the isles, though not
bound to them.

True, at one period, as to some **extent** at the present day, large fleets of
whalemen cruised for **spermaceti** upon what some seamen call the Enchanted
Ground. But this, as in due place will be **described**, was off the great outer isle of
Albemarle, away from the intricacies of the **smaller** isles, where there is **plenty** of
sea-room; and hence, to that vicinity, the above remarks do not altogether **apply**;
though even there the current **runs** at times with singular force, shifting, too,
with as singular a caprice.

Indeed, there are seasons when currents quite unaccountable **prevail** for a
great distance round about the total group, and are so strong and irregular as to
change a vessel's course against the helm, though sailing at the rate of four or
five miles the hour. The **difference** in the reckonings of navigators, produced by
these causes, along with the light and **variable** winds, long **nourished** a
persuasion, that there **existed** two **distinct** clusters of isles in the parallel of the
Encantadas, about a hundred leagues apart. Such was the idea of their earlier
visitors, the Buccaneers; and as late as 1750, the charts of that part of the Pacific
accorded with the strange **delusion**. And this apparent fleetingness and

Italian

accelerating: accelerando.
accorded: accordato.
afar: lontano.
apply: applicare, applico, applichi, applicano, applicate, applichiamo, applica.
beauty: bellezza.
channels: canali.
current: corrente, attuale.
delusion: illusione.
described: descritto.
difference: differenza.

distinct: distinto.
eddy: gorgo, vortice, mulinello.
existed: esistito.
extent: limite.
nearly: quasi.
ninety: novanta.
nourished: alimentato, nutrito.
nowhere: in nessun luogo, da nessuna parte.
plenty: abbondanza, affluenza, molto.
prevail: prevalere, prevalete, prevalgo, prevalgono, prevali, prevaliamo.

prospective: potenziale.
runs: corre, scorre.
smaller: minore, più piccolo.
spent: speso, passato.
spermaceti: bianco di balena, spermaceti.
sympathizes: compatisce, simpatizza.
tow: rimorchiare, trainare, rimorchio.
unless: a meno che, eccetto che.
unreliable: inattendibile.
variable: variabile.
wood: legno, bosco, selva, legna.

unreality of the **locality** of the isles was most probably one reason for the Spaniards calling them the Encantada, or Enchanted Group.

But not uninfluenced by their character, as they now confessedly **exist**, the modern voyager will be inclined to **fancy** that the **bestowal** of this name might have in part **originated** in that air of spell-bound desertness which so **significantly invests** the isles. Nothing can better suggest the aspect of once living things malignly **crumbled** from ruddiness into ashes. Apples of Sodom, after touching, seem these isles.

However **wavering** their place may seem by reason of the currents, they themselves, at least to one upon the shore, appear invariably the same: fixed, cast, glued into the very body of cadaverous death.

Nor would the **appellation**, enchanted, seem misapplied in still another sense. For concerning the peculiar reptile **inhabitant** of these wilds—whose presence gives the group its second Spanish name, Gallipagos—concerning the tortoises found here, most mariners have long **cherished** a superstition, not more **frightful** than grotesque. They earnestly believe that all wicked sea-officers, more especially commodores and captains, are at death (and, in some cases, before death) **transformed** into tortoises; thenceforth **dwelling** upon these **hot** aridities, **sole** solitary lords of Asphaltum.

Doubtless, so quaintly dolorous a thought was **originally** inspired by the woe-begone landscape itself; but more particularly, perhaps, by the tortoises. For, apart from their strictly physical features, there is something strangely self-condemned in the appearance of these creatures. **Lasting** sorrow and penal hopelessness are in no **animal** form so suppliantly expressed as in theirs; while the thought of their **wonderful longevity** does not fail to enhance the impression.

Nor even at the risk of **meriting** the charge of absurdly **believing** in enchantments, can I restrain the admission that sometimes, even now, when leaving the **crowded** city to wander out July and August among the Adirondack Mountains, far from the **influences** of towns and **proportionally** nigh to the mysterious ones of nature; when at such times I sit me down in the mossy head of some deep-wooded gorge, **surrounded** by prostrate trunks of **blasted** pines

Italian

animal: animale, bestia, l'animale.
appellation: nome, appellativo.
believing: credendo, credere.
bestowal: concessione.
blasted: maledetto.
cherished: adorato.
crowded: affollato.
crumbled: sbriciolato, sgretolato.
dwelling: dimorando, abitando, dimora, abitazione.
exist: esistere, esisto, esistono, esisti, esistete, esistiamo.

fancy: figurarsi, capriccio, immaginazione.
frightful: spaventevole.
hot: caldo, piccante.
influences: influenza.
inhabitant: abitante.
invests: investe.
lasting: durevole, duraturo, permanente, continuo.
longevity: longevità.
meriting: meritare.

originally: originalmente.
originated: disceso.
proportionally: proporzionalmente.
significantly: significativamente.
sole: sogliola, solo, suola, pianta, unico.
surrounded: circondato.
transformed: trasformato.
unreality: irrealtà.
wavering: esitando.
wonderful: meraviglioso, stupendo, splendido.

and recall, as in a dream, my other and far-distant rovings in the **baked** heart of
the charmed isles; and **remember** the sudden glimpses of **dusky** shells, and long
languid necks **protruded** from the **leafless** thickets; and again have **beheld** the
vitreous inland rocks worn down and **grooved** into **deep** ruts by ages and ages
of the slow draggings of **tortoises** in quest of **pools** of **scanty** water; I can **hardly**
resist the feeling that in my time I have indeed slept upon **evilly** enchanted
ground.

Nay, such is the vividness of my memory, or the magic of my fancy, that I
know not whether I am not the occasional **victim** of **optical delusion** concerning
the Gallipagos. For, often in scenes of social **merriment**, and **especially** at revels
held by candle-light in old-fashioned mansions, so that shadows are thrown into
the further recesses of an **angular** and spacious room, making them put on a look
of haunted **undergrowth** of lonely woods, I have drawn the **attention** of my
comrades by my fixed gaze and sudden change of air, as I have seemed to see,
slowly emerging from those imagined solitudes, and heavily crawling **along** the
floor, the ghost of a gigantic tortoise, with "Memento * * * * *" **burning** in **live**
letters upon his back.

SKETCH SECOND
Two Sides to a Tortoise

"Most ugly shapes and horrible aspects,
   Such as Dame Nature selfe mote feare to see,
   Or shame, that ever should so fowle defects
   From her most **cunning** hand escaped **bee**;
   All dreadfull pourtraicts of deformitee.
   No wonder if these do a man **appall**;
   For all that here at home we dreadfull hold
   Be but as bugs to fearen **babes** withall

Italian

along: lungo.
angular: angolare.
appall: atterrisci, atterrite, atterrisco, atterriamo, atterriscono, atterrire.
attention: attenzione.
babes: pupe, bambole.
baked: cotto.
bee: ape, l'ape.
beheld: guardato.
burning: bruciare, bruciatura.
cunning: astuzia, astuto, furbo.
deep: profondo, fondo, intenso, cupo.

delusion: illusione.
dusky: tetro.
especially: soprattutto, specialmente, principalmente.
evilly: malvagiamente.
grooved: scanalato.
hardly: appena, a malapena, a stento.
leafless: sfrondato.
letters: lettere.
live: vivere, vivete, vivono, viviamo, vivi, vivo, abitare, abiti, abita, abitano, abitate.

merriment: allegria.
optical: ottico.
pools: piscina, totocalcio.
protruded: sporto.
remember: ricordare, ricordiamo, ricorda, ricordano, ricordate, ricordi, ricordo.
scanty: scarso.
tortoise: tartaruga.
undergrowth: sottobosco, boscaglia.
victim: vittima.
vitreous: vitreo.

Compared to the creatures in these isles' **enthrall**

*   *   *   *   *

"Fear **naught**, then said the palmer, well avized,
For these same monsters are not there indeed,
But are into these fearful shapes disguized.

*   *   *   *   *

"And **lifting** up his vertuous staffe on high,
Then all that dreadful armie fast gan flye
Into great Zethy's bosom, where they hidden lye."

In view of the description given, may one be gay upon the Encantadas? Yes:
that is, find one the gayety, and he will be gay. And, indeed, **sackcloth** and ashes
as they are, the isles are not perhaps **unmitigated** gloom. For while no spectator
can **deny** their **claims** to a most solemn and superstitious **consideration**, no more
than my firmest resolutions can **decline** to behold the spectre-tortoise when
emerging from its shadowy **recess**; yet even the tortoise, dark and melancholy as
it is upon the back, still **possesses** a bright side; its calipee or breast-plate being
sometimes of a faint **yellowish** or golden tinge. Moreover, every one knows that
tortoises as well as **turtle** are of such a make, that if you but put them on their
backs you **thereby expose** their bright sides without the **possibility** of their
recovering themselves, and turning into view the other. But after you have done
this, and because you have done this, you should not **swear** that the tortoise has
no dark side. **Enjoy** the bright, keep it turned up **perpetually** if you can, but be
honest, and don't deny the black. Neither should he, who cannot turn the
tortoise from its natural position so as to **hide** the darker and expose his livelier
aspect, like a great October **pumpkin** in the **sun**, for that cause declare the
creature to be one total **inky** blot. The tortoise is both black and bright. But let us
to particulars.

Italian

claims: rivendicazioni.
consideration: corrispettivo, considerazione.
decline: declinare, declino, deperire, peggiorare, ribasso, regressione.
deny: negare, negate, negano, neghi, neghiamo, nego, nega.
enjoy: fruire, godere.
enthrall: affascinare, affascino, affascina, affascinano, affascinate, affascini, affasciniamo, incantare.
expose: esporre, esponete, espongo,

espongono, esponi, esponiamo.
hide: nascondere, nascondo, nascondiamo, nascondono, nascondete, nascondi, pelle, nascondersi, pellame, celare, occultare.
inky: sporco d'inchiostro.
lifting: sollevamento, sollevare.
naught: nulla, zero.
perpetually: perennemente, perpetuamente.
possesses: possiede.

possibility: possibilità, eventualità.
pumpkin: zucca, la zucca.
recess: recesso, alcova, rientranza.
sackcloth: tela di sacco.
sun: sole.
swear: giurare, giura, giuro, giuriamo, giuri, giurano, giurate, bestemmiare, imprecare.
thereby: con ciò.
turtle: tartaruga.
unmitigated: non mitigato.
yellowish: giallastro.

Some months before my first stepping ashore upon the group, my ship was cruising in its close vicinity. One noon we found **ourselves** off the South Head of Albemarle, and not very far from the land. **Partly** by way of freak, and partly by way of spying out so strange a country, a boat's crew was sent ashore, with orders to see all they could, and besides, bring back whatever tortoises they could **conveniently** transport.

It was after sunset, when the adventurers returned. I looked down over the ship's high side as if looking down over the **curb** of a well, and dimly saw the **damp** boat, deep in the sea with some unwonted weight. Ropes were dropt over, and presently three huge antediluvian-looking tortoises, after much straining, were landed on deck. They seemed hardly of the **seed** of earth. We had been broad upon the waters for five long months, a period **amply** sufficient to make all things of the land **wear** a **fabulous** hue to the dreamy mind. Had three Spanish custom-house officers boarded us then, it is not unlikely that I should have curiously stared at them, felt of them, and stroked them much as savages serve civilized guests. But instead of three custom-house officers, behold these really wondrous tortoises — none of your **schoolboy** mud-turtles — but black as widower's weeds, heavy as chests of **plate**, with vast shells medallioned and orbed like **shields**, and dented and blistered like shields that have breasted a **battle**, shaggy, too, here and there, with dark green moss, and **slimy** with the spray of the sea. These **mystic** creatures, suddenly translated by night from **unutterable** solitudes to our peopled deck, affected me in a manner not easy to **unfold**. They seemed newly **crawled** forth from beneath the foundations of the world. **Yea**, they seemed the **identical** tortoises whereon the Hindoo plants this total **sphere**. With a **lantern** I **inspected** them more **closely**. Such **worshipful** venerableness of aspect! Such **furry** greenness mantling the rude **peelings** and healing the fissures of their **shattered** shells. I no more saw three tortoises. They expanded — became **transfigured**. I seemed to see three Roman Coliseums in **magnificent decay**.

Ye oldest **inhabitants** of this, or any other isle, said I, pray, give me the **freedom** of your three-walled towns.

Italian

amply: ampiamente.
battle: battaglia, combattimento.
closely: attentamente.
conveniently: convenientemente, utilmente, comodamente.
crawled: strisciato.
curb: barbazzale, tenere a freno, freno.
damp: umido.
decay: decadimento, carie, decadere.
fabulous: favoloso.
freedom: libertà.
furry: di pelliccia.

identical: identico.
inhabitants: fruitori della casa.
inspected: ispezionato.
lantern: lanterna.
magnificent: magnifico.
mystic: mistico.
ourselves: ci.
partly: in parte, parzialmente.
peelings: buccia.
plate: piatto, lastra, piastra, placca, lamiera, targa.
schoolboy: scolaro.

seed: seme, seminare, germe.
shattered: frantumato.
shields: schermi.
slimy: limaccioso, fangoso.
sphere: sfera.
transfigured: trasfigurato.
unfold: spiegare.
unutterable: inesprimibile.
wear: portare, usura, logoramento, indossare.
worshipful: venerabile.
ye: voi, tu.

The great feeling inspired by these creatures was that of age: — dateless, indefinite **endurance**. And in fact that any other creature can live and breathe as long as the tortoise of the Encantadas, I will not readily believe. Not to hint of their known capacity of sustaining life, while going without food for an entire year, consider that **impregnable armor** of their living mail. What other bodily being possesses such a **citadel** wherein to resist the assaults of Time?

As, lantern in hand, I **scraped** among the moss and beheld the ancient scars of bruises received in many a sullen fall among the marly mountains of the isle — scars strangely **widened**, **swollen**, half **obliterate**, and yet **distorted** like those sometimes found in the **bark** of very **hoary** trees, I seemed an **antiquary** of a **geologist**, studying the bird-tracks and ciphers upon the **exhumed** slates trod by incredible creatures whose very ghosts are now defunct.

As I lay in my hammock that night, overhead I heard the slow weary draggings of the three **ponderous** strangers along the **encumbered** deck. Their stupidity or their resolution was so great, that they never went aside for any **impediment**. One ceased his movements altogether just before the mid-watch. At sunrise I found him butted like a battering-ram against the immovable foot of the **foremast**, and still **striving**, **tooth** and **nail**, to force the impossible passage. That these tortoises are the victims of a penal, or malignant, or perhaps a **downright** diabolical **enchanter**, seems in nothing more likely than in that strange **infatuation** of hopeless **toil** which so often possesses them. I have known them in their journeyings **ram** themselves **heroically** against rocks, and long abide there, nudging, wriggling, wedging, in order to **displace** them, and so hold on their inflexible path. Their **crowning** curse is their drudging impulse to **straightforwardness** in a belittered world.

Meeting with no such hinderance as their companion did, the other tortoises merely fell foul of small stumbling-blocks — buckets, blocks, and coils of rigging — and at times in the act of crawling over them would slip with an **astounding rattle** to the deck. Listening to these draggings and concussions, I thought me of the haunt from which they came; an isle full of metallic ravines and gulches, sunk bottomlessly into the hearts of splintered mountains, and

Italian

antiquary: antiquario.
armor: armatura, corazza.
astounding: sbalorditivo.
bark: corteccia, abbaiare, scorza, latrare, abbaio.
citadel: cittadella.
crowning: corona, supremo.
displace: spostare, spostiamo, sposto, sposti, spostate, spostano, sposta.
distorted: falsato, distorto.
downright: completamente, schietto.
enchanter: mago, incantatore.

encumbered: ingombrato, gravato.
endurance: resistenza, pazienza.
exhumed: esumato, riesumato.
foremast: albero di trinchetto.
geologist: geologo.
heroically: eroicamente.
hoary: pruinoso, canuto, canescente.
impediment: impedimento, ostacolo.
impregnable: inespugnabile.
infatuation: infatuazione.
nail: chiodo, unghia, inchiodare.
obliterate: cancellare, cancellano,

cancellate, cancelli, cancelliamo, cancello, cancella, obliterare.
ponderous: pesante, ponderoso.
ram: montone, ariete.
rattle: sonaglio, rantolo.
scraped: raschiato.
straightforwardness: schiettezza.
striving: sforzandosi.
swollen: gonfio.
toil: faticare, fatica, duro lavoro.
tooth: dente, il dente.
widened: allargato.

covered for many miles with **inextricable** thickets. I then pictured these three straight-forward monsters, century after century, writhing through the shades, **grim** as blacksmiths; crawling so slowly and ponderously, that not only did toad-stools and all **fungus** things **grow** beneath their **feet**, but a sooty moss **sprouted** upon their backs. With them I **lost** myself in **volcanic** mazes; brushed away endless boughs of rotting thickets; till finally in a dream I found myself sitting crosslegged upon the foremost, a Brahmin **similarly** mounted upon either side, forming a **tripod** of foreheads which **upheld** the **universal** cope.

Such was the **wild nightmare** begot by my first impression of the Encantadas tortoise. But next evening, strange to say, I sat down with my shipmates, and made a **merry** repast from tortoise steaks, and tortoise stews; and **supper** over, out knife, and **helped convert** the three **mighty concave** shells into three fanciful soup-tureens, and polished the three **flat** yellowish calipees into three **gorgeous** salvers.

SKETCH THIRD
ROCK RODONDO

"For they this **tight** the Rock of vile Reproach,
　　A dangerous and dreadful place,
　　To which nor fish nor fowl did once approach,
　　But yelling meaws with sea-gulls hoars and bace
　　And cormoyrants with birds of **ravenous race**,
　　Which still sit waiting on that dreadful clift."

　　　　*　　*　　*　　*　　*

"With that the rolling sea **resounding soft**
　　In his big **base** them fitly answered,
　　And on the Rock, the waves **breaking** aloft,

Italian

base: base, basare, fondare, zoccolo, basamento.
breaking: rottura.
concave: cavo, concavo.
convert: convertito, convertire.
feet: piedi.
flat: piano, appartamento, piatto, bemolle.
fungus: fungo.
gorgeous: magnifico, bellissimo.
grim: torvo, truce.
grow: crescere, crescete, crescono,
cresco, cresci, cresciamo, coltivare, coltiviamo, coltivo, coltivi, coltivate.
helped: aiutato.
inextricable: inestricabile.
lost: perso, perduto, smarrito.
merry: allegro, festoso, gaio.
mighty: poderoso, forte, possente, potente.
nightmare: incubo.
race: razza, corsa, correre.
ravenous: vorace.
resounding: risuonando, echeggiando,
riecheggiando, risonante, clamoroso.
similarly: similmente.
soft: dolce, molle, soffice, morbido, tenero.
sprouted: germogliato.
supper: cena.
tight: stretto, impermeabile.
tripod: treppiedi, tripode, treppiede.
universal: universale.
upheld: sostenuto.
volcanic: vulcanico.
wild: selvaggio, feroce, selvatico.

A solemn ineane unto them measured."

*   *   *   *   *

"Then he the boteman bad **row** easily,
And let him heare some part of that **rare** melody."

*   *   *   *   *

"Suddeinly an **innumerable flight**
Of harmefull fowles about them fluttering cride,
And with their wicked wings them oft did smight
And sore annoyed, groping in that griesly night."

*   *   *   *   *

"Even all the **nation** of unfortunate
And fatal birds about them **flocked** were."

To go up into a high **stone tower** is not only a very fine thing in itself, but the
very best mode of gaining a **comprehensive** view of the **region** round about. It is
all the better if this tower stand solitary and alone, like that mysterious Newport
one, or else be sole survivor of some perished **castle**.

Now, with **reference** to the Enchanted Isles, we are **fortunately supplied**
with just such a noble point of observation in a remarkable **rock**, from its
peculiar figure called of old by the Spaniards, Rock Rodondo, or Round Rock.
Some two hundred and **fifty** feet high, rising **straight** from the sea ten miles from
land, with the whole **mountainous** group to the south and **east**. Rock Rodondo
occupies, on a large **scale**, very much the position which the **famous** Campanile
or detached Bell Tower of St. Mark does with **respect** to the tangled group of
hoary edifices around it.

Ere **ascending**, however, to gaze **abroad** upon the Encantadas, this sea-tower
itself claims attention. It is visible at the distance of **thirty** miles; and, **fully**
participating in that enchantment which **pervades** the group, when first seen afar

Italian

abroad: all'estero, fuori.
ascending: salendo, ascendente,
  ascendendo.
castle: castello, torre.
comprehensive: comprensivo.
east: est, levante, orientale.
famous: famoso, rinomato, celebre.
fifty: cinquanta.
flight: volo, fuga.
flocked: affollato.
fortunately: fortunatamente, per
  fortuna.

fully: completamente, pienamente.
hoary: pruinoso, canuto, canescente.
innumerable: innumerevole.
mountainous: montagnoso,
  montuoso.
nation: nazione, popolo.
occupies: occupa.
pervades: pervade.
rare: raro, al sangue.
reference: riferimento, referenza.
region: regione, zona.
respect: rispettare, rispetto, stima.

rock: roccia, masso, cullare, dondolare,
  ondeggiare.
row: fila, riga, remare, filare.
scale: squama, scala, bilancia, scaglia,
  gamma, scalare.
stone: pietra, calcolo, sasso, la pietra,
  ciottolo.
straight: diritto, destro, dritto,
  direttamente.
supplied: fornito.
thirty: trenta.
tower: torre.

invariably is mistaken for a sail. Four leagues away, of a golden, hazy noon, it seems some Spanish Admiral's ship, **stacked** up with glittering canvas. Sail ho! Sail ho! Sail ho! from all three masts. But coming nigh, the enchanted **frigate** is transformed **apace** into a craggy keep.

My first visit to the spot was made in the gray of the morning. With a view of fishing, we had lowered three boats and pulling some two miles from our vessel, found ourselves just before dawn of day close under the moon-shadow of Rodondo. Its aspect was heightened, and yet **softened**, by the strange double **twilight** of the hour. The great full moon burnt in the low west like a half-spent **beacon**, casting a soft **mellow** tinge upon the sea like that cast by a **waning** fire of **embers** upon a midnight hearth; while along the entire east the invisible sun sent pallid intimations of his coming. The wind was light; the waves languid; the stars **twinkled** with a faint effulgence; all nature seemed **supine** with the long night watch, and half-suspended in **jaded** expectation of the sun. This was the critical hour to catch Rodondo in his perfect mood. The twilight was just enough to reveal every **striking** point, without tearing away the dim **investiture** of wonder.

From a broken stair-like base, **washed**, as the steps of a water-palace, by the waves, the tower rose in entablatures of **strata** to a shaven summit. These **uniform** layers, which **compose** the mass, form its most peculiar feature. For at their lines of junction they project flatly into **encircling shelves**, from top to bottom, rising one above another in **graduated** series. And as the **eaves** of any old barn or abbey are alive with swallows, so were all these rocky ledges with **unnumbered** sea-fowl. Eaves upon eaves, and nests upon nests. Here and there were long birdlime streaks of a ghostly white staining the tower from sea to air, readily **accounting** for its sail-like look afar. All would have been bewitchingly quiescent, were it not for the **demoniac** din created by the birds. Not only were the eaves **rustling** with them, but they flew **densely** overhead, **spreading** themselves into a **winged** and continually shifting canopy. The tower is the resort of **aquatic** birds for hundreds of leagues around. To the north, to the east, to the west, stretches nothing but eternal ocean; so that the man-of-war **hawk** coming from the coasts of North America, Polynesia, or Peru, makes his first

Italian

accounting: contabilità, ragioneria, contabile.
apace: di buon passo.
aquatic: acquatico.
beacon: gavitello, boa, faro.
compose: comporre, componi, componiamo, compongo, compongono, componete.
demoniac: demoniaco.
densely: densamente.
eaves: gronda.
embers: brace.

encircling: circondando.
frigate: fregata.
graduated: laureato, graduato.
hawk: falco.
investiture: investitura.
jaded: spossato, affaticato.
mellow: maturo.
rustling: fruscio.
shelves: ripiani, scaffali.
softened: ammorbidito.
spreading: spandimento, spalmatura, propagazione.

stacked: accatastato.
strata: strati.
striking: impressionante.
supine: supino.
twilight: crepuscolo.
twinkled: scintillato, brillato, luccicato.
uniform: uniforme, divisa.
unnumbered: non numerato.
waning: declinando.
washed: lavato.
winged: alato.

land at Rodondo. And yet though Rodondo be terra-firma, no land-bird ever lighted on it. Fancy a red-robin or a **canary** there! What a falling into the hands of the Philistines, when the poor **warbler** should be surrounded by such locust-flights of strong **bandit birds**, with long bills **cruel** as daggers.

I know not where one can better study the Natural History of strange sea-fowl than at Rodondo. It is the **aviary** of Ocean. Birds light here which never touched **mast** or tree; hermit-birds, which ever **fly** alone; cloud-birds, familiar with unpierced zones of air.

Let us first glance low down to the lowermost shelf of all, which is the widest, too, and but a little space from high-water mark. What outlandish beings are these? **Erect** as men, but hardly as **symmetrical**, they stand all round the rock like sculptured caryatides, supporting the next range of eaves above. Their bodies are **grotesquely** misshapen; their bills short; their feet seemingly legless; while the members at their sides are neither **fin**, **wing**, nor arm. And **truly** neither fish, **flesh**, nor fowl is the **penguin**; as an **edible**, pertaining neither to Carnival nor Lent; without **exception** the most **ambiguous** and least lovely creature yet discovered by man. Though dabbling in all three elements, and indeed possessing some rudimental claims to all, the penguin is at home in none. On land it stumps; **afloat** it sculls; in the air it **flops**. As if ashamed of her **failure**, Nature **keeps** this **ungainly** child hidden away at the ends of the earth, in the Straits of Magellan, and on the **abased** sea-story of Rodondo.

But look, what are yon wobegone regiments drawn up on the next shelf above? what rank and file of large strange fowl? what sea Friars of Orders Gray? Pelicans. Their **elongated** bills, and heavy leathern pouches suspended **thereto**, give them the most **lugubrious** expression. A pensive race, they stand for hours together without motion. Their dull, **ashy plumage imparts** an aspect as if they had been **powdered** over with cinders. A **penitential** bird, indeed, fitly haunting the shores of the clinkered Encantadas, whereon tormented Job himself might have well sat down and scraped himself with potsherds.

Italian

abased: degradato.
afloat: a galla.
ambiguous: ambiguo, equivoco.
ashy: cinereo.
aviary: voliera, uccelliera.
bandit: bandito, brigante.
bird: uccello, l'uccello.
canary: canarino.
cruel: crudele.
edible: commestibile, mangiabile.
elongated: allungato.
erect: eretto, fondere, erigere, diritto,

alzare.
exception: eccezione.
failure: fallimento, guasto, avaria, insuccesso, fiasco, rottura.
fin: pinna, aletta, la pinna.
flesh: carne, polpa.
flops: flops.
fly: volare, voli, volate, voliamo, vola, volo, volano, mosca.
grotesquely: grottescamente.
imparts: impartisce.
keeps: osserva, conserva, trattiene.

lugubrious: lugubre.
mast: albero.
penguin: pinguino.
penitential: penitenziale.
plumage: piumaggio.
powdered: polvere, in polvere.
symmetrical: simmetrico.
thereto: in calce.
truly: davvero, infatti, veramente.
ungainly: sgraziato.
warbler: uccello canoro.
wing: ala, l'ala.

Higher up now we mark the gony, or gray **albatross**, anomalously so called, an unsightly unpoetic bird, unlike its storied **kinsman**, which is the snow-white ghost of the haunted Capes of Hope and Horn.

As we still **ascend** from shelf to shelf, we find the tenants of the tower **serially** disposed in order of their magnitude: — gannets, black and **speckled** haglets, jays, sea-hens, sperm-whale-birds, gulls of all varieties: — thrones, princedoms, powers, **dominating** one above another in senatorial array; while, **sprinkled** over all, like an ever-repeated fly in a great piece of broidery, the stormy petrel or Mother Cary's chicken sounds his continual challenge and alarm. That this mysterious **hummingbird** of ocean — which, had it but **brilliancy** of hue, might, from its **evanescent liveliness**, be almost called its **butterfly**, yet whose **chirrup** under the stern is ominous to mariners as to the **peasant** the death-tick sounding from behind the chimney jamb — should have its special haunt at the Encantadas, **contributes**, in the seaman's mind, not a little to their dreary spell.

As day **advances** the **dissonant** din **augments**. With ear-splitting cries the wild birds celebrate their **matins**. Each moment, flights push from the tower, and join the aerial **choir** hovering overhead, while their places below are supplied by darting myriads. But down through all this **discord** of **commotion**, I hear clear, silver, bugle-like notes **unbrokenly** falling, like **oblique** lines of swift-slanting rain in a cascading shower. I gaze far up, and behold a snow-white **angelic** thing, with one long, lance-like **feather** thrust out behind. It is the bright, inspiriting chanticleer of ocean, the beauteous bird, from its bestirring whistle of musical invocation, fitly styled the "Boatswain's Mate."

The winged, life-clouding Rodondo had its full **counterpart** in the finny hosts which peopled the waters at its base. Below the water-line, the rock seemed one honey-comb of grottoes, **affording labyrinthine** lurking-places for swarms of fairy fish. All were strange; many exceedingly beautiful; and would have well graced the costliest glass **globes** in which gold-fish are kept for a show. Nothing was more striking than the complete **novelty** of many individuals of this

Italian

advances: avanzamenti.
affording: permettendo.
albatross: albatro.
angelic: angelico.
ascend: salire, salgo, salite, saliamo, salgono, Sali, ascendere, ascendono, ascendo, ascendete, ascendi.
augments: ingrandisce, aumenta.
brilliancy: splendore.
butterfly: farfalla.
chirrup: cinguetta, cinguettano, cinguettate, cinguetti, cinguettiamo,
cinguetto, cinguettare.
choir: coro.
commotion: agitazione, commozione, scandalo, confusione.
contributes: contribuisce.
counterpart: controparte.
discord: disaccordo.
dissonant: dissonante.
dominating: dominando.
evanescent: evanescente.
feather: penna, piuma.
globes: globi.
hummingbird: colibrì.
kinsman: parente.
labyrinthine: labirintico.
liveliness: vivacità.
matins: mattutino.
novelty: novità.
oblique: obliquo.
peasant: contadino.
serially: in serie.
speckled: maculato.
sprinkled: spruzzato.
unbrokenly: intattamente.

multitude. Here hues were seen as yet unpainted, and figures which are unengraved.

To show the multitude, **avidity**, and **nameless** fearlessness and tameness of these fish, let me say, that often, marking through clear spaces of water — temporarily made so by the **concentric** dartings of the fish above the surface — certain **larger** and less **unwary** wights, which swam slow and deep; our anglers would **cautiously essay** to drop their **lines** down to these last. But in vain; there was no passing the uppermost **zone**. No sooner did the **hook** touch the sea, than a hundred infatuates **contended** for the honor of capture. Poor fish of Rodondo! in your **victimized** confidence, you are of the number of those who inconsiderately **trust**, while they do not understand, human nature.

But the dawn is now **fairly** day. Band after band, the sea-fowl sail away to **forage** the deep for their food. The tower is left solitary **save** the fish-caves at its base. Its birdlime gleams in the golden rays like the **whitewash** of a tall lighthouse, or the lofty sails of a **cruiser**. This moment, doubtless, while we know it to be a dead desert rock other voyagers are taking **oaths** it is a glad populous ship.

But ropes now, and let us ascend. Yet soft, this is not so easy.

SKETCH FOURTH
A PISGAH VIEW FROM THE ROCK

— "That done, he **leads** him to the **highest mount**,
From whence, far off he unto him did show:" —

If you seek to ascend Rock Rodondo, take the following **prescription**. Go three voyages round the world as a main-royal-man of the tallest frigate that floats; then serve a year or two **apprenticeship** to the **guides** who conduct strangers up the Peak of Teneriffe; and as many more **respectively** to a rope-dancer, an Indian **juggler**, and a **chamois**. This done, come and be rewarded by

Italian

apprenticeship: apprendistato.
avidity: avidità.
cautiously: prudentemente.
chamois: camoscio.
concentric: concentrico.
contended: conteso.
cruiser: incrociatore.
essay: saggio.
fairly: abbastanza, equamente.
forage: foraggio.
guides: guide.
highest: sommo.

hook: gancio, amo, uncino, agganciare, aggancio, arpione.
juggler: giocoliere.
larger: più grande.
leads: conduce, guida.
lines: linee.
mount: montare, montatura, supporto, monte, cavalcatura, affusto.
nameless: senza nome.
oaths: giuramenti.
prescription: prescrizione, ricetta, ricetta medica.

respectively: rispettivamente.
save: salvare, salvi, salviamo, salvate, salvano, salvo, salva, risparmiare, risparmiate, risparmiano, risparmiamo.
trust: fiducia, trust, confidenza, affidamento.
unwary: incauto.
victimized: perseguitato, immolato, sacrificato, vittimizzato.
whitewash: imbiancare.
zone: zona, fascia.

the view from our tower. How we get there, we alone know. If we sought to tell
others, what the wiser were they? Suffice it, that here at the **summit** you and I
stand. Does any **balloonist**, does the outlooking man in the moon, take a broader
view of **space**? Much thus, one fancies, **looks** the universe from Milton's **celestial**
battlements. A **boundless** watery Kentucky. Here Daniel Boone would have
dwelt content.

Never heed for the present **yonder** Burnt District of the Enchanted Isles. Look
edgeways, as it were, past them, to the south. You see nothing; but permit me to
point out the direction, if not the place, of certain **interesting objects** in the vast
sea, which, **kissing** this tower's base, we **behold** unscrolling itself towards the
Antarctic Pole.

We stand now ten miles from the Equator. Yonder, to the East, some six
hundred miles, lies the **continent**; this Rock being just about on the parallel of
Quito.

Observe another thing here. We are at one of three **uninhabited** clusters,
which, at pretty nearly uniform distances from the main, **sentinel**, at long
intervals from each other, the entire coast of South America. In a peculiar manner,
also, they terminate the South American **character** of country. Of the
unnumbered Polynesian chains to the **westward**, not one **partakes** of the
qualities of the Encantadas or Gallipagos, the isles of St. Felix and St. Ambrose,
the isles Juan-Fernandez and Massafuero. Of the first, it **needs** not here to speak.
The second lie a little above the Southern Tropic; lofty, **inhospitable**, and
uninhabitable rocks, one of which, presenting two round hummocks connected
by a low reef, **exactly resembles a huge** double-headed shot. The last lie in the
latitude of 33°; high, wild and **cloven**. Juan Fernandez is sufficiently famous
without further description. Massafuero is a Spanish name, expressive of the fact,
that the isle so called lies *more without*, that is, further off the main than its
neighbor Juan. This isle Massafuero has a very **imposing** aspect at a distance of
eight or ten miles. Approached in one direction, in cloudy weather, its great
overhanging height and **rugged contour**, and more especially a peculiar slope of
its broad summits, give it much the air of a vast **iceberg** drifting in tremendous

Italian

balloonist: aeronauta da pallone.	giustamente, precisamente.	**partakes**: partecipa.
behold: guardare.	**huge**: enorme, immenso.	**resembles**: rassomiglia.
boundless: illimitato.	**iceberg**: iceberg.	**rugged**: ruvido.
celestial: celeste, celestiale.	**imposing**: imponente, imponendo.	**sentinel**: sentinella.
character: carattere, natura, indole,	**inhospitable**: inospitale.	**space**: spazio, intervallo.
segno.	**interesting**: interessante.	**summit**: cima, punta, vertice, vetta,
cloven: spaccato, fesso.	**kissing**: baciare.	culmine, sommità.
continent: continente.	**latitude**: latitudine, latitudine di posa.	**uninhabitable**: inabitabile.
contour: contorno, profilo.	**looks**: guarda.	**uninhabited**: disabitato.
edgeways: di traverso.	**needs**: necessità, bisogno.	**unnumbered**: non numerato.
eight: otto.	**neighbor**: vicino.	**westward**: verso ovest.
exactly: esattamente, giusto,	**objects**: oggetti.	**yonder**: là, laggiù.

poise. Its sides are split with dark **cavernous** recesses, as an old **cathedral** with its gloomy lateral chapels. Drawing nigh one of these gorges from sea, after a long voyage, and **beholding** some tatterdemalion **outlaw**, staff in hand, descending its steep rocks toward you, **conveys** a very queer emotion to a lover of the picturesque.

On fishing parties from ships, at various times, I have chanced to visit each of these **groups**. The impression they give to the stranger pulling **close** up in his boat under their grim cliffs is, that surely he must be their first discoverer, such, for the most part, is the **unimpaired** ... silence and solitude. And here, by the way, the mode in which these isles were really first lighted upon by Europeans is not unworthy of mention, especially as what is about to be said, likewise **applies** to the original **discovery** of our Encantadas.

Prior to the year 1563, the voyages made by Spanish ships from Peru to Chili, were full of **difficulty**. Along this coast, the winds from the South most **generally** prevail; and it had been an invariable custom to keep close in with the land, from a superstitious **conceit** on the part of the Spaniards, that were they to lose sight of it, the eternal trade-wind would waft them into **unending** waters, from whence would be no return. Here, **involved** among **tortuous** capes and headlands, shoals and reefs, beating, too, against a continual head wind, often light, and sometimes for days and **weeks** sunk into **utter** calm, the **provincial** vessels, in many cases, **suffered** the extremest hardships, in passages, which at the present day seem to have been **incredibly protracted**. There is on record in some collections of **nautical** disasters, an account of one of these ships, which, starting on a voyage whose duration was **estimated** at ten days, spent four months at sea, and indeed never again entered harbor, for in the end she was cast away. Singular to tell, this craft never **encountered** a gale, but was the **vexed sport** of malicious calms and currents. Thrice, out of provisions, she put back to an intermediate port, and started **afresh**, but only yet again to return. **Frequent** fogs **enveloped** her; so that no observation could be had of her place, and once, when all hands were **joyously anticipating** sight of their destination, lo! the vapors lifted and disclosed the mountains from which they had taken their first

Italian

afresh: di nuovo, ancora, da capo.
anticipating: anticipando.
applies: applica.
beholding: guardando.
cathedral: duomo, cattedrale, la cattedrale.
cavernous: cavernoso.
conceit: presunzione.
conveys: trasporta.
difficulty: difficoltà.
discovery: scoperta.
encountered: incontrato.

enveloped: avviluppato.
estimated: stimato.
frequent: frequente, bazzicare.
generally: generalmente.
groups: gruppi.
incredibly: incredibilmente.
involved: coinvolto.
joyously: gioiosamente.
lose: perdere, perdiamo, perdete, perdi, perdo, perdono.
nautical: nautico.
outlaw: bandito, fuorilegge.

protracted: prolungato.
provincial: provinciale.
sport: sport.
suffered: sofferto, patito.
tortuous: tortuoso.
unending: interminabile.
unimpaired: inalterato.
utter: totale, completo, proferire, emettere.
vexed: irritato, indispettito, vessato, contrariato.
weeks: settimane.

departure. In the like **deceptive** vapors she at last struck upon a reef, whence ensued a long series of calamities too sad to **detail**.

It was the famous pilot, Juan Fernandez, **immortalized** by the island named after him, who put an end to these **coasting** tribulations, by **boldly** venturing the experiment—as De Gama did before him with respect to Europe—of standing broad out from land. Here he found the winds favorable for getting to the South, and by running westward till beyond the influences of the trades, he regained the coast without difficulty; making the passage which, though in a high degree **circuitous**, proved far more **expeditious** than the **nominally direct** one. Now it was upon these new tracks, and about the year 1670, or thereabouts, that the Enchanted Isles, and the rest of the sentinel groups, as they may be called, were discovered. Though I know of no account as to whether any of them were found **inhabited** or no, it may be **reasonably** concluded that they have been **immemorial** solitudes. But let us return to Redondo.

Southwest from our tower lies all Polynesia, **hundreds** of leagues away; but straight west, on the precise line of his parallel, no land rises till your keel is beached upon the Kingsmills, a nice little sail of, say 5000 miles.

Having thus by such distant references—with Rodondo the only possible ones—settled our **relative** place on the sea, let us consider objects not quite so remote. Behold the grim and charred Enchanted Isles. This nearest crater-shaped **headland** is part of Albemarle, the largest of the group, being some sixty miles or more long, and **fifteen** broad. Did you ever **lay** eye on the real genuine Equator? Have you ever, in the largest sense, toed the Line? Well, that identical crater-shaped headland there, all **yellow lava**, is cut by the Equator exactly as a knife **cuts** straight through the centre of a pumpkin **pie**. If you could only see so far, just to one side of that same headland, across yon low dikey ground, you would **catch** sight of the isle of Narborough, the loftiest land of the **cluster**; no **soil** whatever; one seamed **clinker** from top to bottom; **abounding** in black caves like smithies; its metallic shore **ringing** under foot like **plates** of iron; its central volcanoes standing **grouped** like a gigantic chimney-stack.

Italian

abounding: abbondando.
boldly: audacemente, arditamente.
catch: prendere, prendi, prendono, prendete, prendiamo, prendo, fermo, colpire, colpiscono, colpisco, colpiamo.
circuitous: indiretto, tortuoso.
clinker: clinker.
cluster: gruppo, grappolo, cluster.
coasting: costiero, costa.
cuts: tagli.
deceptive: ingannevole.

detail: dettaglio, particolare.
direct: diretto, guidare, destro, condurre, dirigere.
expeditious: sollecito, sbrigativo.
fifteen: quindici.
grouped: raggruppato.
headland: promontorio, capo.
hundreds: centinaia.
immemorial: immemorabile.
immortalized: immortalato.
inhabited: abitato.
lava: lava.

lay: posare, posiamo, poso, posi, posate, posano, posa, laico.
nominally: nominalmente.
pie: pasticcio.
plates: piastre, ripiani.
reasonably: ragionevolmente.
relative: parente, relativo, familiare.
ringing: scampanellio, oscillazione transitoria, suono, sonoro.
soil: sporcare, suolo, terra, insudiciare, terreno.
yellow: giallo.

Narborough and Albemarle are neighbors after a quite **curious fashion**. A familiar **diagram** will **illustrate** this strange **neighborhood**:

E

Cut a **channel** at the above **letter joint**, and the middle **transverse limb** is Narborough, and all the rest is Albemarle. **Volcanic** Narborough lies in the black **jaws** of Albemarle like a wolf's **red tongue** in his open month.

If now you desire the **population** of Albemarle, I will give you, in round **numbers**, the **statistics**, **according** to the most **reliable estimates** made upon the **spot**:

Men,	none.
Ant-eaters,	unknown.
Man-haters,	unknown.
Lizards,	500,000.
Snakes,	500,000.
Spiders,	10,000,000.
Salamanders,	unknown.
Devils,	do.
Making a clean **total** of	11,000,000.

exclusive of an incomputable **host** of fiends, ant-eaters, man-haters, and salamanders.

Albemarle **opens** his **mouth** towards the setting sun. His distended jaws form a great **bay**, which Narborough, his tongue, **divides** into **halves**, one whereof is called Weather Bay, the other Lee Bay; while the volcanic promontories,

Italian

according: secondo.
bay: baia, campata, baio, abbaiare, latrare.
channel: canale, condotto, alveo.
curious: curioso.
diagram: diagramma, schema, progetto, grafico, figura.
divides: divide, separa.
estimates: stima.
exclusive: esclusivo.
fashion: moda, modo.
halves: dimezza.

host: ospite, folla, ostia.
illustrate: illustrare, illustra, illustrano, illustrate, illustri, illustriamo, illustro.
jaws: ganasce.
joint: giunto, articolazione, comune, giunzione, paritetico, giuntura.
letter: lettera, la lettera.
limb: membro, arto.
mouth: bocca, imboccatura, foce, la bocca, apertura.
neighborhood: vicinato, vicinanza, quartiere.

numbers: numeri.
opens: apre.
population: popolazione.
red: rosso.
reliable: affidabile, attendibile, fidato.
spot: luogo, macchia, punto, posto, spot, macchiare.
statistics: statistica.
tongue: lingua, linguetta, la lingua.
total: totale, completo.
transverse: trasversale.
volcanic: vulcanico.

terminating his coasts, are styled South Head and North Head. I note this, because these bays are famous in the **annals** of the Sperm Whale Fishery. The whales come here at certain seasons to **calve**. When ships first cruised hereabouts, I am told, they used to **blockade** the entrance of Lee Bay, when their boats going round by Weather Bay, passed through Narborough channel, and so had the Leviathans very **neatly** in a pen.

The day after we took fish at the base of this Round Tower, we had a fine wind, and shooting round the north headland, suddenly descried a **fleet** of full thirty sail, all beating to **windward** like a **squadron** in line. A brave sight as ever man saw. A most harmonious **concord** of rushing keels. Their thirty kelsons hummed like thirty harp-strings, and looked as straight whilst they left their parallel traces on the sea. But there proved too many hunters for the game. The fleet broke up, and went their separate ways out of sight, leaving my own ship and two trim gentlemen of London. These last, finding no **luck** either, likewise vanished; and Lee Bay, with all its appurtenances, and without a **rival**, devolved to us.

The way of cruising here is this. You keep hovering about the entrance of the bay, in one beat and out the next. But at times — not always, as in other parts of the group — a **racehorse** of a current sweeps right across its mouth. So, with all sails set, you carefully **ply** your tacks. How often, standing at the foremast head at sunrise, with our patient prow pointed in between these isles, did I gaze upon that land, not of cakes, but of clinkers, not of streams of sparkling water, but **arrested** torrents of tormented lava.

As the ship runs in from the open sea, Narborough **presents** its side in one dark craggy mass, **soaring** up some five or six thousand feet, at which point it hoods itself in heavy clouds, whose **lowest** level fold is as clearly defined against the rocks as the snow-line against the Andes. There is **dire** mischief going on in that upper dark. There toil the demons of fire, who, at intervals, **irradiate** the nights with a strange **spectral illumination** for miles and miles around, but **unaccompanied** by any further **demonstration**; or else, suddenly **announce** themselves by terrific concussions, and the full drama of a volcanic **eruption**. The

Italian

annals: annali.
announce: annunciare, annunciate, annunci, annuncia, annunciamo, annunciano, annunziare, annuncio, annunziate, annunzi, annunzia.
arrested: arrestato.
blockade: blocco, bloccare.
calve: figli, figlia, figliamo, figliano, figliate, figlio, partoriamo, partorisci, partorisco, partoriscono, partorite.
concord: accordo.
demonstration: dimostrazione,

manifestazione, prova.
dire: tremendo, spaventoso, atroce.
eruption: eruzione.
fleet: flotta, veloce.
illumination: illuminazione.
irradiate: irradiare, irradi, irradia, irradiamo, irradiano, irradiate, irradio.
lowest: infimo.
luck: fortuna.
neatly: ordinatamente.
ply: maneggia, maneggiate, maneggio,

maneggi, maneggiamo, maneggiano, piallaccio, capo, maneggiare, piega.
presents: presenta.
racehorse: cavallo da corsa, corsa di cavalli.
rival: rivale.
soaring: volo a vela.
spectral: spettrale.
squadron: squadrone.
unaccompanied: senza accompagnamento, solo.
windward: sopravvento.

blacker that cloud by day, the more may you look for light by night. Often whalemen have found themselves cruising nigh that burning mountain when all **aglow** with a ball-room **blaze**. Or, rather, glass-works, you may call this same vitreous isle of Narborough, with its tall chimney-stacks.

Where we still stand, here on Rodondo, we cannot see all the other isles, but it is a good place from which to point out where they lie. Yonder, though, to the E.N.E., I **mark** a distant dusky **ridge**. It is Abington Isle, one of the most northerly of the group; so solitary, remote, and blank, it looks like No-Man's Land seen off our **northern** shore. I **doubt** whether two human beings ever touched upon that spot. So far as yon Abington Isle is **concerned**, Adam and his billions of **posterity remain** uncreated.

Ranging south of Abington, and quite out of sight behind the long spine of Albemarle, lies James's Isle, so **called** by the early Buccaneers after the luckless Stuart, Duke of York. Observe here, by the way, that, excepting the isles **particularized** in comparatively recent times, and which mostly **received** the names of famous Admirals, the Encantadas were first **christened** by the Spaniards; but these Spanish names were generally **effaced** on English charts by the subsequent christenings of the Buccaneers, who, in the middle of the seventeenth century, called them after English noblemen and kings. Of these **loyal** freebooters and the things which **associate** their name with the Encantadas, we shall hear anon. Nay, for one little item, **immediately**; for between James's Isle and Albemarle, lies a fantastic islet, strangely known as "Cowley's Enchanted Isle." But, as all the group is deemed enchanted, the reason must be given for the **spell** within a spell involved by this particular **designation**. The name was **bestowed** by that **excellent** Buccaneer himself, on his first visit here. Speaking in his **published** voyages of this spot, he says—"My fancy led me to call it Cowley's Enchanted Isle, for, we having had a sight of it upon several points of the **compass**, it appeared always in so many different **forms**; sometimes like a ruined **fortification**; upon another point like a great city," etc. No wonder though, that among the Encantadas all sorts of **ocular** deceptions and mirages should be met.

Italian

aglow: ardente.
associate: associare, unirsi, socio, associato.
bestowed: concesso, tributato.
blaze: vampa, fiammata.
christened: battezzato.
compass: bussola, la bussola, compasso.
concerned: interessato.
designation: designazione.
doubt: dubitare, dubbio.
effaced: cancellato.

excellent: eccellente, esimio, ottimo.
forms: moduli.
fortification: fortificazione.
immediately: immediatamente, subito, direttamente, fra poco.
led: condotto, guidato.
loyal: fedele, leale.
mark: segno, marcare, marco, marchio, contrassegnare, marca, segnare, contrassegno, voto.
northern: settentrionale, nordico.
ocular: oculare.

particularized: particolareggiato, dettagliato.
posterity: posterità.
published: pubblicato.
received: ricevuto, accolto.
remain: rimanere, rimangono, rimani, rimango, rimanete, rimaniamo, restare, restiamo, resti, restate, restano.
ridge: cresta, crinale.
spell: compitare, sillabare, incantesimo, sortilegio.

That Cowley linked his name with this self-transforming and bemocking isle, **suggests** the possibility that it conveyed to him some **meditative** image of himself. At least, as is not impossible, if he were any relative of the mildly-thoughtful and self-upbraiding **poet** Cowley, who **lived** about his time, the conceit might **seem unwarranted**; for that sort of thing **evinced** in the naming of this isle runs in the blood, and may be seen in pirates as in poets.

Still south of James's Isle lie Jervis Isle, Duncan Isle, Grossman's Isle, Brattle Isle, Wood's Isle, Chatham Isle, and various lesser isles, for the most part an **archipelago** of aridities, without inhabitant, **history**, or **hope** of either in all time to come. But not far from these are rather **notable** isles—Barrington, Charles's, Norfolk, and Hood's. Succeeding chapters will reveal some ground for their **notability**.

SKETCH FIFTH

THE FRIGATE, AND SHIP FLYAWAY

"Looking far forth into the ocean wide,
  A **goodly** ship with banners **bravely** dight,
  And flag in her top-gallant I espide,
  Through the main sea making her merry **flight**."

Ere quitting Rodondo, it must not be omitted that here, in 1813, the U.S. frigate Essex, Captain David Porter, came **near leaving** her bones. **Lying becalmed** one morning with a **strong** current setting her **rapidly** towards the rock, a strange sail was **descried**, which—not out of **keeping** with alleged enchantments of the neighborhood—seemed to be **staggering** under a **violent** wind, while the frigate lay lifeless as if spell-bound. But a light air springing up, all sail was made by the frigate in chase of the **enemy**, as supposed—he being deemed an English whale-ship—but the rapidity of the current was so great, that

Italian

archipelago: arcipelago.
becalmed: acquietato.
bravely: coraggiosamente.
descried: scorto, intravisto.
enemy: nemico.
evinced: manifestato.
goodly: bonariamente.
history: storia, la storia.
hope: speranza, sperare, spera, sperano, sperate, speri, speriamo, spero.
keeping: conservando, osservando, trattenendo.
leaving: abbandonando, lasciando, partendo.
light: luce, leggero, accendere, chiaro, illuminare, fanale, lampada, luminoso, debole.
lived: vissuto, abitato.
lying: mentire, bugiardo, giacente.
meditative: meditativo.
near: vicino, prossimo, presso.
notability: notabilità.
notable: notevole, notabile.
poet: poeta.
rapidly: rapidamente.
seem: parere, paiono, paiamo, pari, paio, parete, sembrare, sembra, sembrano, sembrate, sembri.
staggering: traballio, traballamento, sbalorditivo, barcollante, barcollamento.
strong: forte, robusto.
suggests: propone, suggerisce.
unwarranted: ingiustificato.
violent: violento.

soon all sight was lost of him; and, at meridian, the Essex, spite of her **drags**, was **driven** so close under the foam-lashed cliffs of Rodondo that, for a time, all hands gave her up. A smart breeze, however, at last helped her off, though the escape was so **critical** as to seem almost **miraculous**.

Thus saved from **destruction herself**, she now made use of that **salvation** to **destroy** the other vessel, if possible. Renewing the chase in the direction in which the stranger had disappeared, sight was **caught** of him the following morning. Upon being **descried** he hoisted American colors and stood away from the Essex. A calm ensued; when, still **confident** that the stranger was an Englishman, Porter dispatched a cutter, not to board the enemy, but drive back his boats engaged in towing him. The cutter succeeded. Cutters were **subsequently sent** to capture him; the stranger now showing English colors in place of American. But, when the frigate's boats were within a **short** distance of their hoped-for **prize**, another sudden breeze sprang up; the stranger, under all sail, bore off to the westward, and, ere night, was hull down **ahead** of the Essex, which, all this time, lay **perfectly** becalmed.

This enigmatic craft—American in the morning, and English in the evening—her sails full of wind in a calm—was never again beheld. An enchanted ship no doubt. So, at least, the sailors swore.

This **cruise** of the Essex in the Pacific during the war of 1812, is, perhaps, the strangest and most stirring to be found in the history of the American navy. She captured the furthest **wandering** vessels; visited the remotest seas and isles; long hovered in the charmed vicinity of the enchanted group; and, finally, **valiantly** gave up the ghost fighting two English frigates in the harbor of Valparaiso. Mention is made of her here for the same reason that the Buccaneers will likewise **receive** record; because, like them, by long cruising among the isles, tortoise-hunting upon their shores, and generally **exploring** them; for these and other reasons, the Essex is peculiarly associated with the Encantadas.

Here be it said that you have but three, eye-witness **authorities worth** mentioning touching the Enchanted Isles:—Cowley, the Buccaneer (1684); Colnet the whaling-ground **explorer** (1798); Porter, the **post** captain (1813). Other than

Italian

ahead: avanti, davanti.
authorities: autorità.
caught: preso, colpito.
confident: fiducioso.
critical: critico.
cruise: crociera.
descried: scorto, intravisto.
destroy: distruggere, distruggono, distruggo, distruggiamo, distruggete, distruggi.
destruction: distruzione.
drags: trascina.

drive: azionamento, comando, guidare, impulso, trasmissione, spingere.
driven: guidato.
explorer: esploratore.
exploring: esplorando.
herself: stesso, sè.
miraculous: miracoloso.
perfectly: perfettamente.
post: posta, palo, impiego, funzione, posto, montante, imbucare.
prize: premio.

receive: ricevere, ricevono, ricevo, riceviamo, ricevi, ricevete, accogliere, accogliete, accolgo, accogliamo, accogli.
salvation: salvezza.
sent: mandato, spedito.
short: corto, breve, basso.
subsequently: successivamente, dietro, dopo.
valiantly: valorosamente.
wandering: vagando, peregrinazione.
worth: valore.

these you have but **barren**, bootless allusions from some **few** passing voyagers or compilers.

SKETCH SIXTH

BARRINGTON ISLE AND THE BUCCANEERS

"Let us all **servile** base **subjection scorn**,
 And as we be sons of the earth so wide,
 Let us our father's **heritage divide**,
 And **challenge** to ourselves our portions **dew**
 Of all the **patrimony**, which a few
 Now hold on hugger-mugger in their hand."

*   *   *   *   *

"Lords of the world, and so will **wander** free,
 Whereso us listeth, uncontroll'd of any."

*   *   *   *   *

"How **bravely** now we live, how **jocund**, how near the first **inheritance**, without fear, how free from little troubles!"

Near two centuries **ago** Barrington Isle was the **resort** of that famous wing of the West Indian Buccaneers, which, upon their **repulse** from the Cuban waters, **crossing** the Isthmus of Darien, ravaged the Pacific side of the Spanish colonies, and, with the **regularity** and **timing** of a **modern** mail, waylaid the royal treasure-ships **plying** between Manilla and Acapulco. After the toils of piratic war, here they came to say their **prayers**, enjoy their free-and-easies, **count** their crackers from the **cask**, their doubloons from the **keg**, and **measure** their silks of Asia with long Toledos for their yard-sticks.

Italian

ago: fa.
barren: sterile.
bravely: coraggiosamente.
cask: barile, botte, fusto.
challenge: contestare, sfida, sfidare, disputare.
count: contare, calcolare, conteggio, conte, calcolo, conteggiare.
crossing: attraversamento, incrocio, traversata, passaggio.
dew: rugiada.
divide: dividere, dividete, dividiamo, divido, dividono, dividi, separare, separa, separi, separiamo, separate.
few: pochi, poco.
heritage: eredità, retaggio, patrimonio.
inheritance: eredità.
jocund: giocondo.
keg: bariletto.
measure: misura, misurare, provvedimento.
modern: moderno.
patrimony: patrimonio.
plying: maneggiando.
prayers: preghiere.
regularity: regolarità.
repulse: rifiuto, respingere.
resort: ricorso, ricorrere, complesso turistico.
scorn: disprezzo, disprezzare.
servile: servile.
subjection: sottomissione, soggezione.
timing: cronometraggio.
wander: vagare, vago, errare, vaghiamo, vaga, vagano, vaghi, vagate, vagabondare.

As a secure retreat, an undiscoverable hiding-place, no spot in those days could have been better fitted. In the centre of a vast and silent sea, but very little traversed — surrounded by islands, whose inhospitable aspect might well drive away the chance navigator — and yet within a few days' sail of the **opulent countries** which they made their prey — the unmolested Buccaneers found here that tranquillity which they **fiercely denied** to every civilized harbor in that part of the world. Here, after **stress** of weather, or a temporary drubbing at the hands of their vindictive foes, or in swift flight with golden **booty**, those old marauders came, and lay **snugly** out of all harm's **reach**. But not only was the place a harbor of safety, and a bower of ease, but for **utility** in other things it was most admirable.

Barrington Isle is, in many respects, singularly adapted to **careening**, refitting, **refreshing**, and other seamen's purposes. Not only has it good water, and good anchorage, well sheltered from all winds by the high land of Albemarle, but it is the least **unproductive** isle of the group. Tortoises good for food, trees good for **fuel**, and long **grass** good for **bedding**, abound here, and there are pretty **natural walks**, and several landscapes to be seen. Indeed, though in its locality belonging to the Enchanted group, Barrington Isle is so unlike most of its neighbors, that it would hardly seem of kin to them.

"I once landed on its **western** side," says a sentimental voyager long ago, "where it faces the black **buttress** of Albemarle. I walked beneath groves of trees — not very lofty, and not palm trees, or **orange** trees, or **peach** trees, to be sure — but, for all that, after long sea-faring, very **beautiful** to walk under, even though they supplied no **fruit**. And here, in calm spaces at the heads of glades, and on the shaded tops of slopes commanding the most **quiet** scenery — what do you think I saw? Seats which might have served Brahmins and presidents of peace societies. Fine old ruins of what had once been **symmetric** lounges of stone and turf, they bore every mark both of artificialness and age, and were, **undoubtedly**, made by the Buccaneers. One had been a long **sofa**, with back and arms, just such a sofa as the poet Gray might have loved to throw himself upon, his Crebillon in hand.

Italian

beautiful: bello, carino, bella, bellissimo.
bedding: biancheria da letto, lettiera.
booty: bottino.
buttress: contrafforte.
careening: carenando.
countries: paesi.
denied: negato.
fiercely: ferocemente.
fruit: frutta, frutto, la frutta.
fuel: carburante, combustibile, benzina.

grass: erba, l'erba.
natural: naturale.
opulent: opulento.
orange: arancione, arancia, arancio.
peach: pesca, la pesca.
quiet: calmare, tranquillo, placare, quieto, calmo, zitto, silenzioso, quiete.
reach: arrivare, portata, raggiungere, pervenire, estendersi.
refreshing: rinfrescante.
snugly: comodamente.

sofa: divano, sofà.
stress: accento, tensione, stress, accentare, sollecitazione, sforzo.
symmetric: simmetrico.
undoubtedly: indubbiamente, si capisce.
unproductive: improduttivo.
utility: profitto, servizio pubblico, programma di utilità, vantaggio, utilità.
walks: cammina.
western: occidentale.

"Though they sometimes tarried here for months at a time, and used the spot for a storing-place for **spare** spars, sails, and casks; yet it is **highly improbable** that the Buccaneers ever **erected** dwelling-houses upon the isle. They never were here except their ships remained, and they would most likely have slept on board. I mention this, because I **cannot** avoid the thought, that it is **hard** to impute the **construction** of these **romantic** seats to any other **motive** than one of pure **peacefulness** and kindly **fellowship** with nature. That the Buccaneers **perpetrated** the greatest outrages is very true—that some of them were mere cutthroats is not to be denied; but we know that here and there among their host was a Dampier, a Wafer, and a Cowley, and likewise other men, whose worst reproach was their desperate fortunes—whom persecution, or **adversity**, or secret and unavengeable wrongs, had driven from Christian society to seek the melancholy solitude or the guilty adventures of the sea. At any rate, long as those ruins of seats on Barrington remain, the most singular monuments are furnished to the fact, that all of the Buccaneers were not unmitigated monsters.

"But during my **ramble** on the isle I was not long in discovering other tokens, of things quite in **accordance** with those wild traits, **popularly**, and no doubt truly enough, imputed to the freebooters at large. Had I **picked** up old sails and rusty hoops I would only have thought of the ship's carpenter and **cooper**. But I found old cutlasses and **daggers** reduced to mere threads of rust, which, doubtless, had stuck between Spanish ribs ere now. These were **signs** of the murderer and **robber**; the reveler likewise had left his trace. Mixed with shells, fragments of broken jars were lying here and there, high up upon the beach. They were **precisely** like the jars now used upon the Spanish coast for the **wine** and Pisco spirits of that country.

"With a rusty dagger-fragment in one hand, and a **bit** of a wine-jar in another, I sat me down on the ruinous **green** sofa I have spoken of, and bethought me long and **deeply** of these same Buccaneers. Could it be possible, that they **robbed** and murdered one day, reveled the next, and rested themselves by turning meditative philosophers, **rural** poets, and seat-builders on the third? Not very improbable, after all. For **consider** the vacillations of a man. Still, strange as it

Italian

accordance: concordanza, accordo.	**erected**: eretto.	**precisely**: precisamente.
adversity: sfortuna, avversità.	**fellowship**: compagnia.	**ramble**: giro, passeggiata, vagare.
bit: pezzo, morso, punta, pezzetto, bit.	**green**: verde, acerbo.	**rate**: tasso, stimare, valutare, aliquota,
cannot: non potere.	**hard**: duro, pesante, difficile, dura,	tariffa, apprezzare, ritmo,
consider: considerare, consideri,	solido.	percentuale.
considerano, consideriamo,	**highly**: altamente, estremamente.	**robbed**: derubato.
considera, considerate, considero,	**improbable**: improbabile.	**robber**: ladro, rapinatore, ladrone.
guardare.	**motive**: motivo, movente, ragione.	**romantic**: romantico.
construction: costruzione.	**peacefulness**: serenità, pace.	**rural**: rurale.
cooper: bottaio.	**perpetrated**: perpetrato.	**signs**: segnaletica.
daggers: pugnali.	**picked**: staccato, punto, rotto, scelto.	**spare**: risparmiare, scorta.
deeply: profondamente.	**popularly**: popolarmente, popolare.	**wine**: vino.

may seem, I must also **abide** by the more **charitable** thought; **namely**, that among these **adventurers** were some **gentlemanly**, **companionable** souls, **capable** of genuine **tranquillity** and virtue."

SKETCH SEVENTH

CHARLES'S ISLE AND THE DOG-KING

—So **with** outragious cry,
A **thousand** villeins round about him swarmed
Out of the rocks and caves **adjoining** nye;
Vile caitive wretches, **ragged**, rude, **deformed**;
All threatning death, all in straunge manner armed;
Some with unweldy clubs, some with long speares.
Some **rusty** knives, some staves in fier warmd.

*   *   *   *   *

We will not be of any **occupation**,
Let such **vile** vassals, born to base **vocation**,
Drudge in the world, and for their **living** droyle,
Which have no wit to live withouten toyle.

Southwest of Barrington lies Charles's Isle. And **hereby** hangs a history which I **gathered** long ago from a **shipmate** learned in all the lore of **outlandish** life.

During the successful revolt of the Spanish provinces from Old Spain, there fought on behalf of Peru a certain Creole adventurer from Cuba, who, by his **bravery** and good fortune, at length advanced himself to high rank in the **patriot** army. The war being ended, Peru found itself like many **valorous** gentlemen, free and independent enough, but with few shot in the **locker**. In other words,

Italian

abide: aspettare, aspettiamo, aspetta, aspettano, aspetti, aspetto, aspettate, restare, sopportare.
adjoining: adiacente, limitrofo, contiguo.
adventurer: avventuriero.
bravery: coraggio.
capable: capace, abile, idoneo, adatto.
charitable: caritatevole, misericordioso.
companionable: socievole.
deformed: deforme, deformato.

gathered: raccolto.
gentlemanly: signorile, da gentiluomo.
hereby: in tal modo, con il presente, con ciò.
living: vivendo, abitando, vivo, vivente.
locker: armadietto.
namely: cioè, vale a dire.
occupation: occupazione, mestiere, professione, impiego, lavoro.
outlandish: inconsueto, esotico,

straniero, strano, bizzarro.
patriot: patriota.
ragged: cencioso, logoro.
rusty: arrugginito, rugginoso.
shipmate: compagno di bordo.
thousand: mille.
tranquillity: tranquillità.
valorous: prode, valoroso.
vile: abietto.
vocation: vocazione.
wit: arguzia.

Peru had not **wherewithal** to pay off its troops. But the Creole—I forget his
name—volunteered to take his pay in lands. So they told him he might have his
pick of the Enchanted Isles, which were then, as they still remain, the **nominal
appanage** of Peru. The **soldier** straightway **embarks** thither, **explores** the group,
returns to Callao, and says he will take a deed of Charles's Isle. Moreover, this
deed must **stipulate** that thenceforth Charles's Isle is not only the sole property
of the Creole, but is forever free of Peru, even as Peru of Spain. To be short, this
adventurer **procures** himself to be made in effect Supreme Lord of the Island,
one of the princes of the powers of the earth.[A]

[Footnote A: The American Spaniards have long been in the habit of making
presents of islands to **deserving** individuals. The pilot Juan Fernandez procured
a deed of the isle named after him, and for some years **resided** there before
Selkirk came. It is supposed, however, that he eventually contracted the **blues**
upon his **princely** property, for after a time he returned to the main, and as
report goes, became a very **garrulous** barber in the city of Lima.]

He now sends forth a **proclamation inviting** subjects to his as yet
unpopulated kingdom. Some **eighty** souls, men and women, **respond**; and being
provided by their leader with **necessaries**, and **tools** of various sorts, together
with a few cattle and **goats**, take ship for the promised land; the last arrival on
board, prior to sailing, being the Creole himself, accompanied, strange to say, by
a **disciplined cavalry** company of large grim dogs. These, it was observed on the
passage, refusing to **consort** with the emigrants, remained **aristocratically**
grouped around their master on the elevated quarter-deck, casting disdainful
glances forward upon the inferior **rabble** there; much as, from the ramparts, the
soldiers of a **garrison**, thrown into a **conquered** town, eye the **inglorious** citizen-
mob over which they are set to watch.

Now Charles's Isle not only resembles Barrington Isle in being much more
inhabitable than other parts of the group, but it is double the size of Barrington,
say forty or fifty miles in **circuit**.

Safely debarked at last, the company, under direction of their lord and **patron**,
forthwith proceeded to build their capital city. They make considerable advance

Italian

appanage: appannaggio.	**garrison**: guarnigione, presidio,	dichiarazione, pubblicazione, bando.
aristocratically: aristocraticamente.	presidiare.	**procures**: procura.
blues: blues.	**garrulous**: loquace.	**rabble**: marmaglia, folla.
cavalry: cavalleria.	**goats**: capre.	**resided**: risieduto.
circuit: circuito.	**inglorious**: inglorioso.	**respond**: rispondere, rispondete,
conquered: conquistato.	**inhabitable**: abitabile.	rispondo, rispondiamo, rispondi,
consort: consorte, coniuge.	**inviting**: invitando, invitare, invitante.	rispondono, reagire, replicare,
deserving: meritando, meritevole.	**necessaries**: necessario.	replico, replichi, replicate.
disciplined: disciplinato.	**nominal**: nominale.	**soldier**: soldato, militare.
eighty: ottanta.	**patron**: patrono, mecenate.	**stipulate**: stipulare.
embarks: imbarca.	**princely**: principe, principesco.	**tools**: attrezzi.
explores: esplora.	**proclamation**: proclamazione,	**wherewithal**: mezzi.

in the way of walls of clinkers, and lava floors, **nicely** sanded with cinders. On the least barren hills they pasture their cattle, while the goats, adventurers by nature, explore the far inland solitudes for a scanty **livelihood** of lofty **herbage**. Meantime, **abundance** of fish and tortoises supply their other wants.

The disorders incident to **settling** all **primitive** regions, in the present case were heightened by the peculiarly **untoward** character of many of the pilgrims. His Majesty was forced at last to **proclaim martial** law, and actually hunted and shot with his own hand several of his rebellious subjects, who, with most questionable intentions, had clandestinely encamped in the interior, whence they stole by night, to **prowl** barefooted on tiptoe round the precincts of the lava-palace. It is to be remarked, however, that prior to such stern proceedings, the more reliable men had been judiciously picked out for an **infantry** body-guard, subordinate to the cavalry body-guard of dogs. But the state of politics in this unhappy nation may be somewhat imagined, from the circumstance that all who were not of the body-guard were downright **plotters** and malignant traitors. At length the death penalty was tacitly **abolished**, owing to the timely thought, that were strict sportsman's justice to be **dispensed** among such subjects, ere long the Nimrod King would have little or no remaining game to shoot. The human part of the life-guard was now **disbanded**, and set to work **cultivating** the soil, and raising potatoes; the regular army now solely **consisting** of the dog-regiment. These, as I have heard, were of a singularly ferocious character, though by severe training rendered docile to their master. Armed to the teeth, the Creole now goes in state, surrounded by his **canine** janizaries, whose terrific bayings prove quite as **serviceable** as bayonets in keeping down the surgings of revolt.

But the **census** of the isle, sadly **lessened** by the **dispensation** of justice, and not **materially recruited** by **matrimony**, began to fill his mind with sad mistrust. Some way the population must be increased. Now, from its possessing a little water, and its comparative **pleasantness** of aspect, Charles's Isle at this period was occasionally visited by foreign whalers. These His Majesty had always levied upon for port charges, thereby **contributing** to his revenue. But now he had additional designs. By **insidious** arts he, from time to time, **cajoles** certain

---

Italian

abolished: abolito.
abundance: abbondanza, ricchezza, affluenza.
cajoles: alletta, lusinghe.
canine: canino.
census: censimento.
consisting: consistendo, constando.
contributing: contribuendo.
cultivating: coltivando.
disbanded: sciolto.
dispensation: dispensa.
dispensed: distribuito.

herbage: erbe.
infantry: fanteria.
insidious: insidioso.
lessened: diminuito.
livelihood: sostentamento, mezzi di sussistenza, mezzi di sostentamento.
martial: marziale.
materially: materialmente.
matrimony: matrimonio.
nicely: piacevolmente.
pleasantness: piacevolezza.
plotters: plotter.

primitive: primitivo.
proclaim: proclamare, proclami, proclamiamo, proclamate, proclamano, proclamo, proclama, pubblicare.
prowl: aggirarsi.
recruited: reclutato.
serviceable: utilizzabile.
settling: regolando, saldando, sistemando, assestamento, regolare, sedimentazione.
untoward: sfavorevole.

sailors to desert their ships, and enlist beneath his **banner**. Soon as missed, their captains crave permission to go and hunt them up. Whereupon His Majesty first hides them very carefully away, and then freely permits the search. In consequence, the delinquents are never found, and the ships retire without them.

Thus, by a two-edged policy of this **crafty** monarch, foreign nations were **crippled** in the number of their subjects, and his own were greatly **multiplied**. He particularly petted these renegado strangers. But **alas** for the deep-laid schemes of **ambitious** princes, and alas for the vanity of **glory**. As the foreign-born Pretorians, **unwisely** introduced into the Roman state, and still more unwisely made favorites of the Emperors, at last **insulted** and **overturned** the throne, even so these **lawless** mariners, with all the rest of the body-guard and all the **populace**, broke out into a terrible mutiny, and **defied** their master. He **marched** against them with all his dogs. A deadly battle ensued upon the beach. It raged for three hours, the dogs fighting with determined **valor**, and the sailors reckless of everything but victory. Three men and **thirteen** dogs were left dead upon the field, many on both sides were wounded, and the king was forced to fly with the **remainder** of his canine **regiment**. The enemy **pursued**, stoning the dogs with their master into the wilderness of the **interior**. Discontinuing the pursuit, the victors returned to the village on the shore, stove the spirit casks, and proclaimed a Republic. The dead men were **interred** with the **honors** of war, and the dead dogs ignominiously thrown into the sea. At last, forced by stress of suffering, the fugitive Creole came down from the hills and offered to treat for peace. But the rebels refused it on any other terms than his **unconditional banishment**. Accordingly, the next ship that arrived carried away the ex-king to Peru.

The history of the king of Charles's Island **furnishes** another **illustration** of the difficulty of **colonizing** barren islands with **unprincipled** pilgrims.

Doubtless for a long time the **exiled** monarch, **pensively** ruralizing in Peru, which afforded him a safe **asylum** in his **calamity**, watched every arrival from the Encantadas, to hear news of the failure of the Republic, the consequent **penitence** of the rebels, and his own recall to **royalty**. Doubtless he deemed the

Italian

alas: ahimè.
ambitious: ambizioso.
asylum: asilo, ricovero, rifugio.
banishment: esilio, bando.
banner: bandiera, striscione.
calamity: calamità.
colonizing: colonizzando.
crafty: astuto.
crippled: zoppo.
defied: sfidato.
exiled: esiliato.
furnishes: fornisce.

glory: gloria.
honors: onore.
illustration: illustrazione.
insulted: insultato.
interior: interno, interiore.
interred: seppellito.
lawless: dissoluto, senza legge, licenzioso, illegale.
marched: marciato.
multiplied: moltiplicato.
overturned: capovolto.
penitence: penitenza.

pensively: pensosamente.
populace: popolino.
pursued: perseguito.
regiment: reggimento.
remainder: resto, rimanenza.
royalty: royalty, diritti di utilizzo, diritti d'autore, diritto di concessione.
thirteen: tredici.
unconditional: incondizionato.
unprincipled: senza scrupoli.
unwisely: imprudentemente.
valor: valore, coraggio.

Republic but a miserable **experiment** which would soon **explode**. But no, the insurgents had confederated themselves into a **democracy** neither Grecian, Roman, nor American. Nay, it was no democracy at all, but a **permanent** *Riotocracy*, which gloried in having no law but lawlessness. Great **inducements** being offered to deserters, their ranks were **swelled** by **accessions** of scamps from every ship which touched their shores. Charles's Island was proclaimed the asylum of the oppressed of all navies. Each **runaway** tar was hailed as a **martyr** in the cause of freedom, and became immediately **installed** a ragged **citizen** of this universal nation. In vain the captains of **absconding** seamen strove to **regain** them. Their new compatriots were **ready** to give any number of **ornamental** eyes in their behalf. They had few cannon, but their fists were not to be trifled with. So at last it came to pass that no vessels acquainted with the character of that country durst touch there, however **sorely** in want of refreshment. It became Anathema—a sea Alsatia—the unassailed lurking-place of all sorts of desperadoes, who in the name of liberty did just what they pleased. They continually **fluctuated** in their numbers. Sailors, deserting ships at other islands, or in boats at sea anywhere in that vicinity, steered for Charles's Isle, as to their sure home of refuge; while, **sated** with the life of the isle, numbers from time to time crossed the water to the **neighboring** ones, and there presenting themselves to strange captains as **shipwrecked** seamen, often succeeded in getting on board vessels bound to the Spanish coast, and having a compassionate **purse** made up for them on landing there.

One **warm** night during my first visit to the group, our ship was floating along in languid stillness, when some one on the **forecastle shouted** "Light ho!" We looked and saw a beacon burning on some obscure land off the **beam**. Our third mate was not **intimate** with this part of the world. Going to the captain he said, "Sir, shall I put off in a boat? These must be shipwrecked men."

The captain laughed rather grimly, as, shaking his fist towards the beacon, he rapped out an oath, and said—"No, no, you **precious** rascals, you don't juggle one of my boats ashore this blessed night. You do well, you thieves—you do benevolently to **hoist** a light yonder as on a dangerous **shoal**. It **tempts** no wise

Italian

absconding: fuggendo, scappando.
accessions: entrate.
beam: trave, raggio, fascio, subbio, baglio, sciopero, traversa.
citizen: cittadino.
democracy: democrazia.
experiment: esperimento, prova, fare esperimenti, sperimentare, esperienza.
explode: esplodere, esplodete, esplodiamo, esplodo, esplodono, esplodi.

fluctuated: fluttuato.
forecastle: castello di prua.
hoist: montacarichi, paranco, argano, sollevamento, sollevare.
inducements: incitamenti.
installed: installato.
intimate: intimo.
martyr: martire.
neighboring: vicino.
ornamental: ornamentale.
permanent: permanente, costante.
precious: prezioso.

purse: borsa, borsellino, portamonete.
ready: pronto, disposto.
regain: ricuperare, riprendere.
runaway: fuggiasco.
sated: sazio.
shipwrecked: naufragato, naufragio.
shoal: secca, bassofondo.
shouted: gridato.
sorely: dolorosamente.
swelled: gonfiato.
tempts: tenta.
warm: caldo, caloroso, scaldare.

man to pull off and see what's the matter, but bids him **steer** small and keep off **shore** — that is Charles's Island; **brace** up, Mr. **Mate**, and keep the light astern."

SKETCH EIGHTH

NORFOLK ISLE AND THE CHOLA WIDOW

"At last they in an island did espy
 A **seemly** woman sitting by the shore,
 That with great **sorrow** and sad **agony**
 Seemed some great **misfortune** to **deplore**;
 And **loud** to them for **succor** called evermore."

"Black his eye as the midnight sky.
 White his **neck** as the driven snow,
 Red his cheek as the morning light; —
 Cold he lies in the ground below.
 My love is **dead**,
 Gone to his death-bed,
 All under the **cactus** tree."

"Each **lonely** scene shall **thee restore**,
 For thee the **tear** be **duly** shed;
 Belov'd till life can **charm** no more,
 And **mourned** till Pity's **self** be dead."

Far to the **northeast** of Charles's Isle, **sequestered** from the rest, lies Norfolk Isle; and, however **insignificant** to most voyagers, to me, through sympathy, that lone island has become a spot made **sacred** by the strangest trials of **humanity**.

Italian

agony: agonia, angoscia.
brace: parentesi graffa, sostegno.
cactus: cactus.
charm: fascino, incanto.
dead: morto.
deplore: deplorare.
duly: debitamente.
humanity: umanità.
insignificant: insignificante.
lone: solitario, solo.
lonely: solitario, solo.
loud: forte, alto, rumoroso.

mate: accoppiare, compagno, accoppiarsi.
misfortune: sfortuna, traversia, disgrazia.
mourned: pianto.
neck: collo, pomiciare, il collo.
northeast: nordest.
restore: ripristinare, ripristiniamo, ripristini, ripristinano, ripristinate, ripristina, restaurare, ripristino, restaura, restauriamo, restauri.
sacred: sacro, santo.

seemly: conveniente.
self: stesso.
sequestered: confiscato, sequestrato.
shore: costa, riva, sponda, puntello, puntellare.
sorrow: tristezza, cordoglio.
steer: manzo, sterzare, governare.
succor: soccorrere, soccorso, aiutare.
tear: strappo, lagrima, strappare, lacerare, lacrima.
thee: te.

It was my first visit to the Encantadas. Two days had been spent ashore in **hunting** tortoises. There was not time to capture many; so on the third afternoon we loosed our sails. We were just in the act of getting under way, the **uprooted** anchor yet suspended and **invisibly** swaying beneath the **wave**, as the good ship gradually turned her **heel** to leave the isle behind, when the seaman who **heaved** with me at the windlass paused **suddenly**, and directed my attention to something **moving** on the land, not along the beach, but somewhat back, fluttering from a height.

In view of the sequel of this little story, be it here narrated how it came to pass, that an object which partly from its being so small was quite lost to every other man on board, still caught the eye of my handspike companion. The rest of the crew, myself included, **merely** stood up to our spikes in **heaving**, **whereas**, unwontedly **exhilarated**, at every turn of the ponderous windlass, my **belted comrade** leaped atop of it, with might and main giving a **downward**, thewey, **perpendicular** heave, his **raised** eye bent in cheery animation upon the slowly **receding** shore. Being high lifted above all others was the reason he perceived the object, otherwise unperceivable; and this elevation of his eye was owing to the elevation of his spirits; and this again—for truth must out—to a **dram** of Peruvian pisco, in guerdon for some kindness done, secretly **administered** to him that morning by our mulatto steward. Now, certainly, pisco does a deal of mischief in the world; yet seeing that, in the present case, it was the means, though **indirect**, of rescuing a **human** being from the most dreadful fate, must we not also needs admit that sometimes pisco does a deal of good?

Glancing across the water in the direction **pointed** out, I saw some white thing **hanging** from an inland rock, perhaps half a **mile** from the sea.

"It is a bird; a white-winged bird; perhaps a—no; it is—it is a handkerchief!"

"Ay, a handkerchief!" echoed my comrade, and with a louder shout apprised the captain.

Quickly now—like the running out and **training** of a great gun—the long cabin spy-glass was thrust through the mizzen rigging from the high **platform** of

Italian

administered: amministrato.
belted: cintura.
comrade: camerata.
downward: verso il basso.
dram: dram.
exhilarated: esilarato.
hanging: impiccagione.
heave: sollevamento.
heaving: sollevamento.
heel: tallone, calcagno, tacco.
human: umano.
hunting: cacciando, caccia.

indirect: indiretto.
invisibly: invisibilmente.
merely: soltanto.
mile: miglio.
moving: toccante, commovente, spostamento.
perpendicular: perpendicolare.
platform: piattaforma, palco, marciapiede, banchina, tribuna.
pointed: appuntato, appuntito, acuto, aguzzo.
quickly: presto, rapidamente,

velocemente.
raised: a rilievo, garzato.
receding: recedendo.
suddenly: improvvisamente, ad un tratto.
training: addestramento, formazione, allenamento, istruzione, educazione.
uprooted: sradicato.
wave: onda, ondata, sventolare, l'onda, ondeggiare.
whereas: durante, mentre, premesso che.

the poop; whereupon a human figure was plainly seen upon the inland rock, eagerly waving towards us what seemed to be the handkerchief.

Our captain was a prompt, good fellow. Dropping the **glass**, he lustily ran forward, ordering the anchor to be dropped again; hands to stand by a boat, and lower away.

In a half-hour's time the swift boat returned. It went with six and came with seven; and the seventh was a woman.

It is not **artistic** heartlessness, but I wish I could but draw in crayons; for this woman was a most touching sight; and crayons, **tracing softly** melancholy lines, would best **depict** the **mournful** image of the dark-damasked Chola **widow**.

Her story was soon told, and though given in her own strange language was as quickly understood; for our captain, from long trading on the Chilian coast, was well **versed** in the Spanish. A Cholo, or half-breed Indian woman of Payta in Peru, three years gone by, with her young new-wedded husband Felipe, of pure Castilian blood, and her one only Indian **brother**, Truxill, Hunilla had taken passage on the main in a French **whaler**, commanded by a **joyous** man; which vessel, bound to the cruising **grounds** beyond the Enchanted Isles, proposed passing close by their vicinity. The object of the little party was to procure tortoise oil, a fluid which for its great **purity** and **delicacy** is held in high **estimation wherever** known; and it is well known all along this part of the Pacific coast. With a **chest** of clothes, tools, **cooking** utensils, a rude **apparatus** for trying out the oil, some casks of biscuit, and other things, not omitting two **favorite dogs**, of which faithful animal all the Cholos are very **fond**, Hunilla and her companions were safely landed at their **chosen** place; the Frenchman, according to the contract made ere sailing, engaged to take them off upon returning from a four months' cruise in the westward seas; which interval the three adventurers deemed quite sufficient for their purposes.

On the isle's lone beach they **paid** him in silver for their passage out, the stranger having declined to carry them at all except upon that condition; though **willing** to take every means to **insure** the due **fulfillment** of his promise. Felipe had **striven** hard to have this **payment** put off to the period of the ship's return.

Italian

apparatus: apparecchio, apparato.	**estimation**: stima, valutazione.	**mournful**: triste.
artistic: artistico.	**favorite**: preferito, favorito.	**paid**: pagato.
brother: fratello, il fratello.	**fond**: tenero, affettuoso, affezionato.	**payment**: pagamento.
chest: petto, torace, cassapanca, cassa.	**fulfillment**: adempimento,	**purity**: purezza, pulizia.
chosen: scelto, eletto.	appagamento.	**softly**: morbidamente.
cooking: cucina.	**glass**: vetro, bicchiere, cristallo.	**striven**: sforzato, si sforzato.
delicacy: delicatezza.	**grounds**: fondamento, stessa	**tracing**: tracciato, lucido.
depict: descrivete, descriviamo,	connessione a terra.	**versed**: versato, esperto.
descrivo, descrivono, ritraiamo,	**insure**: assicurare, assicuri,	**whaler**: baleniere, baleniera.
dipingi, dipingo, dipingiamo,	assicuriamo, assicurate, assicurano,	**wherever**: dovunque, laddove.
descrivi, ritrai, ritraggono.	assicura, assicuro.	**widow**: vedova.
dogs: cani.	**joyous**: gioioso.	**willing**: disposto, volenteroso.

But in vain. Still they thought they had, in another way, **ample pledge** of the good faith of the Frenchman. It was **arranged** that the **expenses** of the passage home should not be **payable** in silver, but in tortoises; one hundred tortoises ready captured to the returning captain's hand. These the Cholos meant to secure after their own work was done, against the **probable** time of the Frenchman's coming back; and no doubt in prospect already felt, that in those hundred tortoises—now somewhere ranging the isle's interior—they **possessed** one hundred hostages. Enough: the vessel sailed; the gazing three on shore answered the loud **glee** of the singing crew; and ere evening, the French **craft** was hull down in the distant sea, its masts three faintest lines which quickly faded from Hunilla's eye.

The stranger had given a **blithesome** promise, and anchored it with oaths; but oaths and anchors equally will **drag**; naught else **abides** on **fickle** earth but unkept **promises** of joy. Contrary winds from out **unstable** skies, or contrary moods of his more **varying** mind, or shipwreck and sudden death in solitary waves; whatever was the cause, the blithe stranger never was seen again.

Yet, however dire a calamity was here in store, misgivings of it ere due time never **disturbed** the Cholos' busy mind, now all intent upon the **toilsome** matter which had brought them hither. Nay, by swift **doom** coming like the **thief** at night, ere seven weeks went by, two of the little party were removed from all anxieties of land or sea. No more they sought to gaze with **feverish** fear, or still more feverish hope, beyond the present's horizon line; but into the furthest future their own silent spirits sailed. By **persevering** labor beneath that burning sun, Felipe and Truxill had brought down to their **hut** many scores of tortoises, and tried out the oil, when, **elated** with their good success, and to **reward** themselves for such hard work, they, too **hastily**, made a **catamaran**, or Indian raft, much used on the Spanish main, and merrily started on a fishing trip, just without a long reef with many **jagged** gaps, running parallel with the shore, about half a mile from it. By some bad **tide** or hap, or natural **negligence** of **joyfulness** (for though they could not be heard, yet by their gestures they seemed singing at the time) forced in deep water against that iron bar, the ill-

Italian

abides: aspetta.
ample: ampio.
arranged: sistemato, predisposto, ordinato.
blithesome: gaio, allegro, gioioso.
catamaran: catamarano.
disturbed: disturbato.
doom: condannare, destino.
drag: trascinare, trascina, trascino, trasciniamo, trascini, trascinate, trascinano, tirare, resistenza.
elated: esaltato, esultante.

expenses: spese.
feverish: febbrile, febbricitante.
fickle: incostante, volubile.
glee: allegria, gioia.
hastily: frettolosamente.
hut: capanna, baracca, rifugio.
jagged: frastagliato, dentellato.
joyfulness: gioia.
negligence: negligenza, trascuratezza, condotta negligente.
payable: pagabile, esigibile.
persevering: perseverando.

pledge: pegno, impegno.
possessed: posseduto.
probable: probabile.
promises: promette.
raft: zattera.
reward: ricompensare, ricompensa, premiare, compenso.
thief: ladro, ladra.
tide: marea.
toilsome: faticoso.
unstable: instabile.
varying: variando, variare.

made catamaran was overset, and came all to pieces; when dashed by broad-chested swells between their broken logs and the sharp **teeth** of the reef, both **adventurers** perished before Hunilla's eyes.

Before Hunilla's eyes they sank. The real **woe** of this event **passed** before her sight as some sham tragedy on the stage. She was seated on a rude bower among the **withered** thickets, crowning a lofty **cliff**, a little back from the beach. The thickets were so disposed, that in looking upon the sea at large she peered out from among the branches as from the **lattice** of a high balcony. But upon the day we speak of here, the better to watch the adventure of those two hearts she loved, Hunilla had withdrawn the branches to one side, and held them so. They formed an oval frame, through which the bluely boundless sea rolled like a **painted** one. And there, the invisible **painter** painted to her view the wave-tossed and **disjointed** raft, its once level logs slantingly upheaved, as **raking** masts, and the four **struggling** arms **indistinguishable** among them; and then all **subsided** into smooth-flowing creamy waters, slowly drifting the splintered wreck; while first and last, no sound of any sort was heard. Death in a silent picture; a dream of the eye; such vanishing shapes as the mirage shows.

So instant was the scene, so trance-like its mild **pictorial** effect, so distant from her blasted bower and her common sense of things, that Hunilla gazed and gazed, nor raised a finger or a **wail**. But as good to sit thus dumb, in **stupor staring** on that dumb show, for all that otherwise might be done. With half a mile of sea between, how could her two enchanted arms **aid** those four **fated** ones? The distance long, the time one **sand**. After the lightning is beheld, what fool shall stay the thunder-bolt? Felipe's body was washed ashore, but Truxill's never came; only his gay, braided hat of golden straw — that same **sunflower** thing he waved to her, pushing from the strand — and now, to the last **gallant**, it still **saluted** her. But Felipe's body **floated** to the marge, with one arm encirclingly outstretched. Lock-jawed in grim death, the lover-husband softly clasped his **bride**, true to her even in death's dream. Ah, heaven, when man thus keeps his faith, **wilt thou** be **faithless** who **created** the faithful one? But they cannot break faith who never plighted it.

Italian

adventure: avventura.
aid: aiutare, aiuto, assistere, assistenza, soccorrere, assistente, soccorso.
bride: sposa, fidanzata, novella sposa.
cliff: scogliera, rupe.
created: creato.
disjointed: disgiunto, sconnesso.
faithless: sleale.
fated: destinato.
floated: galleggiato.
gallant: galante, coraggioso, valoroso.

indistinguishable: indistinguibile.
lattice: reticolo, traliccio.
painted: dipinto, verniciato.
painter: pittore.
passed: passato.
pictorial: pittorico, illustrato.
raking: rastrellare, rastrellamento, rastrellatura.
saluted: salutato.
sand: sabbia, insabbiare, rena.
staring: fissare.
struggling: lottare.

stupor: stupore.
subsided: abbassato, calato, cessato, sprofondato.
sunflower: girasole.
teeth: denti, dentatura.
thou: tu.
wail: gemere.
wilt: appassire, appassisco, appassiscono, appassisci, appassiamo, appassite.
withered: appassito.
woe: dolore, calamità, afflizione.

It needs not to be said what nameless misery now wrapped the lonely widow. In telling her own story she passed this almost **entirely** over, simply recounting the event. Construe the comment of her features as you might, from her mere words little would you have weened that Hunilla was **herself** the **heroine** of her tale. But not thus did she **defraud** us of our **tears**. All hearts **bled** that grief could be so brave.

She but showed us her soul's lid, and the strange ciphers thereon **engraved**; all within, with pride's **timidity**, was withheld. Yet was there one exception. Holding out her small **olive** hand before her captain, she said in mild and slowest Spanish, "Señor, I buried him;" then paused, **struggled** as against the **writhed** coilings of a **snake**, and cringing suddenly, leaped up, repeating in **impassioned pain**, "I buried him, my life, my soul!"

Doubtless, it was by half-unconscious, **automatic** motions of her hands, that this heavy-hearted one **performed** the final office for Felipe, and planted a rude **cross** of withered sticks—no green ones might be had—at the head of that lonely grave, where rested now in lasting un-complaint and quiet haven he whom untranquil seas had **overthrown**.

But some dull sense of another body that should be interred, of another cross that should **hallow** another grave—unmade as yet—some dull anxiety and pain touching her undiscovered brother, now haunted the oppressed Hunilla. Her hands fresh from the **burial** earth, she slowly went back to the beach, with unshaped purposes wandering there, her spell-bound eye bent upon the incessant waves. But they bore nothing to her but a **dirge**, which **maddened** her to think that murderers should **mourn**. As time went by, and these things came less dreamingly to her mind, the strong persuasions of her Romish faith, which sets peculiar store by consecrated urns, prompted her to resume in **waking** earnest that **pious search** which had but been **begun** as in **somnambulism**. Day after day, week after week, she trod the cindery beach, till at length a **double** motive edged every eager glance. With equal longing she now looked for the living and the dead; the brother and the captain; alike vanished, never to return. Little **accurate** note of time had Hunilla taken under such emotions as were hers,

Italian

accurate: esatto, preciso, accurato.
automatic: automatico.
begun: cominciato, iniziato.
bled: sanguinato.
burial: sepoltura, inumazione.
cross: croce, attraversare, irato, incrociare, incrocio, varcare, valicare, traversare, accavallare.
defraud: defraudare.
dirge: nenia.
double: doppio, sosia, raddoppiare, duplice.

engraved: inciso.
entirely: completamente, interamente.
hallow: santificare.
heroine: eroina.
hers: suo.
impassioned: appassionato.
maddened: impazzito, esasperato.
mourn: piangere, piangi, piangiamo, piango, piangono, piangete.
olive: oliva, olivastro.
overthrown: rovesciato.
pain: dolore, male, addolorare, pena,

affliggere.
performed: eseguito.
pious: pio.
search: ricerca, cerca, ricercare, cercare, perquisizione.
snake: serpente.
somnambulism: sonnambulismo.
struggled: lottato.
tears: lacrime.
timidity: timidezza.
waking: svegliare.
writhed: storto, torto.

and little, **outside** herself, served for **calendar** or **dial**. As to poor Crusoe in the self-same sea, no saint's bell pealed forth the **lapse** of week or month; each day went by unchallenged; no chanticleer announced those sultry dawns, no lowing herds those **poisonous** nights. All **wonted** and steadily **recurring** sounds, human, or **humanized** by sweet fellowship with man, but one stirred that **torrid** trance— the cry of dogs; save which naught but the rolling sea invaded it, an all-pervading **monotone**; and to the widow that was the least loved voice she could have heard.

No wonder, that as her thoughts now wandered to the unreturning ship, and were beaten back again, the hope against hope so struggled in her soul, that at length she **desperately** said, "Not yet, not yet; my foolish heart runs on too fast." So she forced patience for some further weeks. But to those whom earth's sure indraft draws, patience or impatience is still the same.

Hunilla now sought to settle precisely in her mind, to an hour, how long it was since the ship had sailed; and then, with the same **precision**, how long a space remained to pass. But this proved impossible. What present day or month it was she could not say. Time was her **labyrinth**, in which Hunilla was entirely lost.

And now follows—

Against my own purposes a pause **descends** upon me here. One knows not whether nature doth not impose some **secrecy** upon him who has been **privy** to certain things. At least, it is to be doubted whether it be good to **blazon** such. If some books are deemed most **baneful** and their **sale** forbid, how, then, with deadlier **facts**, not dreams of doting men? Those whom books will **hurt** will not be **proof** against events. Events, not books, should be forbid. But in all things man sows upon the wind, which bloweth just there **whither** it listeth; for ill or good, man **cannot** know. Often ill comes from the good, as good from ill.

When Hunilla—

Dire sight it is to see some silken **beast** long **dally** with a golden **lizard** ere she **devour**. More terrible, to see how **feline** Fate will sometimes dally with a human soul, and by a nameless magic make it **repulse** a sane despair with a

Italian

baneful: pernicioso.
beast: bestia, animale.
blazon: blasone.
calendar: calendario.
cannot: non potere.
dally: ozio, oziate, oziano, oziamo, ozia, ozi, oziare.
descends: scende, discende.
desperately: disperatamente.
devour: divorare, divorano, divora, divorate, divoriamo, divoro, divori.
dial: quadrante.

facts: fatti.
feline: felino.
humanized: umanizzato.
hurt: ferire, far male, ferita, dolere.
labyrinth: labirinto.
lapse: scivolare, sbaglio, intervallo, passare, errore, periodo.
lizard: lucertola.
monotone: tono uniforme.
outside: fuori, esterno, esterne.
poisonous: velenoso, tossico, venefico.
precision: precisione, accuratezza.

privy: al corrente, privato.
proof: prova, bozza, dimostrazione, provino, impermeabilizzare, resistente.
recurring: ricorrendo, ritornando, ricorrente.
repulse: rifiuto, respingere.
sale: vendita, smercio, svendita.
secrecy: segretezza.
torrid: torrido.
whither: dove.
wonted: usuale, consueto, solito.

hope which is but mad. Unwittingly I **imp** this cat-like thing, **sporting** with the heart of him who **reads**; for if he feel not he reads in vain.

— "The ship sails this day, to-day," at last said Hunilla to herself; "this gives me certain time to stand on; without **certainty** I go mad. In loose **ignorance** I have **hoped** and hoped; now in firm **knowledge** I will but wait. Now I live and no longer **perish** in bewilderings. **Holy** Virgin, aid me! Thou wilt waft back the ship. Oh, past length of weary weeks — all to be dragged over — to buy the certainty of to-day, I freely give ye, though I tear ye from me!"

As mariners, tost in tempest on some **desolate** ledge, patch them a boat out of the remnants of their vessel's wreck, and **launch** it in the self-same waves, see here Hunilla, this lone shipwrecked soul, out of **treachery invoking** trust. Humanity, thou strong thing, I **worship** thee, not in the laureled victor, but in this **vanquished** one.

Truly Hunilla leaned upon a **reed**, a real one; no **metaphor**; a real Eastern reed. A piece of hollow cane, drifted from unknown isles, and found upon the beach, its once jagged ends rubbed smoothly even as by sand-paper; its golden **glazing** gone. Long ground between the sea and land, upper and **nether** stone, the **unvarnished** substance was filed **bare**, and wore another polish now, one with itself, the polish of its agony. **Circular** lines at intervals cut all round this surface, **divided** it into six **panels** of **unequal** length. In the first were scored the days, each **tenth** one marked by a longer and deeper **notch**; the second was scored for the number of sea-fowl **eggs** for **sustenance**, picked out from the rocky nests; the third, how many fish had been caught from the shore; the fourth, how many small tortoises found inland; the fifth, how many days of sun; the **sixth**, of clouds; which last, of the two, was the greater one. Long night of busy numbering, misery's **mathematics**, to weary her too-wakeful soul to sleep; yet sleep for that was none.

The panel of the days was deeply worn — the long tenth notches half effaced, as alphabets of the blind. Ten thousand times the longing widow had traced her finger over the bamboo — dull **flute**, which played, on, gave no sound — as if

Italian

bare: nudo, denudare.
certainty: certezza.
circular: circolare.
desolate: desolato.
divided: diviso, separato.
eggs: uova, le uova.
flute: flauto, scanalatura.
glazing: vetrata.
holy: santo, sacro.
hoped: sperato.
ignorance: ignoranza.
imp: folletto.

invoking: invocando.
launch: lancio, varare, varo, lancia, lanciare.
ledge: sporgenza, cengia.
mathematics: matematica.
metaphor: metafora.
nether: inferiore.
notch: tacca, intaglio, incisione, incavo.
panels: pannelli campione o pannelli espositivi, pannelli.
perish: perire.

reads: legge.
reed: canna, ancia.
sixth: sesto, sesta.
sporting: sportivo.
sustenance: sostentamento.
tenth: decimo.
treachery: tradimento.
unequal: ineguale, disuguale.
unvarnished: non verniciato.
vanquished: sconfitto, vinto.
worship: adorare, venerare, culto, venerazione.

counting birds flown by in air would **hasten** tortoises **creeping** through the woods.

After the one hundred and **eightieth** day no further mark was seen; that last one was the faintest, as the first the deepest.

"There were more days," said our Captain; "many, many more; why did you not go on and **notch** them, too, Hunilla?"

"Señor, **ask** me not."

"And meantime, did no other vessel pass the isle?"

"Nay, Señor; — but —"

"You do not speak; but *what*, Hunilla?"

"Ask me not, Señor."

"You saw ships pass, far away; you waved to them; they passed on; — was that it, Hunilla?"

"Señor, be it as you say."

Braced against her **woe**, Hunilla would not, durst not trust the weakness of her tongue. Then when our Captain asked whether any whale-boats had —

But no, I will not **file** this thing **complete** for scoffing souls to **quote**, and **call** it **firm** proof upon their side. The half shall here remain **untold**. Those two unnamed events which befell Hunilla on this isle, let them **abide** between her and her God. In nature, as in law, it may be **libelous** to speak some truths.

Still, how it was that, although our vessel had lain three days **anchored nigh** the isle, its one human **tenant** should not have discovered us till just upon the point of sailing, never to **revisit** so lone and far a spot, this needs **explaining** ere the **sequel** come.

The place where the French captain had landed the little party was on the further and opposite end of the isle. There, too, it was that they had afterwards **built** their hut. Nor did the widow in her **solitude** desert the spot where her loved ones had dwelt with her, and where the dearest of the twain now slept his

---

Italian

abide: aspettare, aspettiamo, aspetta, aspettano, aspetti, aspetto, aspettate, restare, sopportare.
anchored: ancorato.
ask: chiedere, chiedi, chiediamo, chiedo, chiedete, chiedono, domandare, domando, domandate, domandi, domandiamo.
built: costruito.
call: chiamare, chiami, chiamiamo, chiamo, chiamano, chiama, chiamate, chiamata, appello.

complete: completo, completare, pieno, ultimare, finire.
counting: contare, conteggio.
creeping: strisciando, strisciante.
eightieth: ottantesimo.
explaining: spiegando.
file: lima, archivio, file, pratica, schedario, incartamento, fascicolo, limare, fila, archiviare.
firm: ditta, azienda, impresa, stabile, saldo, sodo, fermo.
hasten: affrettarsi, affrettare.

libelous: diffamatorio.
nigh: vicino.
notch: tacca, intaglio, incisione, incavo.
quote: citare, citazione, quotare.
revisit: rivisitano, rivisito, rivisitiamo, rivisiti, rivisita, rivisitate, rivisitare.
sequel: seguito.
solitude: solitudine.
tenant: affittuario, inquilino, locatario.
untold: non detto.
woe: dolore, calamità, afflizione.

last long **sleep**, and all her plaints awaked him not, and he of husbands the most faithful during life.

Now, high, broken land rises between the opposite extremities of the isle. A ship **anchored** at one side is invisible from the other. Neither is the isle so small, but a **considerable** company might wander for days through the wilderness of one side, and never be seen, or their halloos heard, by any stranger holding aloof on the other. Hence Hunilla, who **naturally** associated the possible coming of ships with her own part of the isle, might to the end have remained quite ignorant of the presence of our vessel, were it not for a mysterious **presentiment**, borne to her, so our mariners **averred**, by this isle's **enchanted** air. Nor did the widow's **answer undo** the thought.

"How did you come to cross the isle this morning, then, Hunilla?" said our Captain.

"Señor, something came **flitting** by me. It touched my cheek, my heart, Señor."

"What do you say, Hunilla?"

"I have said, Señor, something came through the air."

It was a **narrow** chance. For when in crossing the isle Hunilla gained the high land in the centre, she must then for the first have perceived our masts, and also marked that their sails were being loosed, perhaps even heard the **echoing** chorus of the **windlass song**. The strange ship was about to sail, and she behind. With all haste she now **descends** the height on the **hither** side, but soon **loses** sight of the ship among the sunken jungles at the mountain's base. She struggles on through the **withered** branches, which seek at every step to bar her **path**, till she comes to the **isolated** rock, still some way from the water. This she climbs, to **reassure** herself. The ship is still in plainest sight. But now, worn out with over **tension**, Hunilla all but **faints**; she fears to step down from her **giddy** perch; she is fain to pause, there where she is, and as a last resort **catches** the **turban** from her head, **unfurls** and waves it over the jungles towards us.

Italian

anchored: ancorato.
answer: risposta, rispondere, replicare, rispondere a.
averred: asserito.
catches: prende, colpisce.
considerable: considerevole, notevole, ragguardevole, rilevante.
descends: scende, discende.
echoing: risuonare.
enchanted: incantato.
faints: sviene.
flitting: svolazzando, aleggiando.

giddy: stordito.
hither: qui, quà.
isolated: isolato.
loses: perde.
narrow: stretto, ristretto, angusto.
naturally: naturalmente.
path: sentiero, percorso, viottolo, traiettoria, cammino, viale, via.
presentiment: presentimento.
reassure: rassicurare, rassicuri, rassicuriamo, rassicuro, rassicurano, rassicura, rassicurate.

sleep: sonno, dormire, dormi, dormiamo, dormite, dormo, dormono.
song: canzone, canto.
tension: tensione.
turban: turbante.
undo: disfare, disfate, disfa', disfacciamo, disfaccio, disfai, disfanno.
unfurls: spiega.
windlass: argano, verricello.
withered: appassito.

During the telling of her story the mariners formed a voiceless circle round Hunilla and the Captain; and when at length the word was given to man the fastest boat, and pull round to the isle's thither side, to bring away Hunilla's chest and the tortoise-oil, such alacrity of both cheery and sad obedience seldom before was seen. Little ado was made. Already the anchor had been recommitted to the bottom, and the ship swung **calmly** to it.

But Hunilla insisted upon accompanying the boat as indispensable pilot to her hidden hut. So being **refreshed** with the best the steward could **supply**, she started with us. Nor did ever any wife of the most famous **admiral**, in her husband's **barge**, receive more silent reverence of respect than poor Hunilla from this boat's crew.

Rounding many a vitreous **cape** and **bluff**, in two hours' time we shot inside the fatal reef; wound into a secret **cove**, looked up along a green many-gabled lava wall, and saw the island's solitary dwelling.

It hung upon an **impending** cliff, sheltered on two sides by tangled thickets, and half-screened from view in front by juttings of the rude **stairway**, which climbed the **precipice** from the sea. Built of canes, it was thatched with long, mildewed grass. It seemed an abandoned hay-rick, whose haymakers were now no more. The roof inclined but one way; the eaves coming to within two feet of the ground. And here was a simple apparatus to **collect** the dews, or rather doubly-distilled and finest **winnowed** rains, which, in mercy or in **mockery**, the night-skies sometimes drop upon these blighted Encantadas. All along beneath the eaves, a spotted **sheet**, quite weather-stained, was **spread**, **pinned** to short, upright stakes, set in the shallow sand. A small clinker, thrown into the **cloth**, weighed its middle down, thereby straining all **moisture** into a **calabash** placed below. This vessel supplied each drop of water ever **drunk** upon the isle by the Cholos. Hunilla told us the calabash, would sometimes, but not often, be half filled **overnight**. It held six quarts, perhaps. "But," said she, "we were used to thirst. At **sandy** Payta, where I live, no **shower** from heaven ever fell; all the water there is brought on mules from the inland vales."

Italian

admiral: ammiraglio.
barge: chiatta, barcone.
bluff: bluffare.
calabash: zucca.
calmly: con calma.
cape: cappa, capo, promontorio.
cloth: stoffa, tessuto, tela, panno.
collect: raccogliere, raccolgono, raccolgo, raccogliete, raccogliamo, raccogli.
cove: cala, insenatura.
drunk: ubriaco, brillo, ubriacone, bevuto.
impending: imminente.
mockery: derisione.
moisture: umidità.
overnight: di notte.
pinned: appuntato.
precipice: precipizio, abisso, burrone, dirupo.
refreshed: rinvigorito, ristorato, rinfrescato.
sandy: sabbioso, arenoso.
sheet: foglio, lenzuolo, foglia, scotta, lastra.
shower: doccia, fare la doccia, rovescio.
spread: diffondere, spargere, diffusione, spalmare, propagare, scarto.
stairway: scala.
supply: fornitura, rifornimento, fornire, approvvigionamento, erogare, alimentazione, offerta, provvedere, scorta.
winnowed: vagliato.

Tied among the thickets were some **twenty** moaning tortoises, **supplying** Hunilla's lonely **larder**; while hundreds of vast tableted black bucklers, like **displaced**, shattered tomb-stones of dark **slate**, were also scattered round. These were the skeleton backs of those great tortoises from which Felipe and Truxill had made their precious **oil**. Several large **calabashes** and two **goodly** kegs were filled with it. In a pot near by were the **caked crusts** of a **quantity** which had been permitted to **evaporate**. "They meant to have strained it off next day," said Hunilla, as she **turned** aside.

I forgot to mention the most singular sight of all, though the first that greeted us after landing.

Some ten small, soft-haired, ringleted dogs, of a beautiful **breed**, peculiar to Peru, set up a **concert** of glad welcomings when we gained the beach, which was responded to by Hunilla. Some of these dogs had, since her widowhood, been born upon the isle, the **progeny** of the two brought from Payta. Owing to the jagged **steeps** and pitfalls, **tortuous** thickets, sunken clefts and perilous intricacies of all sorts in the interior, Hunilla, **admonished** by the **loss** of one **favorite** among them, never **allowed** these delicate creatures to follow her in her occasional birds'-nests climbs and other wanderings; so that, through long **habituation**, they offered not to follow, when that morning she crossed the land, and her own soul was then too full of other things to heed their lingering behind. Yet, all along she had so clung to them, that, besides what moisture they lapped up at early **daybreak** from the small scoop-holes among the **adjacent** rocks, she had **shared** the dew of her calabash among them; never laying by any considerable store against those prolonged and utter **droughts** which, in some disastrous seasons, **warp** these isles.

Having pointed out, at our desire, what few things she would like transported to the ship—her chest, the oil, not **omitting** the live tortoises which she intended for a **grateful** present to our Captain—we immediately set to work, carrying them to the boat down the long, sloping **stair** of deeply-shadowed rock. While my comrades were thus employed, I looked and Hunilla had disappeared.

Italian

adjacent: adiacente, vicino.
admonished: ammonito.
allowed: permesso.
breed: razza, varietà.
caked: incrostato.
calabash: zucca.
concert: concerto.
crusts: croste.
daybreak: alba.
displaced: spostato.
droughts: siccità.
evaporate: evaporare, evaporate,

evaporo, evapori, evaporano, evapora, evaporiamo, vaporare.
favorite: preferito, favorito.
goodly: bonariamente.
grateful: riconoscente, grato.
habituation: assuefazione.
larder: dispensa.
loss: perdita, danno, smarrimento, deficit.
oil: olio, petrolio, l'olio, lubrificare, oliare.
omitting: omettendo.

progeny: progenie.
quantity: quantità, grandezza.
shared: dividere, condiviso, diviso.
slate: ardesia.
stair: scalino, scala, gradino.
steeps: immerge, bagna.
supplying: approvvigionamento, fornitura.
tortuous: tortuoso.
turned: girato, svoltato, cambiato.
twenty: venti.
warp: ordito, ordire.

It was not curiosity alone, but, it seems to me, something different **mingled** with it, which prompted me to drop my **tortoise**, and once more gaze slowly around. I **remembered** the **husband** buried by Hunilla's hands. A narrow **pathway** led into a dense part of the thickets. Following it through many mazes, I came out upon a small, round, open space, deeply chambered there.

The **mound rose** in the middle; a bare heap of finest sand, like that unverdured heap found at the bottom of an hour-glass run out. At its head stood the cross of **withered** sticks; the dry, **peeled** bark still fraying from it; its **transverse** limb tied up with rope, and forlornly adroop in the silent air.

Hunilla was partly **prostrate** upon the grave; her dark head bowed, and lost in her long, loosened Indian **hair**; her hands extended to the cross-foot, with a little brass **crucifix** clasped between; a crucifix worn **featureless**, like an **ancient graven knocker** long **plied** in vain. She did not see me, and I made no **noise**, but slid aside, and left the spot.

A few moments ere all was ready for our going, she **reappeared** among us. I looked into her eyes, but saw no tear. There was something which seemed strangely **haughty** in her air, and yet it was the air of **woe**. A Spanish and an Indian grief, which would not **visibly lament**. Pride's height in vain **abased** to proneness on the **rack**; nature's pride **subduing** nature's **torture**.

Like **pages** the small and silken dogs surrounded her, as she slowly descended towards the beach. She caught the two most eager creatures in her arms:—"Mia Teeta! Mia Tomoteeta!" and **fondling** them, inquired how many could we take on board.

The mate commanded the boat's crew; not a hard-hearted man, but his way of life had been such that in most things, even in the smallest, **simple** utility was his **leading** motive.

"We **cannot** take them all, Hunilla; our supplies are short; the winds are unreliable; we may be a good many days going to Tombez. So take those you have, Hunilla; but no more."

Italian

abased: degradato.
ancient: antico.
cannot: non potere.
crucifix: crocifisso.
featureless: informe.
fondling: accarezzando.
graven: scolpito, inciso.
hair: capelli, capello, pelo, capigliatura.
haughty: altezzoso.
husband: marito, sposo.
knocker: battente.

lament: lamento, lamentare.
leading: conducendo, guidando.
mingled: mischiato, mescolato.
mound: tumulo.
noise: rumore, schiamazzo.
pages: pagine.
pathway: sentiero.
peeled: sbucciato.
plied: maneggiato.
prostrate: prostrato.
rack: cremagliera, rastrelliera, scaffale, intelaiatura.

reappeared: riapparso.
remembered: ricordato.
rose: rosa.
simple: semplice.
subduing: assoggettando, sottomettendo.
tortoise: tartaruga.
torture: torturare, tortura.
transverse: trasversale.
visibly: visibilmente.
withered: appassito.
woe: dolore, calamità, afflizione.

She was in the boat; the oarsmen, too, were seated; all save one, who stood ready to **push** off and then spring himself. With the **sagacity** of their race, the dogs now seemed aware that they were in the very instant of being deserted upon a barren **strand**. The gunwales of the boat were high; its prow — presented inland — was lifted; so owing to the water, which they seemed instinctively to **shun**, the dogs could not well leap into the little craft. But their **busy** paws hard scraped the prow, as it had been some farmer's door **shutting** them out from shelter in a **winter** storm. A **clamorous** agony of alarm. They did not howl, or **whine**; they all but spoke.

"Push off! Give way!" cried the mate. The boat gave one **heavy** drag and **lurch**, and next moment shot swiftly from the beach, turned on her heel, and **sped**. The dogs ran howling along the water's marge; now pausing to gaze at the **flying** boat, then motioning as if to leap in chase, but mysteriously withheld themselves; and again ran howling along the beach. Had they been human beings, hardly would they have more **vividly** inspired the sense of desolation. The oars were **plied** as **confederate** feathers of two wings. No one spoke. I looked back upon the beach, and then upon Hunilla, but her face was set in a stern dusky calm. The dogs **crouching** in her **lap** vainly licked her rigid hands. She never looked be her: but sat motionless, till we turned a **promontory** of the coast and lost all sights and sounds **astern**. She seemed as one who, having experienced the sharpest of mortal pangs, was **henceforth content** to have all lesser heartstrings riven, one by one. To Hunilla, pain seemed so **necessary**, that pain in other beings, though by love and sympathy made her own, was unrepiningly to be borne. A heart of **yearning** in a frame of steel. A heart of earthly yearning, frozen by the **frost** which falleth from the sky.

The sequel is soon told. After a long passage, vexed by calms and baffling winds, we made the little port of Tombez in Peru, there to recruit the ship. Payta was not very distant. Our captain **sold** the tortoise oil to a Tombez **merchant**; and **adding** to the silver a **contribution** from all hands, gave it to our silent passenger, who knew not what the mariners had done.

Italian

adding: aggiungendo, addizionando.
astern: indietro, a poppa.
busy: occupato, affaccendato, indaffarato.
clamorous: clamoroso.
confederate: confederato.
content: contenuto, contento, soddisfatto, soddisfare.
contribution: contributo, contribuzione.
crouching: rannicchiando.
flying: volando, volare, volante.

frost: gelo, brina, gelata.
heavy: pesante, grave.
henceforth: d'ora in poi, d'ora innanzi.
lap: lappare, grembo.
lurch: barcollare.
merchant: commerciante, negoziante, mercante.
necessary: necessario, occorrente.
plied: maneggiato.
promontory: promontorio.
push: spingere, spinta, urto, pigiare.
sagacity: sagacia.

shun: evitare, eviti, evitiamo, evitano, evita, evitate, evito.
shutting: chiudere, chiusura.
sold: venduto.
sped: accelerato.
strand: trefolo, incagliare.
vividly: vivamente.
whine: uggiolare, piagnucolare, piagnucolio.
winter: inverno, l'inverno.
yearning: brama, desideroso, bramoso, bramando, anelando.

The last seen of **lone** Hunilla she was **passing** into Payta **town**, **riding** upon a small **gray** ass; and before her on the ass's shoulders, she **eyed** the **jointed** workings of the beast's **armorial** cross.

SKETCH NINTH

HOOD'S ISLE AND THE HERMIT OBERLUS

"That darkesome glen they **enter**, where they find
That **cursed** man low sitting on the ground,
Musing full sadly in his sullein mind;
His griesly lockes long gronen and **unbound**,
Disordered hong about his shoulders round,
And hid his face, through which his **hollow** eyne
Lookt **deadly** dull, and stared as **astound**;
His raw-bone cheekes, through penurie and **pine**,
Were shronke into the jawes, as he did never **dine**.
His **garments nought** but many **ragged** clouts,
With thornes together pind and **patched reads**,
The which his naked sides he wrapt abouts."

Southeast of Crossman's Isle lies Hood's Isle, or McCain's Beclouded Isle; and upon its south side is a **vitreous cove** with a wide **strand** of dark pounded black **lava**, called Black Beach, or Oberlus's Landing. It might fitly have been styled Charon's.

It received its name from a wild white **creature** who spent many years here; in the person of a European bringing into this **savage** region qualities more **diabolical** than are to be found among any of the surrounding cannibals.

About half a **century** ago, Oberlus **deserted** at the above-named island, then, as now, a **solitude**. He built himself a **den** of lava and clinkers, about a mile from

Italian

armorial: araldico.
ass: asino, ciuco, somaro, culo.
astound: sbalordite, si stupisci, si stupiscono, si stupite, mi stupisco, stupefaccio, stupefai, stupefacciamo, stupefa', sbalordiscono, stupisciti.
century: secolo.
cove: cala, insenatura.
creature: creatura.
cursed: maledetto.
deadly: mortale.
den: tana.

deserted: abbandonato, deserto.
diabolical: diabolico.
dine: cenare.
enter: entrare, entra, entrano, entrate, entri, entriamo, entro, invio.
eyed: occhio.
garments: indumenti.
gray: grigio.
hollow: cavo, cavità, vuoto, incavare.
jointed: articolato.
lava: lava.
lone: solitario, solo.

nought: zero.
patched: rappezzato.
pine: pino.
ragged: cencioso, logoro.
reads: legge.
riding: equitazione, cavalcata.
savage: selvaggio, crudele.
solitude: solitudine.
strand: trefolo, incagliare.
town: città.
unbound: non rilegato.
vitreous: vitreo.

the Landing, subsequently called after him, in a vale, or **expanded gulch**, containing here and there among the rocks about two acres of soil capable of rude **cultivation**; the only place on the isle not too blasted for that purpose. Here he succeeded in raising a sort of **degenerate potatoes** and pumpkins, which from time to time he exchanged with **needy** whalemen passing, for spirits or dollars.

His appearance, from all accounts, was that of the victim of some malignant **sorceress**; he seemed to have drunk of Circe's cup; beast-like; rags **insufficient** to hide his **nakedness**; his befreckled skin blistered by continual **exposure** to the sun;   nose flat; countenance **contorted**, heavy, **earthy**; hair and beard unshorn, **profuse**, and of fiery red. He struck strangers much as if he were a volcanic creature thrown up by the same **convulsion** which **exploded** into sight the isle. All bepatched and **coiled** asleep in his lonely lava den among the mountains, he looked, they say, as a heaped **drift** of withered leaves, torn from autumn trees, and so left in some hidden nook by the whirling **halt** for an instant of a **fierce** night-wind, which then **ruthlessly** sweeps on, somewhere else to repeat the capricious act. It is also reported to have been the strangest sight, this same Oberlus, of a sultry, cloudy morning, hidden under his **shocking** old black **tarpaulin** hat, **hoeing** potatoes among the lava. So warped and crooked was his strange nature, that the very handle of his hoe seemed gradually to have shrunk and **twisted** in his **grasp**, being a **wretched** bent stick, elbowed more like a savage's war-sickle than a civilized hoe-handle. It was his mysterious custom upon a first encounter with a stranger ever to present his back; possibly, because that was his better side, since it revealed the least. If the encounter chanced in his garden, as it sometimes did — the new-landed strangers going from the sea-side straight through the gorge, to **hunt** up the queer green-grocer reported doing business here — Oberlus for a time hoed on, unmindful of all greeting, **jovial** or bland; as the curious stranger would turn to face him, the **recluse**, hoe in hand, as diligently would avert himself; bowed over, and sullenly revolving round his murphy hill. Thus far for hoeing. When **planting**, his whole aspect and all his gestures were so malevolently and uselessly sinister and secret, that he seemed rather in act of dropping **poison** into wells than potatoes into soil. But among his lesser and more harmless marvels was an idea he ever had, that his visitors came

Italian

coiled: avvolto.
contorted: contorto.
convulsion: convulsione.
cultivation: coltivazione.
degenerate: degenerare, degenerato.
drift: deriva, spostamento.
earthy: terroso.
expanded: espanso.
exploded: esploso.
exposure: esposizione.
fierce: feroce.
grasp: afferrare, stretta, comprendere.

gulch: gola.
halt: fermarsi, fermare, fermata, alt, arresto, sosta.
hoe: zappare, zappa, la zappa.
hoeing: zappatura.
hunt: cacciare, cacci, caccio, cacciate, cacciano, cacciamo, caccia, braccare.
insufficient: insufficiente.
jovial: gioviale.
nakedness: nudità.
needy: bisognoso, indigente, povero.
planting: piantare.

poison: veleno, avvelenare.
potatoes: patate.
profuse: abbondante, profuso.
recluse: eremita.
ruthlessly: spietatamente.
shocking: irritante, scandaloso.
sorceress: maga, strega.
tarpaulin: telone, tela cerata, incerata.
twisted: torto, attorcigliato, contorto, ritorto.
wretched: misero, miserabile, povero, infelice.

equally as well led by longings to behold the mighty **hermit** Oberlus in his royal state of solitude, as simply, to obtain potatoes, or find whatever company might be upon a barren isle. It seems incredible that such a being should **possess** such vanity; a **misanthrope** be **conceited**; but he really had his notion; and upon the strength of it, often gave himself **amusing** airs to captains. But after all, this is somewhat of a piece with the well-known eccentricity of some convicts, **proud** of that very hatefulness which makes them **notorious**. At other times, another unaccountable **whim** would seize him, and he would long **dodge** advancing strangers round the clinkered corners of his hut; sometimes like a stealthy bear, he would **slink** through the withered thickets up the mountains, and refuse to see the human face.

Except his occasional visitors from the sea, for a long period, the only companions of Oberlus were the crawling tortoises; and he seemed more than degraded to their level, having no desires for a time beyond theirs, unless it were for the stupor brought on by **drunkenness**. But sufficiently **debased** as he appeared, there yet lurked in him, only awaiting occasion for discovery, a still further proneness. Indeed, the sole **superiority** of Oberlus over the tortoises was his **possession** of a larger capacity of **degradation**; and along with that, something like an intelligent will to it. Moreover, what is about to be **revealed**, perhaps will show, that **selfish** ambition, or the love of rule for its own sake, far from being the peculiar **infirmity** of noble minds, is shared by beings which have no mind at all. No creatures are so **selfishly tyrannical** as some brutes; as any one who has observed the tenants of the pasture must **occasionally** have observed.

"This island's mine by Sycorax my mother," said Oberlus to himself, **glaring** round upon his haggard solitude. By some means, **barter** or theft—for in those days ships at intervals still kept touching at his Landing—he obtained an old musket, with a few **charges** of **powder** and ball. Possessed of arms, he was **stimulated** to **enterprise**, as a **tiger** that first feels the coming of its claws. The long habit of sole dominion over every object round him, his almost **unbroken** solitude, his never **encountering** humanity except on terms of misanthropic

Italian

amusing: divertente, divertendo, spassoso.
barter: baratto, barattare.
charges: oneri, spese.
conceited: vanitoso, presuntuoso.
debased: avvilito, deprezzato, abbassato, degradato.
degradation: degradazione.
dodge: espediente.
drunkenness: ebbrezza, ubriachezza.
encountering: incontrando.
enterprise: impresa.

glaring: abbagliante, sfolgorante.
hermit: eremita.
infirmity: infermità.
misanthrope: misantropo.
notorious: famigerato, notorio.
occasionally: occasionalmente.
possess: possedere, possedete, possediamo, possiedi, possiedo, possiedono.
possession: possesso.
powder: polvere, cipria, polverina.
proud: orgoglioso, fiero.

revealed: pubblicato, rivelato.
selfish: egoistico, egoista.
selfishly: egoisticamente.
slink: sgattaiolare, sgattaiolano, sgattaioliamo, sgattaiolo, sgattaiola, sgattaiolate, sgattaioli.
stimulated: stimolato.
superiority: superiorità.
tiger: tigre, la tigre.
tyrannical: tirannico.
unbroken: ininterrotto, intatto.
whim: capriccio, fisima.

independence, or mercantile **craftiness**, and even such **encounters** being comparatively but rare; all this must have gradually nourished in him a vast idea of his own **importance**, together with a pure animal sort of scorn for all the rest of the universe.

The unfortunate Creole, who **enjoyed** his brief **term** of royalty at Charles's Isle was perhaps in some degree **influenced** by not unworthy motives; such as prompt other **adventurous** spirits to lead colonists into distant regions and **assume** political preeminence over them. His summary **execution** of many of his Peruvians is quite **pardonable**, considering the desperate characters he had to deal with; while his offering canine battle to the banded rebels seems under the **circumstances** altogether just. But for this King Oberlus and what **shortly** follows, no shade of palliation can be given. He acted out of mere delight in tyranny and cruelty, by virtue of a **quality** in him **inherited** from Sycorax his mother. Armed now with that shocking blunderbuss, strong in the thought of being master of that **horrid** isle, he **panted** for a chance to prove his **potency** upon the first specimen of humanity which should fall unbefriended into his hands.

Nor was he long without it. One day he spied a boat upon the beach, with one man, a negro, standing by it. Some distance off was a ship, and Oberlus immediately knew how matters stood. The vessel had put in for wood, and the boat's crew had gone into the thickets for it. From a convenient spot he kept watch of the boat, till presently a **straggling** company appeared **loaded** with billets. Throwing these on the beach, they again went into the thickets, while the negro proceeded to load the boat.

Oberlus now makes all haste and **accosts** the negro, who, **aghast** at seeing any living being **inhabiting** such a solitude, and especially so **horrific** a one, immediately falls into a panic, not at all lessened by the ursine suavity of Oberlus, who **begs** the favor of assisting him in his labors. The negro stands with several billets on his shoulder, in act of shouldering others; and Oberlus, with a short cord concealed in his bosom, kindly proceeds to **lift** those other billets to their place. In so doing, he persists in keeping behind the negro, who, **rightly** suspicious of this, in vain dodges about to gain the **front** of Oberlus; but Oberlus

Italian

accosts: accosta, avvicina, abborda, approcci.
adventurous: avventuroso.
aghast: atterrito, inorridito.
assume: presumere, presumo, presumono, presumiamo, presumi, presumete, assumere, supporre.
begs: mendica.
circumstances: circostanze.
craftiness: furberia.
encounters: incontra.
enjoyed: piaciuto, fruito, goduto.

execution: esecuzione.
front: fronte, facciata, anteriore, davanti.
horrid: orrendo.
horrific: raccapricciante, orribile.
importance: importanza.
independence: indipendenza.
influenced: influenzato.
inhabiting: abitando.
inherited: ereditato.
lift: ascensore, alzare, sollevare, salire, sollevamento, alzata, passaggio.

load: carico, caricare, peso, carica, colmare.
panted: ansimato.
pardonable: perdonabile.
potency: potenza.
quality: qualità.
rightly: giustamente.
shortly: prossimamente.
straggling: sparso, disperso, girovagando, vagabondando.
term: termine, scadenza, vocabolo, durata.

dodges also; till at last, weary of this bootless attempt at treachery, or fearful of being surprised by the remainder of the party, Oberlus runs off a little space to a **bush**, and **fetching** his blunderbuss, **savagely** commands the negro to **desist** work and follow him. He refuses. Whereupon, presenting his **piece**, Oberlus snaps at him. Luckily the blunderbuss misses fire; but by this time, **frightened** out of his wits, the negro, upon a second **intrepid** summons, drops his billets, surrenders at discretion, and follows on. By a narrow defile familiar to him, Oberlus speedily **removes** out of sight of the water.

On their way up the mountains, he exultingly **informs** the negro, that henceforth he is to work for him, and be his slave, and that his **treatment** would entirely **depend** on his future conduct. But Oberlus, deceived by the first impulsive cowardice of the black, in an evil moment **slackens** his **vigilance**. Passing through a narrow way, and perceiving his leader quite off his guard, the negro, a powerful fellow, suddenly grasps him in his arms, throws him down, **wrests** his musketoon from him, ties his hands with the monster's own cord, shoulders him, and returns with him down to the boat. When the rest of the party arrive, Oberlus is carried on board the ship. This proved an Englishman, and a **smuggler**; a sort of craft not apt to be over-charitable. Oberlus is severely whipped, then handcuffed, taken ashore, and compelled to make known his **habitation** and **produce** his **property**. His potatoes, pumpkins, and tortoises, with a pile of dollars he had hoarded from his mercantile operations were secured on the spot. But while the too vindictive smugglers were busy destroying his hut and **garden**, Oberlus makes his escape into the mountains, and **conceals** himself there in **impenetrable** recesses, only known to himself, till the ship sails, when he ventures back, and by means of an old file which he sticks into a tree, **contrives** to free himself from his **handcuffs**.

Brooding among the ruins of his hut, and the desolate clinkers and extinct volcanoes of this **outcast** isle, the insulted misanthrope now **meditates** a signal **revenge** upon humanity, but conceals his purposes. Vessels still touch the Landing at times; and by-and-by Oberlus is enabled to supply them with some **vegetables**.

Italian

bush: arbusto, cespuglio, boccola, bussola.
conceals: nasconde.
contrives: escogita.
depend: dipendere, dipendete, dipendiamo, dipendo, dipendono, dipendi.
desist: desistere, desisto, desiste, desistiamo, desisti, desistono.
fetching: portando.
frightened: spaventato.
garden: giardino.

habitation: abitazione.
handcuffs: manette.
impenetrable: impenetrabile.
informs: informa.
intrepid: intrepido.
meditates: medita.
outcast: reietto.
piece: pezzo, parte, porzione.
produce: produrre, produciamo, produco, produci, producete, producono, produzione, prodotti, fabbricare, prodotto.

property: proprietà, patrimonio, possesso, fattoria, caratteristica.
removes: toglie, rimuove, asporta.
revenge: vendetta.
savagely: ferocemente, barbaramente, selvaggiamente.
slackens: allenta.
smuggler: contrabbandiere.
treatment: trattamento.
vegetables: verdura, verdure.
vigilance: vigilanza.
wrests: estorce.

Warned by his former failure in **kidnapping** strangers, he now **pursues** a quite different plan. When seamen come ashore, he makes up to them like a free-and-easy comrade, **invites** them to his hut, and with whatever **affability** his red-haired grimness may assume, **entreats** them to drink his **liquor** and be merry. But his guests need little pressing; and so, soon as rendered insensible, are tied hand and foot, and pitched among the clinkers, are there concealed till the ship **departs**, when, **finding** themselves entirely dependent upon Oberlus, alarmed at his changed demeanor, his savage threats, and above all, that shocking blunderbuss, they willingly enlist under him, becoming his humble slaves, and Oberlus the most incredible of tyrants. So much so, that two or three perish beneath his initiating process. He sets the remainder — four of them — to breaking the caked soil; transporting upon their backs **loads** of **loamy** earth, scooped up in **moist** clefts among the mountains; keeps them on the roughest fare; presents his piece at the slightest hint of **insurrection**; and in all respects converts them into reptiles at his feet — plebeian garter-snakes to this Lord Anaconda.

At last, Oberlus contrives to stock his arsenal with four rusty cutlasses, and an added supply of powder and ball intended for his blunderbuss. **Remitting** in good part the labor of his slaves, he now **approves** himself a man, or rather devil, of great **abilities** in the way of **cajoling** or **coercing** others into **acquiescence** with his own ulterior designs, however at first **abhorrent** to them. But indeed, prepared for almost any **eventual** evil by their previous lawless life, as a sort of ranging Cow-Boys of the sea, which had **dissolved** within them the whole **moral** man, so that they were ready to **concrete** in the first offered mould of **baseness** now; **rotted** down from manhood by their **hopeless** misery on the isle; wonted to cringe in all things to their lord, himself the worst of slaves; these wretches were now become wholly **corrupted** to his hands. He used them as creatures of an inferior race; in short, he gaffles his four animals, and makes murderers of them; out of cowards fitly **manufacturing** bravos.

Now, sword or dagger, human arms are but **artificial** claws and fangs, tied on like **false spurs** to the fighting **cock**. So, we repeat, Oberlus, **czar** of the isle,

Italian

abhorrent: ripugnante, orrendo, orribile, avverso, detestabile.
abilities: abilità.
acquiescence: acquiescenza.
affability: affabilità.
approves: approva.
artificial: artificiale, artefatto.
baseness: bassezza.
cajoling: allettando, lusingare.
cock: gallo, cazzo, rubinetto.
coercing: costringendo.
concrete: calcestruzzo, concreto.

corrupted: corrotto.
czar: zar.
departs: parte.
dissolved: dissolto, sciolto.
entreats: supplica.
eventual: finale, eventuale.
false: falso, finto.
finding: fondendo, fondando.
hopeless: disperato, senza speranza.
insurrection: insurrezione.
invites: invita.
kidnapping: rapimento, rapendo,

sequestro di persona.
liquor: liquore.
loads: carica.
loamy: argilloso.
manufacturing: fabbricando, manifatturiero.
moist: umido.
moral: morale.
pursues: persegue.
remitting: annullando.
rotted: marcito.
spurs: derivazione del cablaggio.

gaffles his four subjects; that is, with intent of glory, **puts** four rusty cutlasses into their hands. Like any other **autocrat**, he had a noble army now.

It might be thought a servile war would **hereupon ensue**. Arms in the hands of trodden slaves? how **indiscreet** of Emperor Oberlus! Nay, they had but cutlasses—sad old scythes enough—he a blunderbuss, which by its blind scatterings of all sorts of boulders, clinkers, and other **scoria** would **annihilate** all four mutineers, like four pigeons at one shot. Besides, at first he did not sleep in his accustomed hut; every **lurid** sunset, for a time, he might have been seen wending his way among the riven mountains, there to **secrete** himself till dawn in some **sulphurous pitfall**, undiscoverable to his **gang**; but finding this at last too troublesome, he now each evening tied his slaves hand and foot, hid the cutlasses, and thrusting them into his **barracks**, shut to the door, and lying down before it, beneath a rude shed lately added, slept out the night, blunderbuss in hand.

It is supposed that not content with daily **parading** over a cindery solitude at the head of his fine army, Oberlus now **meditated** the most active mischief; his probable object being to surprise some passing ship touching at his dominions, massacre the crew, and run away with her to parts unknown. While these plans were **simmering** in his head, two ships touch in company at the isle, on the opposite side to his; when his designs **undergo** a sudden change.

The ships are in want of vegetables, which Oberlus promises in great abundance, provided they send their boats round to his landing, so that the crews may bring the vegetables from his garden; informing the two captains, at the same time, that his rascals—slaves and soldiers—had become so **abominably lazy** and good-for-nothing of late, that he could not make them work by **ordinary** inducements, and did not have the heart to be **severe** with them.

The **arrangement** was agreed to, and the boats were sent and **hauled** upon the beach. The crews went to the lava hut; but to their surprise **nobody** was there. After waiting till their patience was exhausted, they returned to the shore, when lo, some stranger—not the Good Samaritan either—seems to have very recently passed that way. Three of the boats were broken in a thousand pieces, and the

Italian

abominably: abominevolmente.
annihilate: annichilire, annientare, annichilisco, annichiliscono, annichilite, annienta, annientano, annientate, annienti, annientiamo, anniento.
arrangement: accomodamento, disposizione, sistemazione, ordinamento, arrangiamento, assestamento, adattamento.
autocrat: autocrate.
barracks: caserma.

ensue: seguire, segui, seguono, seguo, seguiamo, seguite, conseguire, risultare.
gang: compagnia, banda, gang.
hauled: trasportato.
hereupon: in conseguenza di ciò, al che.
indiscreet: indiscreto.
lazy: pigro, indolente.
lurid: acuto.
meditated: meditato.
nobody: nessuno.

ordinary: ordinario, normale, comune.
parading: sfilare.
pitfall: trappola.
puts: mette, pone.
scoria: scoria.
secrete: secernere, secerni, secernono, secerniamo, secernete, secerno.
severe: severo.
simmering: sobbollendo.
sulphurous: solforoso.
undergo: subire, subisci, subisco, subiscono, subite, subiamo.

fourth was **missing**. By hard toil over the mountains and through the **clinkers**, some of the strangers succeeded in **returning** to that side of the isle where the ships lay, when fresh boats are sent to the **relief** of the rest of the hapless party.

However amazed at the treachery of Oberlus, the two captains, **afraid** of new and still more mysterious atrocities — and indeed, half **imputing** such strange events to the enchantments associated with these isles — perceive no **security** but in instant flight; leaving Oberlus and his **army** in quiet possession of the stolen boat.

On the eve of sailing they put a letter in a **keg**, giving the Pacific Ocean intelligence of the affair, and moored the keg in the bay. Some time subsequent, the keg was **opened** by another captain chancing to anchor there, but not until after he had dispatched a boat round to Oberlus's Landing. As may be readily surmised, he felt no little **inquietude** till the boat's return: when another letter was handed him, giving Oberlus's **version** of the affair. This precious **document** had been found pinned half-mildewed to the clinker **wall** of the **sulphurous** and deserted hut. It ran as follows: showing that Oberlus was at least an accomplished **writer**, and no mere **boor**; and what is more, was capable of the most tristful **eloquence**.

"Sir: I am the most unfortunate ill-treated gentleman that lives. I am a patriot, exiled from my country by the cruel hand of tyranny.

"Banished to these Enchanted Isles, I have again and again besought captains of ships to **sell** me a boat, but always have been refused, though I offered the handsomest **prices** in Mexican dollars. At length an **opportunity** presented of possessing myself of one, and I did not let it slip.

"I have been long endeavoring, by hard labor and much solitary suffering, to **accumulate** something to make myself **comfortable** in a **virtuous** though **unhappy** old age; but at various times have been robbed and beaten by men **professing** to be Christians.

Italian

accumulate: accumulare, accumulano, accumulate, accumuli, accumuliamo, accumula, accumulo, accumularsi, ammassare.
afraid: pauroso, inquieto, spaventato, angoscioso, impaurito.
amazed: sbalordito, stupito, si stupito.
army: esercito, armata.
boor: cafone.
clinker: clinker.
comfortable: comodo, confortevole.
document: documento, atto,

documentare, azione.
eloquence: eloquenza.
eve: vigilia.
imputing: attribuendo, imputando.
inquietude: inquietudine.
keg: bariletto.
missing: disperso, mancante.
opened: aperto.
opportunity: opportunità, occasione.
prices: prezzi.
professing: dichiarando, professando.
relief: rilievo, sollievo.

return: ritorno, ritornare, restituire, rientro, contraccambiare, resa, rendere, rivenire, restituzione.
security: sicurezza, garanzia, titolo.
sell: vendere, vendo, vendono, vendiamo, vendi, vendete.
sulphurous: solforoso.
unhappy: infelice, triste.
version: versione.
virtuous: virtuoso.
wall: muro, parete.
writer: autore.

"To-day I sail from the Enchanted group in the good boat Charity bound to the Feejee Isles.

"**FATHERLESS** OBERLUS.

"*P.S.*—Behind the clinkers, **nigh** the **oven**, you will find the old **fowl**. Do not kill it; be **patient**; I **leave** it setting; if it shall have any **chicks**, I hereby bequeath them to you, whoever you may be. But don't count your chicks before they are hatched."

The fowl proved a starveling **rooster**, reduced to a sitting posture by **sheer debility**.

Oberlus declares that he was bound to the Feejee Isles; but this was only to throw pursuers on a false **scent**. For, after a long time, he arrived, alone in his open boat, at Guayaquil. As his miscreants were never again **beheld** on Hood's Isle, it is supposed, either that they **perished** for want of water on the passage to Guayaquil, or, what is quite as probable, were thrown overboard by Oberlus, when he found the water **growing** scarce.

From Guayaquil Oberlus proceeded to Payta; and there, with that **nameless** witchery peculiar to some of the ugliest **animals**, wound himself into the affections of a **tawny damsel**; prevailing upon her to accompany him back to his Enchanted Isle; which doubtless he painted as a Paradise of **flowers**, not a Tartarus of clinkers.

But **unfortunately** for the **colonization** of Hood's Isle with a **choice variety** of animated nature, the **extraordinary** and **devilish** aspect of Oberlus made him to be **regarded** in Payta as a highly suspicious character. So that being found concealed one night, with **matches** in his pocket, under the hull of a small vessel just ready to be **launched**, he was seized and thrown into jail.

The jails in most South American towns are generally of the least wholesome sort. Built of huge cakes of sun-burnt **brick**, and **containing** but one room, without windows or yard, and but one door heavily grated with wooden bars, they present both within and without the grimmest aspect. As public edifices they conspicuously stand upon the hot and dusty Plaza, offering to view, through the gratings, their **villainous** and hopeless inmates, burrowing in all

Italian

animals: animali.	**fatherless**: orfano di padre.	**patient**: paziente.
beheld: guardato.	**flowers**: fiore.	**perished**: perito.
brick: mattone, laterizio.	**fowl**: pollo, gallina, pollame.	**regarded**: considerato.
chicks: pulcino.	**growing**: crescendo, coltivando.	**rooster**: gallo.
choice: scelta.	**launched**: lanciato.	**scent**: profumo, profumare, odore.
colonization: colonizzazione.	**leave**: lasciare, abbandonare, partire,	**sheer**: puro.
containing: contenendo.	lasciano, partono, partite, partiamo,	**tawny**: fulvo.
damsel: donzella.	parti, lasciate, lasciamo, lascia.	**unfortunately**: purtroppo, per
debility: debolezza.	**matches**: fiammiferi.	sfortuna, per fortuna,
devilish: diabolico.	**nameless**: senza nome.	sfortunatamente.
extraordinary: straordinario,	**nigh**: vicino.	**variety**: varietà, variazione.
eccezionale.	**oven**: forno.	**villainous**: infame, malvagio.

sorts of **tragic squalor**. And here, for a long time, Oberlus was seen; the **central** figure of a **mongrel** and assassin band; a creature whom it is religion to **detest**, since it is **philanthropy** to **hate** a **misanthrope**.

Note.—They who may be disposed to question the possibility of the character above **depicted**, are **referred** to the 2d vol. of Porter's Voyage into the Pacific, where they will **recognize** many sentences, for expedition's sake **derived verbatim** from thence, and **incorporated** here; the main difference—save a few passing reflections—between the two **accounts** being, that the present writer has added to Porter's facts **accessory** ones picked up in the Pacific from reliable sources; and where facts conflict, has naturally **preferred** his own authorities to Porter's. As, for instance, *his* authorities place Oberlus on Hood's Isle: Porter's, on Charles's Isle. The letter found in the hut is also somewhat different; for while at the Encantadas he was informed that, not only did it **evince** a certain clerkliness, but was full of the strangest **satiric effrontery** which does not **adequately** appear in Porter's version. I accordingly altered it to suit the general character of its author.

SKETCH TENTH

RUNAWAYS, CASTAWAYS, SOLITARIES, GRAVE-STONES, ETC.

"And all about old stocks and stubs of trees,
   Whereon nor fruit nor leaf was ever seen,
  Did **hang** upon ragged **knotty** knees,
   On which had many wretches hanged been."

Some relics of the hut of Oberlus partially remain to this day at the head of the clinkered **valley**. Nor does the stranger, wandering among other of the Enchanted Isles, fail to **stumble** upon still other solitary **abodes**, long abandoned to the **tortoise** and the **lizard**. Probably few **parts** of earth have, in modern times,

Italian

abodes: residenze.
accessory: accessorio.
accounts: clienti, situazione contabile.
adequately: adeguatamente.
central: centrale.
depicted: dipinto, descritto, ritratto.
derived: derivato.
detest: detestare, detestate, detesto, detesti, detestano, detesta, detestiamo.
effrontery: sfrontatezza.
evince: manifestiamo, manifesto,

manifesti, manifestate, manifestano, manifesta, manifestare.
hang: pendere, appendere, sospendere, impiccare.
hate: odiare, odio, detestare.
incorporated: incorporato.
knotty: nodoso.
lizard: lucertola.
misanthrope: misantropo.
mongrel: bastardo.
parts: ricambi, parte.
philanthropy: filantropia.

preferred: preferito.
recognize: riconoscere, riconoscete, riconosco, riconosciamo, riconoscono, riconosci.
referred: riferito.
satiric: satirico.
squalor: squallore.
stumble: inciampare, incespicare.
tortoise: tartaruga.
tragic: tragico.
valley: valle, vallata.
verbatim: parola per parola.

sheltered so many solitaries. The reason is, that these isles are situated in a
distant sea, and the vessels which occasionally visit them are mostly all whalers,
or ships bound on dreary and protracted voyages, exempting them in a good
degree from both the **oversight** and the memory of human law. Such is the
character of some commanders and some seamen, that under these untoward
circumstances, it is quite impossible but that scenes of **unpleasantness** and
discord should **occur** between them. A sullen **hatred** of the tyrannic ship will
seize the sailor, and he gladly **exchanges** it for isles, which, though blighted as by
a continual **sirocco** and burning breeze, still offer him, in their labyrinthine
interior, a retreat beyond the possibility of capture. To **flee** the ship in any
Peruvian or Chilian port, even the smallest and most rustical, is not **unattended**
with great risk of apprehension, not to speak of jaguars. A reward of five pesos
sends fifty dastardly Spaniards into the wood, who, with long knives, **scour**
them day and night in eager hopes of **securing** their prey. Neither is it, in general,
much **easier** to escape pursuit at the isles of Polynesia. Those of them which have
felt a **civilizing** influence present the same difficulty to the runaway with the
Peruvian ports, the advanced natives being quite as **mercenary** and **keen** of knife
and scent as the **retrograde** Spaniards; while, owing to the bad **odor** in which all
Europeans lie, in the minds of **aboriginal** savages who have chanced to hear
aught of them, to desert the ship among primitive Polynesians, is, in most cases,
a hope not unforlorn. Hence the Enchanted Isles become the voluntary **tarrying**
places of all sorts of refugees; some of whom too sadly experience the fact, that
flight from tyranny does not of itself insure a safe asylum, far less a **happy** home.

Moreover, it has not seldom happened that hermits have been made upon the
isles by the **accidents incident** to tortoise-hunting. The interior of most of them is
tangled and difficult of passage beyond description; the air is sultry and **stifling**;
an intolerable thirst is **provoked**, for which no running **stream** offers its kind
relief. In a few hours, under an **equatorial** sun, reduced by these causes to entire
exhaustion, woe betide the **straggler** at the Enchanted Isles! Their extent is such
as to forbid an adequate search, unless weeks are **devoted** to it. The impatient
ship waits a day or two; when, the missing man remaining undiscovered, up

Italian

aboriginal: aborigeno.
accidents: incidenti.
civilizing: civilizzando, incivilendo.
devoted: devoto.
easier: facile.
equatorial: equatoriale.
exchanges: scambi.
exhaustion: esaurimento, spossatezza.
flee: fuggire, fuggi, fuggiamo, fuggite, fuggono, fuggo.
happy: felice, contento, lieto, beato.
hatred: odio.

incident: incidente, avvenimento, caso.
keen: aguzzo, acuto, tagliente, affilato.
mercenary: mercenario.
occur: succedere, accadere, succedete, succedono, succedo, succediamo, succedi, accado, accadiamo, accadete, accadi.
odor: odore, profumo.
oversight: svista.
provoked: spronato, incitato, provocato.

retrograde: retrogrado.
scour: sfregano, sfrego, sfreghiamo, sfregate, sfrega, sfreghi, sfregare.
securing: fissando.
sirocco: scirocco.
stifling: soffocante.
straggler: ritardatario.
stream: ruscello, corrente, flusso, corso d'acqua.
tarrying: rimanendo.
unattended: incustodito.
unpleasantness: spiacevolezza.

goes a **stake** on the beach, with a letter of **regret**, and a keg of crackers and another of water tied to it, and away sails the craft.

Nor have there been wanting instances where the **inhumanity** of some captains has led them to wreak a secure revenge upon seamen who have given their caprice or pride some singular offense. Thrust ashore upon the **scorching marl**, such mariners are abandoned to perish outright, unless by solitary labors they **succeed** in discovering some precious dribblets of moisture **oozing** from a rock or **stagnant** in a mountain **pool**.

I was well acquainted with a man, who, lost upon the Isle of Narborough, was brought to such extremes by thirst, that at last he only saved his life by taking that of another being. A large hair-seal came upon the beach. He rushed upon it, stabbed it in the neck, and then throwing himself upon the **panting** body quaffed at the living wound; the palpitations of the creature's **dying** heart **injected** life into the drinker.

Another seaman, thrust ashore in a boat upon an isle at which no ship ever touched, owing to its peculiar **sterility** and the shoals about it, and from which all other parts of the group were hidden—this man, feeling that it was sure death to remain there, and that nothing **worse** than death menaced him in quitting it, killed **seals**, and **inflating** their skins, made a **float**, upon which he transported himself to Charles's Island, and joined the **republic** there.

But men, not **endowed** with courage equal to such desperate attempts, find their only **resource** in forthwith **seeking** some watering-place, however **precarious** or scanty; building a hut; catching tortoises and birds; and in all respects **preparing** for a hermit life, till tide or time, or a passing ship **arrives** to float them off.

At the foot of precipices on many of the isles, small rude basins in the rocks are found, partly filled with rotted **rubbish** or **vegetable** decay, or overgrown with thickets, and sometimes a little moist; which, upon **examination**, reveal plain tokens of artificial instruments employed in hollowing them out, by some poor **castaway** or still more miserable runaway. These basins are made in places

Italian

arrives: arriva.
castaway: naufrago.
dying: morendo, morente.
endowed: dotato.
examination: esame, verifica.
float: galleggiante, galleggiare, nuotare, flottante.
inflating: gonfiando.
inhumanity: inumanità.
injected: iniettato.
marl: marna.
oozing: filtrando, stillando,

trasudando.
panting: ansimare.
pool: piscina, unirsi, consorzio.
precarious: precario.
preparing: preparando, allestendo, apprestando.
regret: rincrescere, rammarico, rimpiangere, rimpianto, rincrescimento.
republic: repubblica.
resource: risorsa.
rubbish: rifiuti, spazzatura, macerie,

immondizia.
scorching: cocente.
seals: foche.
seeking: cercando.
stagnant: stagnante.
stake: picchetto, palo.
sterility: sterilità.
succeed: riuscire, riusciamo, riuscite, riescono, riesco, riesci, succedere.
vegetable: legume, verdura, vegetale, ortaggio.
worse: peggiore, peggio.

where it was supposed some scanty drops of dew might **exude** into them from the **upper** crevices.

The relics of hermitages and stone basins are not the only signs of vanishing humanity to be found upon the isles. And, curious to say, that spot which of all others in **settled** communities is most animated, at the Enchanted Isles presents the most dreary of aspects. And though it may seem very strange to talk of post-offices in this barren region, yet post-offices are occasionally to be found there. They consist of a stake and a bottle. The letters being not only **sealed**, but **corked**. They are generally **deposited** by captains of Nantucketers for the **benefit** of passing **fishermen**, and **contain** statements as to what luck they had in **whaling** or tortoise-hunting. Frequently, however, long months and months, whole years **glide** by and no **applicant** appears. The stake rots and falls, presenting no very **exhilarating** object.

If now it be added that grave-stones, or rather grave-boards, are also discovered upon some of the isles, the picture will be complete.

Upon the beach of James's Isle, for many years, was to be seen a rude finger-post, pointing inland. And, perhaps, taking it for some signal of possible hospitality in this otherwise desolate spot—some good hermit living there with his maple dish—the stranger would follow on in the path thus **indicated**, till at last he would come out in a noiseless nook, and find his only welcome, a dead man—his sole greeting the inscription over a grave. Here, in 1813, fell, in a daybreak **duel**, a lieutenant of the U.S. frigate Essex, aged twenty-one: **attaining** his **majority** in death.

It is but fit that, like those old **monastic** institutions of Europe, whose inmates go not out of their own walls to be inurned, but are entombed there where they **die**, the Encantadas, too, should **bury** their own dead, even as the great general monastery of earth does hers.

It is known that burial in the ocean is a pure necessity of sea-faring life, and that it is only done when land is far astern, and not clearly visible from the bow. Hence, to vessels cruising in the vicinity of the Enchanted Isles, they **afford** a convenient Potter's Field. The interment over, some good-natured forecastle poet

Italian

afford: permettere, permettersi, permettono, permettiamo, permettete, permetto, permetti, produrre.
applicant: richiedente, postulante, aspirante, petente, supplicante, candidato.
attaining: arrivando.
benefit: beneficio, profitto, vantaggio, guadagno, prestazione, beneficiare, avvantaggiare.
bury: seppellire, seppelliamo,

seppellisci, seppellisco, seppelliscono, seppellite, sotterrare.
contain: contenere, contenete, contengo, conteniamo, contengono, contieni.
corked: tappato.
deposited: depositato.
die: morire, muoio, muori, muoiono, morite, moriamo, dado, cubo, matrice, stampo.
duel: duello.
exhilarating: esilarando, esilarante.

exude: trasudare.
fishermen: pescatori.
glide: scivolata.
indicated: indicato.
majority: maggioranza.
monastic: monastico.
sealed: sigillato.
settled: regolato, stabilito, stabile, fermo, fisso, popolato, saldato, sistemato, deciso.
upper: tomaia, superiore.
whaling: caccia alla balena.

and **artist seizes** his paint-brush, and **inscribes** a doggerel **epitaph**. When, after a long **lapse** of time, other **good**-natured **seamen chance** to come upon the **spot**, they **usually** make a table of the **mound**, and **quaff a friendly** can to the **poor** soul's **repose**.

As a **specimen** of these epitaphs, take the following, found in a **bleak gorge** of Chatham Isle: —

"Oh, Brother Jack, as you **pass** by,
   As you are now, so once was I.
Just so **game**, and just so **gay**,
   But now, alack, they've **stopped** my pay.
No more I **peep** out of my **blinkers**,
   Here I be — tucked in with clinkers!"

Italian

artist: artista.
bleak: alborella, triste, freddo, afflitto, spiacevole, sgradevole, buio, scuro, brullo.
blinkers: paraocchi.
chance: caso.
epitaph: epitaffio.
friendly: amichevole, cortese, amicale, gradevole, benevole, carino, grazioso.
game: gioco, giuoco, cacciagione, selvaggina, partita.
gay: allegro, gaio.

good-natured: gradevole, cortese.
gorge: burrone, gola, forra.
inscribes: iscrive.
lapse: scivolare, sbaglio, intervallo, passare, errore, periodo.
mound: tumulo.
pass: passare, passaggio, lasciapassare, passata, trascorrere, passo.
peep: occhieggiare, pigolio, pigolare, sbirciare.
poor: povero, cattivo.
quaff: tracannare.

repose: riposo, riposarsi.
seamen: marinai.
seizes: afferra.
specimen: campione, esemplare, provino, saggio.
spot: luogo, macchia, punto, posto, spot, macchiare.
stopped: fermato, cessato, interrotto, smesso, arrestato.
usually: di solito, solitamente.

THE BELL-TOWER

In the south of Europe, nigh a once frescoed **capital**, now with **dank** mould cankering its bloom, central in a plain, stands what, at distance, seems the black mossed **stump** of some **immeasurable** pine, fallen, in forgotten days, with Anak and the Titan.

As all along where the pine tree falls, its **dissolution leaves** a mossy mound — last-flung shadow of the perished **trunk**; never **lengthening**, never **lessening**; unsubject to the fleet falsities of the sun; shade **immutable**, and **true gauge** which cometh by prostration — so westward from what seems the stump, one steadfast **spear** of lichened ruin veins the plain.

From that tree-top, what birded chimes of silver throats had **rung**. A stone pine; a metallic aviary in its **crown**: the Bell-Tower, built by the great **mechanician**, the unblest **foundling**, Bannadonna.

Like Babel's, its base was laid in a high hour of **renovated** earth, following the second **deluge**, when the waters of the Dark Ages had dried up, and once more the green appeared. No wonder that, after so long and deep **submersion**, the **jubilant** expectation of the race should, as with Noah's sons, **soar** into Shinar **aspiration**.

In firm **resolve**, no man in Europe at that period went **beyond** Bannadonna. **Enriched** through **commerce** with the Levant, the state in which he lived voted to have the noblest Bell-Tower in Italy. His repute **assigned** him to be **architect**.

Italian

architect: architetto.
aspiration: aspirazione.
assigned: assegnato.
beyond: oltre, dopo, attraverso, in seguito, poi.
capital: capitale, capitello.
commerce: commercio.
crown: corona.
dank: bagnato, umido.
deluge: diluvio.
dissolution: dissoluzione, scioglimento.

enriched: arricchito.
foundling: trovatello.
gauge: calibro, indicatore, manometro, scartamento.
immeasurable: incommensurabile.
immutable: immutabile.
jubilant: esultante.
leaves: parte, lascia, abbandona.
lengthening: allungando, allungamento.
lessening: diminuendo.
mechanician: meccanico.

renovated: restaurato, ristrutturato, rinnovato.
resolve: risolvere.
rung: piolo.
soar: elevarsi, volare in alto.
spear: lancia.
stump: ceppo, troncone, moncone, mozzicone.
submersion: immersione.
true: vero.
trunk: tronco, baule, proboscide, torso, bagagliaio.

Stone by stone, month by month, the tower rose. Higher, higher; snail-like in **pace**, but **torch** or **rocket** in its pride.

After the masons would depart, the **builder**, standing alone upon its ever-ascending summit, at close of every day, saw that he overtopped still higher walls and trees. He would **tarry** till a late hour there, wrapped in schemes of other and still loftier piles. Those who of **saints'** days thronged the spot — hanging to the rude poles of **scaffolding**, like sailors on yards, or **bees** on boughs, unmindful of **lime** and **dust**, and falling **chips** of stone — their **homage** not the less inspirited him to self-esteem.

At length the **holiday** of the Tower came. To the sound of viols, the climax-stone slowly rose in air, and, amid the **firing** of **ordnance**, was laid by Bannadonna's hands upon the final course. Then **mounting** it, he stood erect, alone, with folded arms, gazing upon the white summits of blue inland Alps, and whiter crests of bluer Alps off-shore — sights invisible from the plain. Invisible, too, from thence was that eye he turned below, when, like the cannon booms, came up to him the people's combustions of applause.

That which stirred them so was, seeing with what **serenity** the builder stood three hundred feet in air, upon an unrailed perch. This none but he durst do. But his **periodic** standing upon the pile, in each stage of its growth — such **discipline** had its last result.

Little remained now but the bells. These, in all respects, must **correspond** with their **receptacle**.

The **minor** ones were **prosperously** cast. A highly enriched one followed, of a singular make, intended for **suspension** in a manner before unknown. The purpose of this bell, its **rotary** motion, and **connection** with the clock-work, also **executed** at the time, will, in the sequel, receive mention.

In the one **erection**, bell-tower and clock-tower were united, though, before that period, such structures had commonly been built distinct; as the Campanile and Torre del 'Orologio of St. Mark to this day attest.

Italian

bees: api.
builder: costruttore.
chips: patatine fritte.
connection: coincidenza, accoppiamento, connessione, collegamento, relazione, banda.
correspond: corrispondere, corrispondete, corrispondi, corrispondiamo, corrispondo, corrispondono, avere la coincidenza.
discipline: disciplina.
dust: polvere, spolverare.

erection: erezione, montaggio, costruzione.
executed: eseguito.
firing: accensione.
holiday: vacanza, giorno festivo, festa.
homage: omaggio.
lime: calce, lime.
minor: minore, secondario.
mounting: montaggio, salita.
ordnance: artiglieria.
pace: passo, andatura, velocità.
periodic: periodico.

prosperously: prosperamente.
receptacle: ricettacolo, recipiente.
rocket: razzo, missile, rucola.
rotary: rotante.
saints: santi.
scaffolding: impalcatura, ponteggio.
serenity: serenità.
suspension: sospensione.
tarry: rimanere, catramoso, rimangono, rimani, rimango, rimanete, rimaniamo.
torch: torcia, fiaccola, cannello.

But it was upon the great state-bell that the **founder** lavished his more daring skill. In vain did some of the less elated **magistrates** here **caution** him; saying that though truly the tower was Titanic, yet limit should be set to the dependent weight of its swaying masses. But undeterred, he prepared his **mammoth** mould, dented with mythological devices; kindled his fires of **balsamic** firs; **melted** his tin and copper, and, throwing in much plate, **contributed** by the public spirit of the nobles, let loose the tide.

The **unleashed metals** bayed like hounds. The workmen shrunk. Through their fright, fatal **harm** to the bell was dreaded. Fearless as Shadrach, Bannadonna, rushing through the **glow**, smote the chief **culprit** with his ponderous **ladle**. From the **smitten** part, a **splinter** was dashed into the **seething** mass, and at once was melted in.

Next day a portion of the work was heedfully **uncovered**. All seemed right. Upon the third morning, with equal satisfaction, it was bared still lower. At length, like some old Theban king, the whole cooled casting was disinterred. All was fair except in one strange spot. But as he suffered no one to attend him in these inspections, he concealed the blemish by some **preparation** which none knew better to **devise**.

The casting of such a mass was deemed no small triumph for the **caster**; one, too, in which the state might not scorn to share. The **homicide** was overlooked. By the charitable that deed was but imputed to sudden transports of **esthetic** passion, not to any flagitious quality. A kick from an Arabian **charger**; not sign of vice, but blood.

His **felony remitted** by the **judge**, **absolution** given him by the priest, what more could even a **sickly** conscience have desired.

Honoring the tower and its builder with another holiday, the republic **witnessed** the hoisting of the bells and clock-work amid shows and pomps superior to the former.

Some months of more than usual solitude on Bannadonna's part ensued. It was not unknown that he was engaged upon something for the **belfry**, intended to complete it, and **surpass** all that had gone before. Most people imagined that

Italian

absolution: assoluzione.
balsamic: balsamico.
belfry: cella campanaria, campanile.
caster: fonditore, rotella.
caution: avvertire, prudenza, avvertenza, cautela.
charger: caricatore.
contributed: contribuito.
culprit: colpevole.
devise: escogitare.
esthetic: estetico.
felony: crimine, delitto.

founder: fondatore, affondare, fonditore.
glow: ardore.
harm: danno, nuocere, danneggiare.
homicide: omicidio, omicida.
honoring: onorare.
judge: giudice, giudicare, critico.
ladle: mestolo, siviera.
magistrates: magistrati.
mammoth: mammut.
melted: fuso, sciolto.
metals: metallo.

preparation: preparazione, allestimento, preparativo.
remitted: annullato.
seething: bollendo, ribollendo.
sickly: cagionevole, malaticcio, malatamente.
smitten: colpito.
splinter: scheggia, frammento.
surpass: sorpassare, superare.
uncovered: scoperto.
unleashed: sguinzagliato.
witnessed: testimoniato.

the design would involve a casting like the bells. But those who thought they had some further **insight**, would shake their heads, with hints, that not for nothing did the mechanician keep so secret. Meantime, his **seclusion** failed not to **invest** his work with more or less of that sort of **mystery** pertaining to the forbidden.

Ere long he had a heavy object hoisted to the belfry, wrapped in a dark **sack** or cloak—a procedure sometimes had in the case of an **elaborate** piece of **sculpture**, or statue, which, being intended to **grace** the front of a new **edifice**, the architect does not desire exposed to critical eyes, till set up, finished, in its appointed place. Such was the impression now. But, as the object rose, a **statuary** present observed, or thought he did, that it was not entirely rigid, but was, in a manner, **pliant**. At last, when the hidden thing had **attained** its final height, and, obscurely seen from below, seemed almost of itself to step into the belfry, as if with little assistance from the **crane**, a **shrewd** old **blacksmith** present **ventured** the suspicion that it was but a living man. This surmise was thought a foolish one, while the general interest failed not to **augment**.

Not without **demur** from Bannadonna, the chief-magistrate of the town, with an associate—both elderly men—followed what seemed the image up the tower. But, arrived at the belfry, they had little **recompense. Plausibly entrenching** himself behind the **conceded** mysteries of his art, the mechanician withheld present **explanation**. The magistrates glanced toward the cloaked object, which, to their surprise, seemed now to have changed its attitude, or else had before been more perplexingly concealed by the violent muffling action of the wind without. It seemed now seated upon some sort of frame, or chair, **contained** within the domino. They observed that nigh the top, in a sort of square, the **web** of the cloth, either from accident or design, had its warp partly withdrawn, and the cross threads plucked out here and there, so as to form a sort of **woven** grating. Whether it were the low wind or no, stealing through the stone lattice-work, or only their own **perturbed** imaginations, is uncertain, but they thought they discerned a slight sort of **fitful**, spring-like motion, in the domino. Nothing, however incidental or insignificant, escaped their uneasy eyes. Among other things, they pried out, in a corner, an **earthen** cup, partly corroded and partly

Italian

attained: arrivato.
augment: ingrandire, ingrandite, ingrandiscono, ingrandisco, ingrandisci, ingrandiamo, aumentare, aumenta, aumentano, aumentate, aumenti.
blacksmith: maniscalco, fabbro ferraio, fabbro.
conceded: concesso.
contained: contenuto.
crane: gru.
demur: esitazione, esitare.

earthen: terrestre, di terra.
edifice: edificio.
elaborate: elaborato, elaborare.
entrenching: trincerando.
explanation: spiegazione.
fitful: irregolare.
grace: grazia.
insight: intuito.
invest: investire, investi, investono, investo, investite, investiamo.
mystery: mistero.
perturbed: perturbato.

plausibly: plausibilmente.
pliant: flessibile.
recompense: compenso, ricompensare.
sack: licenziare, borsa, sacco.
sculpture: scultura, scolpire.
seclusion: isolamento.
shrewd: scaltro, sagace, perspicace, accorto.
statuary: arte statuaria, statuario.
ventured: avventurato.
web: ragnatela.
woven: tessuto.

encrusted, and one whispered to the other, that this cup was just such a one as might, in mockery, be offered to the lips of some **brazen** statue, or, perhaps, still worse.

But, being questioned, the **mechanician** said, that the cup was simply used in his founder's business, and described the purpose; in short, a cup to **test** the condition of metals in **fusion**. He added, that it had got into the **belfry** by the merest chance.

Again, and again, they gazed at the domino, as at some suspicious **incognito** at a Venetian mask. All sorts of vague apprehensions stirred them. They even dreaded lest, when they should descend, the mechanician, though without a flesh and blood companion, for all that, would not be left alone.

Affecting some **merriment** at their **disquietude**, he begged to relieve them, by **extending** a coarse sheet of workman's canvas between them and the object.

Meantime he sought to interest them in his other work; nor, now that the domino was out of sight, did they long remain **insensible** to the artistic wonders lying round them; wonders hitherto **beheld** but in their unfinished state; because, since **hoisting** the bells, **none** but the **caster** had entered within the belfry. It was one **trait** of his, that, even in details, he would not let another do what he could, without too great loss of time, **accomplish** for himself. So, for several preceding weeks, whatever hours were **unemployed** in his secret design, had been devoted to elaborating the figures on the bells.

The clock-bell, in particular, now drew attention. Under a patient **chisel**, the **latent** beauty of its enrichments, before **obscured** by the cloudings incident to casting, that beauty in its shyest grace, was now revealed. Round and round the bell, **twelve** figures of gay **girls**, garlanded, hand-in-hand, danced in a **choral** ring—the **embodied** hours.

"Bannadonna," said the chief, "this bell **excels** all else. No added touch could here improve. Hark!" hearing a **sound**, "was that the wind?"

"The wind, Excellenza," was the light **response**. "But the figures, they are not yet without their faults. They need some touches yet. When those are given, and

Italian

accomplish: compiere, compiamo, compio, compiono, compite, compi, eseguire, arrivare.
beheld: guardato.
belfry: cella campanaria, campanile.
brazen: affrontare con impudenza, di ottone, impudente, svergognato, simile a ottone, sfacciato.
caster: fonditore, rotella.
chisel: scalpello.
choral: corale.
disquietude: inquietudine.

embodied: incarnato, incorporato.
excels: eccelle.
extending: estendendo.
fusion: fusione.
girls: ragazze.
hoisting: sollevamento.
incognito: incognito.
insensible: insensibile.
latent: latente.
mechanician: meccanico.
merriment: allegria.
none: nessuno.

obscured: eclissato, ottenebrato, offuscato, oscurato.
response: risposta, reazione.
sound: suono, sonare, suonare, solido, sondare, sano, scandagliare, rumore, sonda.
test: prova, provare, test, esame, collaudo, collaudare, esaminare, saggio, testare.
trait: caratteristica, tratto.
twelve: dodici.
unemployed: disoccupato.

the—block yonder," pointing towards the canvas screen, "when Haman there, as I merrily call him,—him? *It*, I mean—when Haman is fixed on this, his lofty tree, then, gentlemen, will I be most happy to receive you here again."

The equivocal reference to the object **caused** some return of restlessness. However, on their **part**, the visitors forbore further allusion to it, unwilling, perhaps, to let the foundling see how easily it lay within his **plebeian** art to stir the **placid** dignity of nobles.

"Well, Bannadonna," said the chief, "how long ere you are ready to set the clock going, so that the hour shall be sounded? Our interest in you, not less than in the work itself, **makes** us anxious to be assured of your **success**. The people, too,—why, they are **shouting** now. Say the exact hour when you will be ready."

"To-morrow, Excellenza, if you listen for it,—or should you not, all the same—strange **music** will be heard. The **stroke** of one shall be the first from yonder bell," pointing to the bell **adorned** with girls and garlands, "that stroke shall fall there, where the hand of Una clasps Dua's. The stroke of one shall **sever** that loved clasp. To-morrow, then, at one o'clock, as struck here, precisely here," advancing and placing his finger upon the clasp, "the poor **mechanic** will be most happy once more to give you liege **audience**, in this his littered **shop**. Farewell till then, illustrious magnificoes, and **hark** ye for your vassal's stroke."

His still, Vulcanic face hiding its burning **brightness** like a **forge**, he moved with **ostentatious** deference towards the scuttle, as if so far to **escort** their **exit**. But the **junior magistrate**, a kind-hearted man, troubled at what seemed to him a certain sardonical disdain, lurking beneath the foundling's humble **mien**, and in Christian sympathy more distressed at it on his account than on his own, dimly surmising what might be the **final** fate of such a **cynic solitaire**, nor perhaps uninfluenced by the general **strangeness** of surrounding things, this good magistrate had glanced sadly, sideways from the **speaker**, and thereupon his foreboding eye had started at the expression of the **unchanging** face of the Hour Una.

"How is this, Bannadonna?" he lowly asked, "Una looks unlike her sisters."

Italian

adorned: decorato.
art: arte, l'arte.
audience: udienza, uditorio, pubblico.
brightness: luminosità, lucentezza.
caused: causato.
cynic: cinico.
escort: scortare, scorta, accompagnare, accompagnatore.
exit: uscita, uscire, l'uscita.
final: finale.
forge: forgiare, forgia.
hark: ascoltare.

junior: minore.
magistrate: magistrato.
makes: fa, commette.
mechanic: meccanico.
mien: aspetto.
music: musica, la musica.
ostentatious: ostentato.
placid: placido.
plebeian: plebeo.
sever: stacca, staccate, stacchi, stacco, staccano, disgiungo, disgiungiamo, disgiungi, disgiungete, stacchiamo,

disgiungono.
shop: negozio, spaccio, bottega, officina.
shouting: gridare, urla.
solitaire: solitario.
speaker: oratore, vivavoce, altoparlante, conferenziere.
strangeness: stravaganza, stranezza.
stroke: accarezzare, corsa, apoplessia, colpo, ictus, colpo apoplettico.
success: successo, riuscita.
unchanging: immutabile.

"In Christ's name, Bannadonna," impulsively broke in the chief, his attention, for the first attracted to the figure, by his associate's remark, "Una's face looks just like that of Deborah, the **prophetess**, as painted by the Florentine, Del Fonca."

"Surely, Bannadonna," **lowly resumed** the milder **magistrate**, "you meant the twelve should wear the same jocundly abandoned air. But see, the smile of Una seems but a fatal one. 'Tis different."

While his mild associate was speaking, the chief glanced, **inquiringly**, from him to the **caster**, as if anxious to mark how the **discrepancy** would be accounted for. As the chief stood, his advanced foot was on the scuttle's curb.

Bannadonna spoke:

"Excellenza, now that, following your keener eye, I glance upon the face of Una, I do, indeed **perceive** some little **variance**. But look all round the bell, and you will find no two faces entirely **correspond**. Because there is a law in art—but the cold wind is rising more; these **lattices** are but a poor **defense**. **Suffer** me, magnificoes, to conduct you, at least, partly on your way. Those in whose **well-being** there is a public stake, should be heedfully attended."

"Touching the look of Una, you were saying, Bannadonna, that there was a certain law in art," observed the chief, as the three now **descended** the stone **shaft**, "pray, tell me, then—."

"Pardon; another time, Excellenza;—the tower is damp."

"Nay, I must rest, and hear it now. Here,—here is a wide landing, and through this **leeward slit**, no wind, but **ample** light. Tell us of your law; and at large."

"Since, Excellenza, you **insist**, know that there is a law in art, which bars the possibility of duplicates. Some years ago, you may remember, I graved a small seal for your republic, bearing, for its chief device, the head of your own **ancestor**, its **illustrious** founder. It becoming necessary, for the **customs'** use, to have **innumerable** impressions for bales and **boxes**, I graved an entire plate, containing one hundred of the **seals**. Now, though, indeed, my object was to

Italian

ample: ampio.
ancestor: antenato, ascendente.
boxes: scatole.
caster: fonditore, rotella.
correspond: corrispondere, corrispondete, corrispondi, corrispondiamo, corrispondo, corrispondono, avere la coincidenza.
customs: dogana.
defense: difesa.
descended: sceso, disceso.
discrepancy: discrepanza.

illustrious: illustre.
innumerable: innumerevole.
inquiringly: domandare.
insist: insistere, insistiamo, insisto, insistete, insistono, insisti.
lattices: reticoli.
leeward: sottovento.
lowly: umile.
magistrate: magistrato.
perceive: percepire, accorgersi, scorgere, percepiamo, scorgo, scorgiamo, scorgi, scorgete,

percepite, scorgono, percepiscono.
prophetess: profetessa.
resumed: ripreso.
seals: foche.
shaft: albero, fusto, asse.
slit: fessura, fenditura.
suffer: soffrire, soffri, soffro, soffrono, soffrite, soffriamo, patire, subire, patiamo, patite, patiscono.
variance: varietà, disaccordo.
well-being: benessere.

have those hundred heads identical, and though, I dare say, people think them; so, yet, upon **closely scanning** an uncut impression from the plate, no two of those five-score faces, side by side, will be found alike. **Gravity** is the air of all; but, **diversified** in all. In some, benevolent; in some, ambiguous; in two or three, to a close scrutiny, all but **incipiently malign**, the **variation** of less than a hair's **breadth** in the **linear** shadings round the mouth **sufficing** to all this. Now, Excellenza, transmute that general gravity into **joyousness**, and **subject** it to twelve of those **variations** I have described, and tell me, will you not have my hours here, and Una one of them? But I like—."

Hark! is that—a footfall above?

"**Mortar**, Excellenza; sometimes it drops to the belfry-floor from the **arch** where the stonework was left **undressed**. I must have it seen to. As I was about to say: for one, I like this law forbidding duplicates. It **evokes fine personalities**. Yes, Excellenza, that strange, and—to you—uncertain **smile**, and those fore-looking eyes of Una, suit Bannadonna very well."

"Hark!—sure we left no soul above?"

"No soul, Excellenza; rest assured, no *soul*—Again the mortar."

"It fell not while we were there."

"Ah, in your presence, it better knew its place, Excellenza," **blandly** bowed Bannadonna.

"But, Una," said the milder magistrate, "she seemed intently gazing on you; one would have almost **sworn** that she picked you out from among us three."

"If she did, **possibly**, it might have been her finer apprehension, Excellenza."

"How, Bannadonna? I do not **understand** you."

"No **consequence**, no consequence, Excellenza—but the shifted wind is blowing through the slit. Suffer me to escort you on; and then, pardon, but the toiler must to his tools."

"It may be foolish, Signor," said the milder magistrate, as, from the third landing, the two now went down unescorted, "but, somehow, our great

Italian

arch: arco, volta.
blandly: blandamente.
breadth: larghezza, ampiezza.
close: chiudere, vicino, chiudo, chiudono, chiudiamo, chiudete, chiudi, prossimo, chiuso.
consequence: conseguenza, risultato.
diversified: diversificato, differenziato.
evokes: evoca.
fine: multa, contravvenzione, multare, bello, delicato, carino, eccellente, penale, ammenda.
gravity: gravità.
incipiently: incipientemente.
joyousness: gioia.
linear: lineare.
malign: maligno.
mortar: malta, mortaio.
personalities: personalità.
possibly: forse, possibilmente.
scanning: scansione, scrutando.
smile: sorriso, sorridere.
subject: soggetto, argomento, oggetto, sottoporre, tema, suddito, assoggettato.
sufficing: bastando.
sworn: giurato.
understand: capire, capite, capiamo, capisci, capisco, capiscono, comprendere, comprendono, comprendo, comprendiamo, comprendete.
undressed: svestito.
variation: variazione, variante.
variations: variazioni.

mechanician moves me strangely. Why, just now, when he so superciliously replied, his walk seemed Sisera's, God's vain foe, in Del Fonca's **painting**. And that young, **sculptured** Deborah, too. Ay, and that—."

"Tush, tush, Signor!" returned the chief. "A passing whim. Deborah?— Where's Jael, pray?"

"Ah," said the other, as they now stepped upon the sod, "Ah, Signor, I see you leave your fears behind you with the **chill** and gloom; but mine, even in this sunny air, remain, Hark!"

It was a sound from just within the tower door, whence they had **emerged**. Turning, they saw it closed.

"He has slipped down and **barred** us out," **smiled** the chief; "but it is his custom."

Proclamation was now made, that the next day, at one hour after **meridian**, the clock would strike, and—thanks to the mechanician's powerful art—with unusual accompaniments. But what those should be, none as yet could say. The **announcement** was received with **cheers**.

By the looser sort, who **encamped** about the tower all night, **lights** were seen gleaming through the topmost blind-work, only **disappearing** with the morning sun. Strange sounds, too, were heard, or were thought to be, by those whom anxious watching might not have left **mentally** undisturbed—sounds, not only of some ringing **implement**, but also—so they said—half-suppressed **screams** and plainings, such as might have **issued** from some ghostly **engine**, overplied.

Slowly the day drew on; part of the **concourse chasing** the weary time with songs and **games**, till, at last, the great **blurred** sun rolled, like a **football**, against the plain.

At noon, the **nobility** and principal citizens came from the town in **cavalcade**, a guard of soldiers, also, with music, the more to **honor** the occasion.

Only one hour more. Impatience grew. Watches were held in hands of feverish men, who stood, now **scrutinizing** their small dial-plates, and then, with neck thrown back, gazing toward the **belfry**, as if the eye might **foretell** that

Italian

announcement: annuncio, comunicato, annunzio, avviso, inserzione.	**emerged**: apparso.	**issued**: emesso.
	encamped: accampato.	**lights**: luci.
	engine: motore, macchina, locomotiva, il motore, propulsore.	**mechanician**: meccanico.
barred: sbarrato.		**mentally**: mentalmente.
belfry: cella campanaria, campanile.	**football**: calcio, pallone.	**meridian**: meridiano.
blurred: sfocato.	**foretell**: predire, predi', predici, prediciamo, predico, predicono, predite.	**nobility**: nobiltà.
cavalcade: cavalcata.		**painting**: pittura, dipinto, quadro, verniciatura.
chasing: cesellatura, inseguire.		
cheers: salute, cin cin.	**games**: giochi.	**screams**: grida.
chill: freddo.	**honor**: onore, onorare.	**scrutinizing**: scrutinando.
concourse: atrio, concorso.	**implement**: utensile, attrezzo, implementare, strumento, arnese.	**sculptured**: scolpito.
disappearing: scomparendo.		**smiled**: sorriso.

which could only be made sensible to the ear; for, as yet, there was no **dial** to the tower-clock.

The hour hands of a thousand watches now verged within a hair's **breadth** of the figure 1. A silence, as of the expectation of some Shiloh, **pervaded** the **swarming** plain. Suddenly a dull, mangled sound—naught ringing in it; scarcely **audible**, indeed, to the outer circles of the people—that dull sound dropped heavily from the **belfry**. At the same moment, each man stared at his **neighbor** blankly. All watches were **upheld**. All hour-hands were at—had passed—the figure 1. No bell-stroke from the tower. The **multitude** became **tumultuous**.

Waiting a few moments, the chief magistrate, **commanding** silence, **hailed** the belfry, to know what thing **unforeseen** had happened there.

No response.

He hailed again and yet again.

All continued hushed.

By his order, the soldiers burst in the tower-door; when, **stationing** guards to **defend** it from the now **surging** mob, the chief, accompanied by his **former** associate, climbed the winding stairs. Half-way up, they stopped to listen. No sound. Mounting faster, they reached the belfry; but, at the threshold, started at the spectacle disclosed. A spaniel, which, unbeknown to them, had followed them thus far, stood **shivering** as before some unknown monster in a **brake**: or, rather, as if it snuffed **footsteps** leading to some other world.

Bannadonna lay, **prostrate** and bleeding, at the base of the bell which was **adorned** with girls and garlands. He lay at the feet of the hour Una; his head **coinciding**, in a **vertical** line, with her left hand, clasped by the hour Dua. With **downcast** face **impending** over him, like Jael over **nailed** Sisera in the tent, was the domino; now no more becloaked.

It had limbs, and seemed **clad** in a **scaly** mail, **lustrous** as a dragon-beetle's. It was manacled, and its clubbed arms were uplifted, as if, with its manacles, once more to **smite** its already **smitten** victim. One advanced foot of it was inserted beneath the dead body, as if in the act of spurning it.

Italian

adorned: decorato.
audible: udibile.
belfry: cella campanaria, campanile.
brake: freno, frenare.
breadth: larghezza, ampiezza.
clad: vestito.
coinciding: coincidendo.
commanding: comandare.
defend: difendere, difendi, difendiamo, difendo, difendono, difendete.
dial: quadrante.

downcast: abbattuto.
footsteps: impronte.
former: precedente, passato.
hailed: grandinato.
impending: imminente.
lustrous: lustro.
multitude: affluenza, folla, moltitudine.
nailed: inchiodato.
neighbor: vicino.
pervaded: pervaso.
prostrate: prostrato.

scaly: squamoso.
shivering: rabbrividire.
smite: colpisco, colpiscono, colpisci, colpiamo, colpite, colpire.
smitten: colpito.
stationing: dislocamento.
surging: pompaggio.
swarming: brulichio.
tumultuous: tumultuoso.
unforeseen: imprevisto.
upheld: sostenuto.
vertical: verticale.

Uncertainty falls on what now followed.

It were but natural to suppose that the magistrates would, at first, shrink from **immediate** personal **contact** with what they saw. At the least, for a time, they would stand in involuntary doubt; it may be, in more or less of horrified alarm. Certain it is, that an arquebuss was called for from below. And some add, that its report, followed by a fierce **whiz**, as of the sudden snapping of a main-spring, with a **steely** din, as if a stack of sword-blades should be dashed upon a **pavement**, these blended sounds came ringing to the plain, **attracting** every eye far upward to the belfry, whence, through the lattice-work, thin wreaths of **smoke** were **curling**.

Some averred that it was the spaniel, **gone** mad by fear, which was shot. This, others denied. True it was, the spaniel never more was seen; and, probably, for some unknown reason, it shared the burial now to be **related** of the domino. For, whatever the preceding circumstances may have been, the first instinctive panic over, or else all ground of **reasonable** fear removed, the two magistrates, by themselves, quickly rehooded the figure in the dropped **cloak** wherein it had been hoisted. The same night, it was secretly lowered to the ground, smuggled to the beach, pulled far out to sea, and sunk. Nor to any after **urgency**, even in free **convivial** hours, would the twain ever **disclose** the full secrets of the belfry.

From the mystery **unavoidably investing** it, the **popular** solution of the foundling's fate **involved** more or less of **supernatural agency**. But some few less unscientific minds pretended to find little difficulty in otherwise accounting for it. In the **chain** of **circumstantial** inferences drawn, there may, or may not, have been some absent or **defective** links. But, as the explanation in question is the only one which **tradition** has **explicitly** preserved, in **dearth** of better, it will here be given. But, in the first place, it is requisite to present the supposition entertained as to the entire motive and mode, with their **origin**, of the secret design of Bannadonna; the minds above-mentioned assuming to penetrate as well into his soul as into the event. The disclosure will **indirectly** involve reference to peculiar matters, none of, the clearest, beyond the immediate subject.

Italian

agency: agenzia, rappresentanza, ente, filiale, ufficio.
attracting: attirando, attraendo.
chain: catena, catenina.
circumstantial: particolareggiato, circostanziale.
cloak: mantello, cappa.
contact: contatto.
convivial: conviviale.
curling: arricciare, arricciamento.
dearth: scarsità, penuria.
defective: difettoso, difettivo.

disclose: svelare.
explicitly: esplicitamente.
gone: andato.
immediate: immediato.
indirectly: indirettamente.
investing: investendo.
involve: coinvolgere, coinvolgo, coinvolgiamo, coinvolgi, coinvolgete, coinvolgono, immischiare.
origin: origine, nascita.
pavement: marciapiede, selciato.
popular: popolare.

reasonable: ragionevole, sensato.
related: raccontato, imparentato, congiunto.
smoke: fumo, fumare, fuma, fumi, fumate, fumiamo, fumano, affumicare.
steely: inflessibile.
supernatural: soprannaturale.
tradition: tradizione.
unavoidably: inevitabilmente.
urgency: urgenza.
whiz: fischio.

At that period, no large bell was made to sound otherwise than as at present, by agitation of a tongue within, by means of ropes, or **percussion** from without, either from cumbrous **machinery**, or **stalwart** watchmen, armed with heavy hammers, stationed in the belfry, or in sentry-boxes on the open roof, according as the bell was sheltered or exposed.

It was from observing these exposed bells, with their watchmen, that the foundling, as was opined, derived the first **suggestion** of his **scheme**. Perched on a great mast or **spire**, the human figure, viewed from below, **undergoes** such a **reduction** in its apparent **size**, as to obliterate its intelligent features. It **evinces** no **personality**. Instead of **bespeaking volition**, its gestures rather **resemble** the automatic ones of the arms of a telegraph.

Musing, therefore, upon the purely Punchinello aspect of the human figure thus beheld, it had indirectly occurred to Bannadonna to devise some metallic **agent**, which should strike the hour with its mechanic hand, with even **greater** precision than the vital one. And, moreover, as the vital **watchman** on the roof, sallying from his retreat at the given periods, walked to the bell with uplifted **mace**, to smite it, Bannadonna had resolved that his invention should likewise possess the power of **locomotion**, and, along with that, the appearance, at least, of intelligence and will.

If the conjectures of those who **claimed** acquaintance with the intent of Bannadonna be thus far **correct**, no unenterprising spirit could have been his. But they stopped not here; intimating that though, indeed, his design had, in the first place, been prompted by the sight of the watchman, and confined to the devising of a **subtle** substitute for him: yet, as is not seldom the case with projectors, by insensible gradations, proceeding from comparatively pigmy **aims** to Titanic ones, the original scheme had, in its anticipated eventualities, at last, attained to an unheard of degree of daring.

He still bent his efforts upon the **locomotive** figure for the belfry, but only as a partial **type** of an ulterior creature, a sort of **elephantine** Helot, adapted to further, in a degree scarcely to be imagined, the universal conveniences and glories of humanity; supplying nothing less than a **supplement** to the Six Days'

Italian

agent: agente, rappresentante, mandatario, strumento, arnese.
aims: punta, mira.
bespeaking: prenotando.
claimed: reclamato.
correct: correggere, corretto, giusto, esatto, rettificare.
elephantine: elefantino.
evinces: manifesta.
greater: maggiore.
locomotion: locomozione.
locomotive: locomotiva.
mace: mazza.
machinery: macchinario.
musing: meditabondo, meditazione.
percussion: percussione.
personality: personalità.
reduction: riduzione, diminuzione.
resemble: rassomigliare, rassomiglio, rassomigliate, rassomigliano, rassomigliamo, rassomiglia, rassomigli, assomigliare, somigliare.
scheme: progetto, schema, piano.
size: dimensione, grandezza, formato, taglia, grossezza, misura.
spire: guglia, spira.
stalwart: coraggioso, vigoroso.
subtle: sottile.
suggestion: suggerimento, proposta, suggestione.
supplement: supplemento, integrare.
type: tipo, scrivere a macchina, specie, modello, digitare.
undergoes: subisce.
volition: volizione.
watchman: guardiano, sorvegliante.

Work; **stocking** the earth with a new **serf**, more useful than the **ox**, swifter than the dolphin, stronger than the lion, more cunning than the **ape**, for industry an **ant**, more fiery than serpents, and yet, in patience, another ass. All excellences of all God-made creatures, which served man, were here to receive **advancement**, and then to be combined in one. Talus was to have been the all-accomplished Helot's name. Talus, iron slave to Bannadonna, and, through him, to man.

Here, it might well be thought that, were these last conjectures as to the foundling's secrets not **erroneous**, then must he have been **hopelessly infected** with the craziest chimeras of his age; far **outgoing** Albert Magus and Cornelius Agrippa. But the contrary was averred. However marvelous his design, however apparently **transcending** not alone the bounds of human invention, but those of divine creation, yet the proposed means to be employed were alleged to have been confined within the sober forms of sober reason. It was affirmed that, to a degree of more than **skeptic** scorn, Bannadonna had been without sympathy for any of the vain-glorious irrationalities of his time. For example, he had not concluded, with the visionaries among the metaphysicians, that between the finer mechanic forces and the ruder animal **vitality** some **germ** of **correspondence** might prove discoverable. As little did his scheme partake of the enthusiasm of some natural philosophers, who hoped, by **physiological** and **chemical inductions**, to arrive at a knowledge of the source of life, and so **qualify** themselves to manufacture and improve upon it. Much less had he aught in common with the **tribe** of alchemists, who sought, by a species of incantations, to **evoke** some surprising vitality from the laboratory. Neither had he imagined, with certain sanguine theosophists, that, by faithful **adoration** of the Highest, unheard-of powers would be vouchsafed to man. A practical **materialist**, what Bannadonna had aimed at was to have been reached, not by logic, not by **crucible**, not by conjuration, not by altars; but by plain vice-bench and **hammer**. In short, to solve nature, to steal into her, to **intrigue** beyond her, to procure some one else to **bind** her to his hand;—these, one and all, had not been his objects; but, asking no favors from any element or any being, of himself, to rival her, outstrip her, and rule her. He stooped to **conquer**. With him, common sense

Italian

adoration: adorazione, venerazione.
advancement: progresso, avanzamento.
ant: formica.
ape: scimmia, imitare.
bind: legare, rilegare.
chemical: chimico, prodotto chimico.
conquer: conquistare, conquistate, conquisto, conquisti, conquistano, conquistiamo, conquista.
correspondence: corrispondenza, carteggio.
crucible: crogiolo.
erroneous: erroneo.
evoke: evocare, evochi, evochiamo, evoca, evocano, evoco, evocate.
germ: germe, germoglio.
hammer: martello, martellare, martelletto, il martello.
hopelessly: disperatamente.
inductions: induzioni.
infected: infettato, contagiato, infetto.
intrigue: intrigo, brigare, intrigare.
materialist: materialista.
outgoing: uscente.
ox: bue.
physiological: fisiologico.
qualify: qualificare, qualificate, qualifichi, qualifichiamo, qualifico, qualificano, qualifica.
serf: servo della gleba, servo, schiavo.
skeptic: scettico.
stocking: calza.
transcending: trascendendo.
tribe: tribù.
vitality: vitalità.

was theurgy; machinery, **miracle**; Prometheus, the **heroic** name for **machinist**; man, the true God.

Nevertheless, in his **initial** step, so far as the **experimental automaton** for the belfry was concerned, he allowed fancy some little play; or, perhaps, what seemed his fancifulness was but his **utilitarian** ambition collaterally extended. In figure, the creature for the belfry should not be **likened** after the human **pattern**, nor any animal one, nor after the ideals, however wild, of ancient **fable**, but equally in aspect as in **organism** be an original **production**; the more terrible to behold, the better.

Such, then, were the suppositions as to the present scheme, and the reserved intent. How, at the very threshold, so unlooked for a **catastrophe** overturned all, or rather, what was the conjecture here, is now to be set forth.

It was thought that on the day preceding the fatality, his visitors having left him, Bannadonna had **unpacked** the belfry image, **adjusted** it, and placed it in the retreat provided — a sort of sentry-box in one **corner** of the belfry; in short, **throughout** the night, and for some part of the ensuing morning, he had been engaged in arranging everything connected with the domino; the issuing from the sentry-box each sixty **minutes**; **sliding** along a grooved way, like a **railway**; advancing to the clock-bell, with uplifted manacles; striking it at one of the twelve junctions of the four-and-twenty hands; then wheeling, circling the bell, and **retiring** to its post, there to bide for another sixty minutes, when the same process was to be repeated; the bell, by a cunning **mechanism**, meantime turning on its vertical **axis**, so as to present, to the descending mace, the clasped hands of the next two figures, when it would strike two, three, and so on, to the end. The **musical metal** in this time-bell being so **managed** in the fusion, by some art, **perishing** with its **originator**, that each of the clasps of the four-and-twenty hands should give forth its own peculiar **resonance** when parted.

But on the magic metal, the magic and metallic stranger never struck but that one stroke, drove but that one nail, served but that one clasp, by which Bannadonna clung to his ambitious life. For, after winding up the creature in the sentry-box, so that, for the present, skipping the **intervening** hours, it should not

Italian

adjusted: aggiustato, regolato.
automaton: automa.
axis: asse, assale, perno.
catastrophe: catastrofe, disastro.
corner: angolo.
experimental: sperimentale.
fable: favola.
heroic: eroico.
initial: iniziale, siglare.
intervening: intervenendo.
likened: paragonato.
machinist: macchinista.

managed: diretto.
mechanism: meccanismo, congegno.
metal: metallo.
minutes: verbale, contravvenzione, minuti.
miracle: miracolo.
musical: musicale, musical.
organism: organismo.
originator: originatore, mittente.
pattern: modello, schema, motivo, disegno, configurazione.
perishing: perendo.

production: produzione.
railway: ferrovia.
resonance: risonanza.
retiring: ritirando, riservato.
sliding: scorrevole, scorrimento, slittamento, scivolare.
throughout: dappertutto, in tutto, completamente, per tutto.
unpacked: disimballato, sballato, disfatto.
utilitarian: utilitaristico, utilitarista, utilitario.

emerge till the hour of one, but should then infallibly emerge, and, after deftly **oiling** the grooves whereon it was to **slide**, it was surmised that the **mechanician** must then have hurried to the bell, to give his final touches to its sculpture. True artist, he here became absorbed; and **absorption** still further intensified, it may be, by his striving to **abate** that strange look of Una; which, though, before others, he had **treated** with such **unconcern**, might not, in secret, have been without its thorn.

And so, for the interval, he was oblivious of his creature; which, not oblivious of him, and true to its **creation**, and true to its **heedful** winding up, left its post precisely at the given moment; along its well-oiled **route**, slid **noiselessly** towards its mark; and, aiming at the hand of Una, to ring one clangorous note, dully smote the intervening brain of Bannadonna, turned **backwards** to it; the manacled arms then instantly up-springing to their hovering poise. The falling body clogged the thing's return; so there it stood, still impending over Bannadonna, as if whispering some post-mortem terror. The chisel lay dropped from the hand, but beside the hand; the oil-flask spilled across the iron **track**.

In his unhappy end, not **unmindful** of the rare genius of the mechanician, the republic decreed him a stately **funeral**. It was resolved that the great bell — the one whose casting had been **jeopardized** through the **timidity** of the ill-starred workman — should be rung upon the entrance of the **bier** into the cathedral. The most **robust** man of the country round was assigned the office of bell-ringer.

But as the pall-bearers entered the cathedral porch, naught but a broken and disastrous sound, like that of some lone Alpine land-slide, fell from the tower upon their ears. And then, all was hushed.

Glancing backwards, they saw the groined belfry crashed sideways in. It afterwards appeared that the powerful peasant, who had the bell-rope in charge, wishing to test at once the full glory of the bell, had swayed down upon the rope with one **concentrate** jerk. The mass of quaking metal, too ponderous for its frame, and strangely feeble somewhere at its top, loosed from its **fastening**, tore sideways down, and tumbling in one sheer fall, three hundred feet to the soft sward below, buried itself inverted and half out of sight.

Italian

abate: diminuire, diminuisci, diminuisco, diminuite, diminuiscono, diminuiamo, ridurre.
absorption: assorbimento.
backwards: indietro, a rovescio, all'indietro, supino.
bier: bara.
concentrate: concentra, concentro, concentriamo, concentri, concentrano, concentrate, concentrare, concentrarsi.
creation: creazione, creato.

emerge: apparire, appaio, appaiono, appari, appariamo, apparite, emergere.
fastening: fissando, fissaggio, legatura.
funeral: funerale, funebre.
heedful: attento, cauto.
jeopardized: arrischiato, compromesso, pregiudicato, messo a repentaglio.
mechanician: meccanico.
noiselessly: tranquillamente.

oiling: oliatura.
robust: robusto.
route: strada, cammino, itinerario, via, pista, percorso, corsia, tracciato, rotta.
slide: diapositiva, vetrino, scorrere, scivolare, scivolo.
timidity: timidezza.
track: pista, traccia, binario, cingolo.
treated: trattato.
unconcern: noncuranza.
unmindful: immemore.

Upon its disinterment, the main **fracture** was found to have started from a small spot in the ear; which, being **scraped**, revealed a **defect**, deceptively minute in the **casting;** which defect must subsequently have been pasted over with some unknown compound.

The remolten metal soon **reassumed** its place in the tower's **repaired superstructure.** For one year the **metallic choir** of birds sang **musically** in its belfry-bough-work of **sculptured blinds** and traceries. But on the first **anniversary** of the tower's completion—at early **dawn**, before the **concourse** had **surrounded** it—an **earthquake** came; one **loud crash** was heard. The stone-pine, with all its **bower** of songsters, lay **overthrown** upon the **plain**.

So the blind **slave obeyed** its blinder lord; but, in **obedience**, slew him. So the **creator** was killed by the **creature**. So the bell was too heavy for the tower. So the bell's main **weakness** was where man's blood had flawed it. And so pride went before the fall.

Italian

anniversary: anniversario, compleanno.
blinds: acceca.
bower: ancora di prora, pergolato.
casting: assegnazione delle parti, getto, colata.
choir: coro.
concourse: atrio, concorso.
crash: crollare, collisione, precipitare, caduta, schianto, crollo, scontro, tracollo, fragore, fracasso, disastro.
creator: creatore.

creature: creatura.
dawn: alba, aurora, albeggiare.
defect: difetto, imperfezione, mancanza.
earthquake: terremoto.
fracture: frattura, fratturare, rottura.
loud: forte, alto, rumoroso.
metallic: metallico.
musically: musicalmente.
obedience: ubbidienza, obbedienza.
obeyed: ubbidito, obbedito.
overthrown: rovesciato.

plain: piano, pianura, evidente, distinto, chiaro.
reassumed: riassunto.
repaired: riparato.
scraped: raschiato.
sculptured: scolpito.
slave: schiavo, sgobbare.
superstructure: sovrastruttura.
surrounded: circondato.
weakness: debolezza.

GLOSSARY

abased: degradato
abashment: confusione
abate: diminuire, diminuisci, diminuisco, diminuite, diminuiscono, diminuiamo, ridurre
abated: diminuito, ridotto
abbot: abate
aberration: aberrazione, errore, sbaglio
abhorrent: ripugnante, orrendo, orribile, avverso, detestabile
abide: aspettare, aspettiamo, aspetta, aspettano, aspetti, aspetto, aspettate, restare, sopportare
abides: aspetta
abiding: durevole, permanente, continuo, aspettando
abode: residenza, appartamento, alloggio, dimora
abodes: residenze
abominably: abominevolmente
aboriginal: aborigeno
abound: abbondare, abbondano, abbondate, abbondi, abbondiamo, abbondo, abbonda
abounding: abbondando
abridge: abbreviare, abbreviate, abbrevi, abbrevia, abbreviamo, abbreviano, abbrevio, limitare, accorciare, compendiare, ridurre
abrogation: abrogazione, abolizione
absconding: fuggendo, scappando
absenteeism: assenteismo
absolution: assoluzione
absurdly: assurdamente
abundance: abbondanza, ricchezza, affluenza
accelerating: accelerando
accessions: entrate
accessory: accessorio
accidentally: accidentalmente
acclivity: pendio
accomplish: compiere, compiamo, compio, compiono, compite, compi, eseguire, arrivare
accomplishing: compiendo
accordance: concordanza, accordo

accorded: accordato
according: secondo
accost: abbordare, avvicinare
accosted: abbordato, accostato, avvicinato
accosts: accosta, avvicina, abborda, approcci
accumulate: accumulare, accumulano, accumulate, accumuli, accumuliamo, accumula, accumulo, accumularsi, ammassare
accustomed: consueto, abituato, usuale, solito, avvezzo
aching: dolorante, dolente
acquaintance: conoscenza, conoscente
acquainted: informato
acquiesced: acconsentito
acquiescence: acquiescenza
acquiescent: acquiescente
acrid: acre, aspro, pungente
acuteness: acutezza
additionally: inoltre
adhered: aderito
adhering: aderendo
adieu: addio
adjoining: adiacente, limitrofo, contiguo
adjourn: aggiornare, rimandare
adjunct: aggiunta
adjusting: aggiustando, regolando
admirable: ammirabile, ammirevole, mirabile
admitting: confessando, ammettendo
admonished: ammonito
admonition: ammonimento, ammonizione, esortazione
admonitory: ammonitorio
ado: rumore
adoration: adorazione, venerazione
adorned: decorato
adrift: alla deriva
adroit: abile, destro, sveglio, lesto
adulterated: adulterato
advancement: progresso, avanzamento
advantageous: vantaggioso, utile

adventurer: avventuriero
adventurous: avventuroso
adversity: sfortuna, avversità
aerial: antenna, aereo
afar: lontano
affability: affabilità
affectionate: affettuoso
affirmed: affermato
afflicted: afflitto
affliction: afflizione
afflicts: affligge
afforded: permesso
affording: permettendo
affront: affronto, insulto, insultare
afloat: a galla
afresh: di nuovo, ancora, da capo
aft: a poppa
afternoons: pomeriggi
aggravated: aggravato
aggravates: aggrava
aghast: atterrito, inorridito
agitated: agitato
agitation: agitazione
aglow: ardente
agreeable: gradevole, piacevole, amabile
agreeably: piacevolmente
ague: febbre
airy: arioso
ajar: socchiuso
alacrity: entusiasmo, alacrità
alarmed: allarmato
alarming: allarmante
alas: ahimè
albatross: albatro
ale: birra
allaying: alleviando
allude: alludere, alludi, alludiamo, alludo, alludono, alludete
alluded: alluso
alluding: alludendo
allusion: allusione
alms: elemosina
aloft: in alto
aloof: appartato, in disparte, alla larga, a distanza, distante
alpine: alpino

alps: Alpi
altercation: lite, alterco
alternate: alternare, alterno, alternato
alternately: alternativamente, alternatamente
altitude: altitudine, altezza, quota
amazement: stupore, meraviglia
amends: emenda, ammenda
amidships: a mezza nave
amidst: tra, fra
amiss: male, inopportuno
amphitheatre: anfiteatro
amply: ampiamente
anaconda: anaconda
ancestor: antenato, ascendente
anchor: ancora, ancorare, ancoraggio, àncora, l'ancora
anchorage: ancoraggio
anchored: ancorato
andes: Ande
anew: di nuovo, ancora
angelic: angelico
angular: angolare
animated: animato
animation: animazione, vivacità
annals: annali
annihilate: annichilire, annientare, annichilisco, annichiliscono, annichilite, annienta, annientano, annientate, annienti, annientiamo, anniento
annoying: irritante
anomaly: anomalia
answerable: responsabile
ant: formica
antarctic: antartico, Antartide, Polo Sud
anthracite: antracite
antic: bizzarro, grottesco
anticipating: anticipando
antiquary: antiquario
apace: di buon passo
apathetic: apatico
apathy: apatia
ape: scimmia, imitare
apostatize: apostatate, apostati, apostato, apostatiamo, apostatano, apostata, apostatare
appall: atterrisci, atterrite, atterrisco, atterriamo, atterriscono, atterrire
appanage: appannaggio
apparel: vestimento, abito
apparition: apparizione
appellation: nome, appellativo
applause: applauso
appointing: nominando
apprehension: apprensione, arresto
apprehensive: apprensivo
apprehensively: timorosamente, apprensivamente
apprentice: apprendista
apprenticeship: apprendistato

apprise: avvertono, informo, informiamo, informi, informate, informano, informa, avviso, avvisiamo, avvisi, avvisate
apprised: informato, avvisato, avvertito
approves: approva
apron: grembiule, grembiale
apt: adatto
aquatic: acquatico
arabian: arabo
archipelago: arcipelago
arduous: arduo
aries: Ariete
aristocratically: aristocraticamente
armor: armatura, corazza
armorial: araldico
armory: arsenale, armeria
aromatic: aromatico
arranging: sistemando, predisponendo, ordinando
artificially: artificialmente
ascend: salire, salgo, salite, saliamo, salgono, Sali, ascendere, ascendono, ascendo, ascendete, ascendi
ascendancy: predominio, ascendente
ascending: salendo, ascendente, ascendendo
ascent: ascesa, ascensione
ascertain: constatare, constatiamo, constati, constatate, constato, constatano, constata, accertare, accerto, accertiamo, accerti
ascertainable: accertabile
ascribe: attribuire, attribuite, attribuiscono, attribuisci, attribuiamo, attribuisco
ascribed: attribuito
ashes: cenere
ashore: a terra
ashy: cinereo
askance: di traverso, sospettosamente, obliquamente
aspiration: aspirazione
ass: asino, ciuco, somaro, culo
assailant: assalitore, aggressore
assailed: assalito
assassin: assassino
assassination: assassinio
assign: assegnare, assegnate, assegni, assegnano, assegna, assegniamo, assegno
assisting: assistendo, aiutando
assorting: assortendo
assuring: assicurando
astern: indietro, a poppa
astonished: stupito, si stupito
astonishment: stupore, meraviglia, sorpresa
astound: sbalordite, si stupisci, si stupiscono, si stupite, mi stupisco, stupefaccio, stupefai, stupefacciamo,

stupefa', sbalordiscono, stupisciti
astounding: sbalorditivo
astral: astrale
atheist: ateo
athletic: atletico
attaches: attacca, fissa, allega
attain: arrivare, arrivi, arriviamo, arrivate, arrivano, arriva, arrivo, ottenere, raggiungere, conseguire
attained: arrivato
attaining: arrivando
attendant: custode, compagno, inserviente
attentively: attentamente
attenuated: assottigliato, attenuato
attest: attestare, attesto, attestiamo, attesti, attestate, attesta, attestano
attesting: attestando
attic: soffitta, attico
attire: abbigliare, abbigliamento
attracting: attirando, attraendo
audible: udibile
audibly: udibilmente
augment: ingrandire, ingrandite, ingrandiscono, ingrandisco, ingrandisci, ingrandiamo, aumentare, aumenta, aumentano, aumentate, aumenti
augmented: ingrandito, aumentato
augments: ingrandisce, aumenta
augury: presagio, augurio
aurora: aurora, alba
austere: austero
autocrat: autocrate
automaton: automa
avail: giovare, essere utile, servire, utilizzare
availed: servito
avalanche: valanga
avenge: vendicare, vendico, vendica, vendicano, vendicate, vendichi, vendichiamo
averred: asserito
averse: avverso
aversion: avversione, ripugnanza
avert: evitate, eviti, distogli, distogliete, evitiamo, evitano, evita, evito, distolgo, distogliamo, allontaniamo
averted: evitato, allontanato, distolto
averting: distogliendo, evitando, allontanando
aviary: voliera, uccelliera
avidity: avidità
avowed: dichiarato
awaken: svegliamo, svegliano, svegli, risvegliate, risvegliano, risvegliamo, risvegli, svegliate, risveglia, sveglia, risveglio
awakening: risveglio
azure: azzurro
babes: pupe, bambole

babylon: babilonia
backward: indietro, a rovescio, supino, deficiente
baffled: sconcertato
baffling: sconcertante
baggy: cascante, gonfio, rigonfio
baked: cotto
balconies: balconi
bald: calvo, pelato
balloonist: aeronauta da pallone
balmy: fragrante
balsamic: balsamico
balustrade: parapetto, balaustra, balaustrata
balustrades: balaustrate
bandit: bandito, brigante
baneful: pernicioso
banished: bandito
banishment: esilio, bando
banister: ringhiera
banisters: parapetto, ringhiera
banner: bandiera, striscione
baptist: battista
barbarous: barbaro
barbary: Barberia
barber: barbiere, parrucchiere
barge: chiatta, barcone
bark: corteccia, abbaiare, scorza, latrare, abbaio
barracks: caserma
barred: sbarrato
barren: sterile
barricade: barricata, barricare
barter: baratto, barattare
baseness: bassezza
beacon: gavitello, boa, faro
beads: rosario
beak: becco, rostro
beamed: irradiato
bearings: cuscinetti
becalmed: acquietato
beckon: accenna, accennano, accennate, accenni, accenniamo, accenno, accennare
beckoned: accennato
beckoning: accennando
bedding: biancheria da letto, lettiera
bee: ape, l'ape
befallen: successo
befalling: succedendo
beforehand: in anticipo
befriend: aiutiamo, aiuto, aiuti, aiutano, aiuta, aiutate, aiutare
begged: mendicato
begging: mendicando
begs: mendica
behaved: agito, comportato
behavior: condotta, comportamento
beheld: guardato
behold: guardare
beholding: guardando
belfry: cella campanaria, campanile

belted: cintura
benefactor: benefattore
benevolent: benevolo
benign: benigno, benevolo
berries: bacche
berry: bacca
berth: cuccetta, ancoraggio, attraccare
beseeching: implorando, scongiurando, supplicando, supplichevole, implorante
bespeaking: prenotando
bestowal: concessione
bestowed: concesso, tributato
betake: recarsi
betray: tradire, tradisci, tradite, tradisco, tradiamo, tradiscono
betrayed: tradito
betraying: tradendo
bewilderment: perplessità
bidding: offerta, licitazione, comando
bier: bara
birch: betulla
biscuit: biscotto
bishopric: diocesi, vescovado
biting: pungente, mordace
blackberry: mora
blackening: annerendo
blacking: nero, annerire, lucido nero
blackish: nerastro
blacksmith: maniscalco, fabbro ferraio, fabbro
bland: dolce, blando
blandly: blandamente
blasted: maledetto
blaze: vampa, fiammata
blazed: arso
blazon: blasone
bled: sanguinato
blemish: difetto
blending: mescolanza, miscela
bless: benedire, benedi', benedite, benedicono, benedico, benedici, benediciamo
blinds: acceca
blinkers: paraocchi
blithe: allegro
blithesome: gaio, allegro, gioioso
blockade: blocco, bloccare
bloom: fiore, fiorire, fioritura
blot: macchia
blotted: macchiato
blueberry: mirtillo, bacca di mirtillo
bluff: bluffare
blurred: sfocato
boarded: imbarcato
boarding: abbordaggio, tavolato, imbarco
boatswain: nostromo
boldly: audacemente, arditamente
bolting: bullonatura
bolts: bulloni
boor: cafone

booty: bottino
bosom: petto, seno
boundless: illimitato
bower: ancora di prora, pergolato
bowing: archeggio
bows: archetti
bowsprit: bompresso
brace: parentesi graffa, sostegno
braces: bretelle
brake: freno, frenare
brakes: freni
bravado: bravata
bravely: coraggiosamente
bravery: coraggio
brazen: affrontare con impudenza, di ottone, impudente, svergognato, simile a ottone, sfacciato
breadth: larghezza, ampiezza
breeches: brache, calzoni alla zuava
brethren: fratelli, confratelli
brewed: fermentato
bridle: briglia, freno, imbrigliare
brightly: luminosamente
brightness: luminosità, lucentezza
brilliancy: splendore
brine: salamoia, acqua salata
brisk: vivace, attivo
briskness: vivacità
broach: spiedo, spillare, broccia
broadside: fiancata
bronzed: bronzo
brooding: cova
broth: brodo
browbeaten: intimidito
browse: sfogliare, brucare
bubbling: gorgogliare, gorgoglio, ribollimento, bolla
buccaneer: pirata
buckler: protezione, scudo
budge: spostarsi, muoversi
buggy: carrozzino, calesse, carrello, calessino
bulb: lampadina, ampolla, lampada, bulbo
bullion: lingotto
bunting: pavese
burglar: ladro, scassinatore
bust: busto
butterfly: farfalla
buttoned: abbottonato
buttoning: abbottonare
buttress: contrafforte
buzzing: ronzio
cables: cavi
cactus: cactus
cadaverous: cadaverico
cadaverously: cadavericamente
cajoles: alletta, lusinghe
cajoling: allettando, lusingare
caked: incrostato
calabash: zucca
calamities: calamità

calamitous: calamitoso
calamity: calamità
calcined: calcinato
calked: calafatato
calve: figli, figlia, figliamo, figliano, figliate, figlio, partoriamo, partorisci, partorisco, partoriscono, partorite
calves: figlia, partorisce, vitelli
campanile: campanile
canary: canarino
cane: bastone, canna, canna da zucchero
canine: canino
cannon: cannone
cannot: non potere
canopy: baldacchino, tettuccio, calotta
canton: cantone
capped: avente come limite superiore
caprice: capriccio
capricious: capriccioso
captains: capitani
careening: carenando
carelessly: negligentemente
carnival: carnevale
carpenter: falegname, carpentiere
carrion: carogna
carthage: Cartagine
cascade: cascata
cask: barile, botte, fusto
castaway: naufrago
caster: fonditore, rotella
castile: Castiglia
castilian: castigliano
castles: castelli
catamaran: catamarano
catastrophe: catastrofe, disastro
catches: prende, colpisce
cavalcade: cavalcata
cavalry: cavalleria
cavernous: cavernoso
ceaseless: incessante
celestial: celeste, celestiale
centaur: centauro
ceremonious: cerimonioso
certify: certificare, certifichiamo, certifico, certifichi, certificano, certifica, certificate
cessation: cessazione
chained: incatenato
chalky: gessoso
chamois: camoscio
chanced: successo
changeable: variabile, mutevole
charcoal: carbone di legna
charger: caricatore
charitably: caritatevolmente
charmed: affascinato
charred: carbonizzato
chatty: chiacchierino
cheaply: economicamente
cheerfully: allegramente

cheerfulness: contentezza, allegria
cheery: allegro
cherish: adoriamo, adori, adorate, adorano, adora, adoro, adorare, curare teneramente
cherished: adorato
cherishing: adorando
chicks: pulcino
childless: senza figli
chill: freddo
chilled: raffreddato
chimney: camino, fumaiolo
chirrup: cinguetta, cinguettano, cinguettate, cinguetti, cinguettiamo, cinguetto, cinguettare
chisel: scalpello
choleric: collerico
chooses: sceglie, elegge
choral: corale
christened: battezzato
chuckle: riso soffocato, ridacchiare
churn: zangola
cider: sidro
cinders: cenere
circuitous: indiretto, tortuoso
circumstance: circostanza
circumstantial: particolareggiato, circostanziale
cistern: cisterna
citadel: cittadella
civility: civiltà, cortesia
civilized: civilizzato
civilizing: civilizzando, incivilendo
clad: vestito
clamber: arrampicarsi
clamorous: clamoroso
clap: applaudire, battere le mani, applauso
clapping: applaudire
clasp: fermaglio
clatter: sferragliare, ticchettio, acciottolio, sferragliamento
clearness: limpidezza, chiarezza
cleaving: spaccando, fendendo, spaccatura
clenched: serrato
climax: punto culminante
cling: aderite, aderiscono, aderiamo, aderisco, aderisci, aggrapparsi, aderire
clinker: clinker
clipping: tosatura, taglio
closet: armadio
clouded: annuvolato
cloudless: sereno
cloudy: nuvoloso, torbido
clout: colpire, colpo
clove: chiodo di garofano
cloven: spaccato, fesso
cloyed: saziato
clumsy: goffo, maldestro, impacciato
clutch: frizione, afferrare

coarse: rozzo, grossolano
coarseness: grossolanità, ruvidezza
coasting: costiero, costa
coaxing: blandendo, persuadendo
cock: gallo, cazzo, rubinetto
cockpit: abitacolo, cabina di guida
coercing: costringendo
coil: bobina, rotolo
coiled: avvolto
coinciding: coincidendo
coldness: freddezza
collusion: collusione
colonization: colonizzazione
colonizing: colonizzando
color: colore, colorare
colored: colorato
coloring: coloritura, colorante
colors: colori
colossal: colossale
colt: puledro
comb: pettine, pettinare, favo
combativeness: combattività
commanding: comandare
commandment: comandamento
commenced: cominciato
commencing: cominciando
committing: commettendo
commotion: agitazione, commozion scandalo, confusione
communicated: comunicato
communicating: comunicando
companionable: socievole
compass: bussola, la bussola, compasso
compassion: compassione
compassionate: compassionevole
compatriot: compatriota
compelled: costretto, forzato
compiled: compilato
complaisance: compiacenza
complexion: carnagione
complicity: complicità
complied: accondisceso, ottemperat
compliment: complimento
compliments: complimenti
compose: comporre, componi, componiamo, compongo, compongono, componete
comprehend: comprendere, comprendo, comprendono, comprendiamo, comprendi, comprendete
comprehended: compreso
comrade: camerata
con: contro
concave: cavo, concavo
conceals: nasconde
conceit: presunzione
conceited: vanitoso, presuntuoso
conceivable: concepibile
conceive: concepire, concepiamo, concepisci, concepisco, concepiscor

concepite
concentric: concentrico
concord: accordo
concourse: atrio, concorso
condensation: condensazione
condescend: degna, degnano, degnate, degni, degniamo, degno, degnare
condescended: degnato
condescending: degnando, condiscendente
condolence: condoglianza
condor: condor
conductor: conduttore, bigliettaio, capotreno
confederate: confederato
conferred: conferito
confess: confessare, confessa, confessano, confessa, confessi, confessiamo, confesso
confessed: confessato
confession: confessione
confidant: confidente
confinement: reclusione, prigionia, confinamento
confirming: confermando
conflagration: conflagrazione
conflicting: conflitto
confound: confondere
congenially: congenialmente
congratulating: felicitando
conjecture: congettura
conjoined: congiunto
conjured: evocato
connecting: legando, collegando
conquer: conquistare, conquistate, conquisto, conquisti, conquistano, conquistiamo, conquista
conquered: conquistato
conscientious: coscienzioso
consecutively: successivamente
considerately: premurosamente
consisted: consistito, constato
consisting: consistendo, constando
consort: consorte, coniuge
conspicuously: cospicuamente
conspirator: cospiratore
constancy: costanza
consternation: sbigottimento, costernazione
constrained: costretto
constraint: costrizione, vincolo
construe: interpreti, analizzate, interpreto, interpretiamo, interpretano, interpreta, analizzo, interpretate, analizza, analizziamo, analizzi
construing: analizzando, interpretando
contagion: contagio
contemplating: contemplando
contemptuous: sprezzante

contended: conteso
contentment: soddisfazione
continual: continuo, costante
contorted: contorto
contour: contorno, profilo
contracted: contratto
contrary: contrario
contrasting: contrastante
contributes: contribuisce
contrition: contrizione
contrives: escogita
convalescence: convalescenza
conveniently: convenientemente, utilmente, comodamente
conversational: conversazionale, loquace, colloquiale
conveyed: trasportato
conveys: trasporta
convivial: conviviale
convulsion: convulsione
cooled: raffreddato
coolly: frescamente
copied: copiato
copying: copia, copiatura, riproduzione
copyist: copista
coral: corallo
cordial: cordiale
corked: tappato
correcting: correggere
corroborated: confermato, corroborato
corroded: corroso
corrupted: corrotto
costume: costume, abito
costumes: costumi
cot: lettino, branda
coughing: tosse, tossire
countenance: approvare, viso
countryman: compatriota
coupling: accoppiamento, innesto, giunto, manicotto
courteous: cortese
courteously: cortesemente
courtier: cortigiano
cove: cala, insenatura
covert: nascosto, rifugio, riparo
cowardice: codardia, vigliaccheria
craftiness: furberia
crafty: astuto
crane: gru
crave: bramare
craven: codardo
crawled: strisciato
creaking: cigolando, stridendo, cigolio, scricchiolio
creamy: cremoso
creator: creatore
credence: credenza
credible: credibile
creditable: lodevole
credited: accreditato

credulous: credulo
creep: strisciare, strisci, strisciamo, strisciano, strisciate, strisciamento, striscia, striscio
creeper: pianta rampicante
creeping: strisciando, strisciante
creole: creolo
crescent: mezzaluna
crest: cresta
criminality: delinquenza
crimson: cremisi
cripple: storpio, storpiare
crippled: zoppo
crisp: croccante, crespo
crooked: storto, disonesto
crosswise: trasversalmente
crotch: forca
crouched: rannicchiato, accoccolato
crouching: rannicchiando
crowding: folla, affollamento
crowning: corona, supremo
crucible: crogiolo
crucifix: crocifisso
cruiser: incrociatore
crumbled: sbriciolato, sgretolato
crumpled: sgualcito, spiegazzato
crunching: sgranocchiando
crusade: crociata
crusts: croste
crutch: stampella, gruccia
cuban: cubano
cue: stecca
culminate: culminare, culmini, culminiamo, culminate, culminano, culmina, culmino
culprit: colpevole
cultivated: coltivato
cultivating: coltivando
cultivation: coltivazione
cunning: astuzia, astuto, furbo
cupola: cupola
curb: barbazzale, tenere a freno, freno
curl: arricciare, ricciolo, riccio
curling: arricciare, arricciamento
curse: bestemmiare, maledire, imprecare, maledizione, imprecazione
cursed: maledetto
cushion: cuscino
cutter: taglierina, fresa, tagliatore, coltello, taglierino
cynic: cinico
czar: zar
dabbling: bagnando, sguazzando
dagger: pugnale, daga
daggers: pugnali
dainty: delicato
dally: ozio, oziate, oziano, oziamo, ozia, ozi, oziare
dampness: umidità
damsel: donzella
danced: ballato, ballavo ballava

dandelions: dente di leone
dangerously: pericolosamente
dank: bagnato, umido
daring: osando, audace
dashed: tratteggiato
daybreak: alba
dazzling: abbagliare, abbagliante, accecante
deafness: sordità
dearth: scarsità, penuria
debased: avvilito, deprezzato, abbassato, degradato
debating: dibattere
debility: debolezza
debonair: affabile
decayed: decrepito
decease: decedere, decesso
deceit: frode
deceive: ingannare, ingannano, inganniamo, ingannate, inganna, inganni, inganno, truffare, truffate, truffano, truffiamo
deceived: ingannato, truffato
decency: decenza
decently: decentemente
deceptive: ingannevole
decks: adorna
declares: dichiara
decorous: decente, decoroso
decoy: esca
deeds: gesta
deem: credere, crediamo, credete, credi, credo, credono, ritenere, giudicare, guardare
deeming: credendo
deepened: approfondito
deepens: approfondisce
defense: difesa
deference: deferenza
deficient: deficiente, carente, difettoso, insufficiente
defied: sfidato
defile: gola
deformed: deforme, deformato
defraud: defraudare
defray: risarcite, risarciscono, risarcisco, risarcisci, risarciamo, risarcire
defunct: defunto
degenerate: degenerare, degenerato
degradation: degradazione
degraded: degradato
deity: divinità
dejection: deiezione, abbattimento, scoraggiamento, depressione
delegated: delegato
delicacy: delicatezza
delirious: delirante
deluge: diluvio
delusion: illusione
delusive: ingannevole, illusorio
demented: demente

demoniac: demoniaco
demur: esitazione, esitare
den: tana
denoting: denotando
denouncing: denunciando
densely: densamente
dented: ammaccato
denying: negando
depart: partire, partite, partiamo, parti, partono, parto, andarsene
departed: partito
departing: partendo
departs: parte
depended: dipeso
depict: descrivete, descriviamo, descrivo, descrivono, ritraiamo, dipingi, dipingo, dipingiamo, descrivi, ritrai, ritraggono
depicted: dipinto, descritto, ritratto
deplore: deplorare
deploring: deplorando
deploy: schierare
deponent: deponente
deportment: condotta, comportamento
deposited: depositato
deposition: deposizione
depravity: depravazione
depress: deprimere
deranged: squilibrato
deriving: derivando
descend: scendere, scendiamo, scendono, scendi, scendete, scendo, discendere, discendono, discendo, discendiamo, discendi
descended: sceso, disceso
descending: scendendo, discendendo
descends: scende, discende
descried: scorto, intravisto
deserving: meritando, meritevole
designation: designazione
desirous: desideroso
desist: desistere, desisto, desistete, desistiamo, desisti, desistono
desisted: desistito
desolate: desolato
desolation: desolazione, devastazione
despairing: disperare
desperation: disperazione
despotic: dispotico
destined: destinato
detained: ritenuto
detest: detestare, detestate, detesto, detesti, detestano, detesta, detestiamo
devilish: diabolico
devise: escogitare
devour: divorare, divorano, divora, divorate, divoriamo, divoro, divori
dew: rugiada
diabolical: diabolico

diagonal: diagonale
dial: quadrante
dictate: dettare, dettano, dettate, det dettiamo, detta, detto
dictated: dettato
dictatorship: dittatura
diffident: timido
digesting: digerire
digestion: digestione
dignified: dignitoso
dilated: dilatato
diligence: diligenza
dimly: pallidamente
dimmed: oscurato
din: rumore
dine: cenare
dined: pranzato, cenato
dip: intingere, inclinazione, immersione
dipping: immersione
dire: tremendo, spaventoso, atroce
dirge: nenia
disappearing: scomparendo
disarmed: disarmato
disarming: disarmando
disarray: scompiglio
disbanded: sciolto
discerned: distinto, discernuto, percepito
disciplined: disciplinato
disclose: svelare
disconcerted: sconcertato, turbato
disconnecting: disinnestando, sconnettendo
discontent: malcontento
discontinuing: interrompendo
discord: disaccordo
discourtesy: scortesia
discoverer: scopritore
discovering: scoprendo
discrepancy: discrepanza
disdain: sdegno, sdegnare
disdainful: sdegnoso, sprezzante
diseased: malato
disenchanted: disilluso, disincantato
disengaged: disimpegnato, disinnestato
disentangled: districato
disgraceful: disgraziata, vergognoso, disonorevole
disguised: travestito
dishonor: disonorare, disonore
disinterested: disinteressato, imparziale
disinterestedness: disinteresse
disjointed: disgiunto, sconnesso
dismal: triste, buio, mostruoso, misero, sgradevole, miserabile, banale, afflitto, povero, schifoso, scuro
dismantled: smontato
dismayed: costernato**

dismissing: licenziando
dismount: scendere, scendete, scendi, scendiamo, scendo, scendono, smontare
disorderly: disordinato
disown: rinnegano, ripudiate, ripudiano, ripudiamo, ripudia, ripudi, rinnego, rinneghiamo, rinnegate, rinnega, disconoscono
dispassionate: spassionato
dispatch: dispaccio, invio, spedizione
dispatched: spedito
dispatching: spedire
dispel: dissipare
dispensation: dispensa
dispense: distribuire, distribuiamo, distribuiscono, distribuite, distribuisci, distribuisco, dispensare
dispensed: distribuito
displace: spostare, spostiamo, sposto, sposti, spostate, spostano, sposta
displaced: spostato
displeased: scontentato, scontento
displeasure: scontento, dispiacere
disposed: disposto
disposition: disposizione, predisposizione, ingegno, talento
disqualified: squalificato
disquietude: inquietudine
disrepair: rovina, sfacelo
disservice: danno, disservizio
dissipate: dissipare
dissipated: dissipato
dissipation: dispersione, dissipazione
dissonant: dissonante
distorted: falsato, distorto
distressed: afflitto
distressing: doloroso, penoso, angoscioso
distribute: distribuire, distribuite, distribuiscono, distribuiamo, distribuisco, distribuisci
distrust: diffidenza
distrustful: sospettoso, diffidente
diversified: diversificato, differenziato
divides: divide, separa
divulge: divulgare
docile: arrendevole, mansueto
docility: docilità
doddered: tremato
dodge: espediente
dodging: mascheratura in stampa
dolorous: doloroso
dolphin: delfino
dome: cupola
dominating: dominando
dominion: dominio
donkey: asino, ciuco
doom: condannare, destino
dormitory: dormitorio
dote: essere rimbambito

doubly: doppiamente
downcast: abbattuto
downright: completamente, schietto
downward: verso il basso
downy: lanuginoso
drags: trascina
dram: dram
draping: drappeggiando
dread: temere
dreamy: sognante
drearily: tristemente
dreary: triste, scuro, afflitto, schifoso, sgradevole, mostruoso, spiacevole, buio, abominevole
drilling: trapanazione, perforazione, trivellazione
drinker: bevitore
dripping: sgocciolatura, stillicidio, gocciolamento
dross: scoria
drought: siccità
droughts: siccità
drown: annegare, annega, annego, anneghiamo, anneghi, annegate, annegano, annegarsi, affogare
drowned: annegato
drowning: annegando, annegamento, annegare
drowsy: sonnolento
drudge: sgobbone
drunkenness: ebbrezza, ubriachezza
duel: duello
duplicity: duplicità
dusk: crepuscolo
dusky: tetro
dwell: abitare, dimorare, dimorate, dimoro, dimori, dimorano, dimora, abitiamo, abiti, abitate, abitano
dwelling: dimorando, abitando, dimora, abitazione
dwells: abita, dimora
eagerness: impazienza
earnest: serio, caparra
earnestly: seriamente
earthen: terrestre, di terra
earthly: terrestre, terreno, mondano
earthquake: terremoto
earthy: terroso
eats: mangia
eaves: gronda
eccentric: eccentrico, stravagante
eccentricity: eccentricità
echoing: risuonare
eddy: gorgo, vortice, mulinello
edgeways: di traverso
edible: commestibile, mangiabile
edifice: edificio
effaced: cancellato
effectual: efficace
efficacy: efficacia
effrontery: sfrontatezza
eightieth: ottantesimo

elapse: trascorrere, trascorriamo, trascorro, trascorri, trascorrete, trascorrono, decorrere
elated: esaltato, esultante
elegance: eleganza
elephantine: elefantino
elevated: elevato
elevating: elevando
elevation: elevazione, altezza, prospetto
elicit: suscitate, suscito, susciti, suscitano, suscita, suscitiamo, suscitare
elm: olmo
elongated: allungato
eloquence: eloquenza
elucidate: delucidare
embalming: imbalsamando, imbalsamare
embarks: imbarca
embers: brace
embodied: incarnato, incorporato
embossed: stampato in rilievo
emigrant: emigrante
eminently: eminentemente
emphasizing: accentuando, enfatizzando
emphatic: enfatico
emphatically: enfatico, enfaticamente
empowered: autorizzato
emptiness: vuoto
enact: decretare, decreto, decretiamo, decreti, decretate, decreta, decretano
enacting: decretando
encamped: accampato
enchanted: incantato
enchanter: mago, incantatore
enchantment: incantesimo, incanto
encircled: circondato
encircling: circondando
encountering: incontrando
encounters: incontra
encumbered: ingombrato, gravato
endangered: mettere in pericolo
endeavor: cercare, sforzarsi, sforzo, tentativo
endowed: dotato
endurance: resistenza, pazienza
endure: sopportare, sopporta, sopporto, sopportiamo, sopporti, sopportano, sopportate, tollerare, durare, duriamo, dura
energetic: energico, energetico
engraved: inciso
enigmatic: enigmatico
enlarged: ingrandito, ampliato
enlightened: illuminato
enlist: arruolare, arruoliamo, arruoli, arruolo, arruolano, arruola, arruolate
enlisted: arruolato
enlists: arruola

ennobled: nobilitato
enraged: irritato, arrabbiato, incollerito, adirato
enriched: arricchito
ensign: insegna, alfiere
ensue: seguire, segui, seguono, seguo, seguiamo, seguite, conseguire, risultare
ensued: seguito
ensuing: seguendo
entangled: intrappolato, ingarbugliato, impigliato, imbrogliato, aggrovigliato
enterprising: intraprendente
entertain: intrattenere, intrattenete, intrattieni, intratteniamo, intrattengo, intrattengono, ricevere
entertained: intrattenuto
entertains: intrattiene
enthrall: affascinare, affascino, affascina, affascinano, affascinate, affascini, affasciniamo, incantare
entice: attirare
entreat: supplicare
entreated: supplicato
entreating: supplicando, supplicare
entreats: supplica
entrenched: trincerato
entrenching: trincerando
enveloped: avviluppato
envoy: inviato
envy: invidia, invidiare, invidio, invidiate, invidiano, invidi, invidiamo
epitaph: epitaffio
equator: equatore
equatorial: equatoriale
equivocal: ambiguo, equivoco
equivocally: equivocamente
erect: eretto, fondere, erigere, diritto, alzare
erection: erezione, montaggio, costruzione
err: errare, errano, errate, erri, erriamo, erro, erra, sbagliarsi
errand: messaggio, commissione
erroneous: erroneo
eruption: eruzione
escort: scortare, scorta, accompagnare, accompagnatore
essayed: provato
esthetic: estetico
estimation: stima, valutazione
eternity: eternità
evanescent: evanescente
evaporate: evaporare, evaporate, evaporo, evapori, evaporano, evapora, evaporiamo, vaporare
evergreen: sempreverde
everlasting: eterno
evermore: sempre
evilly: malvagiamente

evince: manifestiamo, manifesto, manifesti, manifestate, manifestano, manifesta, manifestare
evinced: manifestato
evinces: manifesta
evincing: manifestando
evoke: evocare, evochi, evochiamo, evoca, evocano, evoco, evocate
evoked: evocato
evokes: evoca
exalts: esalta
exasperated: esasperato
exasperating: esasperando
exceeding: eccedendo
exceedingly: estremamente
exceeds: eccede
excels: eccelle
excepting: salvo
exclaiming: esclamando
exclamation: esclamazione
execrable: esecrabile
exert: praticare, esercitare, eserciti, pratico, pratichiamo, pratichi, praticate, praticano, pratica, esercitiamo, esercitate
exerting: esercitando, praticando
exertion: sforzo
exhaustion: esaurimento, spossatezza
exhibited: esibito
exhilarated: esilarato
exhilarating: esilarando, esilarante
exhorted: esortato
exhumed: esumato, riesumato
exiled: esiliato
expectancy: aspettativa
expeditious: sollecito, sbrigativo
expertly: espertamente
expiration: scadenza, espirazione
expire: scadere, morire, scadi, scadono, muoio, scadiamo, scadete, muori, muoiono, moriamo, scado
expired: morto, scaduto
explode: esplodere, esplodete, esplodiamo, esplodo, esplodono, esplodi
exploded: esploso
explorer: esploratore
explores: esplora
expose: esporre, esponete, espongo, espongono, esponi, esponiamo
exposing: esponendo
expressive: espressivo
exquisite: squisito
exterior: esteriore, esterno
extinct: estinto
extracted: estratto
extremity: estremità
exude: trasudare
eyed: occhio
fable: favola
facilitated: facilitato, agevolato
fades: svanisce

fading: svanendo, scolorimento
fainted: svenuto
fainting: svenendo
faintness: debolezza
faints: sviene
faithfully: fedelmente
faithless: sleale
faltered: balbettato
faltering: balbettando
familiarity: dimestichezza
familiarly: familiarmente
famously: famosamente
fanciful: fantasioso, fantastico
farther: più lontano
fastened: fissato
fastening: fissando, fissaggio, legatura
fatality: fatalità
fated: destinato
fatherless: orfano di padre
fathom: scandagliare
fatigue: fatica, affaticare, stancare, stanchezza, affaticamento
faulty: difettoso
favor: favore, favorire, cortesia
favorable: favorevole
favored: favorito
favorite: preferito, favorito
fawn: cerbiatto
fearless: intrepido, impavido
feather: penna, piuma
featureless: informe
febrile: febbrile
feeble: debole
feline: felino
fellowship: compagnia
felony: crimine, delitto
fencing: scherma
fern: felce
ferocious: feroce
ferryman: traghettatore
fertilizing: concimando
fervid: fervido
fetching: portando
feverish: febbrile, febbricitante
feverishly: febbricitantemente
fickle: incostante, volubile
fictitious: fittizio
fidelity: fedeltà
fidgety: agitato, irrequieto
fiery: infuocato
filial: filiale
fin: pinna, aletta, la pinna
fished: pescato
fitful: irregolare
fitfully: irregolarmente
fixture: attrezzatura, apparecchiatura, attrezzo
flake: scaglia, fiocco
flank: fianco
flatter: lusingare, lusingate, lusingo, lusinghi, lusingano, lusinghiamo,

lusinga, adulare
flattering: lusingando, adulatorio
flavoring: aroma, condimento
flaw: difetto, screpolatura, fessura, crepa, imperfezione, incrinatura
flayed: scuoiato, si scorticato
flee: fuggire, fuggi, fuggiamo, fuggite, fuggono, fuggo
fleece: vello
flighty: capriccioso
flitted: aleggiato, svolazzato
flitting: svolazzando, aleggiando
floated: galleggiato
flocked: affollato
flops: flops
florentine: fiorentino
florid: florido
flourishing: fiorendo, fiorente
fluctuated: fluttuato
flume: canale
flushing: flussaggio, lavaggio
flute: flauto, scanalatura
foam: schiuma, spuma, schiumare
foamed: espanso
foe: nemico
folding: pieghevole, piegamento, piegatura
foliage: fogliame
folio: foglio
folks: gente
fondling: accarezzando
fondness: affezione, passione
font: fonte battesimale, carattere, tipo di carattere
foolishly: scioccamente
footing: punto d'appoggio
footnote: nota a piè pagina, nota in calce, nota a piè di pagina
footstep: passo
forage: foraggio
forbear: antenato, astenersi
forbearing: indulgente, paziente
forbid: vietare, vieti, vietate, vietano, vietiamo, vieta, vieto, proibire, proibite, proibiamo, proibisci
forbidding: vietando, proibendo, ostile, spaventevole
fore: anteriore, parte anteriore
foreboding: presentimento
forecastle: castello di prua
foremast: albero di trinchetto
foremost: primo
foreseeing: prevedendo
foreseen: previsto
foreshadowing: prefigurando
foretell: predire, predi', predici, prediciamo, predico, predicono, predite
forewarned: prevenuto, preavvertito, preavvisato
forge: forgiare, forgia
forger: falsificatore, falsario

forgetful: dimentico, smemorato
forlorn: derelitto, abbandonato, misero
formality: formalità
forthwith: immediatamente
fortification: fortificazione
foundling: trovatello
fowl: pollo, gallina, pollame
fowler: uccellatore
fracture: frattura, fratturare, rottura
frantic: frenetico
frantically: freneticamente
fraternal: fraterno
freak: capriccio
freebooter: pirata
freed: liberato
freemason: massone
frenchman: francese
frenzied: delirante, frenetico
freshen: rinfrescare
friar: frate
friction: attrito, frizione, sfregamento
frigate: fregata
fright: paura, spavento, timore, angoscia
frighten: spaventare, spaventiamo, spaventi, spaventate, spaventano, spaventa, spavento, impaurire, intimorire
frightful: spaventevole
frock: vestito, tonaca, abito
frosted: brinato
frugal: frugale
fruitless: infruttuoso, inutile
frustrate: frustrare, frustrano, frustrate, frustri, frustriamo, frustro, frustra
fugitive: fuggitivo
fulfillment: adempimento, appagamento
fumbling: armeggiando, brancolando, annaspando, frugando
fumes: vapore, esalazione, fumi
functionary: funzionario
fungus: fungo
furnish: fornire, fornite, forniscono, fornisco, fornisci, forniamo, arredare
furnished: ammobiliato, fornito
furnishes: fornisce
furnishing: fornendo, arredamento
furrow: solco, solcare
furry: di pelliccia
furthest: il più lontano
furtive: furtivo
fused: fuso
gaily: gaiamente
gainsay: nego, nega, negano, negate, neghi, neghiamo, negare
gala: gala
gale: burrasca
gallant: galante, coraggioso, valoroso
gallantly: galantemente

gangway: passerella, passaggio, corsia
garments: indumenti
garnish: guarnire
garrison: guarnigione, presidio, presidiare
garrulous: loquace
gash: sfregiare, taglio
gauntlet: guanto
gawky: goffo
generality: generalità
generalize: generalizzare, generalizziamo, generalizzo, generalizzi, generalizzate, generalizzano, generalizza
generosity: generosità
genially: genialmente
gentility: raffinatezza, nascita elevata
gentlemanly: signorile, da gentiluomo
gentleness: delicatezza
geologist: geologo
germ: germe, germoglio
ghastly: orribile, orrendo, sgradevole, spiacevole, abominevole
ghetto: ghetto
ghostly: spettrale
gibbet: patibolo, condannare all'impiccagione, forca
gibraltar: Gibilterra
giddy: stordito
gigantic: gigantesco
gild: indorare, dorare
gilded: dorato
gilds: dora, indora
gilt: doratura
ginger: zenzero
gingerly: cauto
girdle: cintura
gladly: volentieri, con piacere
glaring: abbagliante, sfolgorante
glazed: satinato
glazing: vetrata
gleam: luccicare, barlume
glee: allegria, gioia
glide: scivolata
glittering: scintillare, brillio, brillare, scintillio
globes: globi
globular: globulare
glowing: raggiante, ardente
glued: incollato
glum: accigliato
gnawed: rosicchiato, roso
goats: capre
gobble: ingurgitare, ingozzare, ingollare, ingoiare, trangugiare
good-humored: di buon umore
goodly: bonariamente
good-natured: gradevole, cortese
gorge: burrone, gola, forra
gorgeous: magnifico, bellissimo

graceful: grazioso, aggraziato
graduated: laureato, graduato
grandeur: grandiosità
granite: granito
grasped: afferrato
grasping: avido
grassy: erboso
grate: griglia, grattugiare, graticola, grata, grattare
grated: grattuggiato
gratification: gratificazione, soddisfazione
gratified: gratificato
gratify: gratificare, gratificano, gratifico, gratifichiamo, gratifichi, gratificate, gratifica
grating: grata, griglia, stridente, carabottino, inferriata
gravely: tomba, seriamente
graven: scolpito, inciso
grayness: grigiore
graze: graffio, escoriazione, sfiorare, pascolare, pascere
grecian: greco
greedy: avido, bramoso, goloso, ghiotto, ingordo
greenish: verdognolo, verdastro
greenland: Groenlandia
greenness: verde
greeting: salutando, saluto, accoglienza
grieved: accorato, addolorato
grimy: sudicio
grind: macinare, molare, triturare, rettificare
grinding: rettifica, macinazione, molitura
grizzled: brizzolato
grizzly: grigio, brizzolato, grigiastro, orso grigio
grooved: scanalato
groped: brancolato
groping: brancolando
grotesque: grottesco
grotesquely: grottescamente
grotto: grotta
grouped: raggruppato
growling: ringhiare
guarded: guardingo, custodito
guarding: guardia
gulch: gola
gusty: burrascoso, tempestoso
habitation: abitazione
habituation: assuefazione
hacked: tagliato
haggard: sparuto
hailed: grandinato
hairs: capelli, peli
hallow: santificare
halves: dimezza
halyard: drizza
hammock: amaca

handcuffs: manette
hapless: sfortunato, disgraziato
harangued: arringato, concionato
harassing: molestando, tormentando, assillante
harbor: porto
hardened: indurito, temprato
hark: ascoltare
harlequin: arlecchino
harmed: nociuto
harmonious: armonioso, armonico
harpoon: arpione, fiocina
harshly: duramente
haste: fretta, furia
hasten: affrettarsi, affrettare
hastened: affrettato, sollecitato
hasty: affrettato, frettoloso
hatched: covato
hatchet: accetta, ascia
hatchway: boccaporto
haughtiness: alterigia
haughty: altezzoso
hauled: trasportato
haunt: frequentare
haunted: frequentato, perseguitato
haunting: ossessionante
haven: porto
havoc: rovina, devastazione
hawk: falco
haze: foschia, caligine
hazy: nebbioso
headland: promontorio, capo
headsman: carnefice
healing: guarendo, guarigione, guarire
hearth: focolare
heartless: insensibile
heave: sollevamento
heaving: sollevamento
hectic: frenetico, etico
heed: cura, attenzione
heedful: attento, cauto
heedless: sbadato, disattento
heighten: innalzare
heightened: innalzato
heightening: innalzando
helm: timone, remo
helmsman: timoniere
hemlock: cicuta
hemp: canapa
hempen: di canapa
henceforth: d'ora in poi, d'ora innanzi
heraldry: araldica
herbage: erbe
hereabouts: qui vicino
hereafter: in futuro
hereby: in tal modo, con il presente, con ciò
hereupon: in conseguenza di ciò, al che
hermetically: ermeticamente

hermit: eremita
hermitage: eremitaggio, eremo
heroic: eroico
heroically: eroicamente
heroine: eroina
hesitancy: esitazione
hides: nasconde
hindrance: impaccio, ostacolo
hinted: suggerito
hiss: fischiare, sibilo, sibilare
hither: qui, quà
hive: alveare, arnia
hoar: canuto
hoary: pruinoso, canuto, canescente
hobgoblin: spiritello maligno
hoe: zappare, zappa, la zappa
hoeing: zappatura
hoist: montacarichi, paranco, argano, sollevamento, sollevare
hoisting: sollevamento
hollowness: falsità, cavità
homage: omaggio
homeward: verso casa
homicide: omicidio, omicida
honeysuckle: caprifoglio
honor: onore, onorare
honorable: onorevole
honoring: onorare
honors: onore
hooked: gancio, adunco, agganciato
hop: luppolo
hopelessly: disperatamente
horrid: orrendo
horrific: raccapricciante, orribile
horrified: impressionato, inorridito, atterrito, far inorridire
horseback: groppa, dorso del cavallo
hospitable: ospitale
hovered: gironzolato
hovering: librarsi
howl: muggire, ululare, ululato, urlare
hubbub: fracasso, chiasso, baraonda, baccano
hue: tinta
hulk: carcassa
hum: ronzio
humane: umano
humanized: umanizzato
humanizing: umanizzando
humming: ronzante, ronzio
hummingbird: colibrì
humor: umore, umorismo
humorous: umoristico, divertente
humped: gobba
hunted: cacciato
hurriedly: affrettatamente
husky: rauco, pieno di bucce
hybrid: ibrido
hypochondriac: ipocondriaco
iceberg: iceberg
ignorant: ignorante

illiberal: illiberale
illuminating: illuminando, accendendo
illumination: illuminazione
illusory: illusorio
illustrious: illustre
illy: malatamente
imagining: immaginando
immeasurable: incommensurabile
immemorial: immemorabile
immobility: immobilità
immoral: immorale
immortalized: immortalato
immovable: immobile
immutable: immutabile
imp: folletto
impairing: danneggiando
impartiality: imparzialità
imparts: impartisce
impassioned: appassionato
impatience: impazienza
impatient: impaziente
impatiently: impazientemente
impediment: impedimento, ostacolo
impelled: costretto, incitato
impended: incombito
impending: imminente
impenetrable: impenetrabile
imperative: imperativo
imperceptibly: impercettibilmente
imperfect: imperfetto
imperfectly: imperfettamente
impertinence: impertinenza
impious: empio
impostor: impostore
imposture: impostura, inganno
impotent: impotente
impregnable: inespugnabile
impress: impressionare, imprimere
imprisoned: imprigionato
improbable: improbabile
impromptu: improvvisato, estemporaneo
impropriety: scorrettezza, improprietà
imprudently: imprudentemente
impulsive: impulsivo
imputation: imputazione
impute: attribuire
imputed: attribuito, imputato
imputing: attribuendo, imputando
inadequately: inadeguatamente, insufficientemente
inadvertence: inavvertenza
inadvertently: inavvertitamente
inasmuch: in quanto
inboard: entrobordo
incautious: imprudente, incauto
incensed: incenso
incessant: incessante
incidental: fortuito, incidentale
incipient: incipiente

incipiently: incipientemente
incited: incitato, spronato
inclosure: recinzione
inclusive: inclusivo, compreso
incognito: incognito
incoherent: incoerente
incompetence: incompetenza, insufficienza
incongruous: incongruo
incontinently: incontinentemente
inconvenience: inconvenienza, disagio, disturbo
inconvenient: difficile, pesante, inconveniente, incomodo
incredulity: incredulità
incubus: incubo
incurable: incurabile, inguaribile, insanabile
incurring: incorrendo
indecorous: indecoroso
indecorously: indecorosamente
indefinite: indefinito
indefinitely: indefinitamente
indifference: indifferenza
indifferent: indifferente
indifferently: indifferentemente
indigestion: indigestione, cattiva digestione
indignant: indignato
indignation: indignazione, sdegno
indigo: indaco
indiscreet: indiscreto
indiscriminate: indiscriminato
indispensable: indispensabile
indisposed: indisposto
indisposition: indisposizione
indisputable: indiscutibile
indistinguishable: indistinguibile
individuality: individualità
indocility: indocilità
indolence: indolenza
induce: dedurre, concludere, indurre, induci, inducono, induciamo, inducete, deducono, deduco, deduciamo, deducete
inducements: incitamenti
inducing: deducendo, inducendo, concludendo
inductions: induzioni
indulge: indulgere
indulged: compiaciuto, indulto
indulgence: indulgenza
indulgent: indulgente
industrious: diligente
ineffectual: inefficace, vano
inefficiency: inefficienza
inexperienced: inesperto
inextricable: inestricabile
infantile: infantile
infantry: fanteria
infatuation: infatuazione
infer: dedurre, deducete, deduco,

deduciamo, deducono, deduci, concludere, concludi, concludiamo, concludete, concludo
inference: conclusione, illazione, inferenza, deduzione
inferiority: inferiorità
inferred: dedotto, concluso
infidel: miscredente, infedele
infirmity: infermità
inflamed: infiammato
inflaming: infiammando
inflating: gonfiando
inflexible: inflessibile, rigido
inflicted: inflitto
inflicting: infliggendo
informally: senza formalità, informalmente
informing: informando
informs: informa
ingenious: ingegnoso
inglorious: inglorioso
inhabitable: abitabile
inhabitant: abitante
inhabited: abitato
inhabiting: abitando
inhospitable: inospitale
inhumane: inumano
inhumanity: inumanità
iniquitous: iniquo
iniquity: iniquità
injected: iniettato
injure: danneggiare, danneggia, danneggiamo, danneggiano, danneggiate, danneggio, danneggi, ferire, ferisco, feriscono, feriamo
ink: inchiostro
inkling: accenno
inkstand: calamaio
inky: sporco d'inchiostro
innate: innato, congenito
innocuous: innocuo
innumerable: innumerevole
inquietude: inquietudine
inquired: domandato
inquiring: domandando, domandare
inquiringly: domandare
inquisitively: curiosamente
insane: matto, insano, demente, folle
inscribes: iscrive
inscription: iscrizione
inscrutable: inscrutabile
insensible: insensibile
insertion: inserzione, inserimento
insidious: insidioso
insignificance: banalità, futilità
insignificant: insignificante
insolence: insolenza
insolent: insolente
inspect: ispezionare, ispezioni, ispezioniamo, ispezionate, ispezionano, ispeziona, ispeziono, controllare

inspected: ispezionato
inspire: ispirare, ispira, ispirate, ispiri, ispiro, ispirano, ispiriamo
instantaneously: istantaneamente
instep: collo del piede
instinctive: istintivo
instinctively: istintivamente
insubordination: insubordinazione
insulted: insultato
insure: assicurare, assicuri, assicuriamo, assicurate, assicurano, assicura, assicuro
insurrection: insurrezione
intending: intendendo
intensified: intensificato
intentional: intenzionale
intently: intensamente
intercepted: intercettato
interfered: interferito
interiors: interno
interment: inumazione
interred: seppellito
interrogated: interrogato
interruption: interruzione
intervening: intervenendo
interweaving: intessendo, intrecciandosi, intreccio
intimation: accenno
intolerable: intollerabile
intolerably: intollerabilmente, intollerabile
intonation: intonazione, cadenza
intrepid: intrepido
intrepidly: intrepidamente
intricacy: complessità, complicazione
intricately: complicato, intricatamente
intrigue: intrigo, brigare, intrigare
intriguing: intrigante
intruded: imposto
invade: invadere, invadi, invadiamo, invado, invadono, invadete
invaded: invaso
invading: invadendo, invadere
invalid: non valido, invalido
invariable: invariabile
inverted: invertito
investing: investendo
investiture: investitura
invests: investe
invisibly: invisibilmente
invites: invita
inviting: invitando, invitare, invitante
invitingly: invitare
invocation: invocazione
invoking: invocando
involuntarily: involontariamente
involuntary: involontario
inward: interno
irksome: seccante
irradiate: irradiare, irradi, irradia,

irradiamo, irradiano, irradiate, irradio
irradiated: irradiato
irregularly: irregolarmente
irreparable: irreparabile
irresistible: irresistibile
irresistibly: irresistibilmente
irreversible: irreversibile
irritability: irritabilità
irritable: irritabile
irritated: irritato
islet: isoletta, isolotto
isolate: isolare, isolate, isolo, isoli, isoliamo, isola, isolano
issuing: emittente, emettere, emanazione, di emissione, emissione
isthmus: istmo
jackal: sciacallo
jaded: spossato, affaticato
jagged: frastagliato, dentellato
jar: giara, barattolo
jaws: ganasce
jeopardized: arrischiato, compromesso, pregiudicato, messo a repentaglio
jerk: scossa, sobbalzo, scossone
jew: ebreo
jewel: gioiello, gemma, gioia
jocose: giocoso
jocund: giocondo
jointed: articolato
jostle: spingere, spintone
jot: annotare in fretta
jovial: gioviale
joyfulness: gioia
joyless: senza gioia, mesto
joyous: gioioso
joyously: gioiosamente
joyousness: gioia
jubilant: esultante
judicious: giudizioso, assennato
juggler: giocoliere
juncture: giuntura
junk: giunca
jupiter: giove
keel: chiglia
keg: bariletto
kidnap: rapire, rapiamo, rapisci, rapisco, rapiscono, rapite
kidnapping: rapimento, rapendo, sequestro di persona
kindled: acceso
kindling: accendendo, accensione
kinsman: parente
kisses: baci
kissing: baciare
kith: amici
knave: canaglia, farabutto, briccone, furfante
knob: manopola, tenaglie, bottone, pomo, pomello

knocker: battente
knots: nodi
knotted: nodo
knotting: annodamento
knotty: nodoso
labor: fatica, lavoro
labyrinth: labirinto
labyrinthine: labirintico
ladle: mestolo, siviera
lament: lamento, lamentare
landward: verso terra
languid: languido
languor: languore
lantern: lanterna
lapel: risvolto
lapse: scivolare, sbaglio, intervallo, passare, errore, periodo
larboard: babordo
larder: dispensa
lark: allodola
lash: sferza, frusta
lashing: frustatura, rizza, frustata, fustigazione
latent: latente
lateral: laterale
lather: schiuma, insaponare
latitude: latitudine, latitudine di pos
lattice: reticolo, traliccio
lattices: reticoli
launching: lancio, lanciare, varo
lava: lava
lavishly: generosamente
lawless: dissoluto, senza legge, licenzioso, illegale
lax: molle
leaden: di piombo
leafless: sfrondato
leanly: magramente
leaped: saltato
leaping: saltare
ledge: sporgenza, cengia
lees: sedimento, feccia
leeward: sottovento
leisurely: comodo
lengthened: allungato
lengthening: allungando, allungamento
lengthwise: longitudinalmente, per i lungo
lessen: diminuire, diminuiamo, diminuisci, diminuisco, diminuiscono, diminuite
lessened: diminuito
lessening: diminuendo
lest: affinchè non, per paura che
lethargic: letargico
levant: Levante
leveled: livellato
libelous: diffamatorio
license: licenza
lifeless: esanime
lighted: illuminato

lighten: alleggerire, alleggerisci, alleggerite, alleggerisco, alleggeriamo, alleggeriscono, illuminare
lightning: fulmine, baleno, lampo
likened: paragonato
lima: Lima
limb: membro, arto
lime: calce, lime
lingered: indugiato
lingering: indugiando, indugiare, prolungato
lint: garza
liquor: liquore
livelihood: sostentamento, mezzi di sussistenza, mezzi di sostentamento
liveliness: vivacità
lividly: lividamente
lizard: lucertola
lizards: lucertole
loam: argilla
loamy: argilloso
locker: armadietto
locomotion: locomozione
lodged: alloggiato
lofty: alto, elevato
loiter: bighelloniamo, gironzolo, gironzoliamo, gironzoli, gironzolate, gironzolano, gironzola, bighelloni, bighellonate, bighellonano, bighellona
loneliness: solitudine
lonesome: solitario
longevity: longevità
longing: bramoso
loosened: allentato, sciolto
loosening: allentando, allentamento, sciogliendo
loth: riluttante
lowly: umile
lowness: bassezza
lucifer: Satana
luckless: sfortunato
lugubrious: lugubre
lunacy: pazzia
lunatic: pazzo, lunatico
lurch: barcollare
lure: allettare
lurid: acuto
lurk: nascondersi
lustrous: lustro
lye: liscivia
mace: mazza
machinist: macchinista
maddened: impazzito, esasperato
madras: madras
magically: magicamente
magnified: ingigantito, ingrandito
mahogany: mogano
maidenly: puro, verginale
maim: mutilare
majestic: maestoso

majesty: maestà
malachite: malachite
malady: malattia
malay: malese
malicious: maligno, doloso, malizioso
malign: maligno
malignant: maligno
mammoth: mammut
mandate: mandato
manhood: virilità
manifest: manifesto, manifestare, palese
manifestation: manifestazione
manipulated: manipolato
manoeuvre: manovra, manovrare
mantle: mantello, manto
maple: acero
mariner: marinaio
maritime: marittimo
marl: marna
marshal: schierare, maresciallo
martial: marziale
martyr: martire
marvel: meraviglia, stupirsi
marvelous: meraviglioso
masked: mascherato
masking: mascheramento
masonry: muratura
massacre: massacro, strage, carneficina, massacrare
mast: albero
masterly: magistrale
mat: stuoia
materialist: materialista
materially: materialmente
matins: mattutino
matrimony: matrimonio
matted: coperto di stuoie
matting: stuoia
matured: maturo, maturato
maturing: maturando
meadow: prato
meagre: scarso
mechanic: meccanico
mechanically: meccanicamente
mechanician: meccanico
meditate: meditare, mediti, meditiamo, meditate, meditano, medita, medito
meditated: meditato
meditates: medita
meditative: meditativo
meekly: umilmente
melancholy: malinconia, malinconico
mellow: maturo
melody: melodia
melted: fuso, sciolto
memento: memoria
menaced: minacciato
mending: riparazione
menial: umile

mercenary: mercenario
merchantman: mercantile
merge: incorporiamo, uniscono, unisco, fondiamo, unisci, unite, uniamo, incorporo, incorpori, incorporate, incorporano
merged: incorporato, unito, fuso
meridian: meridiano
meriting: meritare
meritorious: meritorio, benemerito
merrily: allegramente
merriment: allegria
merry: allegro, festoso, gaio
metallic: metallico
methodically: metodicamente
mexican: messicano
mid: mezzo
midway: a metà strada
mien: aspetto
mildly: dolcemente, gentilmente
mildness: mitezza
millstone: mola
minced: tritato
mingled: mischiato, mescolato
mingling: mescolando, mischiando
miraculous: miracoloso
mirage: miraggio
mirrored: replicato
misanthrope: misantropo
misanthropic: misantropico
misbehavior: cattiva condotta
mischief: birichinata
misconception: idea sbagliata
miserably: miserabilmente, miseramente
misfortune: sfortuna, traversia, disgrazia
misgivings: dubbi
missal: messale
misshapen: deforme
mistrust: diffidenza, sfiducia
misty: nebbioso
misunderstood: incompreso, frainteso
mitigates: mitiga
mob: folla, plebaglia, gentaglia
mock: deridere, deridono, derido, deridiamo, deridi, deridete, finto, beffare
mocked: deriso
mockery: derisione
moist: umido
moisten: umettare, inumidire
moistening: inumidendo, umettando
mostly: umido
moisture: umidità
mole: talpa, molo, neo
mollified: addolcito, ammollito, ammorbidito
momentary: momentaneo
monastery: monastero
monastic: monastico

mongrel: bastardo
monk: monaco
monotone: tono uniforme
monotonous: monotono, uniforme
monumentally: monumentalmente
moodiness: broncio, malumore
moody: triste
moonlight: chiaro di luna
moralize: moraleggiare, moralizzare
morbid: morboso
morbidly: morboso
morose: imbronciato, cupo
morsel: boccone
mortal: mortale
mortar: malta, mortaio
mortified: mortificato
moss: muschio
mossy: muschioso
motionless: immobile
mouldy: ammuffito, muffito
mound: tumulo
mountainous: montagnoso,
  montuoso
mounting: montaggio, salita
mourn: piangere, piangi, piangiamo,
  piango, piangono, piangete
mourned: pianto
mournful: triste
mourning: lutto, piangendo
mulatto: mulatto
mule: mulo
mulish: testardo
multiplied: moltiplicato
multitude: affluenza, folla,
  moltitudine
multitudinous: innumerevole
munched: sgranocchiato
murderous: omicida
muscular: muscolare, muscoloso
musically: musicalmente
musing: meditabondo, meditazione
musket: moschetto
mute: muto
muteness: mutismo, mutezza
mutineer: ammutinato
mutinous: ammutinato
mutiny: ammutinamento,
  ammutinarsi
mutually: reciprocamente
mysteries: misteri
mysteriously: misteriosamente
mystic: mistico
mystify: mistificare, mistifichi,
  mistifichiamo, mistificano, mistifica,
  mistifico, mistificate
mythological: mitologico
nail: chiodo, unghia, inchiodare
nailed: inchiodato
nakedness: nudità
nameless: senza nome
namesake: omonimo
napkin: tovagliolo, salvietta,

pannolino
narrated: raccontato, narrato
naught: nulla, zero
nautical: nautico
navigated: navigato
navigating: navigando
navigation: navigazione
navigator: navigatore
nay: anzi
nearness: vicinanza
near-sighted: miope
necessaries: necessario
necklace: collana
needless: inutile
needy: bisognoso, indigente, povero
negotiator: negoziatore
negro: negro
neighbor: vicino
neighborhood: vicinato, vicinanza,
  quartiere
neighboring: vicino
neighborly: da buon vicino
nervousness: nervosismo, nervosità
nested: intercalato
nether: inferiore
nettled: irritato
newfoundland: Terranova
nigh: vicino
nightfall: imbrunire, crepuscolo
nile: Nilo
nimrod: nembrod
noiseless: silenzioso
noiselessly: tranquillamente
nominally: nominalmente
nonchalance: noncuranza
nonsensical: assurdo, privo di senso
nook: angolino, cantuccio
northeast: nordest
northerly: settentrionale
northward: verso nord
notability: notabilità
notary: notaio
notch: tacca, intaglio, incisione,
  incavo
noticing: notare
nought: zero
nourished: alimentato, nutrito
novelty: novità
nudity: nudità
numbered: numerato
numbering: numerazione
nut: dado, noce, madrevite, capotasto
oaf: zoticone
oaken: di quercia
oaks: querce
oar: remo
oars: remo, remi
oarsman: rematore, vogatore
oath: giuramento, imprecazione
oaths: giuramenti
oats: avena
obedience: ubbidienza, obbedienza

obedient: ubbidiente, obbediente
obediently: ubbidientemente
obeyed: ubbidito, obbedito
obeying: ubbidendo, obbedendo
obligingly: servizievole,
  cortesemente
oblique: obliquo
obliterate: cancellare, cancellano,
  cancellate, cancelli, cancelliamo,
  cancello, cancella, obliterare
obliterates: cancella
oblivious: immemore, dimentico
obscured: eclissato, ottenebrato,
  offuscato, oscurato
obscurely: oscuramente
observable: osservabile, visibile
obstacle: ostacolo
obstinate: ostinato
obtruded: imposto
obtuse: ottuso, spuntato, smussato
occupancy: occupazione
occupant: occupante
occupies: occupa
occupying: occupando
oceanic: oceanico
octagonal: ottagonale
ocular: oculare
odor: odore, profumo
offal: frattaglie
offend: offendere, offendiamo,
  offendo, offendi, offendete,
  offendono, insultare, insulto, insulti,
  insultate, insultano
offended: offeso, insultato,
  oltraggiato
offense: offesa
officious: ufficioso, invadente
offing: mare al largo
oft: spesso
oiling: oliatura
oily: oleoso, untuoso, unto
olive: oliva, olivastro
olympus: Olimpo
ominous: sinistro, di malaugurio,
  infausto
omission: omissione
omit: omettere, omettete, ometti,
  omettiamo, omettono, trascurare,
  ometto
omitting: omettendo
omnibus: autobus
oozing: filtrando, stillando,
  trasudando
oppressed: premuto, oppresso,
  serrato, stretto
oppressive: oppressivo
opulent: opulento
orchard: frutteto
orderliness: ordine, regolarità
ordinarily: ordinariamente
ordnance: artiglieria
orientally: orientale

originated: disceso
originating: discendendo
originator: originatore, mittente
ornament: ornamento, decorare,
 soprammobile
ornamental: ornamentale
ostentatious: ostentato
outcast: reietto
outgoing: uscente
outlandish: inconsueto, esotico,
 straniero, strano, bizzarro
outlaw: bandito, fuorilegge
outlive: sopravvivere a
outright: diretto, completamente
outstretched: disteso
oval: ovale
overboard: in mare, fuoribordo, fuori
 bordo
overcast: coperto
overhauling: aggiustando,
 revisionando, riparando,
 sorpassando, verificando
overheard: origliato
overhearing: origliando
overlook: trascurare
overpowering: sopraffacendo,
 opprimente, prepotente,
 schiacciante
oversight: svista
overstep: oltrepassare
overtake: sorpassare, sorpassa,
 sorpassano, sorpassate, sorpassi,
 sorpassiamo, sorpasso
overthrow: rovesciare, rovesciate,
 rovesciano, rovesci, rovesciamo,
 rovescia, rovescio
overthrown: rovesciato
overturn: capovolgere, rovesciare
overturned: capovolto
owing: dovere
ox: bue
paces: pace
pacified: pacificato
pacifying: pacificando
pacing: pacing
padded: imbottito
paddle: pala, pagaia, remo
padlock: lucchetto
pagan: pagano
pagoda: pagoda
pained: addolorato, afflitto, dolore
painters: pittori
palaces: palazzi
paling: palizzata
pall: coltre, cappa
pallid: pallido
pallor: pallore
paltry: meschino
panegyric: panegirico
panoramic: panoramico
pantaloons: pantaloni
panted: ansimato

panting: ansimare
parading: sfilare
paraguay: Paraguay
paramount: supremo
parched: disseccato
pardonable: perdonabile
partake: partecipo, partecipa,
 partecipano, partecipate, partecipi,
 partecipiamo, partecipare
partakes: partecipa
participant: partecipante
particularized: particolareggiato,
 dettagliato
particulars: particolari
parting: separazione, divisione
partitioning: partizione
passively: passivamente
passivity: passività
pasteboard: cartone
pastime: passatempo
pasture: pascolo, pastura
patched: rappezzato
pathway: sentiero
patiently: pazientemente
patrimony: patrimonio
patriot: patriota
paw: gamba, zampa, piede
peacefully: pacificamente
peacefulness: serenità, pace
peach: pesca, la pesca
peal: scampanio
pebbles: ciottoli
pebbly: sassoso
peculiarly: particolarmente
pecuniary: pecuniario
peddle: vendere al minuto
pedestal: piedistallo
peeled: sbucciato
peelings: buccia
peep: occhieggiare, pigolio, pigolare,
 sbirciare
peevish: permaloso, stizzoso
penetrate: penetrare, penetri,
 penetriamo, penetrate, penetrano,
 penetra, penetro
penetrating: penetrando, penetrante
penguin: pinguino
penitence: penitenza
penitential: penitenziale
penniless: squattrinato
pensive: pensoso, pensieroso
pensively: pensosamente
perceives: percepisce, scorge,
 intravede
perceiving: percependo, scorgendo,
 intravedendo
perceptible: percettibile
perch: persico, pesce persico,
 appollaiarsi
percussion: percussione
perilous: pericoloso
periodic: periodico

perish: perire
perished: perito
perishing: perendo
pernicious: pernicioso
perpendicular: perpendicolare
perpetrated: perpetrato
perpetual: perpetuo
perpetually: perennemente,
 perpetuamente
perplexed: confuso, turbato,
 perplesso
perplexity: perplessità
persecute: perseguitare, perseguito,
 perseguita, perseguitano,
 perseguitate, perseguiti,
 perseguitiamo, perseguire
persecution: inseguimento,
 persecuzione
persevering: perseverando
persist: persistere, persistono,
 persisto, persistiamo, persisti,
 persistete
persisted: persistito
persisting: persistendo
persists: persiste
personage: personaggio
persuasion: persuasione
pertaining: concernendo,
 riguardando, spettando
perturbed: perturbato
peruvian: peruviano
pervaded: pervaso
pervades: pervade
pervading: pervadendo
perverse: perverso
phantom: fantasma
philanthropically: filantropicamente
philanthropy: filantropia
phlegmatic: flemmatico
physician: medico, dottore
physiognomy: fisionomia
physiological: fisiologico
pictorial: pittorico, illustrato
picturesque: pittoresco
piecemeal: frammentario
pierced: perforato
pigeon: piccione, colombo
piles: emorroidi
pilgrim: pellegrino
pillar: colonna, pilastro
pinnacle: pinnacolo
pinned: appuntato
pious: pio
pirate: pirata
pitcher: brocca, lanciatore
pitfall: trappola
pitiable: pietoso
pitiably: pietosamente
pitying: compatire, pietà
placid: placido
plague: peste
planter: fioriera, piantatore,

seminatrice
platter: piatto
plausibly: plausibilmente
playful: giocoso
plaza: piazza
pleasantly: piacevolmente
pleasantness: piacevolezza
pleasing: piacevole
plebeian: plebeo
pledge: pegno, impegno
plenipotentiary: plenipotenziario
pliant: flessibile
plied: maneggiato
plotter: plotter
plotters: plotter
ploughing: aratura
pluck: rompere, staccare, cogliere,
  spennare, strappare, fegato
plumage: piumaggio
plume: penna, pennacchio, piuma
ply: maneggia, maneggiate,
  maneggio, maneggi, maneggiamo,
  maneggiano, piallaccio, capo,
  maneggiare, piega
plying: maneggiando
poacher: bracconiere
poise: equilibrio
poisoning: avvelenamento,
  intossicazione, avvelenare
poisonous: velenoso, tossico,
  venefico
polynesian: polinesiano
pondered: meditato, ponderato
ponderous: pesante, ponderoso
poop: poppa
populace: popolino
popularly: popolarmente, popolare
populous: popoloso
porch: veranda, porticato
portent: augurio
portly: corpulento
portuguese: portoghese
possesses: possiede
possessing: possedendo
possessor: possessore
posterity: posterità
postpone: rimandare, rimanda,
  rimandano, rimandate, rimandi,
  rimandiamo, rimando, rinviare,
  posporre
postponing: rimandando
posture: postura, posizione,
  atteggiamento
potency: potenza
pouch: sacchetto, borsa
powdered: polvere, in polvere
powerless: impotente
prairie: prateria
praising: lodare
prayed: pregato
preached: predicato
preacher: predicatore, pastore

precarious: precario
precautions: precauzioni
precede: precedere, precedo,
  precedono, precediamo, precedi,
  precedete
precipice: precipizio, abisso, burrone,
  dirupo
preface: prefazione
preferring: preferendo
prefers: preferisce
preliminaries: preliminare,
  preliminari
prepossessing: affascinante, attraente
prescription: prescrizione, ricetta,
  ricetta medica
presentiment: presentimento
preserves: conserve
presume: supporre, supponiamo,
  supponi, suppongono, suppongo,
  supponete, presumere, presumiamo,
  presumo, presumi, presumete
presumed: supposto, presunto
presuming: supponendo,
  presumendo, presumere
pretended: finto
pretense: pretesa, finta, finzione
prevail: prevalere, prevalete,
  prevalgo, prevalgono, prevali,
  prevaliamo
prevailed: prevalso
princely: principe, principesco
privy: al corrente, privato
proceeding: procedendo,
  procedimento
proclaim: proclamare, proclami,
  proclamiamo, proclamate,
  proclamano, proclamo, proclama,
  pubblicare
proclaimed: proclamato
proclamation: proclamazione,
  dichiarazione, pubblicazione, bando
procure: procurare, procurate,
  procuro, procuri, procurano,
  procuriamo, procacciare, procura
procured: procurato
procures: procura
procuring: procurando
profane: profanare
professing: dichiarando, professando
professionally: professionalmente
profoundly: profondamente
profuse: abbondante, profuso
profusion: profusione
progeny: progenie
projection: proiezione, sporgenza
promontory: promontorio
prompt: preciso, esatto, sollecito,
  pronto
prompting: suggerimento
pronouncing: pronunciando
prophesied: predetto
prophetess: profetessa

proportionally: proporzionalmente
proprietor: proprietario
propriety: convenienza
prospectively: eventualmente
prosperously: prosperamente
prostrate: prostrato
protracted: prolungato
protruded: sporto
proverbially: proverbialmente
providence: provvidenza
provocation: provocazione
provoke: spronare, provocare,
  incitare, provochi, sproniamo,
  sprono, sproni, spronate, spronano
  sprona, provoco
prow: prua
prowl: aggirarsi
prudence: prudenza
prudent: prudente, sensato
prudential: prudenziale
puddle: pozzanghera
pulmonary: polmonare
pumpkin: zucca, la zucca
punchinello: Pulcinella
punctual: esatto, puntuale, preciso
punctuality: puntualità
puny: gracile
purgatory: purgatorio
purposely: intenzionalmente
purse: borsa, borsellino, portamone
pursues: persegue
purveyor: fornitore
pyrenees: Pirenei
quadrant: quadrante
quadruplicate: quadruplicare
quadruplicates: quadruplica
quaff: tracannare
quake: tremito, tremare
quart: quarto, quarto di gallone
queer: strano, omosessuale
questionable: discutibile, dubbio
questioner: interrogante
quickness: prontezza, rapidità,
  lestezza
quiescent: quiescente
quietness: quiete, calma
quietude: calma, quiete
quito: Quito
quits: abbandona
quitting: abbandonando
quivering: tremare
rabble: marmaglia, folla
racehorse: cavallo da corsa, corsa di
  cavalli
rack: cremagliera, rastrelliera, scaffa
  intelaiatura
racket: baccano
radiance: radianza
radiant: radiante, raggiante
radiated: irradiato
radius: raggio, radio
raft: zattera

rag: straccio, cencio
ragged: cencioso, logoro
raggedly: logoramente
rags: stracci
rainbow: arcobaleno, l'arcobaleno
raking: rastrellare, rastrellamento, rastrellatura
ramble: giro, passeggiata, vagare
rampant: rampante, violento, dilagante
rapidity: rapidità, velocità
rapids: rapide
rapt: rapito
rash: eruzione, avventato, eruzione cutanea
rashness: avventatezza
raspberry: lampone, pernacchia
ratified: ratificato
rattle: sonaglio, rantolo
raved: delirato, farneticato, vaneggiato
ravenous: vorace
razor: rasoio
readiness: prontezza
readjusted: riaggiustato
readjusting: riaggiustando
reappear: riapparire, riapparite, riappaio, riappaiono, riappari, riappariamo
reappeared: riapparso
reasoned: ragionato
reassumed: riassunto
reassure: rassicurare, rassicuri, rassicuriamo, rassicuro, rassicurano, rassicura, rassicurate
reassured: rassicurato
rebelled: ribellato
rebellious: ribelle
rebuff: secco rifiuto
receding: recedendo
receptacle: ricettacolo, recipiente
recess: recesso, alcova, rientranza
reciprocal: reciproco
reciprocally: reciprocamente
recital: concerto, recital, dizione
reckless: spericolato
recluse: eremita
recognizing: riconoscendo
recoil: balzo indietro, rinculare, contraccolpo, indietreggiare, rinculo
recollect: rammenta, rammentano, rammentate, rammenti, rammentiamo, rammento, rammentare, ricordarsi
recompense: compenso, ricompensare
reconciled: conciliato, riconciliato
recondite: recondito
recurred: ricorso, ritornato
recurring: ricorrendo, ritornando, ricorrente
reddened: arrossato, arrossito

redirected: reinstradato, riorientato
reef: scogliera, terzarolare
refectory: refettorio, mensa
refined: raffinato, delicato
refrain: ritornello, astenersi
refresh: ristorare, rinfrescare
refreshed: rinvigorito, ristorato, rinfrescato
refreshing: rinfrescante
refreshment: rinfresco, ristoro
refutes: confuta
regain: ricuperare, riprendere
regained: riacquistato, riconquistato, ricuperato, riguadagnato, ripreso
regaining: riacquistando, riprendendo, riguadagnando, riconquistando, ricuperando
regards: considera, saluti
regretted: rammaricato
regularity: regolarità
regulate: regolare, regolano, regolate, regoli, regoliamo, regolo, regola
regulated: regolato
rehearsing: provando
reinforcement: rinforzo, armatura
rejoin: riuniamo, riunite, riuniscono, riunisco, riunisci, riunire, ricongiungersi
rejoined: riunito
relapse: ricaduta
relaxes: rilassa
relenting: cedendo
relentless: inflessibile
relic: reliquia
relieving: alleviando
relinquish: cedere, cedete, cedono, cedo, cedi, cediamo, abbandonare
relinquishing: cedendo
remarking: osservare
reminding: ricordando
remit: annullare, annullano, annullo, annulliamo, annullate, annulla, annulli, condonare, rimettere
remitted: annullato
remitting: annullando
remnant: scampolo, resto
remorse: rimorso
remorseless: spietato
removes: toglie, rimuove, asporta
remunerative: rimunerativo
rendered: reso
rendering: rendering, rendendo, traduzione
renegade: rinnegato
renew: rinnovare, rinnova, rinnovano, rinnovate, rinnovi, rinnoviamo, rinnovo
renewing: rinnovando
renouncing: rinunciando
renovated: restaurato, ristrutturato, rinnovato
repaired: riparato

repairing: riparazione, riparare
repeating: ripetendo
repentant: pentito
repose: riposo, riposarsi
repressed: represso
reprimand: rimprovero, rabbuffo
reproach: rimprovero, rimproverare, riprendere
reproachful: di rimprovero
reproaching: rimproverare
reproduced: riprodotto
reptile: rettile
repulse: rifiuto, respingere
repulsion: repulsione
repulsively: ripulsivamente
repute: giudicare, reputazione
requisite: requisito
resemble: rassomigliare, rassomiglio, rassomigliate, rassomigliano, rassomigliamo, rassomiglia, rassomigli, assomigliare, somigliare
resembled: rassomigliato
resembles: rassomiglia
resembling: rassomigliando
resentful: risentito, astioso
resided: risieduto
residing: risiedendo
residue: residuo, residui
resisting: resistendo
resolute: risoluto, deciso
resonance: risonanza
resounding: risuonando, echeggiando, riecheggiando, risonante, clamoroso
respectful: rispettoso
respectfully: rispettosamente
respecting: rispettare
respite: tregua
responsive: sensibile
restive: restio
restlessness: inquietudine, irrequietezza
restrain: dominare, domina, domino, dominiamo, dominano, dominate, domini, reprimere, governare
restrained: dominato
restraining: dominando
resuming: riprendendo
retiring: ritirando, riservato
retort: replica, storta
retorts: replica
retribution: castigo
retrograde: retrogrado
retrospectively: retrospettivamente
reunited: riunito
reverberated: riecheggiato, rimbombato, riverberato
reverence: riverenza
reverential: reverenziale
reverted: ritornato
revisit: rivisitano, rivisito, rivisitiamo, rivisiti, rivisita, rivisitate, rivisitare

revived: rianimato
reviving: rianimando
revolted: rivoltato
revolved: girato, ruotato
revolving: ruotando, girando,
 girevole
richness: opulenza
rig: attrezzatura
rigging: attrezzatura, manovra,
 sartiame
rim: orlo, cerchione, bordo, cerchio
ringleader: capobanda, caporione
ripe: maturo
ripped: strappato
ripple: ondulazione, increspatura
rippling: increspatura
risked: rischiato
robbed: derubato
robber: ladro, rapinatore, ladrone
robbing: derubando
rocket: razzo, missile, rucola
rooster: gallo
rooted: radicato
rosary: rosario
rotary: rotante
rots: marcisce
rotted: marcito
rotting: marcendo
rounding: arrotondamento
rouse: stimolare, incitare, spronare,
 stimoli, spronate, sproni, sproniamo,
 sprono, stimola, stimolate,
 stimoliamo
roused: incitato, spronato, stimolato
rousing: incitando, spronando,
 stimolando
rover: girovago
roving: stoppino
royalty: royalty, diritti di utilizzo,
 diritti d'autore, diritto di
 concessione
rub: fregare, strofinare
rubbing: sfregamento
ruddy: rubicondo
rugged: ruvido
ruinous: rovinoso
ruminating: ruminando
rumor: diceria, voce, vociferare
runaway: fuggiasco
rung: piolo
rust: ruggine, arrugginire,
 arrugginirsi, corrodere
rusted: arrugginito
rustling: fruscio
rusts: ruggine
rusty: arrugginito, rugginoso
ruthlessly: spietatamente
sackcloth: tela di sacco
sacks: sacchi
saddened: rattristato
safeguard: salvaguardia,
 salvaguardare

safest: il più sicuro
sagacious: saggio, sagace
sagacity: sagacia
sage: salvia, saggio
sailed: navigato
sailor: marinaio, navigatore
sallow: pallido
salutary: salutare
salutation: saluto
salute: salutare, saluto
saluted: salutato
salver: vassoio
samaritan: samaritano
sameness: uniformità
sane: sensato, sano di mente
sanguine: rubicondo, sanguigno
sap: linfa
sappy: succoso
sarcophagus: sarcofago
sash: fusciacca
sated: sazio
satire: satira
satiric: satirico
satirical: satirico
saturnine: saturnino, malinconico
satyr: satiro
savagely: ferocemente, barbaramente,
 selvaggiamente
scabbard: fodero
scaffolding: impalcatura, ponteggio
scaly: squamoso
scandalizing: scandalizzando
scanning: scansione, scrutando
scanty: scarso
scarce: scarso, raro
scarcity: scarsità
scented: profumato
sceptre: scettro
schemed: progettato
schoolboy: scolaro
scissors: forbici, le forbici
scorching: cocente
scoria: scoria
scorn: disprezzo, disprezzare
scour: sfregano, sfrego, sfreghiamo,
 sfregate, sfrega, sfreghi, sfregare
scourge: frustare
scouring: sfregando, lavatura
scowl: sguardo torvo, cipiglio,
 accigliarsi
scrape: raschiare, scrostare
scraped: raschiato
scraper: raschietto, raschiatore,
 rastrello
scraping: raschiatura
screams: grida
screened: schermato
screw: vite, la vite, avvitare
scroll: rotolo di pergamena, scorrere
scrutinizing: scrutinando
sculptor: scultore
sculptured: scolpito

scurvy: scorbuto
scythes: falci
sealer: isolante, sigillatore
seals: foche
seaman: marinaio
seamen: marinai
seating: posto, corretto
 posizionamento, stabilizzazione
seclusion: isolamento
secrecy: segretezza
secrete: secernere, secerni, secernono
 secerniamo, secernete, secerno
secreted: secreto
sedate: calmo
seedy: pieno di semi
seeming: parendo, sembrando,
 sembrare
seemly: conveniente
seething: bollendo, ribollendo
seize: afferrare, afferro, afferra,
 afferrano, afferrate, afferri,
 afferriamo, acciuffare, acchiappare,
 confiscare, prendere
seizes: afferra
seizing: afferrando, grippaggio
selfishly: egoisticamente
selfishness: egoismo
sends: manda, spedisce
senegal: Senegal
sensibly: assennatamente
sentimental: sentimentale
sentinel: sentinella
sentry: sentinella
sequel: seguito
sequestered: confiscato, sequestrato
serene: sereno
serenity: serenità
serf: servo della gleba, servo, schiavo
serially: in serie
serviceable: utilizzabile
servile: servile
sever: stacca, staccate, stacchi, stacco,
 staccano, disgiungo, disgiungiamo,
 disgiungi, disgiungete, stacchiamo,
 disgiungono
sewing: cucendo, cucito
shackle: anello di trazione
shaded: ombreggiato, ombroso,
 sfumatura
shadowy: ombroso
shaggy: ispido, peloso, irsuto
shakes: scuote
sham: simulare
sharpening: affilando, acuendo
shave: far la barba, rasare, radere
shaved: raso
shaven: sbarbato, raso, rasato
shaving: rasatura, truciolo, radere
sheepish: timido, imbarazzato
sheeting: tela per lenzuola
sheltered: riparato
shipmate: compagno di bordo

shipwreck: naufragio
shipwrecked: naufragato, naufragio
shiver: tremare, brivido, rabbrividire
shivering: rabbrividire
shoal: secca, bassofondo
shocking: irritante, scandaloso
shoots: spara
shoved: spinto
shreds: straccia, tagliuzza
shrewd: scaltro, sagace, perspicace, accorto
shrieking: strillare
shrine: santuario
shrink: restringere, restringersi
shrinking: restringere, contrazione
shroud: protezione, sudario
shrunk: ristretto
shuffle: mescolare
shun: evitare, eviti, evitiamo, evitano, evita, evitate, evito
shunning: evitando
shutting: chiudere, chiusura
shyly: timidamente
sickly: cagionevole, malaticcio, malatamente
siding: parteggiare
sighting: avvistamento
signally: segnale
signified: significato
silken: di seta
silky: serico, di seta
silvery: argenteo
simmering: sobbollendo
simulating: simulando
singular: singolare, strano
singularity: stranezza, singolarità
singularly: singolarmente
sirocco: scirocco
skeleton: scheletro
skeptic: scettico
skimmed: scremato, schiumato
skylight: lucernario
slackens: allenta
slain: ucciso, ammazzato
slanting: obliquo
slate: ardesia
slavery: schiavitù
sleepless: insonne
slimy: limaccioso, fangoso
slings: fasce a tracolla
slink: sgattaiolare, sgattaiolano, sgattaioliamo, sgattaiolo, sgattaiola, sgattaiolate, sgattaioli
slippery: sdrucciolevole, scivoloso
slit: fessura, fenditura
sloped: inclinato
sloping: inclinato
slovenly: sciatto, trascurato
sluggishly: lentamente
slunk: sgattaiolato
sly: furbo, astuto, scaltro
smite: colpisco, colpiscono, colpisci,

colpiamo, colpite, colpire
smitten: colpito
smoothing: spianatura, lisciatura
smuggled: contrabbandato
smuggler: contrabbandiere
snatch: afferrare, presa
snatching: afferrare
snore: russare
snowy: nevoso
snug: accogliente, comodo, raccolto
snugly: comodamente
soar: elevarsi, volare in alto
soaring: volo a vela
sober: sobrio
sociable: socievole
sociably: socievole
sod: zolla erbosa
softened: ammorbidito
softening: ammorbidimento, ritenitura, rammollimento, ammorbidendo
soiled: sporca, sporcano, sporcate, sporchi, sporchiamo, sporco, sporcare
solemn: solenne
solemnly: solennemente
solicit: sollecito, sollecitare, sollecitate, solleciti, sollecitano, sollecita, sollecitiamo
solicitation: sollecitazione
soliloquy: monologo, soliloquio
solitaire: solitario
solitary: solo, solitario
solitude: solitudine
someway: in qualche modo
somnambulism: sonnambulismo
somnambulist: sonnambulo
soot: fuliggine
soothe: calmare, calmano, calmiamo, calmi, calmate, calmo, calma, placare, lenire
soothed: calmato
soothing: calmando, calmante, calmare
sooty: fuligginoso
sorceress: maga, strega
sorely: dolorosamente
sorrow: tristezza, cordoglio
sounding: sondaggio
sourness: acidità, asprezza
southward: verso sud
spade: vanga, vangare
spaniard: spagnolo
spar: longherone
spared: risparmiato
spark: scintilla
sparkle: scintilla, sfavillare, brillare
sparkling: sfavillante
spars: litiga
sparsely: scarsamente
spasmodic: spasmodico
spear: lancia

specie: moneta metallica
speck: bruscolo, pagliuzza, macchiolina, puntino, granello, macchietta
speckled: maculato
spectacle: spettacolo
spectacles: occhiali
spectator: spettatore
spectral: spettrale
spectre: spettro
sped: accelerato
speechless: muto
speedily: rapidamente
speedy: rapido
sperm: sperma, spermatozoo
spermaceti: bianco di balena, spermaceti
spicy: piccante, aromatizzato
spill: versare, rovesciare
spire: guglia, spira
spiritless: avvilito
spite: dispetto
spleen: milza, malumore
splinter: scheggia, frammento
sporting: sportivo
sprawling: che si stravacca
springing: saltare, correzione
sprinkled: spruzzato
sprouted: germogliato
spur: sperone, sprone, spronare
spying: spionaggio
squalor: squallore
squeamishness: schizzinosità
stab: pungere, coltellata, pugnalare, pugnalata
stack: accatastare, pila, catasta, camino, ammucchiare, bica
stacked: accatastato
stagger: barcollare
staggered: sfalsato
staggering: traballio, traballamento, sbalorditivo, barcollante, barcollamento
stagnant: stagnante
staid: serio
staining: mordenzatura
stair: scalino, scala, gradino
stairway: scala
stale: raffermo, stantio, trito e ritrito
stalls: platea, stalle
stalwart: coraggioso, vigoroso
stamping: affrancatura, bollatura
starboard: dritta, tribordo
starry: stellato
starve: affamare
stateliness: grandiosità
stately: imponente
stationary: fisso, stazionario, fermo
stationery: cancelleria, articoli di cancelleria
stationing: dislocamento
statuary: arte statuaria, statuario

stature: statura
steadfast: risoluto, costante
steadiness: costanza, fermezza
steals: ruba
stealthy: nascosto, furtivo, clandestino
steely: inflessibile
steeple: campanile
steeps: immerge, bagna
steer: manzo, sterzare, governare
steering: direzione, sterzo
sterility: sterilità
stern: poppa, severo
stiffened: indurito, irrigidito
stiffly: rigidamente
stifled: soffocato
stifling: soffocante
stillness: calma, immobilità, tranquillità, quiete
stimulated: stimolato
stinging: pungente
stipulate: stipulare
stirring: mescolare, eccitante, agitazione
stocking: calza
stoical: stoico
stormy: tempestoso, temporalesco
stout: forte, corpulento, robusto, birra scura
stove: stufa, fornello
straggler: ritardatario
straggling: sparso, disperso, girovagando, vagabondando
straightforwardness: schiettezza
strained: teso
strangeness: stravaganza, stranezza
strap: cinghia, correggia, cinghia a tracolla, cinturino, strap
strapping: reggiatura
strata: strati
stratagem: stratagemma
strawberries: fragole, fragola
strawberry: fragola
stray: randagio, deviare, smarrirsi
streaked: striato
stricken: colpito
stride: passo
strive: sforzarsi
striven: sforzato, si sforzato
striving: sforzandosi
strop: coramella, stroppo
stubble: stoppia
stubborn: ostinato, testardo, cocciuto, caparbio
stumble: inciampare, incespicare
stumbled: inciampato
stump: ceppo, troncone, moncone, mozzicone
stunned: sbalordito, intontito, stordito, assordato, rintronato, tramortito
stupidity: stupidità

stupidly: stupidamente
stupor: stupore
sturdy: robusto
subdue: sottomettere, assoggettare
subdued: sottomesso
subduing: assoggettando, sottomettendo
subjection: sottomissione, soggezione
submerged: sommerso
submersion: immersione
subordinate: subordinato, subalterno
subsided: abbassato, calato, cessato, sprofondato
subsiding: calando, sprofondando, cessando
substituted: sostituito
subterfuge: sotterfugio
subterranean: sotterraneo
suburbs: sobborgo, periferia
succeeding: riuscendo, successivo
successively: successivamente
succor: soccorrere, soccorso, aiutare
suddenness: subitaneità
suds: saponata
suffice: bastare, basta, bastano, bastate, basti, bastiamo, basto
sufficing: bastando
suffrage: suffragio
suggestive: provocante, suggestivo, indicativo
sulk: essere di cattivo umore, fare il broncio
sulky: imbronciato
sullen: triste
sulphurous: solforoso
sultan: sultano
sultry: soffocante, afoso
summon: convocare, chiamare, intimare, citare
summoning: convocare
summons: citazione, ingiunzione
sundry: diversi
sunflower: girasole
sung: cantato
sunrise: alba, levar del sole
sunset: tramonto
superfluous: superfluo
superfluously: superfluamente
supernatural: soprannaturale
superseded: sostituito, soppiantato, rimpiazzato
superstition: superstizione
superstitious: superstizioso
superstructure: sovrastruttura
supine: supino
supping: cenando
supposition: supposizione
suppressed: soffocato, soppresso
surging: pompaggio
surmise: supporre, congetturare
surname: cognome

surpass: sorpassare, superare
surveyed: esaminato
surveying: agrimensura
survivor: superstite, sopravvissuto
susceptibility: suscettibilità
sustaining: sostenendo, poggiando, sostenere
sustenance: sostentamento
swarming: brulichio
sway: oscillare, ondeggiare, barcollare, oscillazione
swaying: oscillare
sweeper: spazzatrice, spazzino
swelled: gonfiato
swirl: vortice, turbinare, turbine
swollen: gonfio
swoop: piombare, avventarsi
sworn: giurato
syllable: sillaba
symbolical: simbolico
symmetric: simmetrico
symmetrical: simmetrico
sympathizes: compatisce, simpatizza
syrian: siriano
tacit: tacito
tacitly: tacitamente
tact: tatto
talkative: loquace
tame: addomesticare, domestico, domare
tangled: aggrovigliato
tapping: maschiatura, rubinetto, colata
tar: catrame, catramare
tarpaulin: telone, tela cerata, incerata
tarried: rimasto
tarring: catramatura, incatramare
tarry: rimanere, catramoso, rimangono, rimani, rimango, rimanete, rimaniamo
tarrying: rimanendo
tasteful: raffinato
taunting: rinfacciando, schernendo
tawny: fulvo
tearing: strappo, lacerazione, stracciare
telescope: telescopio, cannocchiale
temperate: temperato, moderato
tempest: tempesta
tempting: allettante, tentando
tempts: tenta
tenderness: tenerezza, affettuosità
tending: tendendo
tenor: tenore
terminate: terminare, termino, terminiamo, termini, terminate, termina, terminano, finire
terminated: terminato
terminating: terminando
terraces: terrazze
terrifies: terrifica, terrorizza, atterrisce, spaventa

testified: testimoniato
thankful: riconoscente, grato
thanksgiving: ringraziamento
theatrical: teatrale
thee: te
thence: di là
therein: in ciò
thereto: in calce
thereupon: in merito
thermometer: termometro
thickly: spesso, spessamente
thinker: pensatore
thinly: sottilmente, magramente
thinness: finezza, leggerezza, magrezza, sottigliezza
thirst: sete
thither: là
thorn: spina
thrice: tre volte
throng: calca
thwarting: contrastando, ostacolando
tickle: stimolare, stuzzicare, solleticare, solletico
tides: marea
tier: fila
tiger: tigre, la tigre
tiller: sbarra, barra, barra del timone
timely: tempestivo, opportuno
timid: pauroso, angoscioso, timido, timoroso
timidity: timidezza
timorous: timoroso
tinge: tingere, sfumare, tinta
tingling: formicolio
tint: tinta
titanic: titanico
toil: faticare, fatica, duro lavoro
toilsome: faticoso
token: segno, gettone, prova
tolerable: tollerabile
tomb: tomba, sepolcro
tongs: pinzette
tooth: dente, il dente
topsail: vela di gabbia
torment: tormento
torpor: torpore
torrent: torrente
torrid: torrido
tortoise: tartaruga
tortuous: tortuoso
tortured: torturato
tottered: traballato, barcollato
tottering: barcollando, traballando
touches: tocca
tow: rimorchiare, trainare, rimorchio
towing: traino, alaggio, rimorchio
tracing: tracciato, lucido
tractable: docile, trattabile
trader: commerciante
trailing: trascinare
trait: caratteristica, tratto
tranquil: tranquillo, calmo

tranquilizing: tranquillizzando
tranquillity: tranquillità
transatlantic: transatlantico
transcending: trascendendo
transfigured: trasfigurato
transforming: trasformando
transient: transitorio
transportation: trasporto
transported: trasportato
transverse: trasversale
traveled: viaggiato
traveler: viaggiatore
traveling: viaggiando, viaggiare
travels: viaggia
treacherous: traditore
treacherously: traditormente
treachery: tradimento
trellis: graticcio
trembled: tremato
tremor: tremore, tremito
tremulous: tremante
trespasser: trasgressore
tribulation: tribolazione
trifling: insignificante
trim: rifilare
tripod: treppiedi, tripode, treppiede
tropic: tropico
troublesome: fastidioso, noioso
truce: tregua
trumpet: tromba, barrire
trustful: fiducioso
trusting: fiducioso
tumbled: caduto
tumbling: voltolamento, cadere
tumult: tumulto
tumultuous: tumultuoso
turban: turbante
turbulence: turbolenza
turbulent: turbolento
turf: tappeto erboso, zolla erbosa
turnkey: carceriere
turret: torretta
turtle: tartaruga
twang: vibrazione, dare un suono metallico
twilight: crepuscolo
twinge: dolore lancinante
twinkled: scintillato, brillato, luccicato
twitch: ticchio, contrarsi
tyrannical: tirannico
tyrannized: tiranneggiato
tyranny: tirannia
ulterior: ulteriore
unaccompanied: senza accompagnamento, solo
unaccountable: inesplicabile, irresponsabile
unaffected: spontaneo, non affettato, semplice
unalterable: inalterabile
unanswerable: incontestabile,

irrefutabile
unattended: incustodito
unavoidable: inevitabile
unavoidably: inevitabilmente
unawares: inavvertitamente
unbound: non rilegato
unbounded: illimitato
unbroken: ininterrotto, intatto
unbrokenly: intattamente
unchanging: immutabile
uncharitable: aspro
uncivil: incivile
uncivilized: incivile
uncommonly: insolitamente
unconcern: noncuranza
unconditional: incondizionato
unconsciously: inconsciamente
uncovered: scoperto
undeceived: disingannato
undefined: indefinito
undeniable: innegabile
undergo: subire, subisci, subisco, subiscono, subite, subiamo
undergoes: subisce
undergoing: subendo
undergone: subito
undergrowth: sottobosco, boscaglia
underling: subalterno
undisturbed: indisturbato
undo: disfare, disfate, disfa', disfacciamo, disfaccio, disfai, disfano
undressed: svestito
undulated: ondulatorio
unearthly: misterioso, soprannaturale, non terreno
uneasily: inquietamente
uneasiness: disagio
unending: interminabile
unequal: ineguale, disuguale
unexampled: singolare
unexplained: non spiegato
unfaithfulness: infedeltà
unfavorable: sfavorevole
unfinished: incompiuto
unflagging: instancabile, infaticabile
unfold: spiegare
unforeseen: imprevisto
unfriendly: scortese, ostile
unfurls: spiega
ungainly: sgraziato
ungraceful: sgraziato
ungrateful: ingrato
ungratefully: ingrato
unhappily: infelicemente
unharmed: illeso
unhealthy: malsano, malaticcio
unheard: non sentito
unimpaired: inalterato
uninhabitable: inabitabile
uninhabited: disabitato
unintentional: involontario

uniting: unendo
unjust: ingiusto
unlawfully: illegalmente
unleashed: sguinzagliato
unmindful: immemore
unmitigated: non mitigato
unnumbered: non numerato
unobstructed: non ostruito
unoccupied: vacante, libero
unofficially: ufficiosamente
unpacked: disimballato, sballato,
    disfatto
unpleasantness: spiacevolezza
unprincipled: senza scrupoli
unproductive: improduttivo
unprovided: sprovvisto
unreal: irreale
unreality: irrealtà
unreasonableness: irragionevolezza
unreliable: inattendibile
unrolled: si srotolato, svolto
unruly: indisciplinato
unseemly: sconveniente, indecoroso
unsightly: brutto
unsolicited: non richiesto
unsophisticated: non sofisticato
unspeakably: inesprimibilmente
unsupported: non confermato, non
    eseguibile, senza sostegno, non
    permesso
unsure: incerto
untimely: prematuro
unto: a
untold: non detto
untoward: sfavorevole
unused: non usato, inutilizzato
unutterable: inesprimibile
unvarnished: non verniciato
unwarranted: ingiustificato
unwary: incauto
unwholesome: malsano
unwisely: imprudentemente
unworthy: indegno
upbraided: rimproverato
upbraiding: rimproverando
upheld: sostenuto
upholding: sostenendo
upland: regione montagnosa,
    altopiano
uproar: baccano
uprooted: sradicato
upward: ascendente, verso l'alto, in
    alto
uselessly: inutilmente
usurpation: usurpazione
utilitarian: utilitaristico, utilitarista,
    utilitario
utmost: massimo
vacancy: posto vacante
vacantly: vacantemente
vacated: evacuato, liberato,
    sgombrato

vagrant: vagabondo, ambulante
vain: vanitoso, vano
vainly: vanamente
valiantly: valorosamente
valor: valore, coraggio
valorous: prode, valoroso
vanish: sparire, spariscono, sparisco,
    sparisci, spariamo, sparite, svanire
vanishing: sparendo
vanity: vanità
vanquished: sconfitto, vinto
variance: varietà, disaccordo
vastly: vastamente
vastness: vastità
vault: volta
veering: girando, virando
vegetarian: vegetariano
vehemence: veemenza
vehement: veemente
venerable: venerabile
venetian: veneziano
venomous: velenoso
ventured: avventurato
veracity: veracità
verbatim: parola per parola
verge: orlo, margine, bordo
verification: verifica, accertamento
verified: verificato, controllato
verify: verificare, verifica, verifico,
    verifichiamo, verifichi, verificate,
    verificano, controllare, controllo,
    controlla, controllano
verily: molto
vermilion: cinabro, vermiglio
versed: versato, esperto
vertically: verticalmente
vexation: irritazione
vexatious: irritante
vexed: irritato, indispettito, vessato,
    contrariato
vexing: irritando, vessando,
    contrariando, indispettendo
vibrations: vibrazione, vibrazioni
viceroy: viceré
victimized: perseguitato, immolato,
    sacrificato, vittimizzato
vigilance: vigilanza
vigor: vigore, vigoria
vile: abietto
villain: furfante
villainous: infame, malvagio
vindictive: vendicativo
vintner: vinaio
violate: violare, violo, violiamo,
    violate, violano, violi, viola, assalire,
    aggredire, aggredite, assalite
violets: viola
virtuous: virtuoso
visage: viso, volto
visibly: visibilmente
vitality: vitalità
vitreous: vitreo

vividly: vivamente
vocation: vocazione
vogue: moda
voiceless: muto
volcano: vulcano
volition: volizione
volley: volata, raffica
voluminous: voluminoso
voyaged: viaggiato
voyager: passeggero, viaggiatore
voyages: viaggia
vulgar: volgare, triviale
wafer: cialda, wafer, ostia
waft: spandersi, soffio, diffondere
wagon: vagone
wagons: carri
wail: gemere
wailing: piagnisteo, gemere
waits: aspetta
waive: rinunciare
waked: svegliato
wakeful: sveglio
wakened: svegliato
waking: svegliare
wand: bacchetta
wander: vagare, vago, errare,
    vaghiamo, vaga, vagano, vaghi,
    vagate, vagabondare
wanderer: vagabondo
wanders: vaga
waning: declinando
warbler: uccello canoro
warlike: guerriero, bellicoso,
    battagliero
warp: ordito, ordire
warped: deformato
wastes: spreca
watchfulness: vigilanza
watchman: guardiano, sorvegliante
watery: acquoso
wavered: esitato
wavering: esitando
wayfarer: viandante
wearies: stanco
wearily: stancamente
weariness: fiacca
wearisome: faticoso, tedioso
web: ragnatela
wedging: cassa da morto
weedy: allampanato
weep: piangere, piangete, piangi,
    piangiamo, piangono, piango,
    lacrimare
weighing: pesando, pesatura
weighty: pesante
westward: verso ovest
wetted: bagnato
whale: balena
whaler: baleniere, baleniera
whaling: caccia alla balena
wheeled: ruota
whence: da dove, donde

whereabouts: dove
wherein: dove
whereupon: dopo di che
wherewithal: mezzi
whim: capriccio, fisima
whimsy: capriccio
whine: uggiolare, piagnucolare,
  piagnucolio
whirling: turbinoso, vorticoso
whiskers: baffi
whispering: sussurrio
whit: briciolo
whiteness: punto di bianco,
  bianchezza
whitewash: imbiancare
whither: dove
whiz: fischio
wholesale: all'ingrosso, ingrosso
wholesome: sano, salubre
wickedness: cattiveria
widened: allargato
wilderness: regione selvaggia
willingly: volentieri
willow: salice
wilt: appassire, appassisco,
  appassiscono, appassisci,
  appassiamo, appassite
wilted: appassito
windlass: argano, verricello
windward: sopravvento
winged: alato
wink: ammiccare
winnowed: vagliato
wiping: asciugando, pulendo,
  strofinando
wiry: di filo metallico
wisely: saggiamente
wishfully: desiderosamente
withdrawing: ritirando, prelevando
withered: appassito
withering: avvizzimento, appassendo
withheld: trattenuto
withstand: opporsi a, far fronte a,
  resistere, resisto, resistono,
  resistiamo, resisti, resistete
withstood: resistito
wizard: mago, stregone
woe: dolore, calamità, afflizione
wondrous: meraviglioso
wont: avvezzo, abitudine
wonted: usuale, consueto, solito
woolen: di lana
woolly: lanoso, lanuto
wordiness: verbosità
workman: operaio
worshipful: venerabile
woven: tessuto
wrap: avvolgere
wreak: sfogare, sfogano, sfogate,
  sfoghi, sfoghiamo, sfogo, sfoga
wreck: naufragio, relitto, distruggere
wrests: estorce

wretched: misero, miserabile, povero,
  infelice
wringing: estorcendo
wrinkle: ruga, grinza
wrinkled: spiegazzato
writhed: storto, torto
writhing: storcendo, torcendo
wrought: battuto, lavorato
yearning: brama, desideroso,
  bramoso, bramando, anelando
yellowish: giallastro
yielded: ceduto
yielding: cedendo
yon: laggiù, là, li
yonder: là, laggiù
youthful: giovane, giovanile
zeal: zelo, ardore
zenith: zenit
zigzag: zigzagare, zigzag

Lightning Source UK Ltd.
Milton Keynes UK
UKOW050217230512

193052UK00001BA/81/A